Modern European Tragedy

Anthem Studies in Theatre and Performance

Anthem Studies in Theatre and Performance takes a broad, global approach to cultural analysis to examine and critique a wide range of performative acts from the most traditional forms of theatre studies (music, theatre and dance) to more popular, less structured forms of cultural performance. The twenty-first century in particular has seen theatre and performance studies become a major perspective for examining, understanding and critiquing contemporary culture and its historical roots. Performance is a vital manifestation of culture that is enacted, a form to be experienced, recorded, analysed and theorized. It is among the most useful and dynamic foci for the global study of culture.

Series Editor

S. E. Gontarski – Florida State University, USA

Editorial Board

Alan Ackerman – University of Toronto, Canada
Robson Corrêa de Camargo – Universidade Federal de Goiás, Brazil
Stephen A. Di Benedetto – University of Miami, USA
Herbert Blau – University of Washington, USA
Enoch Brater – University of Michigan, USA
Annamaria Cascetta – Università Cattolica del Sacro Cuore, Milan, Italy
Christopher Innes – York University, Canada
Anna McMullan – University of Reading, UK
Martin Puchner – Harvard University, USA
Kris Salata – Florida State University, USA
W. B. Worthen – Barnard College, Columbia University, USA

Modern European Tragedy

Exploring Crucial Plays

ANNAMARIA CASCETTA

ANTHEM PRESS
LONDON · NEW YORK · DELHI

Anthem Press
An imprint of Wimbledon Publishing Company
www.anthempress.com

This edition first published in UK and USA 2015
by ANTHEM PRESS
75–76 Blackfriars Road, London SE1 8HA, UK
or PO Box 9779, London SW19 7ZG, UK
and
244 Madison Ave #116, New York, NY 10016, USA

First published in hardback by Anthem Press in 2014

Copyright © 2015 Annamaria Cascetta

The author asserts the moral right to be identified as the author of this work.

All rights reserved. Without limiting the rights under copyright reserved above,
no part of this publication may be reproduced, stored or introduced into
a retrieval system, or transmitted, in any form or by any means
(electronic, mechanical, photocopying, recording or otherwise),
without the prior written permission of both the copyright
owner and the above publisher of this book.

British Library Cataloguing-in-Publication Data
A catalogue record for this book is available from the British Library.

Library of Congress Cataloging-in-Publication Data
The Library of Congress has cataloged the hardcover edition as follows:
Cascetta, Annamaria, author.
Modern European tragedy : exploring crucial plays / Annamaria Cascetta. pages cm. –
(Anthem Studies in Theatre and Performance)
Includes index.
ISBN 978-1-78308-153-0 (hardcover : alk. paper)
1. European drama (Tragedy)–History and criticism. 2. European drama–20th century–History
and criticism. 3. Tragedy–History and criticism. I. Title.
Pn1892.C36 2014
809.2'512–dc23
2014007426
9781783084241

ISBN-13: 978 1 78308 424 1 (Pbk)
ISBN-10: 1 78308 424 3 (Pbk)

Cover image: Franco Citti (Oedipus blind), frame from the film *Oedipus Rex* (*Edipo re*) by
Pier Paolo Pasolini, Italy, 1967 (© Reporters Associati, Rome).

This title is also available as an ebook.

For Gigi

CONTENTS

Acknowledgements		ix
Introduction	The Tragic, Tragedy and the Idea of the Limit	1
Chapter 1	Hubris and Guilt: *Gengangere* (*Ghosts*) by Henrik Ibsen	15
Chapter 2	Eve Becomes Mary: *L'annonce faite à Marie* (*The Tidings Brought to Mary*) by Paul Claudel	31
Chapter 3	The School of Hatred: *Mourning Becomes Electra* by Eugene O'Neill	47
Chapter 4	The Destiny of Man Is Man: *Mutter Courage und ihre Kinder* (*Mother Courage and Her Children*) by Bertolt Brecht	59
Chapter 5	The Tragic and the Absurd: *Caligula* by Albert Camus	75
Chapter 6	Dianoetic Laughter in Tragedy: Accepting Finitude: *Endgame* by Samuel Beckett	91
Chapter 7	The Arrogance of Reason and the 'Disappearance of the Fireflies': *Pilade* (*Pylades*) by Pier Paolo Pasolini	101
Chapter 8	The Apocalypse of a Civilization: From *Akropolis* to *Apocalypsis cum figuris* by Jerzy Grotowski	117
A Provisional Epilogue	Between the Experience and the Representation of the Tragic: Towards a Performative Theatre	147
Appendix	Chronology of Productions	163
Notes		199
Index		233

ACKNOWLEDGEMENTS

I am most grateful to Stanley E. Gontarski for his support and encouragement during our many years of collaboration, and give a heartfelt 'thank you' to Marsha Gontarski for making our friendship so special.

I also wish to thank the publisher Laterza for permission to translate Chapters 1–6 and the epilogue of this book, published in Italian in the book *La tragedia del Novecento* (2010).

It is with much gratitude that I thank Maria Rita Gaito for her accurate contribution in compiling the appendix and the illustrations, as well as Giuseppe Gario and Brian Groves for their technical revision of the text.

I wish to record my thanks to Richard Sadleir, who translated this book from Italian with competence, dedication, unabated patience and sincere interest. The translation was made possible thanks to the financial contribution of the Catholic University of Milan.

And, finally, my fondest appreciation to Giusi Lupi.

Introduction

THE TRAGIC, TRAGEDY AND THE IDEA OF THE LIMIT

Relevance of the Tragic, Irrelevance of Tragedy

In a famous essay on the tragic in ancient drama as reflected in the tragic in modern drama, Søren Kierkegaard observed that 'the tragic, after all, is always the tragic' and that the idea of the tragic remains essentially the same, as it remains natural for mankind to weep.[1]

The consciousness of the tragic has traversed Western culture for millennia. It is closely bound up with the intuition of inescapable limits, inseparable from the human condition, the ambiguity and contradictions of the human and the awareness of suffering. Perhaps it can be conjectured that awareness of the tragic is a profound permanent structure of the human, which has its anthropological and cultural development in the West and was given expression in Greek culture at a particular moment in its history, a phase of dialectic and transition between a mythical–heroic horizon and a legal–political horizon. It came to the fore in its representation in the theatre in the great season of tragedy in the fifth century BC, when the theatre was a major religious, ceremonial, aesthetic, political and social experience at the centre of community life.

If the sense of the tragic is a permanent *structure* of human consciousness, tragedy is a *form* into which that structure has historically been translated. It was embodied and expressed in tragic art and the stage, which enabled it to exist. As Péter Szondi rightly points out, it is only modernity that, while decreeing the death of tragedy,[2] and reconstructing its transformations through the centuries,[3] has developed the tragic as a philosophical idea, while a poetic of tragedy has existed ever since Aristotle.[4] Now modernity, since Nietzsche, has fuelled a great debate about tragedy to the point at times of making it the paradigm for the interpretation of human existence and reality.

I begin with a quote from Kierkegaard because he has given us a convincing foundational description of the tragic. It can serve the theatre critic as a still-relevant frame of reference for the formulation of a theoretical scheme that will be useful in picking our way through and interpreting the vast phenomenology of twentieth-century drama related to the category of the tragic.

I believe the key points are as follows. The tragic and tragedy can be distinguished – even though originally, in Western culture, the tragic first appeared and found expression in the historical form of classical Greek tragedy, and in this way the two concepts became fused. The tragic should be considered a fundamental phenomenon, one of the essential human experiences, manifested in the always latent possibility of the corresponding feeling. It cannot be reduced to a simple momentous historical event, nor can it be confused with a specific literary and theatrical form. It is always a possible experience.

Here I am not invoking either the pan-tragic vision or ontology, but the existence of a category offering historical, psychological, ethical and aesthetic valences of the greatest importance and interpretative fruitfulness. Important studies entitled *The Death of Tragedy* or *La métamorphose de la tragedie* do not substantially contradict this perspective.[5]

Interesting confirmation comes from *Modern Tragedy* by Raymond Williams,[6] who takes tragedy beyond the limitations of a literary genre and denies its purported incompatibility with modernity and the supposed optimism of modern ideology. He sees it as an inescapable experience of contemporary history, which intersects, but does not coincide, with the tradition. I differ, however, from his position because I maintain that there is, as we have seen in the distinction between the tragic and tragedy, a permanent core, philosophically definable, that is variously embodied in history, including modernity. Williams, by contrast, rejects this point. Another difference is that I would not speak of the tragic nature of individual or collective history, but of tragic awareness, embodied in experience.

Nineteenth-century philosophy, as is well known, thematized the tragic.[7] The philosophy of the twentieth century, as it gradually acquired a rationalist outlook, explored this theme less, though important thinkers dealt with it authoritatively.[8] Often what seems to be a marginal issue, barely touched on, is central and plays a decisive role constitutive of their whole anthropological design, as in the case of Kierkegaard.[9]

The centre of interest of the tragic lies in the *existence* of humanity. In it, the tragic grasps an irreconcilable contradiction, an irreducible distance between the *limit* that constitutes the finitude of humanity (with its radical figure in the consciousness of death) and the infinite passion by which it is pervaded. The *passion for the infinite* is both structural and destabilizing. It spurs mankind to a constant transgression that is both productive and dangerous, both transparent and obscure in the construction of the self that moves humanity in time.

The tragic is thus an experience, always possible, of consciousness. It starts from its given situation and lives suspended between an unresolved question and answer, whatever its ideological orientations: nihilistic or optimistic, rationalist or fideistic.

In this aspect of consciousness the clarity of reason is entwined with the tremor of emotion.[10] If we call this condition 'destiny', we can say that the tragic is a conscious relationship with destiny, which in ancient tragedy lies beyond mankind, behind its back (as fate, family or state, as Kierkegaard observes), while in modern tragedy it lies in the human heart.

It follows that the action of the tragic performance (in the strict sense of tragedy or some other dramatic and theatrical form) is bound up with the continuously variable *transgression* of this necessary limit, until it reaches the inevitable destructive short circuit between finite and infinite, in the continually defeated presumption to cancel the void between finitude and the passion of the infinite.

The great problem in the definition of the modernity of the tragic and its forms of representation arises from the determination of the proportions of guilt and innocence in this action. Kierkegaard again indicates an approach, which has naturally to be made to the measure of the period with which I deal here. The action of a tragedy is both an action and a suffering (*agere et pati*); but while in ancient tragedy suffering prevails,[11] in modernity action prevails, driven by freedom, resolved into subjectivity and its responsibilities, the categories that have been affirmed by Christianity and Western culture ever since the Renaissance. While in ancient tragedy the theme of punishment prevails over suffering, in modernity suffering prevails, subjectively understood.

The dialectic between guilt and innocence, in equilibrium in ancient tragedy, becomes unbalanced in modernity toward guilt and responsibility. But can we speak of total guilt? In coherence with the idea of the irreducible limit, which I have outlined as structural to humanity, we cannot. The imperfection of human existence, which designs and constructs itself slowly and not straightforwardly in time, and of human nature, which evolves gradually, makes it impossible. It is the imperfection of existence that entails the possibility of tragedy and its expression in various forms, just as it remains receptive to both a rude awakening and a catharsis which, as we shall see, is both emotional relief and a gain in intellectual and moral understanding.

The Tragic Scene in the Twentieth Century: A Selection of Dramatic and Performance Texts and a Hypothesis of Interpretation

The idea of the tragic and the form of tragedy as developed in ancient Greece are a crucial achievement. They provide a frame of reference whenever the tragic consciousness resurfaces, embodied in the different ages and phases of Western civilization, in which, naturally, the established categories of individual, person, freedom and the identification of ethics with the centrality of the will, as compared to the centrality of knowledge, clearly distance its matrix from that of archaic and classical Greece.

In the history of Western dramatic forms, it is principally the presence of an absolute horizon of meaning that permits the tragic genre to attain its highest forms. This horizon is based on ideologies, differing over time. They justify it and at the same time determine the different epochal forms of the nuclei of tragedy described below, neglecting the more specifically formal aspects. Here I am thinking, for example, of the Presocratic philosophy which provided the framework for ancient Greek tragedy, the Christian vision which was the basis of both baroque tragedy and what is called 'spiritual tragedy', and Romantic philosophy, which formed the matrix of nineteenth-century tragedy.

In the twentieth century this absolute horizon of meaning was shattered. A number of partial horizons of meaning coexisted and interacted, becoming relativized. The form of tragedy was also overwhelmed and produced a series of rewritings, reversals and fusions. New frontiers emerged in the history of ideas. New formal models were developed in the history of drama of tragic inspiration. Of the nodal points that define, as we have seen, tragic humanity and its expression in literary and theatrical form, the *ambiguous relationship with the limit* strikes me as offering a key to understanding and ordering the phenomenon in our contemporary world. I have taken it as a unifying thread in this first exploration.

I explore the idea of the limit in a twofold sense:

1) The 'situation' in which man by his very nature is placed and the disproportion between *ens* and *esse* that weighs on man. The Greeks intuited it in terms of *moira*, while it has also been theorized in modern thought, especially in the transcendental phenomenology and Heidegger's reflection on *Dasein*.
2) The urge to transgress the limit to excess, culpable on the ethical plane, unreasonable on the plane of rationality. The Greeks intuited this and called it *hubris*.

The twentieth-century stage has represented the many forms in which this concept is embodied while reflecting both on the ontological structure of man and on the history of the century, one of the most atrocious in human history.

To draw a picture that would be both an attempt at synthesis and a starting point for further research, I have formulated the following questions upon which I have based the choice of texts for analysis:

1) How can we articulate the concept of the limit in much of the twentieth century?
    - It is the *finiteness* of mankind, the prospect *hic et nunc* of our *situation*, so well described by the phenomenological philosophy of the twentieth century, the paucity of our resources and the strength of our physical and animal nature.
    - It is the biological limit, whose radical form is the 'fatal illness' – death.
    - It is the moral limit, namely evil (such as violence, aggression, vice, etc.), of others against us, of us against others and of mankind against itself.
    - It is the limit of the individual in relation to others, the fruit of a culture of repression and exploitation.
    - It is the limit of humanity in establishing relations of meaning, the disruption of the relationship with the whole, with the Other, with the beyond, the mortification of the religious individual.

    How did the twentieth century deal with the experience of the limit articulated more or less in these terms?
2) On which aspects of the limit did the twentieth century focus in reflection and performance? Specifically, in keeping with the main focus of this book, how was the limit represented dramatically? How is the tragic action configured in relation to this limit?
3) Which experiences and which ideas of the limit were embodied in the theatre? With the support and interpretative key of which ideologies? (We should bear in mind that the twentieth century was the century of ideologies.)[12] And which philosophies?
4) And in the context of which historical events was the resurgence of the forms of tragedy made urgent and alarming in our culture?

In the twentieth century tragedy stepped down from the heroic pedestal of tradition and touched the common man, in keeping with much of literature and the arts. It broke the isolation of the hero and grasped the tragic situation of man as part of a group, of a mass, seen against the backdrop of centuries of unconventional wars and genocides. The ideological matrix or the collapse of ideology led to reformulations of the basic concepts of tragedy: hero, limit, transgression, guilt, expiation, sacrifice, fear, pity, catharsis. The *pathos* of the hero gave way to the *passion* of the 'man without qualities'.

Tears gave way to laughter (ironic, humorous, sarcastic); passion gave way to reason and again to the most extreme irrationality. The grotesque and the absurd pervaded tragedy. The course of the great river became karstic, flowing underground.

In the broad and complex history and culture of the twentieth century, it is clear that the theme of the limit and its necessity, on which I intend to focus attention, became extremely complicated. But in the case of dramatic culture, the mirror and project of reality, we can take our bearings by starting from a selection of tragic texts of outstanding artistic value and great literary and dramatic resonance, accompanying the course of the century, so enabling us to identify certain major lines of development and dominant approaches.

I will focus on a limited number of texts – crucial in the context of a theatre still fundamentally of speech, created by authors of literary and philosophical training – and on their great success on the stage, documented in the appendix of this book. They are examples of different orientations of thought that have responded in different ways to tragic consciousness, embodied in coherently different dramatic forms. The reader should be especially aware of the following characteristics of this era:

1) The limit moves from without to within, pressing into the individual, into his or her deepest fibres and unconscious levels. This is the case, for example, with Ibsen's *Gengangere* (*Ghosts*) and O'Neill's *Mourning Becomes Electra*.
2) The limit is the enigma of the human personage as *figura Christi* and the mystery of suffering and innocent sacrifice. This is the case of Claudel's *L'annonce faite à Marie* (*The Tidings Brought to Mary*).
3) It lies in social injustice and the influence of class. This is the viewpoint of Brecht in *Mutter Courage und ihre Kinder* (*Mother Courage and Her Children*).
4) The limit is short-circuited with limitless transgression into an act of absolute arrogance. The limit is a dangerous transgression that threatens the very survival of humanity, through the evil associated with the culture of hatred, violence and genocide. Examples are the theatre of the *Shoah* or *Rwanda 94*, a backdrop to certain vibrant modern revivals of Euripides' *Trojan Women*. Another example is Pasolini's *Pilade*.
5) Finally, the limit is presented as absolute, as an interruption of the relationship with the foundation of meaning in the culture of the absurd and nihilism. This is the case, for example, of Albert Camus's *Caligula* and Samuel Beckett's *Fin de partie* (*Endgame*). In the latter, however, there also emerges a new openness to the recognition of the limit and a wisdom that accepts finiteness and makes humour a resource for understanding.

In my study I have limited the field by choosing a small number of what I have assessed as key texts, seen as embodying the following parameters:

1) A reference to substantial currents of thought in the twentieth century (think of the Kierkegaard revival, Christian personalism, Marxism, Freudianism, nihilism, the absurd and the philosophy of existence).
2) An affiliation of the authors to one of the four basic generations into which the century can be divided (though I have limited myself to the first three, making only a brief foray into the fourth).

3) A lucidly critical position towards dramatic characters who represent disturbing trends in the culture and history of the period: the urge to go beyond the limit at the dawn of the new century, the adventure without limits at the time of the great European civil war, and the slow development of a moral maturity after World War II.
4) A correlation between the embodiment of the limit and the idea of the theatre expressed by the technique of the text's construction. It is as if these texts and these authors embodied on the stage an awareness of reality that their generation lacked and were what their generation was not.

The first part of the book examines the emergence of tragedy and its development in a number of *dramatic texts* which have had an intense life on the stage and renewed the technique of dramatic writing. In most cases, these experiments rest on philosophical principles and concerns and represent the primacy of authorial subjectivity.

The last section, comprising *Akropolis* and *Apocalypsis cum figuris*, considers, but only as the foreshadowing of a process that calls for specific and extensive discussion, the emergence of tragedy and its development in the *performative dramaturgies* which characterized the closing decades of the twentieth century and the transition to the new millennium, a period of so-called postmodernity. In them the concept of authorship generally refers to the work of a director or above all collective and workshop writing. Behind these experiments there has generally been found to lie an anthropological background and sensibility.

Greek Tragedy: An Essential Frame of Reference

For a study of the representation of the tragic in our contemporary world it is therefore relevant to return firstly to its sources, as has been done by almost all the modern artists whose works are discussed in these pages. This is not to confuse or equate all sources with each other. The specificity of individual authors and texts should not be ignored and we also need to take account of the narrowness of the extant corpus of Greek tragedy compared with the original output. But my purpose is to identify certain nuclei which, in the historical development of this form of consciousness and its representation, have sometimes served as models, but above all as points of reference variously transformed and interpreted.

We will identify them essentially on the basis of three texts: the *Oresteia* (the trilogy made up of *Agamemnon*, *The Choephori*, *The Eumenides*) by Aeschylus dating from 458 BC, and two works by Sophocles, *Oedipus the King*, performed no later than 425 BC, and *Antigone*, dating from 442 BC.

The first nucleus is the *necessity (ananke) of a limit*, in which the tragic condition and episode are placed. In Aeschylus's profoundly religious vision, the divine underpins the cosmos and man. Necessity is laid on mankind as a gentle yoke, worthy of acceptance, because it is guaranteed by the justice (*dike*) of Zeus, but it is also a harbinger of fear and dismay. A hidden anguish enfolds Agamemnon on his return to Argos and fear hangs heavy over the palace. Orestes, the avenger who is himself pursued by vengeance, is surrounded by a mysterious oracular atmosphere and a sense of impending fatality. As a force that presses on the characters from without, necessity is connected to the unbroken chain of events running from the first link, the original impious misdeed. A curse has hung over the house of Atreus ever since its founder avenged himself on his brother Thyestes by inviting him to a purported feast of reconciliation at which he was served the flesh of his slain children. Agamemnon is the leader of the victorious Achaean army which sets out to punish Troy for the violation of the sacred laws of hospitality by Paris, the abductor of Helen. His mission is just (*moira*), but it is conducted with excesses of destruction and therefore arouses the divine wrath of Artemis. The goddess exacts the reparatory sacrifice of the young maiden Iphigenia, an act which Agamemnon is compelled to perform through necessity (*epei anankes*) by the seer Calchas, who interprets the prodigy of eagles preying on a pregnant hare as indicating the necessity for the sacrifice. We can describe this, with an oxymoron applied to Antigone, as 'sacred wickedness', yet it serves the purpose marked out by a just destiny to arouse the vengeance of Clytemnestra. But this new violation of the law in turn entails the vengeance of Orestes, driven to this deed by Apollo, whose epithet is Loxias (i.e., the Oblique), and who shares responsibility with Orestes for the act. Everything happens according to necessity and stems from the mechanism (or, rather, deified power) of *ate*, the blindness that prevents us from seeing the consequences of our acts, hence wreaking havoc instead of acting through persuasion:

CHORUS. [...]
>Where will it end? Where will it end,
>Where will the power of Ate be soothed to sleep?[13]

Blood calls for blood, revenge calls for revenge, ruled by the goddesses of the archaic, subterranean world, the Erinyes, until its course is changed by a conversion within the divine itself, with the transition from the Erinyes to the Eumenides, and in the human sphere with the institution of the court of justice in the city of men.

Again in the context of necessity, an *ethos* and a *genos* condition the orientation of Agamemnon. They are entailed by his lineage and a mode of being that cannot be reduced to the categories of individual, person or character as we understand them, since these were not yet culturally acquired in that period of history and thought. They determine a convergence between the hero's decisions, the purpose of the god, and the demon who acts through him with justice. The wise voice of the city, the chorus of elders, interprets this theme:

CHORUS. [...] Impious deeds beget a numerous brood, like their progenitors.[14]

Mankind is insatiable in its desire for happiness, but its fate is steeped in tragedy. And above all, mankind lives within the limits of its frailty, like a shadow, a drawing traced in the sand. This is the great theme of Cassandra, long silent, then harrowing in her prophecy of the calamities that appear to her as visions, and finally submissive and courageous as she goes to her fate:

CASSANDRA. [...] Alas for poor mortality! When careering prosperously, a shadow may turn it back, and once unfortunate a wet sponge thrown blurs the picture.[15]

Sophocles' more decidedly humanistic vision and his more enigmatic and indecipherable sense of the divine sheds a more chequered light on the theme of the limit than that of Aeschylus, but it is just as strong. Oedipus and Antigone submit to it as both heroes and victims. The order of the gods is invoked in the *parode* of *Oedipus the King*, but it is revealed by Apollo, referred to by the recurrent epithet of Loxias (the Oblique). The oracles give only general guidance as to adversity; they do not explicitly denounce anyone or anything. Man has to accept the risk of interpreting them. Besides, those who are deputed to oversee this order, moving between cosmic order and political order, such as kings, have a transient and uncertain fate. If Oedipus at first sees clearly and is skilled at solving riddles, within a short time, Tiresias admonishes him, he will see darkness and realize that his fate has brought him to ruin. As we develop our analysis of the concept of necessity, we see that the legacy of the *genos*, the inheritance of the house of Laius, to which Oedipus and Antigone belong, forms the chain of events which sweeps them away one after the other. Laius will die at the hands of his son; Oedipus will kill his father and sleep with his mother. All attempts at escape are in vain. The tragic irony reveals the pathos of their efforts. Necessity is the hero's 'situation' itself; it is his *ethos*, his pride in his human wisdom, his ability to solve riddles, the ability he shows in the *rhesis* of the first episode, when he clashes with his accuser, the soothsayer Tiresias. It is precisely his determination to get to the bottom of things, despite Jocasta's resistance and attempts at dissuasion, that leads to his final downfall. Antigone sees necessity as an unwritten law, but one that has always been valid for mankind:

ANTIGONE. [...]
    Nor thought I thy commandment of such might
    That one who is mortal thus could overbear
    The infallible, unwritten laws of Heaven.[16]

And it is her *ethos* that leads her to compare herself with her father Oedipus, making her inflexible and heroic in committing the 'sacred wickedness' (*hosia panourghetata*, v. 74).

The Aeschylean theme of *ate*, the power that blinds, returns in these works by Sophocles.[17] The power of fate is terrible[18] and no human is permitted to struggle against necessity.[19]

Another shaping nucleus of the ancient form of the tragic is the *excess* of the hero's actions, *hubris* (ὔβρις), the arrogant transgression of the limits of what is right. It is the theme of the first *stasimon* of *Agamemnon*, a hymn to moderation by the wise elders of Argos. It is even more explicitly the theme of the second stasimon, when the chorus expresses its disquiet, its covert fears at the signs it sees of an old arrogance renewed, emerging in the course of the trilogy in the actions of Agamemnon, Clytemnestra and Orestes.

In Sophocles this concept is explored and becomes more ambiguous.[20] Hubris is also found in Antigone and in her expression of piety. She is moved by the imperative to break the civil laws (the rule established by Creon, who defends order in the city), in obedience to yet another law which she regards as higher and inviolable: the defence of the unwritten laws of justice of the 'gods below'. Her sister Ismene shares Antigone's values but criticizes her for seeking to do things that exceed the measure, especially for a woman: 'Small wisdom were it to overpass the bound.'[21] Creon repeatedly speaks of hubris in relation to Antigone's 'misdeed' and her pride in boasting of what she has done.[22] The reflection on hubris in *Oedipus the King* reveals an even more marked semantic and valuational oscillation. The impulse to transgress, the theme of the chorus's famous second stasimon, is analogous to the concept expressed by Aeschylus.[23] The chorus rejects transgression and reaffirms the justice of submitting to the order established by the god. But the complex vicissitudes of Oedipus seem to indicate the presence of another hubris that configures the term as a *vox media*, a twofold concept. It seems that in *Oedipus* Sophocles intuited that, in following the path to knowledge, the urge to transgress the limit is structurally inherent in mankind, being bound up with the poverty of its situation but also with the richness that transcends it, making humanity feel cramped in scope and intolerant of its limitations. In this way the hubris of Oedipus is his pride in his penetrating intelligence. This makes him take issue with the passive and divinatory knowledge of Tiresias and leads him, after committing his first error and encountering the first resistance, to conduct an implacable investigation, with stringent logic, pressing his interrogation in the form of *stichomythia*, accepting the risk, as he tears away the veils from the truth.

His frequent use of the pronoun 'I' is significant ('I put a stop to the Sphinx', 'I want to know my origin', 'I suffer as no one has ever done'). This leads us to another nucleus of the tragic: responsibility (*proairesis, aitia*).

Is man truly the source of his actions? This problem is lucidly explored by Jean Pierre Vernant and Pierre Vidal-Naquet in the wake of the studies of Louis Gernet.[24] I will briefly go over their arguments. While to us the will is an essential dimension of the person, responsible for his or her actions, inwardly involved, unique, permanent and continuous, this was not the case in Greek tragedy. There was no word in the language that corresponded to 'will'. The Greek could not choose but recognize necessity of a religious order, from which an individual was unable to escape and, thanks to his *ethos* (that is, his whole disposition), he made this necessity his own. Decision without choice, partial and shared causality and responsibility: this was the lot of the tragic hero. And yet the act emanates from the individual, who will rightly have to suffer its consequences.[25] This point needs to be clearly understood. It separates ancient ethics from the subsequent history of ethics and our own, in which notions of freedom, free will, action and individual responsibility are consolidated. The cases of Agamemnon and Oedipus are emblematic in this respect.

Related to this is the issue of another node of the tragic: guilt. But this term is bound up with a framework of ideas closer to our own, to the Judaeo-Christian tradition rather than to that of archaic and classical Greece. The Greeks spoke rather of error (ἁμαρτία, *hamartia*), in accordance with their intellectualized vision. The passage in Aristotle is well known: 'There remains, then, the character between these two extremes [or *metaxu*] – that of a man who is not eminently good and just, yet whose misfortune is not brought about by vice or depravity [*eis dustuchian me dia mochtherion*], but by some error or failing [*di'hamartian*].'[26] A paradigmatic example is the story of Oedipus and the reversal in his position from being a strong and beloved sovereign, wealthy, the guarantor of the safety and prosperity of the citizens and pleasing to the gods, to a *pharmakos*, a criminal, a reprobate hated by the gods, who has to be driven out as an exile and a beggar.

The action takes the form of a radical position, an *irreducible conflict*, which leaves the chorus hesitant (saying 'it is difficult to judge'),[27] but not the hero, all of a piece, who clashes with an equally radical position. Examples are Clytemnestra and Agamemnon (representing maternal piety and the laws of the military leader and king), Clytemnestra and Orestes (the law of the mother and the law of the father), the Erinyes and Athena with the Areopagus (the law of vengeance, the reasonable law of an institution of the *polis*), Oedipus and Tiresias (the intelligence of reason, the prophecy of the oracle), Antigone and Creon (the unwritten laws of the gods of the underworld, the written laws of the city; family pietas, the *polis*).

This tension goes back to the *contradictions* and ambiguities characteristic of humanity. This is the theme of the first great stasimon of *Antigone*, a hymn to mankind, described as *deinoteron*, awesome above all other things, inspiring both anguish and admiration, as suggested by the polysemic term used by the chorus. Man is equipped to encounter all things, but not death. His technical inventiveness is great, but 'at one time he moves toward evil, and at another time toward good'.[28]

On the stage in the city of Athens (not in its decline but in the period of its greatest vitality, expansion, creative fervour and pride in its Greek heritage – the 'school of Hellas'), the performances of tragedy accompanied the debate and development of ideas, values and institutions, in an intensely dynamic context. This should not be forgotten when evaluating another nucleus of the model, namely punishment and expiation (*pathos*), in the form of misfortunes such as death on the stage, suffering and injuries. I believe that the calming, stabilizing effect associated with catharsis (which I discuss below) should not be understood as outright restoration of the status quo, as in a literal interpretation of the sacrifice of a scapegoat – though the tragic hero also has affinities with that archetype, justified by the context and its powerful presence in the collective imagination.

One can perhaps conjecture that Greek tragedy accompanies the emergence of the *consciousness of time* in Greek culture, in a transitional phase which oscillates between the cyclical scheme of time as eternally recurrent and the still-indefinite intuition of linear time. In this the theatre paralleled the writing of history, a discipline which was born at the same time. As Jacqueline de Romilly observes, time is a crucial factor in the structure of Greek tragedy.[29] The term appears more than four hundred times, and above all it is related to an event that breaks time's flow, a point of crisis that changes the situation, the *peripeteia*. This is the reversal which alters the hero's fate, growing out of a closely woven sequence of events amid a climate of profound disquiet. In the tragic action, what happens is binding on the future, but it is inscribed in the cyclical time of the festival, the flow in time of a deeply human action, yet draws heavily on the immutability of myth, its recurrence more or less unchanged in every possible retelling. But the elevated speech, the power of *logos* and the lyrical accents out of which Attic tragedy is woven, while embodying the patterns of archaic myth and sacrifice, transfer its effects onto a more fruitful plane than mere tranquilizing restoration.

Through the complex strategy of the arousal and control of emotions, which the formal structure of the genre embodied, the audiences relieved in tears their anxieties over the changes, contradictions and conflicting values that unfolded before them on the stage, enabling them to distil a wisdom from tragedy. I believe it was not just the moderation with which they accepted the necessity and justice of the gods, but a gradual understanding of the different facets of human life, which played their parts in the 'suspension of disbelief' of the live performance, in the heart of the *polis*. I believe this is the essence of learning by suffering (*anagnōrisis*, as Aristotle says, and *ton pathei mathos*, as the chorus in *Agamemnon* sings at v. 177).[30]

This leads to another important nucleus of ancient tragedy: *catharsis*. Catharsis is a mechanism of release which allows the audience to tolerate a risk-laden emotion, to release an excessive surge of affect associated with a traumatic experience. The cathartic effect has been associated from the earliest times with tragedy. It was Aristotle who thematized it in his theoretical treatment in the *Poetics*. Catharsis enables tragedy to release the dangerous emotion aroused by the representation of the ineluctable limit of existence, the destiny of misfortune and death, the price of transgression. It is a strategy of closure, produced in ancient tragedy by a perfect and sophisticated device (episodes and choruses, speech, with *rēsis*, *kommos*, stichomythia, polymetric verse and music, the stage machinery and all things associated with the festival). It has two facets: one balancing and soothing by the release of feelings, the other embodying an intellectual advance, since it creates the conditions for the distillation of a wisdom.

The problem is to understand how this happens and why the account of the downfall and death of the character induces tranquillity and pleasure in the viewer. Freud also felt moved to deal with this issue. In the case of Greek tragedy, the observations of Aristotle in the *Poetics* (1449b) are authoritative. The term catharsis is certainly connected, as Diego Lanza observes, with ritual experience, the process of decontamination, the physiological process of purifying the body of whatever poisons it.[31] Ancient tragedy induces first a gain, which is psychophysical in nature, causing the alleviation of emotional excess and psychophysical tension. But the cathartic function does not end here. In the *Poetics* (1451b) Aristotle suggests that art is an imitation of the universal and that tragedy, the imitation of an action that is possible and universal in scope, is more philosophical than history, and as such it is a source of knowledge, of *theōresis*, in which man's excellence lies.

How then could the effect of tragedy, catharsis, be confined to the level of a physiological release? This occurs and paves the way for a distillation of knowledge, the acquisition of wisdom. Hence tragedy has a stabilizing function, as Vincenzo Di Benedetto explains, but it is also a guide to a progress and maturation of the collective imagination.[32]

The constant reference of tragedy to the horizon of the *polis* is inscribed in the great horizon of the *sacred*. The city, the community, appoints the chorus as its representative voice. This voice is not marginal but is set at the centre of the spectacle. From what we know of the dramatic status of this collective character, it seems to have been placed within and yet outside the drama, directly involved but less prominent than the actors in relation to audience. The chorus consisted of twelve or fifteen choral dancers. Their costumes were less splendid than those of the actors and included signs that succinctly indicated their age, social status and frame of mind. The chorus would enter performing the steps of a dance and then remain on stage throughout the performance, dramatically unifying the action, at times engaging in dialogue with the actor through the *coryphaeus* (chorus leader), reacting to the action and providing a touchstone by voicing the responses which the audience itself might express, probably in a relatively static dance (though it is difficult to be certain on this much-debated point). Emotions and intellectual tensions were mediated by the richness of the meters that guided the rhythm of the song and directed the dancers' steps.

The chorus of the elders of Argos in *Agamemnon*, for example, represents the historical memory of the city, the pride of belonging to it. It evokes shared ethical principles, expresses the wisdom of the assessment of the human condition as subject to the necessity and suffering, reaffirms the right line of conduct (which lies in moderation) and provides a balanced assessment of the difficulty of judgement. The chorus does not conceal its fears and apprehensions, but speaks up courageously as it vows to resist threats of tyranny. The chorus of the elders of Thebes in *Antigone* expresses the memory of the city, the voice of experience that has understood the ambiguous nature of man, his greatness and his frailty, the strength of vengeance and love, fear, the power of fate and the difficulty of judgment, leaving its members uncertain when faced with a breach of the law committed out of piety.

The chorus of the elders of Thebes in *Oedipus* bears witness to the calamity that has befallen the city. It is the trusting interlocutor of a ruler whom it respects and admires, accepting him as the guarantor of its security; but the chorus also distances itself and isolates him when he loses his authority, philosophizing on the nature of man and the paradigmatic rise and fall of Oedipus. The chorus fulfils the expectations of the community in relation to an event which forms part, as Vincenzo Di Benedetto observes, of an 'institutionalized spectacle' through its final detachment and its final gnomic comment.[33]

The Scenario of the Twentieth Century: Generations in Violence[34]

We cannot understand in depth the themes of the texts analysed in this book without remembering their dramatic context, the resurgence of the tragic consciousness in the four generations of the twentieth century, those that were young or adult respectively in the first, second, third and fourth quarters of the century.

A typical European family of the twentieth century had one of its sons killed or maimed in World War I and sacrificed one of its daughters to a life of solitude, deprived of her role as wife and mother. The surviving children in turn produced children who, with their parents and grandparents, fought a second world war in which, unlike the first, civilians were caught up in the fighting and suffered even more deaths than the military. The wartime violence extended to genocide and was perpetuated in peacetime, because politics was increasingly practised as civil war (in the acute phases of the social crisis which everywhere accompanied industrial growth) and as the government of occupation (in other periods). The roots of this violence lay in the common matrix of horrors, with a structural analogy to so-called peacetime and so-called wartime.

Grandparents, children and grandchildren were involved and took part in the continuous and acute violence, which became extreme in World War II. Whole nations in Europe were exterminated by the use of the industrially most advanced technologies and with the active collaboration of the victors and defeated, blinded by indifference or fear, with some minority exceptions. The acceptance of extreme violence, total for the first time in history, became generalized in World War II and reached its peak with the use, at the end of the conflict, only a few days apart, of two atom bombs which were the products of advanced technology. They destroyed tens of thousands of lives in minutes and tens of thousands more over the years, with the survivors doomed to die of radiation sickness. And the climate of secrecy that allowed genocide to happen continues.[35]

The third generation, the grandchildren of World War I, the children of World War II, spent their formative years in the hysterical climate of the Cold War and the terrorist climate of increasingly powerful nuclear tests, in an overt arms race declared and accepted, continuing the process of military innovation which has been continuous since the last quarter of the nineteenth century. The revolt of this generation against their parents still has to be evaluated, to determine whether it was true opposition or embodied a form of continuity with certain attitudes of the previous generations.

The levers of anthropological, cultural and social change are the result of a long historical process brought about essentially by the Church of the Council and socialism in the last quarter of the century: a race towards moral maturation which paralleled the arms race and was seemingly doomed to failure.

The fourth generation of our great European family is still in a sort of limbo devoid of traditional guidelines and struggling with the individual conflicts between far-flung interests. Violence has taken on new forms, which are subtler and more discontinuous. The new economic forms of violence are no less totalitarian than the tried and tested military methods. The financial instruments are powerful in achieving the twin objectives of violence: to assert dominance and accumulate wealth. The violence which arises from contempt seems never to have been so universal and acute. It shapes all the categories of thought and action invented by modernity to organize, rather than transcend, the impulse to violence of a humanity that is strong in its unflagging technological revolution, but still morally immature.

The century has thus expressed the *great relevance of the limit*, thematized in ancient tragedy, acknowledged by its wisdom, and consigned to the now classic artists of the twentieth-century stage, who have not ceased, amid both unconcern and commitment, to stir the consciences of their contemporaries and of future generations.

Chapter 1

HUBRIS AND GUILT: *GENGANGERE* (*GHOSTS*) BY HENRIK IBSEN

Janus *bifrons*

It makes sense to begin with Ibsen's play, though written in the nineteenth century, if we consider that it dates from a period of momentous transition.

Chamberlain Alving and Oswald Alving, the true tragic characters in the play, are like a diptych, a Janus *bifrons*, with one looking back at the nineteenth century and the other forward to the *fin de siècle* crisis that ushered in the new century. Chamberlain Alving's gaze is fixed on the idea of the omnipotence of the self and he acts accordingly, in keeping with an irrepressible, culpable hubris, whose self-destructive and other-destructive consequences fall on himself and his son. Oswald's gaze is focused on the revelation of deceit, omnipotence and the absolute domination of the ego. He sees the biological and psychological 'humiliations' of the self, which believed it was master in its own house, and its coming defeat, though only after the lapse of a generation. In the former the Romantic, positivist ethos is at work; and in the latter the lurking disquiet to which Darwin and Freud were to give a systematic order. Then followed the currents of thought of the new century, which was shaken and maimed by the blow which war inflicted on the presumption and arrogance of Western man.

Kierkegaard, who had also stigmatized the presumption of his century, was a pillar of Ibsen's thinking. He almost certainly read him in his youth. It is significant that the name of the fiancée who inspired the philosopher and the 'Regina cycle' on the issue of sin is also the name of the young woman in *Ghosts*.[1]

The limit with which Chamberlain and Oswald clash is the aspiration to a full and free life of self-fulfilment and desire. It is frustrated by their social environment, by weakness of character or an unsuspected biological inheritance that are revealed unexpectedly. It is expressed in a dramatic machinery made up of everyday gestures, words uttered and unspoken, and allusions. They open up the abyss of suffering, repressions, unresolved conflicts penned up inside the characters, and the unsuspected heritability and familiarity of diseases. The play is structured like a series of doors left open for the characters to spy on each other, as some critics observe.[2] A perfect correspondence between the two theatrical codes.

The historical setting is Norway in the late nineteenth century, within the narrow horizons of a small bourgeois world and the aspirations and ideals of the creative will to overcome weakness. But there is also the prophetic intuition of a generational fault and the perception of the *continuous return*, to use an expression of Nietzsche, of the dynamics of guilt and innocence.

From Ancient to Modern Tragedy: Ibsen's Sources

First of all, as we have said, Kierkegaard gives Ibsen a perspective in which to transcribe the coordinates of modern tragedy in terms borrowed from the Greek model. Confronting modernity, Kierkegaard argued (above all in his essay 'The Tragic in Ancient Drama Reflected in the Tragic in Modern Drama', published in *Either/Or*) that ancient tragedy reveals the nature of tragedy *tout court*. It lies in the disproportion between the need for a limit and the absolute and infinite tension that drives the tragic character. But it takes different forms in antiquity and in modernity (naturally meaning the kind of tragedy coeval with Kierkegaard, not long before the period when Ibsen wrote his plays). In the ancient world the limit was substantive (objective) in its nature: the state, the family or ancestry, destiny. The downfall and destruction of the hero was both action and suffering, and not wholly a consequence of his or her actions. There was a certain extrinsic factor, 'a situation that from the start involves the subjectivity of the hero yet also goes beyond it'.[3] Guilt was similarly intermediate between acting and suffering: it was not wholly the result of a responsible act. And it aroused pity and fear. But in the hero and the audience the pain, the suffering, were deeper than the sorrow, because the degree of reflectivity was lower and individuality, singularity of consciousness, was not yet so highly developed. We can compare the situation to that of a child who sees an adult suffering: he lacks sufficient power of reflection to feel the other's sorrow; the reasons for the adult's suffering remain obscure, yet the child's feeling of sadness is infinitely deep and mingled with an obscure foreboding. The tragic fault, in this view, is not so much mere subjective guilt as hereditary guilt. Destiny is unchangeable. The wrath of the gods is not ethical in character.

Situation and character are dominant in modern tragedy. The hero acts rather than suffers. Subjectivity has a fundamental role. If tragedy is a tension between guilt and innocence, here, in the absolute freedom of the individual, we tend towards total guilt. The individual bears the burden of his life on his shoulders as his own work. It entails anguish, sorrow, total isolation, desperation and defeat by the tragic itself, which verges on the ridiculous. But in this way the age loses the gentle melancholy of the tragic. It drowns sorrow, pity and tears in the absurdity of the individual, who claims to be absolute, who does not feel immersed in a horizon (God, time, the family, a people) which relativises him, and therefore has no chorus to relate to or dialogue with.

Ibsen had to intuit this state of affairs. And while the absent character of Chamberlain Alving faces towards that 'modern' tragic pattern, the character of his son, as has been mentioned, already looks ahead to a further model, to a modernity that is far closer to our own time, one that in the twentieth century was to recover the melancholy, fear and pity, the tension between guilt and innocence of ancient tragedy.

The great sensibility to existence expressed in Ibsen's *Ghosts* is then Kierkegaardian. The theme of angst is Kierkegaardian. The term and concept of *angst* are key elements in Ibsen's text, as is clearly revealed by the *Concordance*.[4] It is an indefinite disquiet, not a specific dread, which he associates with a Judaeo-Christian strand of feeling. It is closely bound up with the vertigo of freedom, with the consequences of sin. These fall on the individual who commits it and on the whole world, because no one is immune from what happens to others: 'Life proclaims aloud the scriptural doctrine that God punishes the crimes of the fathers in their children to the third and fourth generation.'[5]

Certain qualities of Chamberlain Alving probably stem from Kierkegaard's Don Giovanni: his 'erotic, sensuous genius', his undifferentiated aesthetic, his continuous flitting from thing to thing without ever fixing on a goal, his momentary interests, the flow of desire and intoxication, 'a glass of champagne [...] one effervescent moment', the champagne in which he drowns his life and in which his son, young Oswald, drowns his sorrows.[6]

The basic substrate of the modern reformulation of the tragic comes from the Greeks, but it makes a sharp break with them. This issue has been widely debated in criticism of Ibsen.[7] Ibsen himself was well aware of it and the Greek tragedians entered his development in wholly unacademic ways.[8] The key concepts of ancient tragedy and the tragic were the skeleton on which a new body grew. The limit (*moira*), both guilty and innocent transgression (hubris), error (*hamartia*), necessity (*ananke*), the reversal of fortune (*peripeteia*), recognition of the situation and the truth (*anagnōrisis*), fear (*phobos*) and pity (*eleos*) are transcribed in a new ideological horizon in a profound and comprehensive vision of the reality of modern character. Ibsen, as is well known, did not sketch out his creations but rather sculpted them. He brought them to life without contrivance or preconceptions. He probed them in all their complexity, including their contradictions and ambiguities.

Another factor enters into Ibsen's formulation of the tragic horizon in which the characters move in *Ghosts*. This is the brand of Lutheran Protestantism, felt as a burden that weighs with its load of pessimism on human nature, unable to contribute to its own salvation; permanently cut off by sin from its own sources, and remaining sinful even when 'justified', unable to possess sanctification. The characters in *Ghosts* still bear its mark, though it is not made explicit and does not seem to affect them directly. They are inscribed in a closed, stifling and obsessive world, suffering its negatives without having the strength to embody the positives of Lutheran anthropology: identification with and loyalty to one's calling, the great Kierkegaardian theme, and the thread that runs through Ibsen's own biography.[9] Chamberlain Alving never sought it. Oswald seeks it, but fate cuts short his quest.

And whether his influence was direct or indirect, Ibsen knew Nietzsche, principally through Brandes.[10] Ibsen's work echoed Nietzsche's contemporary speculations.[11] They began with *The Birth of Tragedy*, which straddled philology and philosophy. Leaving aside philological polemics and reservations, the culture of the period was shaped by Nietzsche's particular idea of the fundamental importance of Greek tragedy to Western culture. It revealed that 'the Greeks knew and felt the horrors of existence' and sensed the obscure matrix of all things. In the expression of both the Dionysian and the Apollonian that inform tragedy, he gave a voice and face to this chain of fate and death, sublimating it into the harmony of form and triumphing over the terror into which that vision plunged him.

The theme enters into Ibsen's *Ghosts*, which is entwined with other important Nietzschean ideas: the demythifying attitude that sifts political, moral and religious institutions and unmasks their historical responsibility for contributing to man's tragic destiny.[12] Meditation on the 'return' (which in Nietzsche later became eternal recurrence, as a way of belying the linear, progressive or regressive theory of time) impressed him quite independently of expressive form. These ideas were, of course, present in a different framework of thought, commitment and influence, but were still indicative of a certain kind of climate.

The Tragic Nuclei

We will now concentrate on the nuclei of tragedy which emerge in the text,[13] following a brief plot summary.

Young Oswald, the son of Chamberlain Alving, who died some years before, and of Mrs Alving, has returned home to the fjords of the north after a prolonged stay in Paris. There he had pursued his vocation as a painter by moving in artistic circles, with their relaxed and friendly atmosphere. His return coincides with the dedication of an orphanage, a philanthropic project undertaken by Mrs Alving to use the wealth inherited from Alving and so associate her husband's name and memory with it. But this banal circumstance culminates in a tangled web of confessions and revelations, deceits and debacles, as the past bears down heavily on the present, sweeping away the Alving family's plans and benefiting the profiteering carpenter Engstrand, his stepdaughter Regina and Pastor Manders. The truth emerges: Chamberlain Alving was not the man he was generally believed to be, but a debauched victim of his own vices. Mrs Alving was rejected by Pastor Manders, the man she loved, when she fled to him from her husband. Now she is resigned to her situation and devotes herself to defending her wealth and social position. The maid Regina is Alving's daughter, born after an affair with one of the servants. Alving's son is tainted by his father's legacy. He hopes to regain his health through Regina and the joy of living by working in the southern sun, but his dreams are shattered by dementia and the prison of a regressive relationship with his mother. The commemorative orphanage burns down. Engstrand, acting in complicity (though not explicitly) with Manders and Regina, will use the money to build a shady sailors' home.

The late Chamberlain Alving is a tragic figure, a presence-absence weighing on all that happens in the play. He is evoked in act 1, in the dialogue between Pastor Manders and Mrs Alving, and in the words, gestures and behaviour of young Oswald. He was impatient of the limitations imposed by the need to choose and stand by his choice, as required by the need for self-preservation as well as moral exigencies and to protect his reputation. He continued to transgress until his premature death. But his inhibited transgressions were not a true acceptance of his natural vocation opening onto vital horizons, they were frustrated and stifled in secret, while others spied and sneaked, as Roberto Alonge rightly observes.[14] He indulged his depravity in private, covered by bourgeois hypocrisy and the enforced complicity of his wife, who submitted to practical expediency and a safe respectability. In this Alving was abetted by a natural charm, which made him attractive to others and prevented them from thinking ill of him. His transgressions were all committed in private, in seclusion, screened from others. He embodied, though on a smaller scale, Kierkegaard's tragic symbol of Don Giovanni, representing the aesthetic phase in the path of life, which burns for an instant and falls into the sin of not bowing to the modern law of the limit: the freedom to choose in finiteness knowing that desire is infinite.

So Alving loses everything: his life, the son to whom he has bequeathed his taint (not just syphilis, believed to be hereditary at the time, but a mode of being that breaks through the crust of his upbringing, his love and respect for his mother). This taint destroys Alving's life, his honoured memory. His name will be associated not with the charitable foundation of the orphanage but a brothel disguised as a sailors' home in Little Harbour Street, run by the coarse and ambiguous Engstrand and by Alving's natural daughter, conceived by one of his servants and likewise doomed.

At the end of the day of revelations, in keeping with the classical day traditional in tragedy, Mrs Alving sees her husband clearly and interprets his achievements differently. In his youth he took his *joie de vivre* wherever he went; those who saw him were overwhelmed by his festive air. Indomitable strength and fullness of life were manifest in him; but then he was fated to vegetate in a middling sort of city, ill-suited to any great purpose, frustrated by the mediocrity of business and idle amusements.

> MRS ALVING. He had to live at home here in a half-grown town, which had no joys to offer him – only dissipations. He had no object in life – only an official position. He had no work into which he could throw himself heart and soul; he had only business. He had not a single comrade that could realize what the joy of life meant – only loungers and boon-companions.[15]

This brings out the tragic implications of Alving's life. His drive was shattered by the limits of a basically moderate temperament trapped in a stifling and torpid social milieu. Oswald is his double, another tragic character. Oswald is initially enabled to freely transcend this limited world, and his transgression is sustainable. He rejects the business and official roles of his bourgeois family, choosing to work as a painter, so freeing himself from the trammels of bourgeois life. Something comparable appears in the central character in Thomas Mann's *Buddenbrooks*. Oswald turns away from the endless rain and mist of his homeland to seek the light and sun of the south. He rejects the solitude of the fjords for life in Paris; the uneventful conformism and hypocrisy of a wealthy bourgeois family for the irregularity, passion and sincerity of Parisian art circles, where things are called by their real names and hypocrisy shatters against the revelation that the moralists are great experts in immorality.

> OSWALD. No; do you know when and where I have come across immorality in artistic circles?
> MANDERS. No, thank heaven, I don't!
> OSWALD. Well, then, allow me to inform you. I have met with it when one or other of our pattern husbands and fathers has come to Paris to have a look round on his own account, and has done the artists the honour of visiting their humble haunts. They knew what was what. These gentlemen could tell us all about places and things we had never dreamt of.[16]

He feels the restrictions physically hemming him in, a cage in which he is trapped: the dreariness of 'this endless rain', the landscape shrouded in heavy mist, and the deep gloom of the fjord.[17] He chooses to break through the constraints by making his choice freely and firmly. In Paris he deliberately seeks not libertine escapism so much as the freedom of art and the affections. We are given a glimpse of the milieu of the impressionist painters, where everything that Oswald painted 'turned upon the joy of life – always, always upon the joy of life – light and sunshine and glorious air – and faces radiant with happiness' (act 2, 70). We glimpse irregular families, compared with middle-class ideas of respectability, but love and respect reign on their domestic hearths.

OSWALD. I never noticed anything particularly irregular about the life these people lead. […] Never have I heard an offensive word, and still less have I witnessed anything that could be called immoral.[18]

In Paris he seeks to distance himself from the ideas underlying the world he was born into and his outlook alters as he sheds the pessimism of Lutheran anthropology.

OSWALD. I only mean that here people are brought up to believe that work is a curse and a punishment for sin, and that life is something miserable, something it would be best to have done with, the sooner the better.
MRS ALVING. 'A vale of tears', yes; and we certainly do our best to make it one.
OSWALD. But in the great world people won't hear of such things.[19]

But he discovers the intractable limitation that he is unable to overcome is actually different: it is a disease, syphilis, contracted by inheritance or youthful carelessness (carelessness, but due to an inherited propensity), according to the twofold theory of the origin of Oswald's taint advanced by the Parisian physician. It is an irreversible softening of the brain leading to madness, idiocy, regression to an infantile stage in a new symbiosis with his mother, preceding the manifestation of his similarity to his father and hence the sin of his origin. And the antidote of Regina's healthfulness is unable to heal him. Oswald's substance (today we would say his DNA) has been cast in a weak mould, without the least possibility of redemption, by his father, who manifests himself in gestures imprinted in his fibres, automatisms seemingly induced by the environment, as we know happens, so that he appears the photocopy of his father:

MANDERS. When Oswald appeared there, in the doorway, with the pipe in his mouth, I could have sworn I saw his father, large as life.
OSWALD. No, really?
MRS ALVING. Oh, how can you say so? Oswald takes after me.[20]

His whole tragic substance and the modernity of this tragedy lie in this ambiguity, in the inner conflict between an impulse that drives him to seek to break down the barriers that enclose him and an impulse-defect that drags him back and defeats him. Tracing Oswald's misfortune to 'the consequences of his own free choice' seems simplistic compared to the complexity of the problem.[21] It does not allow us to see the implications on the generational plane that our sensibility today enables us to perceive. His physical actions explicitly reveal this: smoking, wine or sex, for instance. The events we overhear taking place beyond the half-open door, Oswald's advances to Regina, reveal it. He cannot disengage his existence from the world of ghosts (French expresses the concept with a very exact and effective term: *revenants*), which he embodies and bears within him. He fails to soar into freedom. Mrs Alving clearly expresses his state:

MRS ALVING. I am timid and faint-hearted because of the ghosts that hang about me, and that I can never quite shake off.
MANDERS. What do you say hangs about you?
MRS ALVING. Ghosts! When I heard Regina and Oswald in there, it was as though ghosts rose up before me. But I almost think we are all of us ghosts, Pastor Manders. It is not only what we have inherited from our father and mother that 'walks' in us. It is all sorts of dead ideas, and lifeless old beliefs, and so forth. They have no vitality, but they cling to us all the same, and we cannot shake them off. Whenever I take up a newspaper, I seem to see ghosts gliding between the lines. There must be ghosts all the country over, as thick as the sands of the sea. And then we are, one and all, so pitifully afraid of the light.[22]

Oswald gradually acquires the deeply human appearance of youth cut short without any guilt by the hubris of the fathers; and his cries, the flashes of insight filled with candour and yearning that reveal his thwarted hopes of life, are reminiscent of the elevated tones of certain youthful victims of Greek tragedy (think of the lamentations of Antigone or Iphigenia), but without the distance of myth, all with the freshness of a modernity that is close to us and has inspired recent productions in the theatre.[23]

The most affecting scenes – act 2, scene 4 and the final scene of act 3 – recall the great *Pietas* of Western art. But especially, in a world without faith and grandeur, they evoke the contemporary studies of regression to the maternal womb and the primary visceral complicity between mother and child.

OSWALD. (*Crumpling up a newspaper.*) I should have thought it must be pretty much the same to you whether I was in existence or not. [...] (*Stops beside* MRS ALVING.) Mother, may I sit on the sofa beside you?
MRS ALVING. (*Makes room for him.*) Yes, do, my dear boy.[24]

His story has the unconsciousness of ancient sin passed down through the whole human race and engrafted onto original sin, which corrupts human nature and renders it vulnerable. The accents in which he expresses himself distantly and without solemnity echo the cries of the victims in ancient tragedy.

MRS ALVING. My poor boy! How has this horrible thing come upon you?
OSWALD. (*Sitting upright again.*) That's just what I cannot possibly grasp or understand. I have never led a dissipated life, never, in any respect. You mustn't believe that of me, mother! I've never done that.
MRS ALVING. I am sure you haven't, Oswald.
OSWALD. And yet this has come upon me just the same – this awful misfortune![25]

The truth is incomprehensible. Its impenetrability is unfathomable to humanity, which refuses to accept a theological explanation for the roots of its tragic condition. Hence it is better to avoid thinking, which is Oswald's choice (act 2).

The tragic situation is resolved wholly in the intimate and private sphere, in the inwardness of a suffering which, at the end of act 2, is defined by the word *angst* (dread). Once uttered, it is repeated obsessively as if representing a concrete oppression.

OSWALD. Don't refuse me, mother. Do be kind, now! I must have something to wash down all these gnawing thoughts. (*Goes into the conservatory.*) And then – it's so dark here! […] I cannot go on bearing all this anguish of soul alone. […] (*Wanders restlessly about.*) But it's all the torment, the gnawing remorse – and then, the great, killing dread. Oh – that awful dread!
MRS ALVING. (*Walking after him.*) Dread? What dread? What do you mean?[26]

Angst is the key word in the great final scene of the tragedy. Obsessively repeated many times, it expresses the prison which holds Oswald in the walls of the locked room, in the enclosed horizon of hostile nature, in a state of incurable illness, the 'deadly disease'. But Oswald also knows fear, a precise fear. The term emerges in the dialogue with Oswald at the end of act 2:

OSWALD. That is why I'm afraid of remaining at home with you.
MRS ALVING. Afraid? What are you afraid of here, with me?
OSWALD. I'm afraid lest all my instincts should be warped into ugliness.
MRS ALVING. (*Looks steadily at him.*) Do you think that is what would happen?
OSWALD. I know it. You may live the same life here as there, and yet it won't be the same life.[27]

Dread reflects the oppression of the unknown, the fears of madness, imbecility, of death in life. The heady feeling of freedom, once experienced, is now in danger of being stifled. But Oswald fears something that he sees clearly. He fears his most authentic nature will be crushed, and this is the true analogy between Oswald and his father, his father's true legacy, the root of that closeness he felt when his father took him on his lap and told him to smoke the pipe, but his mother snatched it away from him. The joy of living. This passage reveals the true ties between father and son, the source of the tragic repression of the expansive tendency of life, which father and son share. But in the one it is irresponsible hubris, self-destructive and hetero-destructive; in the other it is hubris suffered, which inhibits the flowering of a vocation. Hence it is at this point that Helen Alving can begin to tell her story – now all the pieces have fallen into place.

The other characters fall short of the tragic. Helen Alving once sought, albeit unsuccessfully, to flee from the dangerous irregularities of her husband and her own uncertainties into the arms of the most predictable, obtuse and unresponsive man possible, Pastor Manders. She cultivated libertarian ideas and aspirations only by privately reading books considered daring and revolutionary, but which contained what most people actually think without wishing to admit it. In reality, Helen Alving has followed the beaten track: marriage in accordance with the law and morality to a man possessing a large fortune. In the final edition, all doubts that it had been a marriage of love disappear. Her heart was moved by Manders alone at the time. She mortified (and comes to repent of it) the *joie de vivre* of her brilliant young husband, but tenaciously defended his wealth, supporting him in his private turmoil to dominate him and take his place in the management and expansion of his business interests.

Manders has settled into the roles of tending the network of institutions to which he belongs: the boards and committees: 'You may believe it was not so easy for me to get away. With all the Boards and Committees I belong to' (act 1, 53). He occupies a safe niche based on well-managed money, in the midst of his committees and boards of directors, which absorb all his energies, while remaining stuck in the rut of conformist opinions. If he scents an anomaly, a hint of derangement, a novelty, he reduces it to familiar and harmless schemes, as when he discovers that Helen Alving reads books that are 'dangerous'. Eventually he justifies her interest as expressing a desire to keep up with the ideas her son will encounter in the larger world where he is travelling. With a touch of malice he probes her opinions and pretends to be scandalized. But above all he remains entrenched in his selfishness and defensive indifference, in the aloofness of the morality of expediency and respectability. He shelters himself from tensions and suffering, as well as the joys of feelings, passions, emotions, which are all reduced to the level of propriety and impropriety. There is even a touch of comedy and a vein of caricature in the presentation of his false consciousness of money. He is indignant to learn that Engstrand was bribed into marrying the servant seduced by Alving, but is immediately curious to know how much he made on the deal.[28]

MANDERS. But such a piece of duplicity on his part! And towards me too! I never could have believed it of Jacob Engstrand. I shall not fail to take him seriously to task; he may be sure of that. – And then the immorality of such a connection! For money – ! How much did the girl receive?

MRS ALVING. Three hundred dollars.

MANDERS. Just think of it – for a miserable three hundred dollars, to go and marry a fallen woman![29]

The rhetoric of morality and sacrifice, valid for others, conceals his fear of being troubled and disturbed in his torpid life. This is the significance of the evocation of his youthful decision to reject Helen when she fled from her unfaithful husband in the early days of her marriage.

MANDERS. It is the very mark of the spirit of rebellion to crave for happiness in this life. What right have we human beings to happiness? We have simply to do our duty, Mrs Alving! And your duty was to hold firmly to the man you had once chosen, and to whom you were bound by the holiest ties.

MRS ALVING. You know very well what sort of life Alving was leading – what excesses he was guilty of.

MANDERS. I know very well what rumors there were about him; and I am the last to approve the life he led in his young days, if report did not wrong him. But a wife is not appointed to be her husband's judge. It was your duty to bear with humility the cross which a Higher Power had, in its wisdom, laid upon you. But instead of that you rebelliously throw away the cross, desert the backslider whom you should have supported, go and risk your good name and reputation, and – nearly succeed in ruining other people's reputation into the bargain.[30]

He judges and condemns, contravening the Gospel commandment against passing judgement. He censures Mrs Alving's errors, the wrongs she did to her husband and son, making out she is culpable as both wife and mother. But his censures are based on appearances and break down with the revelation of the hidden truth. All his confidence crumbles pathetically and his brittle certainties are shattered.

Engstrand is despicable. He speculates whenever he can with his shabby cynicism, cunning, little tricks, attempts at blackmail and trivial projects. At the same time, insinuatingly and unctuously, he parades fine sentiments in a vapid language made up of popular clichés and exclamations. He simulates pious sentiments, repeated by rote, in purely residual religious expressions (his references to Jesus and the Devil disguise his inward curses as hypocritical invocations), leading him to shed crocodile tears over improbable paternal feelings.

ENGSTRAND. Lord, how you talk, Regina. (*Limps a step or two forward into the room.*) It's just this as I wanted to say – […] Yes, we're weak vessels, we poor mortals, my girl – […] Well, but that was only when I was a bit on, don't you know? Temptations are manifold in this world, Regina.[31]

ENGSTRAND. Yes, I trust I am. And so I'll say good-bye, ma'am, and thank you kindly; and take good care of Regina for me – (*Wipes a tear from his eye.*) – poor Johanna's child. Well, it's a queer thing, now; but it's just like as if she'd growd into the very apple of my eye. It is, indeed. (*He bows and goes out through the hall.*)[32]

He is quick to pick up the weak points of his interlocutor of least resistance, Pastor Manders, who shares his love of money, his essential cynicism and hypocrisy. Manders is, however, not so coarse and, as Mrs Alving perceptively comments, he is 'and will always be, a great baby'.[33] Engstrand is quick to lead him the way he wants to go, playing on his panic at what might happen and above all the risks to his public image. He is shady and sinister in bringing down to his own level those who are essentially already like him, such as the beautiful Regina, while prudently steering clear of those who do not fall for his wiles, but have little to oppose them with, such as Mrs Alving. He is prompt to seize opportunities. He takes advantage of the altered circumstances to bend Manders to his will, and inveigles Regina into his squalid project, which is also the only realistic and appropriate one in the circumstances. Engstrand also pretends to be a zealous paladin of virtue (a sham which the naive, gullible Manders clings to), and hypocritically exploits his religious reminiscences effectively to overcome the pastor's last resistance.

ENGSTRAND. Jacob Engstrand may be likened to a sort of a guardian angel, he may, your Reverence.
MANDERS. No, no; I really cannot accept that.
ENGSTRAND. Oh, that'll be the way of it, all the same. I know a man as has taken others' sins upon himself before now, I do.[34]

A cheap Machiavellianism lies at the root of all this.

Regina makes the most of her blossoming youth and her half-education, which she flaunts by using French expressions and her elegant manners to attempt to play the usual card: either to marry safely or sell herself. Yet despite her efforts at emancipation through the little education she has received and the prospect of travelling the world with Oswald, before the truth is revealed, her schemes shatter against the fateful recurrence of the past. Her lot will be cast in the same mould as her mother's, but she will be even more degraded. Regina is cut from the same cloth. In her beautiful body, young and healthy, she embodies the worst: she is unscrupulous, she broods over grudges; she is sly, quick to take advantage of situations and careful not to be guided by her sentiments. She encourages Manders's ingenuity and his instinct for absolute self-preservation, then covertly blackmails both Manders and Engstrand by suggesting they are to blame in some way for the fire. By encouraging their cynicism she leads them to commit revealing mistakes.

ENGSTRAND. (*Enters through the hall.*) Your Reverence –
MANDERS. (*Turns round in terror.*) Are you after me here, too?
ENGSTRAND. Yes, strike me dead, but I must – ! Oh, Lord! what am I saying? But this is a terrible ugly business, your Reverence.
MANDERS. (*Walks to and fro.*) Alas! alas!
REGINA. What's the matter?
ENGSTRAND. Why, it all came of this here prayer-meeting, you see. (*Softly.*) The bird's limed, my girl. (*Aloud.*) And to think it should be my doing that such a thing should be his Reverence's doing![35]

True and false values collide. Money, as we have seen, is a key term. Truth and freedom are contrasted with duty, interpreted as defending one's reputation at all costs. The aspiration to happiness and the desire for independence are considered errors by the morality of the cross, mortification and the theology of man's submission as a humble instrument of the Almighty. Here we have one of the great nuclei of the idea and the representation of tragedy: *guilt*. Around it are woven the threads of classical Greek and biblical thought. We know that familiarity with the Bible was customary in a Protestant education, that Ibsen achieved scholastic distinction in this subject, that he absorbed it at home and kept a bible in his study, that he frequently consulted it, as he declared and as his numerous markings of the texts reveal.

The theme is the guilt of origin, a version of original sin, imprinted in human nature, but also the guilt of a generation. Presumably Ibsen had an inkling that the nineteenth century would destroy its children at the dawn of the new century. The success of his work in the early nineteen hundreds gives us a glimpse of the dramatic significance of this insight for understanding the tragedy of our own time.

The fatal results of that paternity cannot be curbed or erased, though Mrs Alving seeks to do so:

> MRS ALVING. And besides, I had one other reason. I was determined that Oswald, my own boy, should inherit nothing whatever from his father. […] My son shall have everything from me – everything. […] But then this long, hateful comedy will be ended. From the day after to-morrow, I shall act in every way as though he who is dead had never lived in this house. There shall be no one here but my boy and his mother.[36]

It is the unwitting guilt of origin, of the old biblical kind. It is rooted in the sins of the fathers, in keeping with an outlook which seems to be transferred, in a climate of positivism and neopositivism, from the anthropological and theological plane to the physiological-genetic, with the result that the apodictic sentence is passed by the doctor who made the diagnosis.

> OSWALD. I didn't understand either, and begged him to explain himself more clearly. And then the old cynic said – (*Clenching his fist.*) Oh – !
> MRS ALVING. What did he say?
> OSWALD. He said, 'The sins of the fathers are visited upon the children.'[37]

Expiation follows; the final fire is a polyvalent symbol of it. The fire helps Pastor Manders erase all traces of those disorders that he cannot bear to see; it helps Engstrand by removing any excuse for Regina not staying with him, but it is also nemesis and purification. Yet there is no catharsis, whether inner or outer: Chamberlain Alving and Oswald succumb unconsciously and in despair. There is no social or cultural achievement, no fecundity in the sacrifice of the victim or the punishment of the guilty. The little bourgeois world is enclosed in itself. There is no chorus to speak as the voice of the community, ready to distil knowledge or heighten devotion. Of Chamberlain Alving all that remains is a social mask that conceals the truth; Oswald is imprisoned in imbecility. Mrs Alving, finally defeated, bows over a regressed child, seeking a pity which she is not, and never has been, capable of. As for the others we shall 'look, and pass on'.[38]

Nor is there any projection in time. There is no development. Time stands still. The present is cast in the mould of the past and there is no future. The tragic experience of an inescapable limitation is not richness that fecundates the future. The dissipation remains in the instant of the brothel or the regression to and fixation in the frozen and exclusive mother–son relationship, which will never thaw and grow. From the beginning, Helen Alving has sought to remove her son from all paternal contacts and influences, keeping everything within her own horizon. Her son leaves the parental home, first for his education, then to follow his vocation as an artist in Paris. He is separated from all the property connected with his father's legacy. But fatality has proved far stronger: the signs of a biological and characterial heritage, imprinted in his body, emerge gradually but inevitably. He has been drawn back into his father's house forever. Time is frozen by the ghosts which continually return unchanged. Bergman was to represent it as a clock without hands in the wild strawberry patch: we are born old, we are born dead. Oswald in act 2 describes his life as a living death.

Down to this point I have preferred to interpret *Ghosts* as a philosophical and existential tragedy, but an unforced historical connection can also be read into it. This lies in what the great Ibsen scholar Régis Boyer called the poet's prophetic power, the extreme sensitivity and freedom with which he read the times and their projection into the future.[39] Nurtured by his experiences, firstly of the Scandinavian world and then of Wilhelmine Germany, he must have had an inkling that a catastrophe was brewing, a tragedy of history that would again present the eternal, inexorable return of the tragic, this time clearly due to human guilt. Hence, with the wisdom of hindsight, we can read the fire that destroys the orphanage as a symbolic foreshadowing of a historical disaster, one in which nineteenth-century Europe would disappear; and the sun, which the demented Oswald invokes at the end of the play like a cracked record, is linked in the minds of some of us with that great 'sun' that was to shine on Hiroshima and Nagasaki as it dissolved the world (though we know that the imagination is now accustomed to such associations, some of them distant).[40]

The Form of Modern Tragedy

Ibsen began to reflect on the tragic and its modern form by exploring a seemingly normal and conformist situation, one faithful to the clichés: a family which suggests the possibility of triangular complications and a plot rich in pathos and melodrama, turning on vice and death, potentially inspiring an equally conformist play with realistic and melodramatic overtones. But the play proved to be quite different. Ibsen delved deeper. He searched for the truth, seeking to create a drama that would range widely and touch the deepest chords, instead of the routine after-dinner entertainments copied from foreign works which had irked him in the fifties as a stage manager in Christiania and Bergen.

Realism and symbolism are interwoven. The lucid observation of reality, the mastery of language and the timing of the dramatic structure, the undercurrents of innuendo with unspoken words passing between the characters, combine to create a gallery of portraits and reciprocal solitudes that are utterly modern in character. But the structure rests on the shoulders of antiquity. The work preserves the concentration of the three unities. The space does not change, but it is not completely enclosed. A large living room overlooks the garden with one door on the left and two on the right: they are closed or half-open. Beyond is a conservatory framed by large windows with a door giving onto the garden. Through the windows we see the endless drizzling rain and the deep and melancholy fjord. The time span is limited to one day. The first act takes place in late morning, the second after lunch, and the third continues through the night until sunrise. There are few characters; the chorus is completely absent, not just as a specific character, outdated by the dramatic conventions of the period, but even as the function of a presence, a gaze, the involvement of a group, the community or the town. The orphanage that was meant to unite it is destroyed by fire.

The structure of the play is skilfully contrived. It is closely woven, urgent in its development and enriched by internal, terminological, thematic and situational symmetries and cross-references. The suspense is adroitly managed. The hints at the mystery and the gradual revelation of the truth about Oswald partly repeat the technique of *Oedipus*: clues are dropped, but Mrs Alving, like Jocasta, denies and represses them. Then the situation quickly precipitates and the climax brings the revelation.

The other elements of mystery are subtly insinuated. One example is the audience's suspicion that the fire is not an unforeseeable accident but an act of arson perpetrated by Engstrand, the sanctimonious organizer of the prayer meeting in the newly completed orphanage, in order to forge invisible bonds between his sinister plan for the brothel in the port, Regina and Manders himself.

Ibsen deftly brings in certain 'inconsistencies' which attentive readers or members of the audience, kept on tenterhooks, wait to see explained: Regina's dialogue with Engstrand is studded with French expressions. How can a servant be so modish? What lies behind it? And why does Mrs Alving overreact to the idea that Regina might go home with Engstrand? Isn't he her father? And why does Manders, who seems thick skinned, indulge an impulse of tenderness by calling Mrs Alving by her first name on one occasion? What is at the bottom of all this?

The play's construction is notable. The penultimate scene of act 2 is interrupted after Mrs Alving tells Manders they can finally talk freely. The suspension is filled by two unexpected events: the announcement that Oswald intends to take Regina away, as his wife if she is willing, and the outbreak of the fire. The scene closes with Manders's words, their double meaning clearly brought out by the French translation: 'pas d'assurance' (And we left it uninsured!).[41]

Ibsen shows great mastery and a shrewd sense of proportion in allowing things to transpire without contrivance and without being too explicit. Moments of subtle and refined technique are interwoven with dialectical moments of stringent rationality; passages of poignant poetry are insinuated into the rigour of the system. This appears in certain passages of tenderness and closeness between Oswald and his mother and in one or two passages where Manders's hidebound manner seems to crack open and deeper feelings surface.

A brief scene in act 1 contains a scattering of clues: the cup of wine in which red mingles with white; Oswald trailing suspiciously after Regina as he makes his exit; the door left ajar, through which the past returns.

Act 3 is shorter, about half the length of act 1 and two-thirds of act 2. As we have seen, it moves rapidly to its climax. It becomes increasingly introverted in the movement of mother and son, who first withdraw into their regressive relationship and then within themselves and at the same time into the prison of their reciprocal and inescapable presence.

OSWALD. Yes. I was quite small at the time. I recollect I came up to father's room one evening when he was in great spirits.
MRS ALVING. Oh, you can't recollect anything of those times. [...] My dear friend, it's only something Oswald has dreamt.[42]

The two conclusive scenes of the finale are powerful. The first is between Mrs Alving, Oswald and Regina, and the second between Mrs Alving and Oswald alone. Certain gestures charge the scene with a profound and moving symbolism. Oswald acquires the character of an innocent victim, a suffering Christ, as Mrs Alving wipes the water and sweat from his face, an act that evokes St Veronica. But he gradually regresses towards the infantile state to which the fatal disease condemns him, bringing him ever closer to his mother. As they sit together on the sofa, he is forlorn, helpless, in her hands:

MRS ALVING. The child has his mother to nurse him. […]
OSWALD. Well, let us hope so. And let us live together as long as we can. Thank you, mother. […]
MRS ALVING. Everything you point to you shall have, just as when you were a little child. […]
OSWALD. (*Repeats, in a dull, toneless voice.*) The sun. The sun.[43]

Then the action is blocked. The 'worm-eaten' brain is fixated on the last words uttered in the state of consciousness: 'the sun'. His tongue repeats it mechanically, dully, while his eyes are fixed on what has now become a hallucination: the fire in which the orphanage blazes and the rising sun are confused. There is no catharsis, no assurance of liberating death, because we do not know whether Mrs Alving can give it to him.

A Perfect Theatrical Machine

Ibsen had a thorough knowledge of dramatic machinery. When barely 20 he had been appointed stage director of the theatre in Bergen. He acquired a mastery of all the theatrical skills. The dramatic structure he fashioned for his tragedy is perfect: the recurrence of strategically placed keywords (money, dread, duty, happiness, sun) catalyses the audience's attention. His accomplished use of pauses creates room for an allusive kind of performance, prompting the actors to provide glimpses of things left unsaid, a world that can be imagined behind and beyond the limits of the action, classically enclosed within the unities of space and time. Graphically, his use of dashes indicates this openness.

The language is suited to the characters. What complexity, what a wealth of facets in this little world! Note, for example, how cautiously and craftily Engstrand goes about unfolding his plan to Regina, his ambiguous complacency about his own unnamed weaknesses, his allusions to 'a new line of business', his arguments, spoken and unspoken, to bring her round and his shady calculations and mischievous allusions to Regina's special interest in the young Oswald. We note Regina's ladylike tone, suggesting an upbringing above her position as a servant, the vulgarities she is tempted to use when she is moved to express contempt, and the pauses she fills with the gestures of serving. There are numerous telling details. For example, she bustles about Pastor Manders, helping him take off his overcoat and putting away his dripping umbrella, as if angling for some advantage and leading the conversation towards herself.

REGINA. Yes, that may be; but all the same – Now, if it were in a thoroughly nice house, and with a real gentleman –
MANDERS. Why, my dear Regina –
REGINA. – one I could love and respect, and be a daughter to –
MANDERS. Yes, but my dear, good child –[44]

We sense Manders's hypocritical and probing hesitation, his moralistic and unrequested admonitions and embarrassing suspicions. He wavers between taking a firm stand and conveniently ignoring unpleasant realities. He mingles cautious business considerations (e.g., the advisability of insuring the orphanage) with accusations and reproaches, flashes of tenderness and stifled regrets:

MANDERS. (*Softly and hesitatingly.*) Helen – if that is meant as a reproach, I would beg you to bear in mind –
MRS ALVING. – the regard you owed to your position, yes; and that I was a runaway wife. One can never be too cautious with such unprincipled creatures.
MANDERS. My dear – Mrs Alving, you know that is an absurd exaggeration –[45]

In Mrs Alving we detect implicit evocations of her youthful love for Manders and his prudent withdrawals. In Oswald we observe the sudden pauses that check his speech as the truth surfaces, at first gradually and then ever more rapidly and inexorably. Pauses and exclamations punctuate the short final scenes of the first act of the discovery.

The restrained stage directions emphasize poses and symbolic gestures with rare icasticity. Take the stage direction at the beginning of act 3: Mrs Alving stands in the conservatory, looking straight ahead, with a large shawl over her head. Regina stands not far behind her in a similar pose. They stare at the fire as it burns the orphanage down to the ground. We sense that their gaze guides their thoughts as they probe the underlying significance of what is happening in the distance.

The history of the reception of Ibsen's play in the theatre has proved its effectiveness in performance and its power to stimulate certain actors to achieve the distinction of the tragic. A perfect and modern construct, in the European consciousness it became a landmark of tragedy, which the new age proved unable to ignore.

Chapter 2

EVE BECOMES MARY: *L'ANNONCE FAITE À MARIE* (*THE TIDINGS BROUGHT TO MARY*) BY PAUL CLAUDEL

An entirely different outlook, profoundly influenced by faith in Christianity and inspired by the Gospels, appears in the dramatic development of the tragic awareness of another great writer of the early twentieth century, Paul Claudel.[1] We can choose *The Tidings Brought to Mary* to explore the theme we are concerned with here.

Tidings is a key text in twentieth-century dramaturgy. The tragic inspiration, sifted through the religious idea of existence and expressed in the modes of high poetry, modulated in lyrical and liturgical patterns, develops into a positive vision.

The text is based on a philosophy of Christian inspiration, fostered by Maritain's personalism and Thomism. Like the works of other great twentieth-century writers, among them T. S. Eliot and Giovanni Testori, it deals with the question, widely discussed by scholars, of the relation between the tragic consciousness and Christian consciousness, and their compatibility.[2]

The tragic action of the character is presented in a very special way, because she is *figura Christi*. In Christ the finite and infinite coexist. This is because he embodies in himself the concreteness of the human person, situated in time and space, even experiencing death, and total intimacy, which coincides with the absoluteness of the divine. The height of the tragic therefore verges on the denial of the possibility of the tragic. Violaine, however, like Thomas Becket in Eliot's play, is not Christ but *figura Christi*. They therefore come close to surpassing the tragic, but they do not fully do so, because they tend towards the divine but do not possess it. Certainly there is not the slightest failing in them, except the presumption of holiness (which in Eliot's Becket is actually expressed as temptation). The tragic condition of Violaine has a different valence from that of the other characters, as we will see in Pierre de Craon and Mara. Their transgression and their guilt lies, Christianly, both in a choice freely made and in the inescapable root of evil, inherited sin, the *mysterium iniquitatis* which requires, in keeping with Claudel's vision, an act of expiation that is embraced by Violaine, *figura Christi*.

Its conception and construction engaged over half a century of the author's life. The work first took shape in a version drafted in 1892, *La jeune fille Violaine* (probably revised later and eventually published in 1926). A second version of this was issued in 1901, followed by a radical revision undertaken in 1909, which led to the publication in 1912 of *L'annonce faite à Marie* (in the *Nouvelle Revue Française*, and shortly thereafter as a book). But its composition was only completed with the final edition in 1948.³

The alterations were certainly due in part to the need to ensure it could be performed in the theatre, as well as in response to requests from directors and actors and the author's own growing stage experience as he developed his distinctive ideas about the theatre. But it was also due to the pressure of the historical period, which saw France suffer in two world wars, become fired up with revanchism, drown in the blood of the carnage at the front, then grow fearful of invasion and seek to recover after it. Above all it was a reflection of Claudel's spiritual development, his probing, all through his life, of the sources of ancient wisdom and the Holy Scriptures, and the most problematical nuclei of existence and faith, suffering, death and redemptive sacrifice – the unconditional response to his vocation and his stubborn questioning of God, to the point of seeking to force a response. But it was also due to the tragic poet's changing awareness under the pressures of personal experiences, the historical and social situation, and his profound cultural studies, in addition to the copious production of a life spent tirelessly in the most remote parts of the world, from the Far East to the Americas, yet always with a tenacious attachment to his homeland in the depths of France.

The History of the Text

The 1912 edition

To favour an understanding of this process, we can examine the sequence of scenes in the 1912 version.

We are at the end of the Middle Ages, as conventionally represented, in the barn of Combernon, a massive building closed by a swinging door coarsely painted with figures of St Peter with the keys and St Paul with the sword. It is nearly dawn. Violaine, a tall and slender figure, barefooted, the young heiress to the property, wrapped in her garments as both peasant and nun, appears before Pierre de Craon, the cathedral builder, who has ridden on horseback into the barn. As the Angelus sounds, the dialogue marks the beginning of the play. Pierre is guilty of having been unable to resist the beauty of Violaine. He sought unsuccessfully to violate her and now he is punished by being stricken with leprosy. Violaine loves another, the young and industrious Jacques Hury, and hopes to be betrothed to him soon. In the fullness of her happiness and generosity, Violaine gives Pierre a twofold gift: the gold ring that Jacques had given her, to add lustre to the new cathedral Pierre is building, and a sisterly kiss on his lips that will cause her to contract leprosy in her innocent body. Unseen, her jealous sister Mara spies on her (prologue).

It is now daytime and the scene is set in the kitchen at Combernon, filled with domestic utensils, rather as in a Bruegel painting. Violaine's mother, bustling about the hearth, and her father, Anne Vercors, the vigorous artificer of Combernon, engage in a dialogue that is first veined with delightful irony and a sense of closeness, then with drama. It is decided: Violaine will marry Jacques, as Anne is to go to Jerusalem on a pilgrimage to redeem France and the Church of Rome from the evil divisions into which they have fallen.

Mara enters and threatens the Mother: if she does not dissuade Violaine from the marriage, she will hang herself. Anne Vercors, Jacques Hury, Violaine, the farm workers and the servants enter. There follows a sample of Anne's paternal and generous justice: instead of punishing a poor peasant caught stealing trees, Anne raises a hymn to the farm and the land and takes his leave in a ceremony with a liturgical ring to it: the breaking of bread blessed with the sign of the cross (act 1, scenes 1–3).

Two weeks have gone by. The scene is set out of doors at noontide in July. Everything is vibrant in the bright sunshine in the orchard, from which the eye can see the opulent extent of Combernon and the side of Monsavierge. The Mother tells Mara she has spoken to Violaine and observes sorrowfully that the girl no longer laughs. Jacques comes to see Violaine. Mara sarcastically repeats her assertion that Violaine has been unfaithful to him, but he refuses to believe it.

Violaine appears 'all golden', 'clothed in a linen gown with a kind of dalmatic of cloth-of-gold decorated with large red and blue flowers'. On her head she wears a diadem. 'Jacques! Bonjour, Jacques.'[4] The greeting is repeatedly evoked throughout the play. But Violaine's words sound strange at a lovers' meeting. There are allusions to the twofold significance of the garment she wears (that of the nuns of Monsavierge and of the local women on the day they are betrothed and the day they die), and doubts about Jacques's right to take for himself what is God's alone. Their words form a crescendo which culminates in the revelation: with the knife that Jacques gives her, Violaine cuts open the gown where it covers her left breast and reveals the first stain of leprosy on it. The young man flares up angrily, his suspicions of betrayal confirmed. He himself accompanies her to the place set apart for lepers.

In the same room as in act 1 Mara eagerly announces that the feared betrothal has been broken off. Violaine, dressed in her travelling clothes, takes leave of her mother, who fails to understand what has happened. Violaine permits none of those present to embrace her, in obedience to a vow. She leaves all her possessions to Mara (act 2, scene 5).

Years later. It is Christmas Eve in the village of Chevoche. A road has been cut through the forest to allow the king to traverse it. Saved by the Maid of Orleans, he is to be crowned at Reims. In the snow a lively popular festival is in full swing, with racy patois, laughter, drunken shifts of mood and belligerence, sudden impulses of cruelty and charity, and burlesque figures, like the two coarsely painted giants made out of barrels and trumpets. A eulogy of sacred architecture by Pierre de Craon's apprentice, sent to lay in a store of sand for his new building, forms a noble counterpoint to the popular festivities. Mara arrives with a mysterious bundle under her cloak. She asks about the leper woman, whose shadow is seen stooping over the snow to gather the food that people throw to her with charity and contempt.

The two set off together in a brief wordless scene dominated by the heath, which glitters coldly amid archaic, disquieting forms in the moonlight. There follows the key scene between Mara and Violaine. Mara urges Violaine to ask God for a miracle: to restore to life the little girl born of her marriage to Jacques Hury, whom she bears dead in her arms. This passage has a dramatic crescendo and presents a closely woven debate on the theme of sacrifice. Violaine retires to her cell where she alone hears the angelic choirs. She obtains the miracle in a climate of tension, while we hear the distant sounds of bells and trumpets receding and Mara reads three passages from a book that a priest has given to Violaine: the prophecy of Isaiah, the sermon of Pope St Leo and the homily of Pope St Gregory on the birth of Jesus. Then comes the surprise: the child's eyes, formerly black like Mara's, are now blue like Violaine's (act 3, scenes 1–3). What can it mean?

The scene returns to the room in Anne Vercors's farmhouse from act 1. It is late at night. Entering stealthily, Mara removes the lamp set on the table, so plunging the stage into a darkness barely lit by the embers.

There is a sudden flurry as Pierre de Craon enters bearing the dying body of Violaine, found in a sandpit where someone had cast it. Jacques is present, but he seems unmoved in his harsh resentment. Then they are left alone and the intimacy of the scene in the garden is recreated, charged with a new intensity. Reclining on the table, Violaine revives sufficiently to greet him with the same accent as in the past: 'Bonjour, Jacques!' There follow explanations and recollections of their love, an encounter between his suffering, unable to give or take anything from her, and her peace as she speaks of communion on the cross, the revelation of what happened on Christmas night, suspicions of Mara as the cause of the fatal accident that struck Violaine, and regret for the monastery of Monsavierge, now deserted following the death of the last recluse. They part with the words from long ago: 'O my betrothed, among the flowery branches, hail!'[5] 'Jacques, bonjours Jacques!' To Pierre de Craon, who carries her out to die, she says, 'But how good it is to die too! / When all is really ended, and over us spreads little by little / The darkness as of a deep shade.'[6]

Anne Vercors, returning unexpectedly from Jerusalem, raises a hymn to his regained homeland. He has brought back some earth from the Holy Land for his burial.

The whole play is recapitulated in the conclusive scene 5. It takes place on the same afternoon at summer's end between Anne Vercors, Jacques Hury and Pierre de Craon, sitting together on the stone seat, its back adorned with lion heads at the bottom of the garden. The trees are laden with fruit; the immense plain, after harvest, is bathed in light. Flocks of sheep graze peacefully. The key themes of the play pass in succession. These are: the earth; forgiveness for Mara (who, on arriving, confesses her crime); the renewal of the seasons and the farm in the young and vigorous hands of Jacques; the gift of life; and the sacred architecture, which makes Pierre the father of churches and the embodiment of a powerful symbolism linking the body of the little martyr Justitia with the body of the new martyr Violaine, whose wedding ring, presented as a gift to Pierre, has turned to light in the stained glass window of the new cathedral. Monsavierge has been repopulated. Anne, stern and proud, takes his leave. Three strokes of the bell ring out. It is not the Angelus but the Communion bell. Pierre utters the closing words, while everyone looks up, waiting: 'The three strokes are gathered like an ineffable sacrifice into the bosom of the Virgin without sin' (act 4, scenes 1–5).[7]

Variants

The 1938 version was shaped, as fully documented in the *Mémoires improvisées*, with the advice of Charles Dullin.[8] After taking over from Jouvet and Copeau the planned performance by the Comédie Française, Dullin advised Claudel to revise act 4. The revisions went well beyond technical alterations. Its length was cut by about a third and the scenes from five to two. There was only a single setting, the chamber in the house of the father, as in act 1. The harsh dialogue between Mara and Jacques reveals the undercurrents of rancour, animosity, resentment and bitterness between them. But it is above all in the long final scene that the greater rigour of inspiration and form in this version emerges clearly. Returning from Jerusalem, Anne Vercors himself enters his home, calvary and tomb, bearing in his arms the dying body of Violaine, whom he has found by the roadside buried in a sandpit. He lays her on the table and covers her with his cloak. The scene focuses on the family, excluding the motif of Pierre de Craon, which diverted attention from the core of the drama. The dialogue is taut and closely woven out of conflicting emotions, but the prevailing atmosphere is one of peace, compassion and closeness between the two wasted bodies: the tired old father and the young woman whose life is ebbing, whose heart he has felt beating ever more weakly all night long, and her feeble voice from her lips close to his ear asking him to take her home, to the house of her father, which now becomes the concrete figure of the House of the Father.

Anne explains the significance of what has happened in scriptural accents: 'L'Ange de Dieu a annoncé à Marie et elle a conçu de l'Esprit-Saint' (The Angel of God has brought the tidings to Mary and she has conceived by the Holy Spirit).[9] The handmaiden of the Lord has given the gift of herself to redeem the inexorable evils of the world, for which Anne himself went on pilgrimage. The theme is the acceptance of the cross, embracing it because the purpose of life is not living but dying. Jacques Hury utters words of love, which Violaine seems unable to hear; but it is Mara who forces her to hear them, as she had already done on that night when she forced Violaine to the depths of her being, compelling her to conceive in the spirit. The character of Mara has an interesting new development. She screams her pride, claims sole credit for what was done; but Anne relates everything to God and reconciles his two daughters in his peace and fatherly understanding. Then Violaine bids them farewell, as if reawakened by the singing of children coming from far away, with the words of the twofold encounter of love: the love between her and Jacques and the love of Mary for the Lord in the Annunciation, and with the motif of the weakening of the body and the peace of death.

Anne Vercors leaves bearing the body of Violaine, to die in her destined resting place. They are followed by the gaze of Jacques, who then returns to Mara and their daughter, as the last notes of the Angelus fade.

The new version tones down many of the almost triumphalist motifs, the celebration of the earth, the homeland and the great works of sacred art. Act 3 is more richly charged with humanity and spirituality, while the reflection on the tragic is more profound. There has been a bloody war, a 'senseless massacre'. The future holds forebodings; the tragedy is revealed for what it is, not a tragedy of heroes but of common people. In his own life the poet had seen the heartbreaking suffering of his sister Camille, the misfortunes of his son and of his illegitimate daughter Louise. The new version, more intimate and reflective, polarizes two motifs: pity for the maimed body, which we have seen in the plot summary, and the theme of Mara. Her character gains in complexity and sheds its schematically allegorical light and shade. Mara is also a suffering creature. She suffers from the contempt by which she has always been surrounded and with which she has always been tolerated: less beautiful, less sunny, less happy, she has always seen Violaine placed before her. Her husband married her on compulsion, while continuing to think of her sister. She has had one child, whom she lost and who was restored to her bearing the indelible mark of her sister in her eyes. She has had faith, but to be heard by God she had to compel it through the 'temptation' of Violaine. She has a penetrating intelligence and a will of iron, but she does not know sweetness or peace and is unable to moderate her obduracy. Her inner life is a torment. She is like a hard metal. The origin of her name seems to derive from either the Latin American name for a rodent with powerful jaws or a Jewish word for a bitter herb.

The final version of the play was composed between 1946 and 1948 and dedicated to Jacques Hébertot when it returned to the stage. Much water had passed under the bridge: Claudel, now an octogenarian, had retired from professional life in 1935 and was experiencing illness in his old age. Europe was steeped in the blood of another war, and it had experienced the silence of God. Violaine kept knocking at the door of the poet's consciousness.

The work was further pared down. Its length was cut by about a fifth and act 4 slightly shortened. The stage directions were made less detailed, leaving greater freedom to the director, but they also emphasized some of the few elements of symbolic importance, such as the crucifix on the wall in the prologue set in the barn of Combernon. Pierre de Craon makes a less theatrical entrance on foot. Proxemics, indicated by the implicit and explicit stage directions, guide the interpretation of the plot, as in Violaine's pauses beneath the candle and beneath the cross. The Latin verses of the prayer of the Angelus are removed, so as not to detract from the dramatic concentration. Gratuitously cultivated and aesthetic descriptive passages are eliminated to focus more sharply on the only symbolic elements that count. Hence we no longer find a detailed Flemish interior but a bare table at Combernon. The characters gain in humanity: greater simplicity and realism as an everyday counterpoint to the old couple (Anne and the Mother), with confidence, closeness, delightful irony, fellowship and respect. Some trivial, superficial gestures are eliminated. After the revelation Jacques no longer looks offended as he gazes at Violaine: it is left to the actor to find the right gestures. Distracting elements or additional topics are removed, so as not to deviate conceptually from the dramatic core, as with all the praise of sacred architecture and stained glass.

The climactic scene of the 'miracle' performed by Violaine is introduced without the descriptions of the landscape in the earlier version. The motif of the analogy between Violaine/Christ and Father/God the Father is emphasized by keeping the cuts and changes made in the second version and introducing important new variants. Violaine's body is no longer taken out to die, but she speaks her last words and dies on the 'Eucharistic' table in the room at Combernon. Her father performs the gesture of raising the hands of Jacques and Mara. Jacques turns his eyes away from Violaine towards Mara's hard and steady gaze.

The presence of Violaine and Mara on stage together seems to invite a comparison between two experiences of the development of the tragic consciousness.

The uncompromising Violaine remains present, composed of mildness and hope, challenging the equally uncompromising Mara, with her desperate defiance. Their confrontation is with death, the radical figure of tragedy made present in the death of the innocent child. 'Et le cri de Mara, et l'appel de Mara, et le rugissement de Mara, et lui aussi, il s'est fait chair au sein de cette horreur' (It is the cry of Mara and the plea of Mara and the roar of Mara. He also became flesh inside this horror). God did it, but, 'J'ai été la plus forte! C'est Mara, c'est Mara qui a fait cela!' (I was the strongest. It's Mara, it's Mara who did this!)[10] We see humanity's titanic pride in her urge to compel God to act as well as in her refusal to share someone with another person, choosing rather to destroy him. This is Mara's logic. Yet she believes in Violaine. It is difficult to give birth to a body; it is even more difficult to give birth to a soul.

The theme of Mara here goes far beyond the hysterical experience of a jealous woman wounded in her pride, or her animal-like possessiveness towards her husband in the other versions.

The Idea of the Tragic

The condition of sorrow

The idea of the tragic grew to full fruition by this path, but the intuition was already lucid in its outlines in the years dealt with in this first part of my study. If the idea of the tragic is bound up with the core experience of the limit, we can say that all the characters experience the limit, against which their own 'absolute' vocation shatters. The idea of the tragic grew to full fruition by this path, but the intuition was already lucid in its outlines in the years dealt with in this first part of my study. If the idea of the tragic is bound up with the core experience of the limit, we can say that all the characters experience the limit, against which their own 'absolute' vocation shatters.

Violaine is beautiful, enamoured, beloved. She is all impulse, led by generosity to share with others the abundance that has been given her.

VIOLAINE. And kiss my sister Justice for me.
PIERRE DE CRAON. (*Looking suddenly at her, as if struck with an idea.*) Is that all you have to give me for her? A bit of gold taken off your finger?
VIOLANE. Will that not be enough to pay for one little stone?
PIERRE DE CRAON. But Justice is a large stone herself.
VIOLANE. (*Laughing.*) I am not from the same quarry.
PIERRE DE CRAON. The stone needed for the base is not the stone needed for the pinnacle.[11]

These are mysterious words, expressing a flash of insight, the unconscious decision to make the sacrifice that will become clear at the end. The kiss that Violaine gives Pierre de Craon out of generosity and mercy[12] is the cause of that 'silver flower' (i.e., her plague sore),[13] the evil which she takes upon herself, like Christ. It is the vocation to accept redemptive sacrificial death, which Anne Vercors sees in Violaine's eyes, like a strange flower, a lily, in the midst of other flowers. Physical illness contaminates her, the violence of others kills her, envy and superstition wound and segregate her.

Anne Vercors, coming to the end of his industrious life, strong and intelligent, grounded in faith, loving of country and family, passionate for the earth,[14] caring for others, merciful and just, strips himself of his dearest affections and abandons all he has constructed, leaving it to others, giving himself naked to death.

Pierre de Craon, the artist who erects temples to God, a giant of creativity and sacred art, pays with the stigma of leprosy for his one crime, committed out of passion – his attempt to violate Violaine; though both of them know that 'tout est *action* de grâces' (everything gives thanks in *action*).[15] His greatness is solitary. He is surrounded by the misunderstanding, coarseness, calumny and envy of little men, like those who quarrel during the feast at Chevoche.

Jacques Hury, the hard-working and a passionate lover, respectful and free from all covetousness, is fated to suffer the sorrow of an unhappy love, an imposed marriage and a burning unfounded suspicion. For him there will never be any happiness:

> VIOLAINE. It is ended, what does that matter? Happiness was never promised to you. Work, that is all that is asked of you.[16]

In contrast with him, Mara is dark, malevolent and wicked. Yet she also has qualities that in time (with the development of the text through its successive drafts, as we have seen) probe her relationship with the limit, with evil and death. Her basic limitation lies in her very nature, with a malevolent lucidity that always seizes on the worst or makes the worst of everything she sees and touches. It lies in her harshness and animosity, in her aloof and rigid beauty, and in the fate that awaits her: a husband compelled into a loveless marriage; a daughter who dies and can only be recovered by forcing God and accepting a 'shared' (*partagée*) motherhood. It lies in the evil she is willing to do: spying, divulging secrets, near blasphemy and violence. But she suffers and her love is born from suffering.

The world is also suffering: it is riven by conflicts, ambitions, abuses of power. As we have seen, Anne Vercors raises a heartfelt lament for the divisions within the kingdom and the Church. A sacrifice is called for.

Sacrifice and meaning

All the characters live in the tragic dimension of existence, but all feel they are inscribed in a horizon of meaning.

> VIOLANE: It is too hard to suffer and to not know why. But that which others do not know, I have learned, and I must share my knowledge. [...] Only that which is ill should perish, and that which should not perish is that which suffers. Happy is he who suffers, and knows why![17]

All the characters recognize they are part of a cosmos that is ordered and not static, where everything is transformed in keeping with the divine plan. They all feel the command to *Homo faber* to continue the creation, but some follow a different path by transforming their human condition of suffering and death into a redeeming sacrifice. The concept of sacrifice is the core of the idea of tragedy that Claudel expresses in this play, which I take as an example of one of the significant trends of twentieth-century culture and dramaturgy. The archaic archetype, which passed into the religious system of pagan antiquity and the Jewish world, has been so profoundly transformed in Christianity that it appears in fact as a nonsacrificial religion.[18] The term 'sacrifice' should be correctly understood in the light of Holy Scripture (in the Gospels and the letters of St Paul, especially Romans and Corinthians) and New Testament theology in its human complexity and richness. This is what Claudel does, so much so as to make it difficult to interpret the story of Violaine, to which the sacrificial pattern seems to apply.

Violaine is the *figura Mariae* in the docility of her response to her calling as a servant of the Lord, in the spirit of the Annunciation and in virginal 'motherhood'. At the same time she is above all the *figura Christi*. The basis of her behaviour is not the primary intention of suffering, as if God had an archaic need of blood, but a fraternal generosity and love that ties her to others and makes her desire to make them partakers of her vitality, her joy and her relation to the divine. For this reason she bestows a kiss on the leper: she accepts the risk and suffering that stem from her act, and those that others (Mara) inflict on her, by continuing to give what she has, of herself. In short, the emphasis is on giving rather than renunciation. This is true to Christian sacrifice in Claudel's imagination: strengthening the relation with God, strengthening the bonds of communion between people, cooperating actively (and not suffering passively, like the archaic sacrificial victim in an external religious ritual) in the reconciliation and redemption of those who have fallen into evil. In the background lies the idea of priesthood and holiness. And it is admirable that Claudel should have drawn the figure of woman into this high orbit.

Violaine is repeatedly linked to the Eucharist and the Passion: in the introduction of the motif of the cross in the prologue to the second edition; in the garment and posture in which she appears to Jacques as an officiant at the altar; in the blessing and distribution of the bread when Anne Vercors leaves home; and in the deposition on the table of her dying body. Death, the radical figure of the tragic, is transcended by the act in which Violaine dispenses life and evokes the resurrection. The theoretical framework is respected; but what brings the figure of Violaine to life, making it real and fascinating, is her simplicity, strength, enthusiasm and vital beauty. The vivid imagination of Claudel is at work, the faculty with which he traversed and commented on the Holy Scriptures in thousands of impassioned pages.

In conclusion, Claudel's text testifies to a profound experience of tragedy, suffering and the *mysterium iniquitatis*. It achieves a positive development in a solid and mature faith which, before the famous 'illumination' on Christmas day 1886, which led to his conversion, had to struggle with remoteness, rejection and an obsession with death, which amid the urgent and almost breathless copiousness of his output gives a glimpse of truth. Despair was transformed into hope. The dread of his youth became the words 'Je n'ai pas peur' (I am not afraid), uttered as death approached.[19]

Sources

Claudel's tragic outlook drew on many sources in his broad culture, assimilated with clarity and passion, and on the highest Western tradition. The first was Holy Scripture. The work, as we have seen, is interwoven with biblical references. There are three guiding images in this 'mystery play'. One is the Gospel episode of the Annunciation and Visitation,[20] centred on the theme of the 'handmaid of the Lord' who answers the call made to her by the angel, an intermediary of God, the soul that 'doth magnify the Lord […] for he hath regarded the lowliness of his handmaiden' (Luke 1:46–8). The other, present principally in the revised version, is the controversial passage from Matthew 11:12: 'The kingdom of heaven suffereth violence', which is engrafted, through the motif of Mara, on the words in John 16:23: 'Whatsoever ye shall ask the Father in my name, he will give it you.' The third is the Deposition.[21] The three planes of meaning, psychological/personal, historical and philosophical/religious, are condensed into a narrative and dramatic framework that presupposes the biblical subtext. It provides the structure of ideas with its evolution from the Old Testament conception of the God of justice and revenge to the New Testament conception of a merciful God who gives his Son and generates not a sacrificial chain of retributive justice but a chain of imitation. This produces a new, free and joyous acceptance, culminating in Jesus' invitation to renounce all worldly goods and follow him, as in the case of Anne Vercors and Violaine. It provides the archetypes within which the phases of the plot are symbolically inscribed: Nativity, Passion and Resurrection. It also provides the symbolism of places and objects: leprosy, the door, the garden, the cross, the bread. It provides the poetic mode: the transvaluation from realism to symbolism, from the narrative/dramatic model to the lyrical and ritual model inspired by the Psalms, in particular Psalm 113 ('In exitu Israël de Aegypto'), the Song of Songs, the voices of the prophets (especially Isaiah), Ecclesiastes, and the great meditation on the fullness of time which structures the work.[22] It also provides an anthropological perspective, one that gives great dignity to woman. The Lord needed her in order to be clothed in that flesh which redeems the world, and for this reason sought to secure her consent. Thousands of virgins, says Claudel, have repeated it down the centuries. It also provides, mediated by the exegetical tradition, an interpretation of events in terms of analogy and therefore their representation as metaphor.[23] The saga of a people is extended to become the great epic of humanity in pilgrimage. The meanings reverberate between the 'two texts written by God. One is the Bible, the other is the world, the immense circle of the Creation'.[24] Finally it is also the path that leads Claudel's tragic awareness to emerge from the shallows of the materialistic, deterministic vision from which he started.[25]

The Bible also provides great inspiration for the poet's language, his theatrical vocation: writing and speech are primarily voice, rhythm and emotion. In one of his thousands of pages as a reader of the Bible, Claudel wrote, 'One should not just read the Bible; one should listen to it.'[26]

His habitual reading of the scriptures as believer and poet was part of a systematic conceptual framework that Claudel drew from Thomism and which provided an important source for the work. These were the years of the cultural programme expressed in 1879 by Leo XIII's encyclical *Aeterni Patris* and the excitement it generated in various parts of Europe. In the 1880s and after, the Roman Church, informed by neo-Thomism, was engaged in vast activity in the most varied spheres, part of a far-reaching project of building a new universal Christian society.[27] Claudel's confessor induced him to read Aquinas, who became his constant companion during the years in China from 1895 to 1899. Claudel struck up a close friendship with the masters of this spiritual guidance, such as Jacques Maritain.[28]

In what ways did Aquinas's work respond to Claudel's needs? It is not so much the instance of a conceptual system that gives order to reality, but the passion and the rigour with which 'everything is ordered' in the theological perspective and the unified structure of his thought. In God, both revealed and approached with logical and rational arguments, all creatures converge as efficient cause, final cause and reparatory cause, the place of origin and return for all creatures in the paternal solicitude of salvation.[29] It is the clarity with which he sees the ultimate end, toward which life moves as the term of good, the desire for happiness. It is the fascination exerted by a realistic, positive and fundamentally optimistic anthropology that identifies the happiness of man in tending toward the supreme end. (This, surely, is the outlook of Violaine and Anne Vercors).

It is the enhancement of the physical and human, not mortified, but perfected by grace. It is the enhancement of human speech, which in Claudel becomes the exaltation of the 'sign' of human speech in the wake of the creating word. It is the enhancement of the corporeity of matter through acceptance of the idea of the symbol, meaning the substantial union of matter and form, the intrinsic unity of the subject, against every dualistic or one-dimensional hypothesis. And finally, it is both the exaltation of the book of nature, written 'with God's finger' and explicable by a free creative act, and the enhancement of the social dimension of human life.

If we reread *Tidings* bearing these categories in mind, we will grasp its coherence and harmony: the love of the earth, life and beauty, the sense of paternity and family, the analogical thread which ties the figures and their lives to the archetypal figures and situations of Holy Scripture, and the offering of the self.[30] These are the strong points against which the tragic turmoil of existence breaks.

Another source is Greek tragedy, which Claudel drew on for at least three fundamental reasons: the idea of the theatre, the form of the verse, and the theme of sacrifice, which in the tragic scheme is characterized as sacrifice performed by women. In the closing years of the nineteenth century and the first fifteen years of the twentieth, the efforts of Claudel were focused on seeking new forms of drama, prosody and metrics suited to the stage. For a long time he immersed himself in Aeschylus and took him as a model. Claudel had sensed a community of spirit since his years at the *lycée* (high school), and to possess the Greek tragedian intimately undertook the labour of translating the *Oresteia*.[31]

The work, as he acknowledged, gave him the prosodic training he needed, forcing him to tackle the problem of gestural and musical techniques and spatial arrangements to embody a highly civic and ritual idea of theatre in modernity. Other crucial events were his meeting with Darius Milhaud, who arranged music for choirs, the discovery of the Hellerau theatre and school and the work of Jacques Dalcroze. The poetry of the Greek chorus led him to reflect on the performative value of speech in the theatre, the primary force of voice, rhythm, timbre. He observed, 'I think the key element is less meaning than intonation [...]. There is no need for the audience to grasp the meaning of each sentence. Sometimes a mysterious whisper will suffice.'[32] Aeschylus confirmed his conviction that the poet can be indifferent to verisimilitude in the theatre. What matter are not so much sociopolitical situations as the profound forces at work which determine the tragic essence of life. 'One might say the poet seems to be hasting to return and cry out again before a half-closed tomb, which, indeed, is the drama, the stupor at death and evil.'[33] The solemnity of certain passages (like the great scene of the pacification of the Eumenides) seemed to foreshadow the striking processional scenes in Christianity and the sacred theatre inspired by it. The technical work, which Claudel performs with an approach that is poetic and dramatic rather than semantic and syntactic, led him to measure himself against what he saw as the true dramatic metre, the iamb, and to the transitions from word to verse to prosody to song to the chorus. He drew on a model of religious and civic art, grasping its phonic and musical aspects; he subsumed the pagan trilogy into the orbit of universal Christianity and related himself conceptually (though not only conceptually) to the climate being created in Paris in those years by the great innovators: Lugné-Poe at the Théâtre de l'Oeuvre, Antoine at the Théâtre Libre, Copeau at the Vieux-Colombier and Dullin at the Atelier.[34] Rediscovering the grandeur of ancient drama meant opposing the poor theatrical aesthetics of those years and rediscovering the contact of the theatre with the radical themes of mankind.

The Tragic in the Form of a Mystery: Tradition and Modernity

Claudel's profound inspiration, drawing on such deep roots, produced a highly original and effective dramatic form, coherent with its poetic and ideological significance. There are two planes to be analysed: the dramatic construction and the phonic level of the text.

A good example is the variety of registers in the opening scene between Pierre de Craon and Violaine. There is lightness and allusiveness, but also the tension and drama of the love scene and the farewell, with passages of coquetry, mischievousness, tenderness, innocence, jealousy, resentment, bitterness and disappointment. The romantic language is coloured by a religious symbolism suited to the builder of cathedrals:

PIERRE DE CRAON: [...] I take away your ring,
    and of its little circle I will make golden seed! [...]
    The soul of Violaine, my child, in whom my heart delights. [...]
    But that which I am going to build will lie under its own shadow like condensed gold,
    and like a pyx full of manna![35]

Greek tragedy serves as a model: there is a ritual solemnity in the scenes of prayer and the leper's kiss; there is a lyricism in the contemplation of the creation and the hymn to beauty, raised by the two characters as they gaze at the distant countryside at dawn;[36] there is a prospect of historical and national celebration (the France of the cathedrals and the war against the English); and there is a striking crescendo that grows out of an everyday situation and rises to the solemnity of a sacrificial spirituality.

The tradition of the medieval sacred theatre and the Shakespearean tradition serve as models. Dialogues in two scenes, group or choreutic, mingle: the almost burlesque procession with the peasant caught stealing a bundle of sticks, the servant who imitates the blaring of a trumpet, and the peasant with the double load of firewood on his back and chest, while a dog barks. Realistic scenes are interwoven with solemn scenes such as the farewell after the breaking of the bread, almost an emblem of a last supper: 'All take your places! Just once more I will cut the bread.'[37]

The movement is frozen in the final scenes (almost *tableaux vivants* or ritual moments) of the prologue and act 1, when all watch Anne Vercors' departure as if petrified, or in the single acts in which the action is emblematically frozen. Again the ceremonial forms and the Greek theatre served as models, in addition to influences absorbed over the years, such as the experiments of Appia and Hellerau, which affected the subsequent versions of the work. What counts in creating the effect of beauty and tragedy is not the gesture, but the attitude, the pose. No artifice, no agitation, but the playwright must beware of creating the impression of a dream.[38]

It is worth dwelling, as an example, on act 3, dramaturgically the most complex and, on the plane of the fabric of sound, among the most effective parts of the work. Many elements contribute to the dramatic rendering: the solemnity of the hour, with Christmas Eve and day passing into night and then dawning again, and the evocation of the setting; the snowy forest in which the festival is celebrated, recalling Bruegel's famous image; Violaine's hovel lit by glimmers from the meagre fire and the dark cell; the contrast between the animated festival and the struggle between Violaine and Mara, which culminates in the 'miracle' of mystic childbirth; and the contrast between the coarse dialectical vitality of the scene with the common people and the stringent dialectic between Violaine and Mara. Violaine urges the reasons for a theology of God's love, of pain as an existential choice of suffering as reparatory, and of herself as a sacrificial victim, one who takes on herself the sorrows and sins of the world. Mara expresses cynicism, resentment and arrogance to the point where she wishes to force God and demands a miracle. The key episode is the scene of the resurrection, Violaine's 'mystical' childbirth, in a crescendo of sounds from far and near. The symbols are interwoven; voices and sounds are fused in a condensation of meaning and a climax of tension and emotion. Mara, increasingly prey to panic, reads the first lesson of each of the three nocturnes of the Christmas mass (the prophecy of Isaiah, the sermon of Pope Leo and Luke's account of the Nativity). We hear the sounds of the royal procession passing through the forest on its way to Reims to celebrate the resurrection of France, the work of the Maid of Orleans. Supernatural songs accompany the reading of Holy Scripture. There is a mystical rapture that restores a human creature transformed.

The coarse and the sacred mingle in an almost Shakespearean mimesis, as Peter Brook would call it. First comes the scene of the peasants with their bawdy talk, coarse language, realistic French dialect, their boastful braggadocio, and the 'harmless' cruelty of their treatment of the poor leper, to whom they also give alms. Then follows the evocation of the solemn ceremony as the king enters Reims Cathedral with a procession of clergy and civil authorities amid the glistening of torches on the white snow, a gesture intended to imitate the entry of Jesus into Jerusalem on an ass.

As for the phonic aspect, it is well known that Claudel followed in the wake of Rimbaud and Mallarmé, making a key contribution amid the crisis and renewal of French versification at the turn of the century. He moved it in the direction of freedom, shifting the focus decisively onto the sounds and the stage action.[39] The rhythms of the human voice, the division into verses based on emotion and breath intervals rather than logic, are functional to the acting.

Act 3 could be described as a score divided into at least three movements: the comic choral movement of the rural feast, the intimate movement of the Mara/Violaine duet and the solemn liturgical movement of the miracle. First the language stoops to a popular register that expresses the festive animation: patois, mispronunciations and popular jingles are mixed with forced, burlesque rhymes, etymological figures, anaphora, exclamations, harmonies, recurrent timbres (such as the vibrant, sibilant, fricative consonants), a rapid tempo, broken rhythms and onomatopoeic exclamations, as in the mimicry of the cold. We can listen carefully to the text (necessarily in the original French) to appreciate its sound:

UNE AUTRE FEMME. C'est le jour de Noël que not'roi Charles revient se faire sacrer.
UNE AUTRE. C'est une simple fille, de Dieu envoyée,
    Qui le ramène à son foyer.
UNE AUTRE. Jeanne, qu'on l'appelle.
UNE AUTRE. La Pucelle!
UNE AUTRE. Qu'est née la nuit de l'Épiphanie!
UNE AUTRE. Qui a chassé les Anglais d'Orléans qu'ils assiégeaient!
UNE AUTRE. Et qui va les chasser de France même-ment tretous! Ainsi soit-il!
UNE AUTRE. (*Fredonnant.*): Noël! Ki Ki Ki Ki Ki Noël! Noël nouvelet! Rrr! qu'i fait froué![40]

Then the qualities of the sounds underscore and bring out the semantic substance: closeness and contrast, intimacy and distance, the leap of the two sisters to another plane, one heavenwards and the other earthwards. The structure of the language links the sisters in an ever more intimate dialogue: terse utterances studded with questions and exclamations, repetitions, anaphora, symmetries, etymological figures and epanalepsis. But it is always the interplay of sounds that reveals the distance separating them and their different fates. The motif of Mara is associated with the recurrence of vibrant velar consonants, indicating aggressiveness, irritability and obstinacy; the motif of Violaine is associated with the recurrence of labiodental consonants (as suggested by their names) to emphasize quiet patience. Then again the sound structure marks the total divergence of their paths and their different tragic experiences. Violaine's leads to sublimation. Her utterances are extended and become closer to the rhythms of verse; the play of metaphor is intensified, the recurrent timbres in assonances and iterations, as in the vibrants, are used in this case to mimic Violaine's stabbing pains:

VIOLANE: [...] Tu m'as vue baiser ce lépreux, Mara? Ah, la coupe de la douleur est profonde,
    Et qui y met une fois la lèvre ne l'en retire plus à son gré![41]

Mara's tragic experience is increasingly enclosed in the loss from which she defends herself tooth and nail. Denials and repeated subjects, anaphora, recurrent timbres (again vibrant), with word groups of similar length mimic an insistent, relentless rhythm.

> MARA. Non! non! non! tu ne me donneras point le change avec tes paroles de béguine! Non, je ne me laisserai point apaiser.
> Ce lait qui me cuit aux seins, il crie vers Dieu comme le sang d'Abel!
> Est-ce que j'ai cinquante enfants à m'arracher du corps? est-ce que j'ai cinquante âmes à m'arracher de la mienne?
> Est-ce que tu sais ce que c'est que de se déchirer en deux et de mettre au-dehors ce petit être qui crie?
> Et la sage-femme m'a dit que je n'enfanterai plus.
> Et quand j'aurai cent enfants, ce ne serait pas ma petite Aubaine.[42]

Again it is the web of sound that emphasizes the breakthrough onto a new plane. The human events, historical and personal, the tragedies of peoples and individual lives, are projected through liturgy, prayer and Holy Scripture onto the sense of time. A pause, then silence, then the bells ringing in the distance, the choir and the angelic voices, and in the foreground the human voice chanting the readings, which embody the culmination of the work: the mystic birth.

Claudel's search for 'Christian tragedy' extended right across the board and included an extraordinary concern for form and the technical aspects engrafted onto the greater tradition. It is a work in the genre crucial to the twentieth century, as testified by its great success on the stage.

Chapter 3

THE SCHOOL OF HATRED: *MOURNING BECOMES ELECTRA* BY EUGENE O'NEILL

In Europe, Thinking of the New Broadway

It will hardly appear surprising that a selection of the key texts of European twentieth-century drama should include a work by Eugene O'Neill, being yet another response to the emergence of the twentieth century's tragic consciousness. Of course he was American, but the matrix of his work is deeply rooted in European culture and theatrical research, with a pessimistic anthropology and a probing of behaviour based on depth psychology (one of the major axes of twentieth-century thought), embedded in a formal structure that is original and innovative compared to the currents of commercial Broadway theatre.[1]

The idea of the limit is here based on the network of familial dynamics, on the affective block caused by the pathological development of the personality, on the condition of solitude of an individual closed to others. The tragic action is configured as a grave transgression driven by blindness and induced by hatred, one face of the evil that lurks in humans and pervades their lives and histories.

O'Neill began writing *Mourning Becomes Electra* in France in October 1929. He worked for several months with stubborn concentration and completed the first draft in February 1930. On returning to the text, after a holiday in Italy, he accentuated its nonrealistic structure by introducing asides and masks and highlighting the symbolic choice through the central and emblematic collocation of the shipboard scene and the theme song *Shenandoah*. By mid-July 1930 the second draft was ready. Then, still at his home in the south of France, which he left occasionally for brief stays in Paris, he returned to work. He eliminated the asides, which slackened the tension of the action and diminished the naturalness of the expression of the characters through their words and soliloquies. The final draft suppressed the masks, asides and soliloquies.

After a stay in the Canary Islands with his wife Carlotta the work was completed. The way was open for production at the Theatre Guild, New York. This was a well-established theatre, founded at a time when a wave of experimentation dominated all the arts, starting from the experiments of the Washington Square Players. It introduced the great European drama to the United States, leading to a breakthrough in American drama reinforced by the influence of the experimental European companies that toured the New World, from the Abbey Theatre to the Vieux Colombier, the Kleine Theatre (Stockholm's theatre) and Moscow Arts Theatre. In 1931 *Mourning Becomes Electra* had a run of 150 performances at the Theatre Guild and was also published in book form.

The work stands at an important crossroads. O'Neill's acute sensibility was nurtured by the ideas of such thinkers as Schopenhauer, Nietzsche, Freud and Jung. Moreover his early contacts, through his upbringing and education, confronted him with the question of the meaning of life derived from Christianity, through the influences of Puritan Protestantism and traditional Irish Catholicism, though he abandoned both at an early age. His craft as a playwright was refined by his contacts with the theatre. (O'Neill is said to have been born on Broadway, in a hotel room where his mother lived with his father, of Irish descent – a famous, gifted popular actor and the manager of a theatre company.) His familiarity with the world backstage and insider's knowledge of the theatre, his training in the drama course established at Harvard by George Baker Pearce, the constant experimentalism evident in the different registers of his work and his versatility in combining and fusing a wide range of influences all made him the father of the American theatre and a bridge between Europe and the United States. Aeschylus, Ibsen and Strindberg can be read between the lines of the work that I am about to consider as emblematic of another strand of tragic development.[2]

Structure and Plot

The work is divided into three parts. The first, *Homecoming*, is in four acts dominated by serried dialogues between two characters; there are ten such dialogues following a short choral entry and four brief dialogues between three characters.

It is a late April afternoon in 1865, shortly before sunset. The set, imbued with symbolic elements, represents the exterior of the Mannon house. It occupies a slightly elevated position and is massive and sombre, but its threatening appearance is concealed, as if masked, by the white porch with its six columns, green shutters and a clump of lilacs, contrasting with the gloomy form of a pine on the right.

Enter a sort of chorus, prying and gossiping. It is the voice of the distant city, a small group of townsfolk, led by Seth, the faithful gardener who has always worked for the Mannons. Seth is witness and confidante, as well acting as the driving force of the story at a certain point by his well-informed insinuations.

Enter two characters: Christine, who is about forty, 'striking-looking' and very 'handsome', dignified, proud and stylish, with her celebrated wavy hair, 'copper brown' and 'bronze gold'; and Lavinia, 23 but looking much older, with a resemblance to her mother that she does all she can to conceal. 'Thin, flat-breasted and angular', she has a military bearing and speaks in dry, peremptory tones. She dresses severely, without feminine charm. Her face has the characteristic expression of the Mannon family, like a living mask.[3]

Enter the young brother and sister Peter and Hazel, 'frank, innocent […] and good'.[4] Their wishes are absolutely normal: Peter hopes to marry Lavinia, and Hazel Lavinia's brother, Orin, who is about to return home from the war. But something great and strange is impending: a mystery. The heralded return of General Ezra Mannon, Christine's husband and the father of Lavinia and Orin, from the victorious war causes turmoil and panic. Adam Brant, a handsome ship's captain, a dreamer who extols the free, primitive and authentic life of the South Sea islands, sometimes comes visiting and pays pressing court to Lavinia, though he is actually Christine's lover. Brant is the illegitimate son of a Mannon who was disowned by his family when he fell in love, like everyone else, with Brant's mother, a beautiful servant with a sunny character. Now Brant is bent on revenge. Alerted by Seth, who is the historical memory of the house and sees the significance of the clues he discovers, Lavinia challenges her mother, whom she hates, having always felt rejected by her and because she has an intense and exclusive bond with her father. Mother and daughter wound, despise and blackmail each other in a struggle for the upper hand.

Christine weaves a plot in which her accomplice is to be Brant, who bears a striking resemblance to the portrait of Ezra, even to his sometimes mask-like face, the distinctive hallmark of the Mannons. Brant procures a lethal drug, used for certain heart conditions, to kill Ezra without attracting suspicion, given that he suffers heart disease. The dialogue is a masterpiece of psychological pressure, complicated interpersonal dynamics and a subtle evil feminine intuition that is reminiscent of Lady Macbeth.

Ezra Mannon's return home opens an intense and suspenseful phase of the drama. Tall and strong, he is in his fifties, stiff and big-boned. His authoritarian voice seems to repress and conceal his feelings. He struggles with himself, but his inner life has evolved: his emotion at his daughter's reception is concealed behind formality, awkwardness, and a severe attitude which prohibits tears. Desire, trepidation, jealousy, suspicion, his discovery of a need for confidences and intimacy press on the composure that he has always imposed on himself. His talk runs on personal issues mingled with general reflections about life and death, astonishing the women, who remain entrenched in themselves. A splendid and mysterious scene sees Mannon and Christine facing each other. A strong current of erotic attraction runs between them, together with fear and foreboding, the need for confession and confidences, embarrassment and simulation. Now that Ezra has understood life on the battlefield, he wants to be loved by her. Christine takes advantage of a moment of calculated seduction to carry out her plan.

The night of lovemaking fails to break down the barrier between them; Christine has given herself to him once more as a body and nothing more. But he has had enough of bodies. Anger, malice and revelations trigger the expected heart attack. When Mannon begs her to bring his medicine, Christine makes him swallow the pill that causes coma and death. Ezra realizes the truth too late, but has time to murmur an accusation which Lavinia hears.

Part 2 (*The Hunted*) consists of five acts. Again urgent, pressing dialogues between paired characters prevail. There are about fifteen of them in all, as compared with a brief choral opening and two short soliloquies. One of the soliloquies, by the drunken chantyman, introduces the scene aboard ship, symbolically at the centre of the work, which evokes the unlikely dream of freedom from self and external conditions. There are five dialogues in all for more than two voices.

Two days after the murder of Ezra Mannon, the scene is the same as in act 1 of the first part. A group of citizens have come to pay their respects to the dead man. They act as a conventional chorus, essentially extraneous to the drama, and take their leave. While awaiting the return of the wounded Orin, a decorated war veteran, Christine seeks Hazel's complicity. Orin arrives: he is young and strikingly similar to

Ezra and Brant, yet his manner contains something contradictory, by turns stiff yet slouching, stern yet tender, arousing maternal feelings and clearly moved by a welter of different impulses. Lavinia seeks to inflame his feelings; Christine works on his Oedipus complex, driving him into regression in order to keep him under her thumb and force him into an exclusive relationship with her. But he has been marked by his experience of war, which has opened his eyes and destroyed his inner world. Christine manipulates his feelings: she finally breaks his tie with his father, whom he had never loved, and seeks to separate him from his sister by claiming she is an unbalanced visionary, anticipating her allegations. She also tries unsuccessfully to divert Orin's suspicions of Brant, which are more stubborn because they are fostered by his jealous love of his mother. The proof of her guilt is patent. Lavinia and Orin exact vengeance, first by ambushing Brant aboard his sailboat, where they slay him by simulating assault and robbery, not uncommon in the docks, and then by driving Christine to commit suicide in despair.

Part 3 (*The Haunted*) consists of four acts. Again they are dominated by dialogues between two characters, totalling thirteen in all and culminating in the struggle between Lavinia and Orin in act 2, when each has become the prisoner of the other. There is an opening choral scene, symmetrical with the openings of the other two parts, and four short dialogues with many voices.

The drunken group of Seth the gardener and his companions are shown spying on the Mannon house, which has lain empty for a year since the murders. The scene is played out entertainingly on dares regarding the characters' fear of the ghosts now said to haunt the house. The humour creates a counterpoint reminiscent of certain scenes in Shakespeare, relieving the nightmare of tragedy. Then a telegram announces the return of Lavinia and Orin from their trip to the South Seas, on which they have tried to forget the past. On their arrival, their relationship appears to reproduce relations between Christine and Orin.

Lavinia returns, dressed in green. Her body has filled out, her movements are far less rigid than before and her beautiful hair is strangely similar to her mother's. She dominates Orin, who is gaunt, wooden, and increasingly regressed. She tries to repress his sense of guilt, his morbid fantasies, forcing him to keep to their official version of events. She cuts him off from others, preventing him from forming other ties and relations, especially with Hazel, who loves him. Lavinia wants to escape from her destiny: she dreams of marrying Peter and leading an open and normal life; but Orin, haggard and increasingly resembling the family portraits, finds no way out and drags Lavinia to the fulfilment of their destiny. He tells Lavinia that he has written the history of their family in order to discover 'in the Mannon past the evil destiny behind our lives'.[5] He describes Lavinia sarcastically as the most interesting criminal of all, the one who embodies all the hidden deeds from the Mannons' past. Orin suffers growing jealousy, an increasing and irrepressible urge to confess, a crazed regression and identification with his father, by which the Oedipus impulse is fulfilled. The situation grows acute: evil and devil are keywords. In the frenzy of the death wish Orin shoots himself with his pistol.

Lavinia's last attempts to escape her destiny are fruitless. She fills the house with flowers and yearns to leave and marry Peter, allowing the house-tomb to fall into ruin in the sun and rain. Her mind is confused. Now alone, she re-enters the house, not to kill herself like Christine and Orin but to atone and preserve the lineage of the Mannons: she is the last Mannon, she has no need of anybody, not even of God, either to forgive herself or punish herself: 'Living alone here with the dead is a worse act of justice than death or prison!'[6]

From Electra to Lavinia

The *Oresteia* furnished O'Neill with the framework on which to construct his trilogy. Analysis of the affinities and differences make it possible to identify exactly his distinctive conception of the tragic and subsequent elaboration of the original form of the tragedy, in continuity with his underlying ideas.

One trilogy (*Homecoming, The Hunted, The Haunted*) is inspired by another (*Agamemnon, The Choephori, The Eumenides*). One opens before the palace of the Atreides, the other before Mannon's house. A chorus, which is the vigilant and wise consciousness of the city, opens Aeschylus' trilogy; a homely, obtuse, imperceptive and garrulous chorus, basely attracted only by curiosity and the wealth of the Mannons, introduces the story recounted by O'Neill, guided by a malicious, insinuating, prying coryphaeus: the gardener Seth who has himself come to resemble the Mannons.

The two plots are in some ways symmetrical: a general returns victorious from a great war that has involved his whole race. Revenge awaits him for the excesses of arrogance in which he indulged even before the expedition, and because another man has taken his place in his wife's heart and his rank as husband, another who harbours similar family grievances against him. (Aegisthus is the thirteenth son of Thyestes, Brant is the bastard son of David Mannon.) He falls into the trap that his wife and her lover lay for him. Then follows the vengeance for vengeance, as the general's daughter and his son join forces to strike down the murderers. Orestes first slays Aegisthus and then his mother Clytemnestra; Orin shoots Brant and indirectly kills his mother Christine by forcing her to commit suicide. After this the two plots diverge sharply. In *The Eumenides* Electra disappears from the scene, which now centres on Orestes, representing the royal line, the institutions of the city state and acting within the horizon of the sacred. Persecuted by the Erinyes, deities of ancestral vengeance, guarantors of an archaic and prelegal order, Orestes is finally reconciled to life, the polis and the sacred. He accompanies the transition to a more mature phase of culture and community, regaining the prestige of a role and status. In *Mourning Becomes Electra* the circle closes increasingly tightly around Lavinia and Orin. Imprisonment in a fixed and unresolved Oedipal bond embroils them in regression and guilt, which destroys one in physical death by suicide and the other in the death of reclusion in the ancestral house-tomb.

The nuclei of the tragic are transformed in the course of this journey into introversion and self-reference. Necessity presses from within: it is a complex, an incestuous relationship, translated into a passion of jealousy and hatred.

The heroic dimension is demystified in the disenchantment and disgust of the returned soldier who has discovered the true face of war: contact with death and its insignificance in the field. He has seen white walls stained with blood, which counts for no more than dirty water, and myriads of rotting bodies, experiencing the banality of evil and the degradation of human indifference.

Hubris is bound up with the excesses of a private ethic, a closed family horizon. But, as we shall see, it also has serious historical and anthropological implications, precisely because of this selfish reclusiveness. It appears in the arrogance and rigidity of Ezra Mannon, the hatred and vengefulness of Christine, Orin and Lavinia, and is resolved into irreducible conflicts expressed in harsh dialogues (between Lavinia and Christine, Christine and Ezra Mannon, Lavinia and Brant), a cruel game in which the characters wound, despise, blackmail and unmask each other, driven to extremes by their reciprocal animosities. The response to the impulse that acts inwardly with a compelling pressure is a free and conscious decision wilfully pursued with an utterly culpable tenacity. Hence the damage the characters inflict upon each other.

ORIN. [...] The only love I can know now is the love of guilt for guilt which breeds more guilt – until you get so deep at the bottom of hell there is no lower you can sink and you rest there in peace! (*He laughs harshly and turns away from her.*)[7]
LAVINIA, (*grimly.*) Don't be afraid. I'm not going the way Mother and Orin went. That's escaping punishment. And there's no one left to punish me. I'm the last Mannon. I've got to punish myself! Living alone here with the death is a worse act of justice than death or prison! [...] It takes the Mannons to punish themselves for being born![8]

But there is no catharsis. Lavinia receives no purification or acquisition of knowledge. Likewise there is no stabilizing or progressive function for the city. The community relationship is shattered: the house of Mannon, though playing an important part in vital sectors such as the business community, judicial institutions and military enterprise, remains distant, inaccessible and even threatening. In the first play of the trilogy there appears a kind of representative sample or delegation from the town embodied in the humbler characters (the gardener, the carpenter and their wives or relations); in the second there is a group of bourgeois figures (the Bordens, the Hills, Dr Blake the physician); and in the third drama there are again humble figures (the gardener, the carpenter, the old clerk from the hardware store, the fishing captain, the lame farmer). This group of timorous drunkards eavesdrop and spy on the family, commenting on events without any proper understanding of their lives and the events that are happening.

Orin refuses to be caught up in the flow of history: the account of his family that he is entrusting to the written page, making himself a writer, is his answer to the need for self-confession and he privately entrusts it to the girl he will never marry. Even the sacred is invoked only to be excluded, wither as the continuous, mortifying *memento mori* of the preaching in the temple of Puritan tradition, evoked with nostalgia by Ezra Mannon,[9] or as a light too dazzling for human meanness.

ORIN. And I find artificial light more appropriate for my workman's light, not God's – man's feeble striving to understand himself, to exist for himself in the darkness! It's a symbol of his life – a lamp burning out in a moon of waiting shadows![10]

Hatred: The Driving Force of the Tragedy

A keyword insinuates itself early into the verbal fabric of the work, appearing first in a secondary passage,[11] but spreading rapidly across the whole field: hatred. The keyword 'hate' and its verbal forms, for example, recur nine times in the harsh dialogue at the start of act 2 of *Homecoming* between Lavinia and Christine.

Lavinia is dominated by hatred: she hates love, she hates whoever claims to love her, she hates the object of her jealousy, her mother Christine.

LAVINIA, *(stiffening-brusquely.)* I do not know anything about love! I do not want to know anything! *(Intensely.)* I hate love! […] *(Intensely.)* I hate the sight of him![12]

The note of hatred, embodied in a desperate cry, appears at the end of act 3 of *Homecoming*, closing the encounter between Ezra, who has just returned from the war, Christine and Lavinia, who, 'in a fit of jealousy and hatred', screams 'I hate you!'[13]

Hatred spreads in the moonlight, which gives things the spectral quality of a nightmare. Lavinia hates her mother, Christine her daughter and husband. Brant hates the Mannon family. In the dramatic dialogue between Christine and Orin in act 2 of *The Hunted*, she seeks to turn away suspicion from herself and tie Orin even more closely to her by driving him into regression. As she taints her son's mind with the suspicion that his father jealously hates him, the iterated forms of 'hate' again pervade her speech.

At the close of the play Lavinia remains the unquiet vestal entombed without peace in the house 'which my grandfather built as a temple of Hatred and Death'.[14] Hatred is the key to understanding the levels of significance of this tragedy. At first it focuses on personal, biographical events, but is then gradually extended symbolically to take in historical and historical-anthropological meanings with a far broader scope. Hatred is generated in Lavinia by frustration due to the lack of love which she feels in childhood, when her mother rejected her as if she were the very daughter of her disgust:

CHRISTINE, *(bitterly.)* No. I loved him once – before I married him – incredible as that seems now! He was handsome in his lieutenant's uniform! He was silent and mysterious and romantic! But marriage soon turned his romance into – disgust!
LAVINIA, *(wincing again – stammers harshly.)* So I was born of your disgust! I've always guessed that, Mother – ever since I was little – when I used to come to you – with love – but you would always push me away! I've felt it ever since I can remember – your disgust! *(Then with a flare-up of bitter hatred.)* Oh, I hate you! It's only right I should hate you!
CHRISTINE, *(shaken – defensively.)* I tried to love you. I told myself it wasn't human not to love my own child, born of my body. But I never could make myself feel you were born of any body but his! You were always my wedding night to me – and my honeymoon![15]

Lavinia's affective life is blocked in the Oedipal phase. Her personality is flattened on her father's, fixed in the rigidity of posture and the mask that unites all the Mannons: the repression of her joy in life, the death wish, concealed behind the façade of appearances.

Likewise, Orin's hostility for his father and hatred for his mother's lover (another Mannon) are the expression of his fixation at the Oedipal level and a regressive tendency that his father sought to overcome by persuading him to enlist as a soldier, while his mother later exploits it to save herself.

CHRISTINE. When will he be well enough to come home?
MANNON. Soon. The doctor advised a few more days' rest. He's still weak. He was out of his head for a long time. Acted as if he were a little boy again. Seemed to think you were with him. That is, he kept talking to 'Mother'.[16]

There is a morbid bond between Orin and Christine, which has its most ambiguously revelatory dialogue in the second act of part 2. In some ways this recalls the relation between Mrs Alving and Oswald in *Ghosts*. Christine's new relationship with her lover has detached her from Orin. Orin feels a dull jealousy, an indefinite fear.

CHRISTINE. [...] that she [Lavinia] will even accuse me of the vilest, most horrible things!
ORIN. Mother! Honestly now! You oughtn't to say that!
CHRISTINE, *(reaching out and taking his hand.)* I mean it, Orin. I wouldn't say it to anyone but you. You know that. But we've always been so close, you and I. I feel you are really – my flesh and blood! She isn't! She is your father's! You are a part of me![17]

Neither of the children is capable of maturing or of overcoming the block that stifles their lives and embroils them in the mutual guilt of torture, as Christine declares.[18] Hatred governs relations in a closed, imploded family, at the same time depressing and making barren the society to which it belongs, and of which it should be the cynosure. The theme of the family has always been central to tragedy and is particularly strong in this phase of American literary culture. Think of *The Sound and the Fury* by Faulkner, *The Grapes of Wrath* by Steinbeck and *The Great Gatsby* by Fitzgerald, with the Joad, Compson and Buchanan families. But hatred also governs broader relationships, fuelling the obsession with power and triggering civil war. So even where the image of the family is positive, united in solidarity and hope, as in Steinbeck's novels, hatred becomes social hatred, fomented by fear, and the word itself continues to be a key term. Its laws block harmonious growth, reciprocal maturation. The world of Cain poisons everything. The play passes from the personal plane to the historical-cultural, to which it imparts a regressive movement and a tragic destiny. This is the diagnosis that O'Neill implicitly presents.

As in Aeschylus' tragedy, events in the play are seen against the backdrop of war, from which Ezra Mannon and young Orin return. Aeschylus presents war within the framework of ancient ethics, as the just punishment for a violation of values, a defence and heroic bulwark, so that even the elders of the chorus yearningly wish they had taken part in it. O'Neill looks at reality. In the greedy, arrogant, overbearing and aggressive tendencies of the civilization which precipitated World War I, the twenties and thirties, followed by the Great Depression and the bloodbath in the West, he sees clearly the mystification of war and the empty rhetoric of justifications for it.

It is the meditation on this reality that probably inspired one of the most beautiful and successful scenes in the play, exploring themes of love, hatred and truth: the dialogue between Ezra and Christine, alone on the steps of the Mannon house on the evening of his homecoming. The experience of war, the daily contact with death, the last landfall of both victory and defeat, the nights in camp with thousands of men around him, have matured the general, who has also been shipowner, judge and mayor of the city. His wartime experience has reawakened his feelings, his need for intimacy and love. It has shattered his rigid armour and loosened his tongue. Death becomes meaningless when it is continuous, prompting him to reflect on life and reviving his urge to live, revealing the inconsistency and deception of an ideology, an oppressive, intimidating and distorted vision of religion.

MANNON. [...] It was seeing death all the time in this war got me to thinking these things. Death was so common, it didn't mean anything. That freed me to think of life. Queer, isn't it? Death made me think of life. Before that life had only made me think of death!

CHRISTINE, (*without opening her eyes.*) Why are you talking of death?

MANNON. That's always been the Mannon's way of thinking. They went to the white meeting-house on Sabbaths and meditated on death. Life was dying. Being born was starting to die. Death was being born. (*Shaking his head with a dogged bewilderment.*) How in hell people ever got such notions! That white meeting-house. It stuck in my mind- clean-scrubbed and whitewashed – a temple of death ! But in this war I've seen too many white walls splattered with blood that counted no more than dirty water. I've seen dead men scattered about, no more important than rubbish to be got rid of. That made the white meeting-house seem meaningless – making so much solemn fuss over death![19]

O'Neill must have drawn on a historical source for this passage. It recalls the famous letter that General William T. Sherman sent his brother on 30 June 1864, describing the worst of war, the spectacle of death and destruction, indifference to the slaughter of 'a couple of thousand men'. By contrast the experience of war has crushed the mind of the young Orin Mannon, aggravating his fixation and confusion. The war has also hardened him, making him indifferent to death. What was taken to be his heroism was only the duty to stay alive at all costs. This was the training he received from his father, whom he identifies with the war, and as a result Orin is now completely indifferent to his death. He speaks ironically, sarcastically. 'Murdering people doesn't improve one's manners', he comments in act 1 of *The Hunted*.[20]

ORIN, (*who is again looking at Hazel, breaks out harshly.*) Do you remember how you waved your handkerchief, Hazel, the day I set off to become a hero? I thought you would sprain your wrist! And all the mothers and wives and sisters and girls did the same! Sometime in some war they ought to make the women take the men's place for a month or so. Give them a taste of murder!

CHRISTINE. Orin!

ORIN. Let them batter each other's brains out with rifle butts and rip each other's guts with bayonets! After that, maybe they'd stop waving handkerchiefs and gabbing about heroes! (*Hazel gives a shocked exclamation.*)[21]

It is impossible to disregard the fact that, not many years before this, Hemingway had published his great novel *A Farewell to Arms* (1929), which expressed antimilitarism, an obsession with the 'dirty crime that constitutes war', endorsed by a generation of artists and intellectuals. Likewise Orin reveals the deceit he sees in the rhetoric of war: there is no nobility in the sacrifice of the soldier's life; evil becomes banal; insensibility prevails, and with it the urge to survive at all costs. Even the much-vaunted act of heroism which earned him his honourable wound and a decoration for bravery was in fact an act of heedlessness, of fear and cowardice.

The American Civil War provides the context for the plot. O'Neill chose it because, before his lifetime, it was the greatest wartime epic experienced by the United States, making it appropriate to evoke the context of the Trojan War for the Greek peoples, which provides the backdrop to the *Oresteia*. But above all he chose it because it embodied the mechanism of the irreducibility of hatred. Hatred brought about the American Civil War between the wealthy, urbanized North, making steady progress in technology, industry, navigation, railways and banking, and the rural South, with little immigration and few railways. It can further be considered the laboratory for the European civil wars, from World War I down to 1945. The use of the machine gun and rifled cannon led to massacres among the combatants that were technically impossible in earlier conflicts. At the centre of the war lay the problem of racism and the idea of the superiority of the white race, an almost insoluble problem fuelled by venom and rancour. The Civil War aimed at the annihilation of the enemy; it called for unconditional surrender, the cessation of the other's existence. And the struggle was desperate, lasting four years, at an appalling cost in money, property and lives. Hundreds of thousands of men on both sides died of wounds or disease in the field. Many parts of the South were devastated. The Shenandoah Valley was ravaged from end to end. It is elicited by the song hummed by Seth the gardener, one of the leitmotifs of O'Neill's play. Hatred between North and South rankled for many decades. The social and moral fibre of the country suffered. The war brought to prominence a coarse, avid and unscrupulous class, with an outlook that was hard, bourgeois, selfish and short-sighted, which O'Neill evokes in the 'chorus' described above. Yet, when the war was over, it went down in the history books as the great phase of the country's unification.

Tragic Pessimism: From the Autobiographical Plane to the Historical and the Philosophical-Anthropological

The mainspring of the tragedy is hatred. It acts on a personal level, spreads to the historical plane and fosters an anthropology hostile to mankind and a fundamentally pessimistic philosophy. The play's historical implications have been indicated above: the hatred unleashed in the greatest war in the historical memory of the United States, the Civil War, and the bloodshed of the 'Great War', recently ended. The law of hatred and vengeance divides the local and human community, preventing harmonious growth.

The world of Cain has gained ground: this is the diagnosis of the age that O'Neill presents, projecting it into the past.

On the first of these three planes, O'Neill's inspiration is nurtured both by autobiographical elements and the categories of Freudian psychoanalysis. Veiled by cultural, scientific or literary patterns, *Mourning Becomes Electra* shadows forth O'Neill's unresolved conflicts and brooding memories of his family, the dynamics that shackled and imprisoned Eugene, his brother Jamie and his mother and father in a tormenting but also intensely affective relationship. When all had died and Eugene was the only survivor, like Lavinia living on in the Mannon house, those conflicts subsided into compassion for old suffering expressed in *Long Day's Journey into Night* (1940), a play written 'in tears and blood', as O'Neill wrote in the dedication to his wife Carlotta, without cultural filters or disguises and with a direct, lucid introspection.

Of Freud, O'Neill claimed to have read only *Totem and Taboo* (1913) and *Beyond the Pleasure Principle* (1920). He also received treatment from at least three psychoanalysts and had a smattering of clinical psychoanalytic knowledge. In conceiving the characters of Lavinia and Orin, he acted on the suggestions of the Oedipus complex and Electra complex,[22] the latter being a term introduced by Jung and rejected by Freud, but applicable to O'Neill's frame of reference by his own admission.[23] These complexes have become 'fixated'. The characters' repression of these drives, their efforts to overcome them and their psychic prehistory, have been inadequate; the reawakening of these impulses forms the core of their psychoneuroses, their unbearable suffering and inexpiable sense of guilt. Their attempt to detach their desires from the primary libidinal object in order to reach out and become a member of the social community, building and expanding it, has been defeated, so blocking their development and destroying them.

The modern perception of tragedy in O'Neill starts from this plane of diagnosis: the psychological roots of a humanity made up of individuals who are acutely neurotic, verging on perversion, inhibited in their normal and constructive development, endowed with a frail, incomplete selfhood and unable to resist the most immature drives.

Lavinia detaches herself early from her first love object, her mother. She feels chilled by her mother's indifference or even hostility towards her; her female development is arrested, hatred prevails, and she turns her exclusive and jealous love towards her father, actually developing the same mask-like expression. Then the drive is diverted to her brother-son, in which she identifies herself with her mother, her father's love object, in a supreme, desperate bid for intimacy. But the manoeuvre fails. The 'fixation' is permanent, hatred prevails and spreads, bringing with it the death instinct.[24]

Lavinia appears as the Vestal Virgin, guardian of Death, the last of the Mannons, for whom the obsession with death, as we have seen, is the prevailing drive that nothing ultimately succeeds in overcoming, though the trauma of wartime seemed for a while to threaten to undermine it. This pessimistic conclusion was naturally influenced, in this phase of his work, by O'Neill's readings of Schopenhauer, whom he explicitly claimed as a source. Schopenhauer's works appear in the library of Edmund Tyrone, Eugene O'Neill's alter ego in the autobiographical *Long Day's Journey into Night*. O'Neill was also influenced by psychoanalytic works, which were to be distilled and reaffirmed (albeit with their conflicts quelled) in *The Iceman Cometh* (1939), which deals with the theme of illusion, and above all in *Long Day's Journey into Night*, in which he explored the seductiveness of death. To be more precise, I would say that this representation of hatred, which plays such a large part in governing human relations and, by analogy, historical events, the very structure of being in these works, stems from a combination of psychoanalytic ideas and philosophical ideas derived from Schopenhauer, two powerful influences on O'Neill's development and with a close affinity for his spirit.[25] The death wish, which Freud associated with the love–hate ambivalence that explodes when the personality is 'fixated' on destruction and self-destruction, was engrafted onto his discovery of the blind 'will to live', the principle, not ethical but ontological, identified by Schopenhauer. He believed it was the *noumenon*, the true reality that exists complete and identical in both things and people, which are the manifestations or expressions of a *principium individuationis* that is no more than the fabric of surface representations. They move in a brutal interplay of oppression and destruction of all that is opposed to them, of absolute selfishness, functional to the 'necessity' of that principle which, filtered through the deceptive veil of Maya, lies beneath the changeful appearances, the interplay of both little lives and great events, the organic and inorganic.

If all this turmoil and suffering, of people who are like 'clockwork which is wound up and goes without knowing why', are to end in nothingness, then wisdom is *noluntas*, the immobility of peace, mortal languor and the contemplation of deceptive appearances as a distant, extraneous picture, Schopenhauer's *via negativa*.[26]

One cannot help identifying this body of ideas with Lavinia's decision to bury herself in the Mannon house, or again behind the 'rot in peace' of Nina Leeds, the central figure in *Strange Interlude* (1928). Again it underlies the aquatic suspension in an alcoholic torpor of the patrons of the saloon at the end of the line, who have renounced their illusions, and the detachment and oblivion sought in morphine by Mary Tyrone in *Long Day's Journey into Night*, the last of his works, in which our playwright presented his most authentically real world without mediation.

Then in paragraph 51 of *The World as Will and Representation* (1818), which O'Neill would have read, we find Schopenhauer's opinion of tragedy to be 'the summit of the poetic art', revealing humanity's sufferings, left to the mercy of fate and compelled to tear one another to pieces. The philosopher was thinking of classical, baroque and Romantic tragedy. The modernist O'Neill turned the inquiring gaze of this noble genre into the truth of a world without heroes.

Chapter 4

THE DESTINY OF MAN IS MAN: *MUTTER COURAGE UND IHRE KINDER* (*MOTHER COURAGE AND HER CHILDREN*) BY BERTOLT BRECHT

The form of tragedy and the traditional mode of expressing man's tragic condition in the theatre were, as is well known, some of Bertolt Brecht's most controversial targets.[1] There are two sets of reasons for this. The first is technical, because classical tragedy and the drama that derives from it belong, as Brecht saw it, to a kind of theatre that does not arouse the critical spirit and the dialectical attitude. The second is philosophical, because they are founded on an idea of destiny and the immutability or universality of human thought, in conflict with Brecht's Marxian principles.[2]

The limit that weighs on life (which Brecht embraced as an object of great love and inexhaustible pleasure, which fascinated him and to which he devoted his life's work)[3] was not so much a natural limit as that entailed by people's responsibility towards others. It was Marx who provided him with the insight into this vital issue for modernity, and Brecht started from this. This point of view constitutes a significant change from that of the works we have examined so far. The limit is bound up with poverty and oppression. It is based on exploitation. It is not predestined and unavoidable, but historical and changeable. Accepting the idea of destiny means accepting one form of alienation which Marx analysed and rejected, that of an absolute, when humanity forgets its only home is the earth. It is the superstructural product of a culture, as are all ideas historically determined by various forms of economic structure in history. It is not people's consciousness that determines their being, but their social being that determines consciousness. Even the most ancestral form of consciousness, the mother's, is no exception to this rule. Brecht deals with this point: *Mother Courage and Her Children* is its greatest embodiment in contemporary tragedy.

The transgression of the limit that I have associated with the tragic action is here articulated in three modes, which clearly reveal Brecht's ideological position. One is the lust for power and wealth. This is the guilty and destructive motivation of the warlords. The second is the petty greed that seeks a refuge and protection in war and descends to compromises for small gains. It seeks to survive, getting what it can; but it ventures too close to the fire and inevitably gets burnt, while being jointly responsible for the history of injustice. The outcome is tragic, as Mother Courage and her children know all too well. The third is of those who feel, albeit only instinctively, like Kattrin, the contradiction and disquiet of the limit inscribed in reality. With a revolutionary act they transgress it at the cost of their lives. This makes it possible to push the limit a little further away, even though, as we have seen, it is essentially impossible for it to be abolished.

The Genesis of the Work

The first draft of the play, perhaps preceded by a sketch during Brecht's Danish exile, dates from the period 27 September to 3 November 1939, and the first public glimpse of the work came when Scene 6 was published in a Moscow magazine.[4] The script (or 'matrix') was published to coincide with the first performance at the Zurich Schauspielhouse on 19 April 1941.

While collaborating with Paul Dessau on the composition of the stage music, which was considered binding on subsequent performances, Brecht altered the text. The work was performed at the Deutsches Theater in Berlin, as the German premiere, on 11 January 1949, and was published for the first time by Suhrkamp (formerly Samuel Fischer in West Berlin and Frankfurt). After the premiere the German text was further revised and finally reissued in 1950 by Suhrkamp. The text as thus established emerged from the experience of performance and the process of learning the principles of epic theatre implemented by the actors under Brecht's direction. From the planned text, as Siro Ferrone would put it, we pass to the consolidated text, which was, however, to become a model for the future. In September 1951 the Berliner Ensemble reformulated the text. So these are not different versions, but varying degrees of development of the same text, with variants that are primarily functional to the staging. There are three basic levels: the 1939 draft, the 1941 script and the 1949 draft with the final changes embodied in the 1950 edition and closely connected with the 'model book', whose basic idea and development were bound up with this performance. It was published in 1958 with additions derived from Brecht's production at the Munich Kammerspiele in 1950, the new production at the Berliner Ensemble in 1951 and the revised texts and a final selection of photographs in 1956.

The Context: Europe in Catastrophe

It is always useful, and in the case of Brecht indispensable, to explore the setting in which a given work developed.[5] Apart from inner or philosophical motives, though these should not be underrated, the sense of urgency that drove Brecht to work at his desk sprang from historical, civil and social concerns. He confessed as much in one of the texts in the fascinating 'lyrical diary' of his poems:

> Inside me contend
> Delight at the apple tree in blossom
> And horror at the house-painter's speeches.
> But only the second
> Drives me to my desk.[6]

Brecht composed the work when he was already an exile, fleeing from Nazi Germany in the aftermath of the Reichstag fire. He settled first in Denmark, then in Sweden and

Finland, still within range of his homeland. 'Germany, pale mother! / How you sit defiled.'[7] Finally he moved to the United States. He revised the work, gave it a stable form for the stage, and finally published it in postwar Berlin, in the heart of Communist Germany when he was running the institution known first as the Deutsches Theater and then the Berliner Ensemble. Struggling with disappointments and regrets, he sought to make it both the conscience and stimulus of the new order and the utopia which he hoped to see realized.

Brecht was an eyewitness to some of the twentieth-century's worst disasters. The earliest were the final phases of World War I, when he was drafted, still very young, as a medical orderly in an Augsburg hospital. Brecht saw clearly what would later become evident to historians. The abyss revealed by the age was not imputable to impersonal or inscrutable problems or forces, as in ancient tragedy, but to the acts of individuals who had conceived ideologies and filled the century with 'murderous ideas', and were therefore responsible for them. The historical context, with the concomitance of grievous errors of perspective and disastrous decisions, reinforced Brecht's view and led him to challenge the idea of destiny, the old assumption underlying tragedy. Once again, his poetry expresses this idea clearly:

> Stop searching, woman, you will never find them!
> But, woman, don't accept that fate is to blame!
> Those murky forces, woman, that torment you,
> Have each of them a face, address and name.[8]

In his work Brecht attacked these errors. They included the widespread combative mindset, the escalation of German militarism and the policy of rearmament; the escalation of the authoritarian state, backed by violence, toward totalitarianism, and the state identified with society; the pursuit of a deep-seated transformation of society in the name of an ideology that pervaded it through propaganda, terror and the work of the secret police; the idealization of violence and racism, and the belief that the driving force of society was conflict; the suppression of all disinterested criticism; the power and increasingly less neutral character of modern science; the difficult, conflicting and at times lengthy and expensive (in human terms) experimentation and development of correctives to capitalism, with profit as its mainspring and ultimate goal; the eclipse of democracy; the aberrant influence of such regimes on culture and its leading representatives; the enigma of consensus; and contempt for the people and the obtuse, dull and supine weakness of their consciences.

Such concerns became obsessions and fuelled Brecht's writings. His first and most harrowing obsession was war. Though his treatment of it is rooted in the analysis of past and present, it also touches the deepest chords of pity, the meaning of life, death and personal responsibility, confined between nature and culture. War was an experience common to Brecht's generation, on which it made a profound impression. Wars involved millions of people, wrenching them from their normal lives and sending them into the front lines and trenches, spreading a culture of regimentation. For the first time in history millions of civilians were subjected to military discipline. Weapons were placed in their hands and they were brought into constant contact with what we have identified as the extreme figure of tragedy: death and the devaluation of life.

Brecht hated and condemned war, though reasons of prudence and expediency led him, above all after World War II, to play down the pacifist element in his work so as not to undermine the revolutionary outlook. Far from being ideological, Brecht's aversion to war was humanitarian, the expression of an independence of mind and unprejudiced awareness that are common to the authors dealt with in this book. They were what their generation might have been and was not, with the disastrous consequences familiar to us.

Brecht and the other intellectuals of the period were strongly influenced by their reading. Brecht's loathing of war was heightened by his response to the success at the time enjoyed by books such as Ivan Bloch's *The Future of War* (1898), with the prophecy that modern warfare would be impossible except at the cost of suicide, Clausewitz's *On War* (1832–35), with the idea of war as a cultural and a political instrument,[9] or *Mein Kampf* (1925), a frenzied expression of a nationalist and racist 'utopia'.

Marxist thinking also played an important part in the debate. Brecht came to it by reading Marx and Engels' *Communist Manifesto* (1848) and *Das Kapital* (1867–94). War is not connatural to humans, structural to the violent relationship that develops between individuals and between organized communities. It is a cultural construct dependent on the economic structure that men have chosen. War is the inevitable product of capitalist accumulation. It is caused by the vicious circle of the accumulation of resources, production of war materials, wars waged to expand markets and profits, and imperialism – a permanent state of war. Rosa Luxemburg had made the same point. Brecht was struck by her insights and the effectiveness of her arguments.

Brecht's poems reveal some of his deepest feelings about this human practice, which on the one hand seeks to exorcise death by inflicting it, and on the other expresses a self-destructive instinct or death wish, violating humanity's only possession (in the dramatist's earthly perspective), namely life and its inalienable fulfilment. His poems suggest the human resonance of the tragic problem in Brecht and parallel the text we are dealing with here. It is a human and cultural background which cannot be ignored without running the risk of offering a reductive and ideological interpretation of Brecht's work. I will try to present the essence of some of the themes he deals with, while referring the reader to the texts themselves. They deserve not to be completely overshadowed by his better-known writings for the theatre.

War is the great inferno of human suffering, the corruption of the body, the deadening of the heart and the frustration of illusions.[10] It is the subversion of the natural order of things.[11] It is the natural outcome of peace when it is administered not as the true opposite of war but as a natural preparation for it: this is the subtlest of the deceptions of those in power.[12] In either state, whether as victors or vanquished, the lot of the ordinary people is hunger and poverty. And what will come to the soldier's woman? At most some gift, some trinket, which will only conceal the approach of her last reward: 'the funeral, the widow's veil'.[13]

Brecht flees from the climate of violence, dictatorship and war. But no peaceful haven, however tenderly contemplated in the silence of nature violated, can prevent the forebodings of disaster.

> In the willows by the Sound,
> These spring nights the screech-owl often calls.
> According to a peasant superstition,
> Your screech-owl informs people that
> They haven't long to live. I,
> Who know full well that I have told the truth
> About the powers that be,
> Don't need a death bird
> To inform me so.[14]

War is the profanation of all human solidarity. *War Primer* is a collection of photographs accompanied by a commentary in the form of epigrams. In this book Brecht reversed the usual wartime manipulation of photographs and denounced it. An example is the epigram on an attack in the Caucasus, giving a voice to the Swabian peasant felled by a bullet fired by a Russian peasant.[15] Another epigram comments on the photograph of an American and the Japanese he has slain, which reveals the absurd human contradiction of that moment:

> We saw each other – it happened very fast –
> I smiled and both of them smiled back at me.
> And at first we stood and smiled, all three.
> One pulled his gun. And then I shot him dead.[16]

War arouses elementary levels of ancestral fears of others and death. While focusing his attention steadily on political and social history, Brecht repeatedly evokes the philosophical motif of the transience of human things, the fading of life like smoke, life deeply loved, enjoyed and savoured. His poems contain reminiscences of one of the books he read most deeply in: the Bible in the Lutheran translation and specifically the themes of Ecclesiastes.[17] His atheistic vision[18] and metaphysical pessimism,[19] which left no room for doubts, further accentuated his radical condemnation of war. The deprivation of the only good mankind possesses – life itself – is the true tragedy. Its loss by violence in war is the greatest sin. Humanity alone is responsible, as an epigram explains in the *War Primer*, commenting on the photograph of a woman who wanders searching through the rubble of a Berlin house destroyed by British bombs.

His wholly human indignation and pity also dwell on the evocation of Christ as an innocent victim of human violence, and on Mary, who suffered the indignity of extreme violence in the flesh of her son. He speaks of the necessary (*nötig*) comfort which has flowed to the poor from them ever since the cold, good night of Christmas,[20] and the example of resistance that comes from Christ's proud and grieving silence before those who, like the stone statue on a tomb, condemned him.[21]

The theme of war, so relevant and yet so ancient, is interwoven in its implications with another archetype, another thread that runs through history and the present, myth and symbol: the theme of the mother. Its depth of resonance provided the inspiration for *Mother Courage*. We can now enter into a more immediate analysis of this work.

A Mother without Tears and a Mute Who Beats the Drum of Vengeance. The Stone Begins to Speak.

We are in the Swedish region of Dalarne in the spring of 1624, on a campaign in the Thirty Years War. A recruiter and a sergeant are seeking to enlist soldiers for the Polish campaign on behalf of the commander-in-chief, Count Oxenstierna. They complain about the intractable inhabitants in these parts, who want to eat without paying their tribute to the war, described as the only source of order. They encounter the canteen wagon run by Mother Courage, a well-known provisioner who lives off the war. By selling victuals she ensures the soldiers go to their deaths happy and better fed. In a witty and dangerous exchange she reveals her trade, the origin of her strange family, the three children she has had by three different fathers. With uncanny shrewdness she reads the fate of those present, which includes death for all. The scene ends as might have been foreseen: Mother Courage earns good money by selling a silver buckle to the sergeant and loses a child, the smart and reckless Eilif, who allows himself to be enrolled. Since she wants to live off the war she has to give it something in return (scene 1).

Two years later, during the Polish campaign, before the fortress of Wallhof, we see Mother Courage in the Swedish camp, in the general's kitchen. She is haggling with the cook over the sale of a capon when the general arrives accompanied by Eilif and the chaplain. Unseen, and without noticing Mother Courage, the general lavishes praise on Eilif for his valour in massacring some peasants and stealing their cattle. Everything has been done by rule, in keeping with the watchword of war: loot. Mother Courage, who in the meantime has made her presence known and embraced her son, does not allow herself to be taken in by his heroism. She drives a hard bargain for the chicken and then slaps her hero, because he failed to follow her sage instructions: never run risks and always put saving your own skin first (scene 2).

Three years have passed. Mother Courage continues to drive her trade, which now includes buying and selling war materials. Her son Swiss Cheese has been made a paymaster. His honesty (or, according to Mother Courage, his stupidity) has earned him the confidence of the regiment, which entrusts its cash box to him. Yvette, a young Frenchwoman who was deceived by her first love, has become the soldiers' prostitute and is suffering from syphilis. She is one of the followers of the cart. The cook and the chaplain arrive. Now serious, now joking, now hypocritical, now sincere, they talk about the motives behind the religious war, the good intentions of those who wish to serve freedom or faith. The scene is homely: a cannon serves to prop up a washing line. Suddenly the peace is shattered by a surprise attack launched by the Catholics. In the confusion Mother Courage tries to salvage whatever she can. She conceals the beauty of her mute daughter Kattrin by smearing her face with ashes to save her from the soldiers' lust. She hides her paymaster son, who has hidden the money chest under the wagon.

Yvette dresses up for the newcomers. The chaplain disguises himself to avoid capture, because as a Protestant his life is in danger. Mother Courage adapts to circumstances. She changes the flag on her cart and continues to supply victuals. Swiss Cheese, overcome by his scruples, decides to escape in order to take the money chest to his regiment. Incautiously he betrays himself to two spies and is captured, despite Kattrin's attempts to forewarn him. To free her son by her usual method of bribery, Mother Courage uses the mediation of Yvette. She falls in with her son's ploy by pretending they do not know each other. She pawns her cart to Yvette, who is financed by her former soldier lover, and thinks of using the money in the chest to save her son, but it has been lost because Swiss Cheese threw it away. The time she wastes by haggling proves fatal and her son is shot. The stretcher with the corpse is brought before her as a ruse, in an attempt to make her forget her caution in her grief and reveal where the chest is hidden. But she and her daughter remain mute and impassive. She denies her son to avoid betraying herself (scene 3).

The cart is again in Mother Courage's possession. It is much the worse for wear and she means to lodge a complaint with the army high command. Her courage and pride are again weakened. Outside the officer's tent she meets a young soldier who likewise intends to complain about an injustice he has suffered. The 'Song of the Great Capitulation' reveals the two characters' change of heart (scene 4)

Two years have passed. Mother Courage's small cart is still on the move, crossing great expanses of territory: Poland, Moravia, Bavaria, Italy. We are now at Tilly's victory at Magdeburg. The wagon has halted in front of a half-destroyed village. Soldiers are looting it, a fundamental practice of the Thirty Years War. Mother Courage defends her wares stubbornly. She refuses to give the chaplain any linen shirts to make bandages for the wounded and represses Kattrin's natural pity and maternal protectiveness. Her daughter and the chaplain continue to press her: he gets the bandages, she her little corner of tenderness with a baby she has saved and is now able to cradle (scene 5).

The action moves to Bavaria. Marshal Tilly's funeral is being held offstage. We learn that the usual religious solemnities, for example the tolling of the church bells to accompany the burial, are out of the question because all the churches and steeples have been destroyed on his orders. Salvoes will be fired instead. Meanwhile Mother Courage attends to her duties as victualler and merchant. She takes stock of her goods and keeps an eye on the soldiers who have received their pay and are drinking at the bar she keeps, deserting the funeral. She expresses her concern that the general's death will be bad for her war business. The chaplain reassures her. She rejects the chaplain's proposed marriage of convenience because it is not worth her while (he is lazy and garrulous). At the same time she reveals a hidden liking for the cook whose pipe she is smoking (he had pawned it to her). She takes advantage of a momentary fall in prices by sending Kattrin to buy goods in the nearby town, endangering her. Kattrin returns injured and violated, but carrying the goods and now with no hope of finding a husband. She angrily refuses Yvette's red boots which her mother has kept and is now willing to give her in the hope of comforting her. The scene ends with Mother Courage cursing war (scene 6).

She soon retracts her curses. In the next scene we see Mother Courage at the height of her business career, wearing a necklace of silver coins around her neck and expressing her pleasure in war by singing a cynical song: war only means dealing in lead instead of cheese; the sedentary and the weak always go to the wall anyway (scene 7).

In that same year, 1632, an old woman and a young peasant are unsuccessfully trying to survive by selling the little they have left to Mother Courage, her cart now well stocked with recent purchases. The pealing of bells announces that the war is over, following the death in battle of Gustavus Adolphus at the very moment of victory. Mother Courage is torn between satisfaction and anxiety. How is she to dispose of all this merchandise? But at least she has saved two of her children, or so she believes. After three years' absence, the general's cook returns. Relations are restored between the three: Mother Courage, the chaplain and the cook. Their livelihood is at stake. Courage's little business is tempting. The two contenders attack and discredit each other in the attempt to prevail. Then a decision is made: the chaplain will resume his old garments and his vocation, while the cook is harnessed to the cart, which he ends up drawing with Kattrin, while her mother sings. Yvette reappears, older and ailing, but enriched by her marriage to a former colonel, now dead. She gets her own back on the first scoundrel who ruined her: the cook.

When Mother Courage goes off to market, her son Eilif appears handcuffed and pale. He is being led off to death for having committed in peacetime the very acts (looting and killing) that had earned him accolades in wartime. He is allowed to take his leave with his family, but his mother is not present and his sister, still under the shock of her disfigurement, refuses to emerge from the wagon. The cook lacks the courage to break the news to Mother Courage. Meanwhile, the war breaks out again and Mother Courage goes off singing cheerfully: Mother Courage is always here (scene 8).

The war is now in its 17th year. It is 1634. Germany is depopulated, desolate, famine-stricken. The cities are reduced to ashes and wolves roam through them. In the mountains, before a ruined shrine, Mother Courage and the cook are forced to beg. They have nothing more to sell, no money to pay for their purchases. The cook receives the news that he has inherited his mother's tavern on her death and suggests Mother Courage should run it with him. She turns down the offer when she learns that Kattrin is excluded from the plan, because the cook fears she will be a burden now she is aging, mute and disfigured. Between the cart and the tavern Mother Courage chooses the old way: her cart. But first the scene is interrupted by the 'Song of Solomon', about death and the unnecessary virtues: wisdom, courage, honesty, selflessness and the fear of God.

Kattrin has overheard the conversation. Partly from pride and partly to avoid being a burden she tries to run away, but not without leaving a mischievous or perhaps malicious sign behind her: the cook's trousers and her mother's skirt laid symbolically side by side. Her mother comes back and stops her in time, but does not give in to emotion. There is the usual display of cynicism: she refused the cook's offer, she says, not out of emotional weakness but for the sake of the cart. They harness themselves to the cart and drag it away. Snow is imminent. The cook arrives and looks blankly at his clothes which Mother Courage has unceremoniously tossed out of the cart. He exits in the opposite direction (scene 9).

All through 1635 Mother Courage and her daughter Kattrin pull their cart through an increasingly ravaged and desolate Germany. They pass by a farmhouse, stopping for a moment to listen to a voice singing of the comfort of a haven (scene 10).

It is 1636. The war still has many more years to run. The cart, now bedraggled and almost empty, is outside a peasant house with a thatched roof. Mother Courage has gone to town to get supplies. It is a January night. An ensign and a soldier enter dragging a peasant and his son out of their house and tell them to show them a path into the town. It is clear that the imperial armies are about to surprise the town of Halle and butcher its inhabitants. To force the peasants to cooperate, the soldiers threaten to deprive them of their livestock, hence their livelihood. The peasants have no choice but to submit and pray. But Kattrin thwarts the soldiers' plans. Instead of joining in the prayer she performs a dangerous and highly effective gesture. She climbs onto the stable roof with a drum which she has jealously preserved and concealed all this time, pulls the ladder up behind her and starts to beat it wildly as a warning to the sleeping town. The soldiers plead with her, promising to save her mother if she stops, while the peasant woman advises them to smash the cart. Their efforts are unavailing, as is the grotesque attempt to drown out the drumming by making other humdrum, everyday noises. Finally, to silence her, they shoot at her. Kattrin gives one last rolling drum beat, followed by a weak one, then slowly crumples up. But the town is awake. We hear the bells ringing and cannons firing (scene 11).

Day breaks to the sound of drums and fifes as the troops march away. Mother Courage keeps vigil over her daughter's body and sings a lullaby, as if detached, without any apparent feeling. She gives the farmer some money for the burial. She clings to the idea that she still has one child to recover, Eilif, since she has yet to learn of his death. She goes off in the wake of the last regiment that passes by, pulling her cart, which she can do now that it is half empty.

Behind the scenes we hear a song that ends (scene 12):

> The spring is come. Christians, revive!
> The snow drifts melt, the dead lie
> And if by chance you're still alive
> It's time to rise and shake a leg.[22]

Sources and Contexts: The Mentality of War

The theatre of war is Mother Courage's field of action. Her cart, her travelling store, follows the marching armies in one of the great wars of European history. Despite its insignificance, it is affected, at a distance and in the midst of ignorance and indifference, by the eddying of important events in which the destinies of nations, great powers and peoples are played out. Through 12 of the 30 years of the 'war of religion', the cart moves from Dalarne in west-central Sweden to Poland, to Wallhof, south of Riga (where King Gustavus Adolphus of Sweden defeats the Poles), then to Moravia, Italy and Bavaria, to Magdeburg (where Tilly defeats the Swedish king), to Breitenfeld (where he is defeated in turn by Gustavus Adolphus), to Ingolstadt in Bavaria (at Tilly's funeral following his defeat by the Swedish king, a few months before the Battle of Lützen in which Gustavus Adolphus dies victorious), and from the German mountains of Fichtel to the roads of central Germany and the city of Halle.

Her life's journey is the journey of the war. Mother War: in this oxymoron lies the powerful image that dominates the work. The mother, Mother Germany, is the matrix of human life. But it is above all the present that inspires Brecht. The Thirty Years War was not just any war, chosen as the setting for the story of Mother Courage. As World War II loomed, a number of writers sought to provide an overall interpretation of the earlier war, and they continued their work in depth in the postwar period.[23] The Thirty Years War was seen as an aid to understanding the present and in its turn an understanding of it was fostered by the dramatic events of modern times. Brecht studied it from the standpoint of the Nordic countries where he was living in exile, first in Denmark just before the German invasion, then Sweden and Finland. There he explored Scandinavian history and criticized the vested economic interests of the countries of Northern Europe, which were dining with the Devil without knowing that to do so requires a very long spoon.

Some analogies between the war three hundred years earlier and the current one could help the critical theatregoer and the epic actor, whom Brecht had in mind, to keep their eyes open. The absorption of Bohemia by the Habsburgs and the destruction of its system of government, with its many degrees of religious and political freedom and tolerance, reflected certain invasions of the present. The clash between blocs in World War II was foreshadowed by the ideological conflicts between religions and cultures: Catholic European humanism and Protestant European humanism, the Spanish–Habsburg universal model and the urbanized model of the bourgeois and Protestant states, the absolute state and the fragmentation of power. The connection between war and capitalism (which came to Brecht from his Marxist reading, but is now evident to many scholars) is clearly exemplified by the Thirty Years War. The practice of war was a significant aspect of early modern capitalism.[24] This was a commercial capitalism, not yet industrialized, focused on financial and banking activities which in a certain sense followed in the wake of the war. And if 'the cruelty and destructiveness of war can never be in doubt [...], there were those who profited, and whose profits were the foundation of capitalist successes.'[25] This led to the circulation of gold, shipbuilding, the armaments industry, metallurgy, mining and the steel industry. 'War helped capitalism in three main ways: in the development of heavy industry for military purposes, the growth of industrial investment, and the financial methods that led to a development of the capital market.'[26]

The war fostered a warlike outlook, the warlike outlook affected peace and its activities: this can be derived even from that distant past. The period of the Thirty Years War heralded the development of the war machine. Military tactics and technology (with the well-known innovations introduced by Gustavus Adolphus and Wallenstein) evolved rapidly and were transferred from one field to another. The war machine had to continue to operate. Then as later, Germany was devastated and destroyed. Brecht was fully and painfully aware of this. But what struck him above all and aroused his profound indignation was the human cost of this senseless and absurd adventure in power: the cruelty, requisitions, sieges, havoc and looting, theorized and institutionalized as ways for keeping armies in the field. The wasted energies, the violence and deportations, the destruction of crops, the systematic impoverishment of the soil, the fires, the ruin of the peasants, the widening gap between rich and poor, the growing numbers of scavengers, the movements of armies in the cold and the resultant famines and epidemics. And death above all. All this is implicit in the text. The episodes that evoke war in these terms are numerous: the city under siege and the poverty of the peasants (scene 2); the theft of the cattle and the killing of the herdsmen who own them out of bravado by Eilif (2); the danger of rape (3); the hypocritical justification of the 'just war'; the war made special by religion and fought for the sake of freedom, so justifying the costs paid by the poor; a war like others with massacres, robberies, the burning of houses (3); permission to plunder (5); casual robberies in farms (7); the farmer's house destroyed by cannon fire (5); and the killing of those who resist (11).

These specific historical facts, in which past and present are linked, though driven by the urgency of the present, reveal a wider horizon of meaning. They also encompass the biblical symbols of the Horsemen of the Apocalypse, the scourges of the prophecies of Ezekiel and Jeremiah: war, plague, famine, exile, the substance of a reading of the Bible which was familiar to Brecht.[27] But obviously, as part of his nonreligious and materialistic vision, responsibility is more effectively assigned not to a God who strikes down transgressors with his punishments and is seen as inexorable fate, but to the men and women who, as we have seen, freely determine the fate of humanity. In this way, by reasoning on the context, Brecht reverses one of the assumptions of the tragic tradition: necessity or fate.

Another of the assumptions of tragedy crumbles when we analyse the character of the text: Courage, the absolute antihero inspired by Hans Jakob Christoffel von Grimmelshausen's *Landstörtzerin Courasche*, the fictional life of another amoral woman named Courage set against the backdrop of the Thirty Years War in Germany, ravaged by the mercenary armies of the European powers.[28] Courage, with her venal trafficking as a merchant and victualler in the wake of the soldiers, continually on the make, occupies the foreground. In the background are ranged the heroes whom we find at the centre of another great German text, which has no part in Brecht's imagery: Friedrich Schiller's *Wallenstein* trilogy, in which the hero is immersed in the rhetoric of war, overwhelmed by the dark and blind power of fate.[29] The elements that, in *Wallenstein's Camp* (act 1, scene 5), were details of the setting (such as the peddlers' stalls, the victualler pouring out the wine, the peasant and his son, and the drum), are here moved to the centre of the stage. Heroism is devalued in the image of the cunning Eilif, a reckless and unscrupulous bully who likes to use his hands, whose merit lies in killing and plundering by deception, and in the image of the gluttonous general of dubious tendencies who buys his soldiers (scene 2).

The Limit and Destiny of Humanity Lies in Others. Tragedy Is Not Inevitable. But Courage Learns Nothing.

Mother Courage lives in the tragedy caused by others, but she learns nothing. She is a mother, but though she has shed all the connotations, sentiments and rhetoric of the *Mater Dolorosa*,[30] she does not gain those of the aware mother who chooses rebellion. Contrast this with Pelageya Vlasova in the play *Die Mutter* (*The Mother*) and her daughter, the true heroine of a modern tragedy, according to Brecht, without any sense of fatality.

The whole drama is pervaded by the theme of the limit, of suffering and death, despite the avoidance of pathos characteristic of the epic style. It is polarized around certain keywords and reflects the symbolic depths of the human condition, but it reflects a condition that is reversible, in part through the iterated allusion to Christ's Passion, reduced to an exclusively human measure.[31]

The black cross (*schwarzes Kreuz*) looms up in the first scene, associated with the word death (*Tod*) in the fortunes that Mother Courage, in the guise of a witch, reads in the future of all the characters on stage (the recruiting soldiers and her children), in the song in which the canteen woman announces her arrival.[32] In the first scene the frailty of the flesh is evident in Kattrin's disability – she can only make hoarse noises when she is distressed. The theme of human frailty reappears in the 'Song of the Girl and the Soldier', sung by Courage and Eilif in scene 2: 'You'll go out like a light! And the sun'll take flight. / For your courage just makes us feel colder.'[33]

The theme of the limit reappears in the 'Song of the Hours', inspired by the sixteenth-century hymn 'Christus, der uns selig macht', in which the Stations of the Cross are divided into the seven canonical hours of the office. The chaplain sings the song to the paymaster Swiss Cheese, Courage's honest and rather simple-minded son, the innocent victim who is compared to the Son of Man (scene 3). It emerges again at Tilly's funeral, in the violence inflicted on Kattrin. The wound that disfigures her face inhibits her desire for love and her maternal vocation (scene 6).

The condition of the limit is embodied in material poverty (scene 11), which subjects the characters to the adversity of nature without any refuge or haven (scene 10), but also in feelings of deprivation and the impoverishment of relationships, a luxury that neither Courage, Kattrin nor the cook can afford. There is no place for Kattrin in the tavern in Utrecht; compassion is a failing, tenderness for one's children a sign of childishness and weakness. The virtues do not pay (scene 9).

But Courage learns nothing, and Brecht, ably supported by his greatest interpreter, Helene Weigel, makes this clear. A hyena of the battlefield ('Hyäne des Schlachtfelds'),[34] as she is described by the chaplain, when she is left alone she continues to live off the war: there is no room for illusion, but things could always get better.

> MOTHER COURAGE.
> Take me along! [...]
> With all its luck and all its danger,
> The war is dragging on a bit.
> The common man won't benefit. [...]
> But still a miracle may save him:
> Tomorrow is another day!
> The new year's come. The watchmen shout!
> The thaw sets in. The dead remain.
> Wherever life has not died out
> It staggers to its legs again.[35]

Courage does not belie her character. She lives on war and nurtures it. In a certain sense she is its accomplice. She advertises her wares (shoes or bread, linen shirts or guns, buckles or bullets) to help the soldiers fight better, sending them well-fed to hell and keeping her purse filled with coins. Lucid, shrewd and cynical, she wants to grow fat on the war but is unwilling to pay the price. She is smooth-tongued and never allows herself to be hoodwinked. She has no illusions. She refuses to swallow the specious justifications for the war, the idea that it is being waged for faith, for the fear of God, or any other ideal. The truth is that 'A war is only what you make it / It's business, not with cheese but lead'[36]. She is tough and determined in the way she plays the game. Peace kills her, because it will leave her with her stock on her hands. She has no qualms about bribery and is indifferent to which side wins. Such knowledge of life as she has gained is expressed in the 'Song of the Great Capitulation' and the 'Song of Solomon'. Wisdom, valour, integrity, selflessness and the fear of God are ruinous. People are better off without them. Rage is short-lived. Pity is repressed. Self-interest always comes to the fore. If a general dies it means one customer less. She has no use for fine talk.

Certainly not all her humanity is dead. She halts a moment to listen to a voice singing of the rose and the snowflake as she travels along the roads of Germany following an increasingly bedraggled army. She leaves some money for Kattrin's burial (though earlier she had the strength to leave her son unburied, denying him after he was shot by a firing squad), and a lullaby comes to her lips. She too feels a brief transport of love for the cook, who has left her the pipe she smokes. But cynicism and the spirit of the huckster prevail.

What lesson does Courage fail to learn that Pelageya, her counterpart in *Die Mutter*, learns clearly? It is this: that the solution to her ills lies not in her private self but in the active and courageous gesture of rebellion, in close union with others who are weak by themselves but act together. Compromise does not pay. It makes things worse and delays the solution. Astuteness serves not to scrape a living, drifting with the stream for a little personal gain, but to organize resistance and rebellion. Intelligence should be used to learn, to gain access to knowledge that seems reserved exclusively to a few, an instrument of privilege and oppression. It is not true that people are always the same, unchanging, that the identity of a mother is fixed by a visceral bond that demands the kind mindless and unyielding resistance typical of a mother hen. The relationship can become more mature and constructive, even at a distance, even in death, through the sharing of a common cause. Forms of behaviour and modes of being are historical and modifiable. It is not true that humanity is helpless before fate: the destiny of man is man.

So we understand that a key character of this new tragedy or epic tragedy is Kattrin the mute. In this work Kattrin is the truly tragic figure. She is a victim who gradually gains awareness and makes a gesture of disobedience and rebellion that costs her her life. By rousing the sleepers she brings change, with an act that pushes at the limits imprisoning humanity. She is Courage's only daughter and half German. She has a soft heart, which is the cross she bears. But she also has a cross in her future, which her mother (who reads palms like all wandering canteen women – part huckster, part merchant, part fortune teller), sees in the helmet. She is mute and naturally given no lines in the play. With her disability, she suffers from the humiliating lessons of others: she refuses to have anything to do with the soldiers, she is happy to be dumb and rather ugly, so that she no longer runs any danger, and puts up with insults (people used to say, 'we don't see the cripple').[37]

Actions are her words: she pulls the cart, always between the shafts, but she is not degraded, her sensibility is unchanged. She is sensitive, strong, intelligent, patient and proud. She reveals her femininity, though frustrated, with naive simplicity by donning the hat and falling for the temptation of Yvette's red boots, which she steals and hides. She is pathetically pleased with the chaplain's unctuous and hypocritical compliment. She trembles with fear when the soldiers, famished for women, are about to arrive, and her mother rubs ashes on her face to make her less attractive. She understands the danger to her brother Swiss Cheese, who hides the money chest of the Finnish regiment when the Catholics are about to arrive. She is quick to grasp the fact that they are spies, but no one believes her, least of all her brother, who is something of a simpleton and ends up with 11 bullets in him. She makes herself useful. When the peasant family refuse to quit their home on the arrival of 'enemy' troops and are wounded, Mother Courage refuses to hand over her shirts to make bandages for them. Kattrin becomes excited and threatens her with a plank. She saves the baby and cradles it, expressing her profound maternal instinct. She receives a disfiguring wound and may also have been raped, certainly violated. She goes to the town to procure goods for her mother and is satisfied with her reward (Yvette's red boots). When she thinks that her mother and the cook are planning to live together without her, she leaves them a witty sign (a pair of the cook's old trousers and an old skirt of her mother's, alluding to their relationship) and tries to run away so as not to be in their way. With her mother she listens to the song of the rose and the snowflake.

Finally there is her heroic action, her purposeful and fruitful self-sacrifice. The peasant woman urges her to pray for the Lord to waken the townspeople and to protect the children sleeping unawares, as the imperial army prepares to attack the city and slay its inhabitants. But Kattrin creeps behind the cart, picks up a drum, conceals it beneath her apron and climbs onto the roof of the peasant house. There, staring into the distance (with a gaze quite unlike the distant gaze of the characters in Beckett) she beats the drum wildly. She beats all the stronger when the soldiers try to drown out the noise by getting the peasants to start chopping wood. The young farmer seems to cooperate with the attackers, but then all at once he seems captivated by her rebellion and stops chopping. Finally, there comes a chain reaction: as Kattrin, stricken, slowly crumples up weeping and dies, the city is aroused, and the noise of bells ringing out mingles with cannon fire. She has succeeded.

Tragedy and the Epic Style

To prevent the tragic from falling into the tragedy inherited from the past and so shape a new experience of knowledge and active engagement through stagecraft, Brecht sought to develop a new dramatic technique and a new mode of theatrical direction and performance.

His material work on the boards of the stage was long, painstaking and fluent, notable for its rigour, energy, clear-sighted intelligence, imagination and simplicity. The methods developed ensured that there would be no backsliding, that the audience would not equivocate. War should not appear timeless or inevitable, Mother Courage should not appear a victim, a *Mater Dolorosa*, nor Kattrin a heroine or a saint, while the play had to avoid falling into pathos or atmospherics (though some productions have done just this and critics have often tried to see it in these terms). Brecht sought to ensure that the production distilled the right knowledge and brought out the primary meaning that he wished to instil into it: ordinary people do not benefit from war. War, a continuation of peace by other means, makes virtues fatal even to those who possess them. No sacrifice is too great in the struggle against war.

The first set of principles he devised concerned the construction of the play. They are all too familiar and regrettably weakened by a mannered Brechtism, evident in this text. Notable features of Brecht's dramaturgy are: the presence of music and songs as separate, anti-illusionistic elements, not arising out of the action but commenting on it; the floodlit stage; the construction of the play as separate scenes, with marked jumps in time, announced by titles and with the locations shown by signs, so avoiding dramatic fluidity; the use of paradoxes (such as the two young men who draw the cart like horses or Courage's name); interiors mounted parallel, like the general's tent and the cook's kitchen; the antiphrastic juxtaposition of contrasting elements: the heroism of a rogue and the war song, the song of the dead soldier and the sound of the spoon on the pot, the cannon and the washing hung out to dry, the contrast between the themes of the dialogue (the general's death, the nature of war and peace, the marriage proposal) and humdrum occupations (the inventory of the goods in the canteen wagon) (scene 6); the inversion of well established *topoi*, such as the impassiveness of the mother who denies she knows her own son rather than a mother mourning over her dead son; the inclusion of almost farcical elements at dramatic moments, such as the emergency halt in the half-destroyed village (scene 5); and the use of pervasive irony.

The second set of principles concerns the staging and acting of the play. We have an essential source in Brecht's *Courage Model 1949*, issued posthumously in 1958 by the Berlin publisher Henschel.[38] The result of a lengthy process,[39] it consists of descriptive stage notes and commentaries, with photographs taken by Ruth Berlau, Heinar Hill and Ruth Wilhelmi of the productions by the Deutsches Theater, the Berliner Ensemble, the Munich Kammerspiele, and of the text of the play. I will confine myself to giving some idea, following the model book, of a few examples of gestures and details that have passed into the annals of epic drama, largely invented by the brilliance and intensity of the unforgettable Helene Weigel.

Courage is above all else a canteen woman: this should never be forgotten. At the end of each bargain over the sale of a buckle (scene 1) or a capon (2), and even when her feelings should be overwhelming, as when paying the peasants for the burial of her slain daughter (12), a distinctive detail is the very clear sound of the snap fastening of the money bag that keeps Courage firmly attached to life. Driving a hard bargain is second nature to a canteen woman, even when a gesture of pity for her dead daughter is involved. So Courage takes the coins from her purse and counts them out in payment for the funeral, but she keeps one back and returns it to her pouch (12). A businesswoman's job is to be suspicious. Even a sergeant's coin has to be bitten to make sure it is good money (1).

Courage's moral obtuseness, her imperviousness, even her callousness, are not those of an individual but rather the class she belongs to. Brecht sees this as the petty bourgeoisie *avant la lettre*, who could only lend their support to the war. (An effective touch is Courage's entry at a run in scene 8, radiant that the peace is over. It is far more convincing than her curse on war (6). Weigel was particularly good at showing how Mother Courage always makes cynicism prevail, sometimes almost angrily repressing her residual weaknesses, the latent contradictions that surface. In this way she teaches the young soldier the 'Song of the Great Capitulation', so as to be able to practise it herself (4), and turns down the cook's proposal, despite her earlier interest in him, so renouncing the advantages of the tavern in Utrecht. She is careful to avoid expressing tenderness or pathos in her response to the voice singing of the sweetness of the hearth, embodying her attitude in an inimitable gesture: she tosses her head, shaking it like a strong but weary horse returning to work. There is no trace of sentimentality in Mother Courage's actions in the last scene, when she sings a lullaby. She ignores the peasants' hostility, bows and marches off. It is clear her mind is already on other things.

Kattrin is not an idealized heroine, with impulses of saintliness, though a suggestion of Antigone is present, as we know, in Brecht's imagery. This is expressed clearly in her gestures, notably in the performance by Angelica Hurwicz referred to in the model book, in the scenes in the camp in a half-destroyed village (5), the 'sign' she leaves for her mother and the cook who are planning to set-up house together (9), and the scene of the drum and the awakening of the city of Halle (11). Her development is incisively expressed. The pantomime of her rescue of the baby, or the way she threatens her mother, who refuses to hand over the shirts to be used as bandages, appear as more than just animal instinct. They are acts of intelligence, as appears again when she wakes the sleeping city. Her acts are expressive of intelligence and wounded pride and a refusal to put up further with the abuses that prevent her from having all that she desires in her normality: love and motherhood. The war certainly changes and destroys her. Fresh and cheerful at first, she becomes resentful, not without malice, rather coarsened, sometimes numbed and slightly childish. At first her gestures express fear for herself and the city. She is a mixture of awkwardness and promptness, recklessness and courage, a tangle of emotions, intelligence and energy.

The 'stone' biblically, begins to speak gradually, through several different stages. She stares coldly from the rooftop at the frightened people; she raises the drumsticks ever higher and beats louder, in a contest to see who makes most noise; there is malicious laughter, groaning, weariness, the momentary defeat, the sobbing without tears and momentarily irresolute movements and fear, until she again draws on all her exhausted energies. The bullet fired by the soldier strikes her as she raises both arms, stoops again and strikes the drum. Her last drum beat comes as her arm falls. Then the drumbeats fade into the sound of the cannons fired by the waking city.

Chapter 5

THE TRAGIC AND THE ABSURD: *CALIGULA* BY ALBERT CAMUS

A great writer and an outstanding moral figure of the twentieth century was responsible for the next text we are to analyse: *Caligula* by Albert Camus. Hannah Arendt, writing to her husband from Paris, described him as 'the best man in France'. Yet in his lifetime the novelist, a Nobel laureate, beloved of thousands of readers, remained, as is well known, at times isolated and unheeded in a period of ideological conflicts, of opposed blocs and the *maîtres à penser* of the century. Today, however, a revaluation is rightly under way. His moral authority, lucidity, courage and intellectual substance are restoring his authority. His distinctive identity is unusual among intellectuals, embracing both his modest origins in the African periphery and the bourgeois circles of the intellectual capital of Europe. His familiarity with literary culture and the true, living culture of the theatre, his militant antifascist engagement and his independent, honesty of judgement – all these qualities today exert a new fascination.

And his position on the theme of the theatre of the tragic today appears both profound and extremely fruitful.[1] The text presents another side of the modern elaboration of the tragic consciousness, the representation of an absolute passion, of life, love, power, creating a short circuit between man and God. This leads to the man becoming a tyrant and mistaking himself for a god against the backdrop of the absurd, the denial of meaning. The results is that he ravages the world and plunges it into chaos.

History of the Text and Contexts

The history of the text begins with a note in Camus's *Carnets* (*Notebooks*) dated January 1937 which, besides giving a brief overview of the projected work, calls it 'Caligula ou le sens de la mort'.[2] Again in 1937, then just 24 years old and the director of a theatre company, Camus sketched out a first draft, with the intention of taking the part of the protagonist himself, but the planned production was shelved. In 1939 the text was extended, and further revised in 1941, but not published. So it is now the product of two phases of work which flowed into two typescripts, both made by his friend Christiane Galindo (the first dating from September 1939, the second from February 1941). This version belongs to the cycle of the absurd, 'les trois Absurdes', together with his novel *L'etranger* (*The Stranger*) and his essay *Le mythe de Sisyphe* (*The Myth of Sisyphus*), and is described by a note in the *Carnets* for 1942 as a 'tragedy'.[3] It was published for the first time by A. James Arnold in volume 4 of the *Cahiers Albert Camus*.[4]

In May 1944 Camus published a new edition of his work, brought to completion during the war years. It was first issued by Gallimard as a single volume with *Le Malentendu*, then republished separately in the same year and reprinted in 1946 and 1947. It belongs to a development of the concept of the absurd which led him to emerge from his impasse and move towards a new moral humanism, rigorous and constructive, expressed principally in fiction and essays. The play was performed for the first time in 1945 at the Théâtre Hébertot, directed by Jacques Hébertot, with sets by Paul Œttly and Gérard Philipe in the part of Caligula. After some adjustments, with a view to its performance at the Festival d'Angers, the edition described as definitive was published in a volume entitled *'Caligula' suivi de 'Le Malentendu'* by Gallimard in the Folio 1958 collection. By this time Camus was close to his tragically early death.

The first *Caligula* (composed between 1937 and 1939 and revised in 1941, as mentioned above) is fundamentally inscribed in the Algerian horizon and the cultural climate of French Africa, which cared for the education of its children by sending out trained teachers who were gifted and ambitious. It was a periphery, of course, compared to the heart of the capital, but far from neglected and very much alive. It happened that a boy, an orphan of war from a poverty-stricken family, filled with talent and joy in life, sensitivity, a desire to learn, craving knowledge, was identified at school by alert and far-sighted teachers, and was assisted and accompanied in a course of education that would take him far. Camus responded with determination, enthusiasm, generosity and rigour. His natural charm, his authenticity and honesty, frankness and independence, his enthusiasm and unsparing effort, his directness, his humour (at times cutting), his propensity for love and affectionate relationships, made him very welcome in Algerian circles (and later in Paris). Writing was an absolute pleasure, and one which his illness, soon evident, never overcame. In fact tuberculosis, though it undermined Camus's health throughout his life, heightened his sensibility and strengthened his perceptions. A hyperesthesia, an introspective tendency, fostered a closer concern with literature, a dialogue with other writers and an early, intimate contact with the problem of death.[5]

The inspiration of *Caligula*, its subject and themes, were nurtured by the experiences of Camus's early Algerian years (he was born in 1913). Classical studies altered his perception of his homeland: the ruins of Imperial Rome in that garden of delights that was North Africa in antiquity nurtured his memory and imagination. At Tipaza, the dead city in the hills of Djémila, 'the ruins covered with flowers, and the light bubbling in the clusters of stone',[6] and 'paths amid the remains of houses, broad paved streets under the gleaming columns, and the immense forum between the triumphal arch and the temple'[7] led him to reflect on the philosophy of history. In the union between the ruins and springtime, the ruins become stones again; history wanes and is overwhelmed by nature. In the confusion of wind and sunshine which mingles light with the ruins, the individual senses his identity with the solitude and silence of the dead city as 'a taste for death we shared'.[8] This setting gave rise to the fusion of individual and nature, the sense of death, the projection into the ancient heart of history, leading Camus to the Roman sources and the figure of Caligula.

Camus was no dreamer. The consciousness of the class to which he belonged by birth, his involvement in the milieu of the progressive youth of Algiers, his closeness to the

Popular Front (which had been fighting since the early thirties for democratic freedoms against the fascist threats), the insistence of his mentors that philosophy must be united with politics and engagement, and the idealization of communism (which in Algeria smacked much less than in Paris of the dictatorial, police-state and anti-egalitarian turn which it had taken with Stalin in the USSR) led him to join the Communist Party, only to abandon it two years later. But his attitude was critical, because the communists ignored the colonial question in favour of proletarian internationalism and the antifascist struggle, and he was filled with sincere utopian and idealistic spirits. His engagement, especially at the Maison de la Culture, with authors dear to young people on the Left, such as Malraux and Gide, stimulated his reflections on power. The Nazi and Fascist successes in Italy, Germany and Spain stimulated reflection on the figure of the dictator and the mechanisms of consensus in the organs of government and among the people. All these ideas fed into *Caligula*.

His work as a journalist on the leftist newspaper *Alger républicain* (alongside the anarchist Pascal Pia, later a resistance fighter) was wholly devoted to the struggle against Nazism, Fascism and Francoism. It offered a fertile ground for imagining a figure who embodied absolute, arbitrary power. The formation of a journalistic ethic, including a brief experience in France with *Paris-Soir*, as a journalist in exile in Paris on the eve of the German occupation, reinforced Camus's outlook, despite the mediocrity of the milieu of the newspaper and his absorption in the writing of his novel *L'étranger*.

The first version of *Caligula* also embodied his powerful sensuousness, his attraction to the female body, his experience of love and his youthful immersion in nature in Algeria. The play is not a parenthesis in his work as novelist. Camus was profoundly a man of the theatre; it was one of the major interests in his life. In the period that concerns us here, before or during the composition of the first version of *Caligula*, Camus was committed to the project of the Théâtre du Travail, with close links to the Communist Party. He founded the troupe and worked as an adapter of texts, manager, actor and organizer. His hectic activity for a popular and political theatre filled a void in the city of Algiers. The purpose at that time was to create a living culture, closer to the people, engaged in the struggle against Fascism and in favour of the proletariat.[9] Above all the novelist also developed a vocation for the concreteness of the stage:

> A whole creation to be realized, tangible, made up of beams and trestles, pots of glue and electrical contacts – just to start with – and on that to organize men, animate them to construct artistic theories thinking we'll have to call in the fire brigade – and once everything gets started, and comes to life in the performance, shaking up the discouraged, joking with them, believing in everything to be performed and played in one evening and of which nothing will remain the next day except the need to sweep up and cast up the accounts. I know of no more exhilarating experience.[10]

Leaving the Théâtre du Travail (and the Communist Party) in October 1937, Camus founded the Théâtre de l'Équipe, which was independent of all political ties. Together with an idea of literature, in those years Camus pursued a theatrical aesthetic, finding it in the echoes that reached Algeria from the stage of Jacques Copeau's Vieux-Colombier in Paris. He took an emblematic phrase from it in as the epigraph of his manifesto: 'Des théâtres dont le mot d'ordre est: travail, recherche, audace, on peut dire qu'ils n'ont pas été fondés pour prospérer mais pour durer sans s'asservir.' (Of theatres whose watchword is work, study, boldness, we can say that they were not founded to prosper but to keep going without submitting.) Camus thought about youthful drama, based on collective creativity, close to the raw truth of life. Copeau was concerned with the repertoire, but also its dramatic inspiration.[11] As an actor he played the part of Ivan in his stage version of *Les Frères Karamazov* and explored the issue of the limits of human freedom within the framework of atheism.

The First Version of Caligula in 'les trois Absurdes'

Camus's meditation on the nuclei of what I have identified as the tragic consciousness, namely the relationship with necessity in its radical figures of the inescapable limit and death, was developed through various stages and pursued throughout his life.[12] It was a journey of thought, consistent with his vocation as a moral philosopher, entrusted to theoretical works as well as fiction and plays, in the belief that 'on ne pense que par image' (we can only think in images) and 'si tu veux être philosophe, écris des romans' (if you want to be a philosopher, write novels).[13] It was a path that paralleled the growth of Camus's experience of life, accompanied by the pursuit of logic, rigour, a close correspondence between thought and practice and a great capacity for human sympathy.

The first phase was the theory of the absurd, which provided the substratum for *Caligula* and had its systematic and striking formulation in *Le mythe de Sisyphe*, begun in 1939 and completed in February 1941: 'Terminé *Sisyphe*. Les trois Absurdes sont achevés.'[14] Camus wished for the simultaneous publication of the three books, *L'étranger*, *Le mythe de Sisyphe* and *Caligula*, which illuminate each other. Hellenism nurtured his thought, yet it was also deeply imbued with a modern sensibility.

To engage in an analysis of the response of *Caligula* to the theme of tragedy requires a brief introduction to this theory. The absurd is a form of sensibility, an attitude of the spirit, common in the twentieth century, says Camus, rather than a philosophy and a metaphysic. The intuition of the absurd can surprise man at any moment, even the most banal and humdrum. It can insinuate that sudden sense of wonder, developing into a movement of awareness, an 'awakening'. It brings into focus the most urgent of questions, that of the meaning of life, which clashes with the opacity and contradiction of the response. What is the starting point? Camus expresses it like this: it means realizing that the world is dense, strange, 'in-human'. It means seeing it folded back on itself and not tending 'reciprocally' towards the 'intention' of the individual, though he or she may be enticed by its colours, moods, tastes, while being repelled by its indifference. It means suddenly feeling like an 'outsider', like Meursault, the protagonist of the novel *L'étranger*, like an actor in relation to the stage, like Roquentin, the character in Sartre's *La nausée* (*Nausea*), who realizes he is 'de trop' and grasps the absolute gratuitousness and contingency of his existence. It is suddenly seeing oneself from outside, as if through a pane of glass that shows the pantomime gestures and excludes the voices, and asking the reason for this distressing agitation. It means stumbling into death, in the elementary and definitive degree of the adventure, and suddenly intuiting the scandal comparable to that of a generalized death sentence for an inexplicable and unascertained culpability – common to Meursault, Caligula's subjects or the citizens of a city in a state of siege. It is the contrast between two evident facts. On the one hand there is the longing for unity, the 'craving for the absolute', the moral and intellectual need for complete transparency. On the other there is the condition of the limit, of fragmentation, of shadow, the thwarting of existence. The first of these facts becomes manifest when one realizes that 'this world, in itself, is not reasonable',[15] that there is an absurd (literally *absurdus*, dissonant) imbalance between the irrational and the desire for absolute clarity whose call echoes in our depths.[16] 'The absurd is born of this confrontation between the human need and the unreasonable silence of the world.'[17]

The sense of estrangement, the sudden realization that the harmony between man and nature is broken, that the analogy between the life and body of man and the life and body of nature cannot be explained, shattering against the alien, inhuman, mechanical, lifeless image of the corpse, is the experience which suddenly gives rise to Caligula's changed behaviour following the death of his sister and lover Drusilla.[18] Absurdity lies not in humanity or the world, but in the combination between them.

At this stage of his thought Camus meant only to take as far as he could, to its extreme consequences, the 'absurd' reasoning embodied in the characters of Meursault and Caligula (though clearly they are poetically much more than this). There is no question of affirming the existence of God, says Camus, since the logic of the absurd does not lead to it, or of affirming the power of reason, since its limits are fixed by the absurd.[19] The question is how to find a way out of the impasse, or how and why to remain beneath this sky of the absurd. Camus formulates the problem lucidly in his theoretical essay and in the imaginary figures he creates in novels and plays. He allows the possible paths to be embodied, in complete depth and autonomy, in the typologies of his characters: Meursault, Caligula, Paneloux, Rieux.

Several different paths are explored. One is to disavow the recognition of the absurd as a radical condition and admit a rationalist philosophy by which everything is reason and the world has a meaning and an explanation. Another is to confirm the evident fact of the absurd, while also proposing a path of escape through what Camus calls the 'forced hope' of irrationalist or existentialist philosophies. Yet another is to cling to the absurd, taking it upon oneself and making oneself a living and willed testimony to it, unmasking it by making oneself its counterpart and speeding up the inevitable outcome by slaying others and oneself. The examples are Meursault and Caligula. Or finally one can cling to the evident fact of the absurd, but give it a positive turn by meeting it with a lucid and disenchanted gaze, with full consciousness and the challenge of a solitary and at the same time sympathetic effort, without any future. At the same time, one recovers the passion for life, living it as fully as possible, itself also an act of revolt, 'an offensive against a hostile heaven'.[20] In this last response the absurd becomes a daily *askesis* in which everything, except the final solution, is freedom, commitment, love, hard work, constructiveness. It fills man's heart as stones fill the heart of Sisyphus in his labour: senseless and useless, but 'one must imagine Sisyphus happy'.[21] This is the great achievement of Dr Rieux in *La Peste* (*The Plague*).

The theory of the absurd is related to the tragic consciousness. It is one of the many facets of the research that the tragic consciousness fosters in modernity, in an ideologically fragmented horizon which no longer gives rise to the form of tragedy and does not permit the emergence of the nuclei of its model, as invariably happened in the past. Underlying the tragic dramaturgy and the dramaturgy of the absurd is an analogical idea of the inevitability of limits, the contradiction between the finite condition of humanity and its boundless love, between the defeat of existence and the provocation of totality. But tragedy is the transgression (and then the reaffirmation) of the fatality of the limit in the name of a 'value', in which the being of the hero is epitomized. Though the foundation of the significance of this value is not guaranteed and the event takes place largely in darkness, this foundation of significance is not excluded: it does not save the hero from suffering because of the threat that strikes him down, but it gives a meaning to his death, which becomes a 'sacrifice'.

The dramaturgy of the absurd lies, by contrast, in the 'indifference' of value. The foundation of significance appears as nostalgia, a mockery of man's nature, without any objective verification. Death, if sought, comes as surrender, an 'accident' caused by weakness in enduring the burden of the absurd. And it is not converted into true sacrifice, capable of projecting its fertility into time and the community. The relationship with the sacred or the absolute, essential to the tragedy, is invoked, if at all, by the absurd in order to better emphasize its destitution. There is truth in what Camus himself observes: in the tragic the yes balances the no, while in the absurd it is the no that prevails. The absurd is the way of *Caligula*.

The Faces of the Absurd: From the First Caligula to the Last

There is, however, an important difference between the version completed in 1941 and the version published in May 1944 by Gallimard as a single volume with *Le Malentendu*, shortly before the beginning of the critical period between the Allied landings in Normandy and the liberation of Paris. In the first the absurd is represented as having a pre-eminently existential connotation; it is the human condition. In the second it also has a strongly historical connotation. As if man's ontological condition were not enough, Camus implies, he makes himself responsible for absurd situations and actions such as totalitarianism, the corruption of power and warfare.

In the meantime Camus's horizons had expanded. He now moved in the orbit of Gallimard in Paris. He was not just an author whose work was issued by this major publishing house, but enjoyed the friendship of the family and began working as a reader for the firm from November 1943. He entered the milieu of Sartre and Beauvoir, made contact with the resistance in the form of the underground cell Combat, becoming editor-in-chief of its homonymous newspaper. He began working on that great metaphor for humanity's condition of suffocation and imprisonment which is *The Plague* and exploring the premises of that further step beyond the absurd which he called revolt. He began the short set of *Lettres à un ami allemand*, the first being written in July 1943. Camus condemns hatred, violence, injustice, the mutilation of the human. He foretells the inevitable defeat of those who choose the absurdity of violence and injustice. Caligula can be seen more clearly now. Caligula is not Camus but a logic of the absurd pushed to the extreme with implacable lucidity. Yet Camus sees another way out, to prevent the absurd from entrapping humanity: 'If nothing had any meaning, you would be right. But there is something that still has meaning.'[22] Further,

> I continue to believe that this world has no ultimate meaning. But I know that something in it has a meaning and that is man, because he is the only creature to insist on having one. This world has at least the truth of man, and our task is to provide its justification against fate itself. [...] You will ask me, 'What do you mean by saving man?' It means not mutilating him, and yet giving a chance to the justice that man alone can conceive.[23]

We can now follow the development from the first to the second *Caligula*. We will start from an overview of the 1941 edition.

In the hall of the imperial palace – furnished with a full-length mirror, a gong and a couch – Caligula's aide Helicon, of whom he asks the moon (i.e., the impossible), and Cherea, the most intelligent and cynical of the senators conspirators, express their concern at the disappearance of Caligula, sought in vain for three days in the countryside. The young Scipio, a friend of the emperor and like him an 'artist', explains that Caligula's madness was triggered when he cried out and stroked the lifeless face of his sister-lover Drusilla. Caligula enters the deserted hall furtively, distraught and hoarse, laughing hysterically at the mirror. He then reveals the reason for his crisis and the change that will become manifest in him soon after: the revelation of the face of death. It is the face of an 'étrangère', which has annihilated the 'chaude et souple' (warm and supple) truth of her body, in harmony with nature, with the countryside, 'where she walked with such harmony that the swaying of her shoulders [was] confused with the outline of the hills on the horizon'.[24] Only Cesonia, his mature mistress, and the young Scipio express sympathy for him, as Caligula proves to be a sentimentalist, lacerated and seared in the fibres of his flesh. But affairs of state are pressing. Caligula announces his decisions: to rigorously apply logic and implacably accept its consequences. While treasure is important, human life is not. Wealthy citizens are required to make their wills in favour of the state. They will be put to death, following a list drawn up arbitrarily and as the needs of the state require it. Power and freedom coincide: 'pas de limites'. If freedom is only what Caligula permits it to be, from now on subjects and senators will only have the freedom of those under sentence of death, to whom everything is indifferent except the blow that will fell them. Meanwhile he speaks only to Cesonia of the evil and disgust he feels on his skin and in his mouth and his longing for Drusilla. Only with her does he rave of his longing when, on 'certain evenings like this, before this pale sky bathed by the soft and brilliant glow of the stars, how not to swoon before all that is pure and consuming in my love?'[25] In solitude his fear grows. He needs victims and absolute freedom. Cesonia must assist him by being cruel and unforgiving (act 1, scene 11).

Some senators gather in Cherea's house to plot rebellion. Caligula humiliates them in every way, ridicules them and makes them run beside his litter when he travels into the countryside. He confiscates their property, slays their children or parents, takes their wives and lies with them or sets them to work in his brothel. He gives their seats at the circus to the common people, calls them by effeminate epithets and takes their money. Cherea calms them and urges them to be prudent, to wait for the right moment. The cold and prudent Cherea is not troubled by these humiliations, but fears the implications of Caligula's new conduct: 'philosophy' and 'poetry' in power. The reversals, the humiliations, the complete gratuitousness of death, the complete dissociation of guilt and punishment, reach their height at the dinner in the scene 5. A senator whose son was killed is forced to laugh; the beloved wife of another senator is forced to submit to a 'little need' of Caligula's. Another senator is addressed with female epithets; other senators are reduced to servants and clear the table. The most unseemly gestures are made casually at table. Everything else disappears before fear. On the one hand Caligula's 'philosophy' and 'logic' continue their development and he is now drafting a treatise on this subject (*Le Glaive*). On the other he enacts a series of measures in which the logic of the absurd is applied ruthlessly: 'Execution relieves and liberates. [...] A man is guilty because he is one of Caligula's subjects. Ergo all men are guilty and shall die. It is only a matter of time and patience', states the treatise.[26] Caligula proclaims the scourge of famine and closes the public granaries. He institutes a new Order of Merit to reward not virtue but vice. Mereia, an old senator, is punished with death by poisoning because Caligula sees him swallowing a medication for asthma, and mistakenly believes he is dosing himself with an antivenin (a crime!). This act ends with the great scene of confrontation between the young Scipio and Caligula, attracted to each other as opposites, driven by extreme passions, the one pure in goodness, the other in evil, both lost in art. Moved by sincerity and falsehood, sympathy and aggression, Caligula permits Scipio to tell the truth at all times. From his hatred for those who killed and tortured his father, Scipio feels close to the young Caligula. He tears off the emperor's mask and discovers the face of his truth: solitude and scorn (act 2, in 14 scenes).

Now Caligula exhibits himself in a grotesque masquerade of the gods. Attired as Venus, on a pedestal, announced by cymbals and drums, he forces the patricians to worship him. He accepts their offerings and then explains his action. It is a sham, a mimetic demonstration of the blindness and absurdity of fate: 'I've merely realized there is only one way of getting even with the gods. All that's needed is to be cruel as they. (*Furious.*) In my sleepless nights I have encountered fate. You cannot imagine what a foolish air it has. And monotonous: it only has a single expression. implacable. Nothing could be easier to imitate.'[27] While Helicon struggles to warn him of the conspiracy being hatched against him, Caligula appears distracted and lost in his impossible dream, which he asks Helicon to fulfil for him: to have the moon, which he had already possessed one August night, when, naked, light and gentle, it came from its milky lake rustling with stars, moving across his room, and lay in his bed. The dream is coloured with delirious lyrical accents in the following monologue: 'After all, why shouldn't Helicon bring it off? One night, perhaps, he'll catch her sleeping in a lake, and carry her here, trapped in a glistening net, all slimy with weeds and water, like a pale, bloated fish drawn from the depths. Why not, Caligula?'[28] The act ends with the 'duel' between Caligula and Cherea. They confront each other wearing the mask of naturalness and sincerity. Fencing skilfully with each other, they make explicit the sense of their incompatibility and the conspiracy which Cherea is hatching against

Caligula, who discovers it yet allows it to proceed. Cherea, he says, without loving or hating Caligula, opposes him because he considers him dangerous to the kind of life that he, like most men, wants: security, not a destabilized world which can be ravaged at any moment by the bizarre, with the absurd taken by implacable logic to its extreme consequences, and in which to kill is to possess. For this reason Caligula has to die (act 3, in 5 scenes).

The fearful senators are made objects of scorn and sarcasm by Cherea himself, who exhorts them to composure and courage. Ultimately Caligula forces them to think. He forces everyone to think. Insecurity: this is what stimulates thought. Caligula, attired as a dancer, his head crowned with flowers, performs in shadow play behind a curtain. There are other mockeries and provocations to humiliate the nobles and throw contempt on them. Cherea shows himself the most lucid, being master of the situation. Then follows another farce: a poetry competition on the theme of death. In his hopeless delirium Scipio wins, while the others are further humiliated and punished by being forced to pass before Caligula licking the tablets on which their doggerel verses are written. The time has come: Cherea nods. Scipio tries to warn Caligula, but Caligula knows. 'Tu as choisi, Caligula' (You asked for it, Caligula).[29] There follows the last intimate dialogue between Caligula and Cesonia. They are united by a 'tendresse honteuse' (shameful tenderness).[30] Caligula begins to think that the last witness of his life must be eliminated now that he is completely free from memory and illusion and knows that nothing lasts. The curtain has to be rung down. When Cesonia calls him 'mon petit', as if offering herself to him, he strangles her. Caligula is now faced with the great void. Before a mirror he cries out his despair. He has sought the impossible, at the confines of the world, the furthest reaches of himself, but Helicon has not yet come. He stretches out his hand, but encounters only himself: 'toujours toi comme un crachat en face de moi' (you always, like spit in my face).[31] He consigns himself to history, where he will still live, and falls, stabbed by the conspirators (act 4, in 11 scenes).

Analysis of the divergences from the 1941 edition reveal the final transition from a lyrical-philosophical emphasis to a political-philosophical emphasis, in the common premise that men die and are not happy. In the first version, on encountering the fact of death Caligula discovers the failure of love and the blind, implacable face of destiny. He decides to embody it in order to unmask it, condemning himself to despair. Negative and positive in a certain sense balance each other out. In the second version, Caligula is the face of the tyrant, the face of the man who makes himself a god from an absolute will to power, without limits, by willing the impossible. The negative prevails decisively. This explains, for example, the following differences.

In act 1, scene 3, the stage direction which represents Caligula as advancing towards the mirror and babbling confused words ('il grommelle des paroles indistinctes'), replaces Caligula's important monologue before the mirror in act 1, scene 4 on love. It is not true that love responds to love; death responds to love. Intimacy with the truth of a warm, soft, beloved body becomes the estrangement of a face stiffened by death. The bond between man and nature, between the sinuous lines of a female body and the outline of the hills, is broken, revealing man absurdly as a stranger.

The Helicon motif is expanded. He is the freed slave faithful to Caligula, received into his palace, the one who should enable him to achieve the impossible by bringing him the moon. He is the one who tries to warn him against the conspirators and is stabbed along with him. In a dialogue added in this version which clarifies his significance (act 4, scene 6), he is contrasted with the cold, cynical and prudent Cherea who despises him:

HELICON. [...]. Despise the slave, Cherea! He is above your virtue because he can still love this miserable master, whom he defends against your noble lies, your perjured mouths.[32]

The tyrant's power base lies in the people, his faithful servants, obedient until death. It does not lie in the Senate, the republican magistracy who want to deal with him as equals and curb his power. Caligula despises the senators (in this edition called 'patriciens') and humiliates them as much as he can. He brings out their mediocrity ('Mais comme c'est commun' [how commonplace he is], he says of Mucius, in act 2, scene 6). In his mature years Camus reflected on the connections between populism and power. It is a sign of his independence of judgement and his insight that that he did not interpret Caligula in terms of the cliché of the mad emperor. Modern historians, as mentioned above, have themselves revised this very cliché.

Again Camus brings out the frequent cowardice of the senators and the treachery of inept politicians, as in the episode, inserted here, of the effeminate old senator who betrays the conspiracy in order to ingratiate himself with Caesar (act 3, scene 4).

In the later version Camus cut the more comic-grotesque provocations of a foul-mouthed, loutish Caligula (act 2, scenes 6 and 7), with references to the sexual performance of Mucius' wife and the embarrassment over what is happening in the other room. In short he avoids distracting the audience from the theme of the brutality and arrogance of power. It also clarifies more explicitly a further reason for the hostility of Cherea, Caligula's antagonist, who has chosen measured prudence, the security of preservation in mediocrity without taking risks, by the addition of scene 1 to act 4 between Cherea and Scipio. Cherea senses that the young Scipio will abandon the other conspirators, though without betraying them, because he feels that a similar flame burns in his heart and Caligula's and that they have a similar source of unhappiness: an absolute passion that leads him 'à tout exiger' (to demand everything) and a lucid intelligence that makes him 'tout comprendre' (understand everything). More than all his other crimes, Caligula has committed that of communicating his despair to a youth, a tragic awareness that is shipwrecked in the consciousness of the absurd.[33] On this point there exists a tacit understanding, as shown by the other brief scene added between Helicon, Scipio and Cherea.

In addition to Caligula's connotations as an unhappy lover, the new version removes the suggestion that Caligula is a 'son' in relation to Cesonia, his mature mistress, felt as a maternal presence. Her dying invocation of 'Mon petit' is replaced by the feeble invocation of 'Caïus'. Also suppressed is the stage direction in act 3, scene 5, which risks lightening the figure of Caligula: 'Il sourit doucement. Il est presque beau.' (He smiles gently. He is almost handsome.)[34] Finally the monologue in act 3, scene 5, corresponding to the monologue of act 4, scene 4 in the 1941 edition, is made tighter and more stringent. The new closing is more incisive:

CALIGULA. [...] [*Furiously.*] Logic, Caligula, we must pursue logic. Power to the end, excess to the end. No, there is no turning back and we have to go on till the end![35]

From the Historical Character to the Tragic-Absurd Character: 'Poetry is More Philosophical and More Important than History'[36]

Camus uses historical sources, particularly Suetonius, combining them with a purpose that is not historical but firstly philosophical and secondarily political-philosophical.[37] He did not bring about the events out of which the work was woven, but manipulated them and reinvented a framework for reflection and dramatic treatment which sought not to represent objective historical facts but the 'truth' of history. His philosophical education made him familiar at an early date with Aristotle's basic insight, expressed in the *Poetics*, that poetry is more philosophical and of greater import than history, since it deals not with things that have really happened, but things that are possible in accordance with the laws of probability and necessity.[38] Camus's interest in the historical figure of Caligula was from the first given a philosophical turn through the teachings of Jean Grenier.[39] The character is fascinating. There are aspects that need to be deciphered, in contrast with the traditional partisan clichés, which are unconvincing. Caligula was an early source of inspiration and for many years the writer mulled over the figure of the emperor. He became part of the everyday landscape of the young Camus, who loved humour as much as seriousness and the passion for life. He called his two cats 'Cali' and 'Gula'. The emperor was an enigma to be understood only by reflecting on him at length.[40]

The data contained in the sources include some features of the absurd condition which emerged in the first phase of composition flowing into the 1941 edition. As ruler of the Roman Empire, Caligula experienced the utmost measure of power and freedom but also the barrier of the limit (in the encounter with death) and the contradiction of the servant–master dynamic, which Sartre was to clarify a little later in *Being and Nothingness* (1943; *L'être et le néant*), and which actually undermines the claim of unlimited freedom and the fulfilment of absolute desire.

Caligula's passion for the theatre, seen or practiced in his disguises and performances, becomes a play of masks and nothingness, in keeping with an insight of Nietzsche's which Camus was familiar with. His sporadic performances in the guise of a deity, which have their historical counterpart in the complex matter of the deification of the emperors, much debated by historians, provided a pretext for representing the indifferent face and empty mask of the divine.[41] The incongruous behaviour of a 'crazy' emperor, according to the cliché of the ancient sources, becomes the lucid unmasking of destiny in its blindness and implacable indifference.

Subsequently the pressure and increasing urgency of the political factor shifted the implications of the data drawn from history towards the image of a tyranny wholly consequential in relation to its premises. In the later version the ruler was represented as the only free person in a nation of slaves, one who exercised power in paranoid fashion. Its outcome could only be tragedy and the absurd of destruction and self-destruction. But through a political 'intelligence' that Camus perceived behind the biased ancient sources, he developed his reading into an extraordinary insight, though still vague, into that revision of the figure of Caligula which contemporary historians have conducted in our own time. Caligula ridicules the powers that he intends to expropriate, annulling them with cynical determination and skilful, sarcastic oratory. He deliberately scrambles the code of communication between senators and emperor, based on simulation, deceit, bad faith and hypocritical servility, and practices duplicitous communication. He dramatizes the exercise of his power as a means of political manipulation and takes it to an extreme.[42] The absurdity of power is closely bound up with the anthropological and metaphysical absurd.

The Absurd and Caligula's Way: Nihilism

Caligula chooses to cling to the absurd, both in the 1941 edition, where the prevailing theme seems to be the despair of the young man who has found death in love, and in the definitive version, in which the connotation of the tyrant emerges more sharply, though it is still inscribed in the philosophical issues of the absurd. The historical-political absurdity of the will to power, which crushes and besieges men, destructive and self-destructive, is related to metaphysical absurdity, *le hasard* (chance), which negates all meaning and value. I will briefly illustrate this development in Caligula, taking quotations and references from the texts of both editions.

Caligula registers the absurd of destiny and unmasks it, but without transgressing it (for example by waging a battle against death or striving to find a meaning). Instead he drives it to an extreme by imitating it, assuming its guise and taking its place in order to comprehend it. He makes himself a blind instrument of death. The outcome is nihilism and a grotesque caricature of tragedy. It closes with the solitude of a face in the mirror, the failure of all understanding, with fear unexorcised and in total opacity, the void: 'I'm frightened. [...] Fear will come to an end. I am going to seek that great emptiness where the heart is at peace.'[43]

Consciousness of the absurd surfaces unexpectedly in Caligula. It is the startling impact of death, encountered, as we saw above, on the 'strange' face of Drusilla, his sister-lover, full of the promise of intimacy, suddenly estranged by the rigidity of her corpse. It is the revelation of the dissociation between a man and the world, where previously he had deluded himself that there was harmony, accord, analogy (a motif evident principally in the 1941 edition) and where there seemed to be a relationship of such close affinity that Caligula could cultivate a hallucination and dream of possessing the moon. The moon, caressed first on the pillar in the garden, appears humanized as a woman.

From this moment on Caligula, as emperor, decides to draw all the consequences of the absurd by uniting logic with power. Unmasking the divine, dismissing the sacred and the whole ethical, axiological approach which could be based on the recognition of it, Caligula makes himself a 'god'. It is not blasphemy, as claimed by Scipio, but clear-sightedness. To match the gods one only needs to be as cruel as they. To match destiny, one need only imitate its 'bête' and 'monotone' face. Always the same face, implacable. Nothing could be easier to imitate.[44] This cannot be identified *tout court* with becoming a tyrant. A tyrant is a man who sacrifices people to his ideas and ambitions, but Caligula has no ideas and no longer has anything to desire in terms of honour or power.

CALIGULA. [...] If I exercise this power it is to compensate.
SCIPIO. For what?
CALIGULA. For the stupidity and hatred of the gods.[45]

The sheer gratuitousness of life and death is expressed by the order of chance: chance instead of social and moral order, chance in decreeing the death of this person or that, the overthrow of all the rules of propriety, family morality, a concern for the common good, feelings, the bestowal of honours and the inversion of the hierarchy of values, because, among other things, 'If the Treasury is essential, human life is not.'[46]

Caligula stages a masquerade of the gods in act 3. Cesonia, as priestess, leads the prayer for Caligula, who appears attired as the goddess Venus on the pedestal. It is a reversal of the divine. The goddess is inverted into the divinity of indifference and contempt. The prayer asks her to teach humanity indifference, to reveal the sole truth of this world, which is that it has no truth, and to endow mankind with the strength to be capable of holding to this truth, hence to bestow aimless passions, sorrows without a reason and joys without a future.

Led purely by his imagination, Caligula wields boundless freedom, which rests on the idea of life as a death sentence carried out with slow and undiscriminating cruelty, based on absolute indifference. He uses theatre to expose life as a phantasmagoria of the ephemeral and of appearance, and humanity as passing interchangeably between the different masks, like a dance between the forms of play, in keeping with Nietzschean ideas, most evident in the 1941 version.[47] He reduces art to rhetoric and adulation, but out of contempt for those who practise it, on whom he inflicts the humiliation of being forced to lick the tablets on which they have written their verses. He cultivates contempt. He lives in the moment, effacing all memory and all projects: 'But now I am again freer than for many years, freed as I am from memory and illusion'.[48] Every day he sheds a part of his humanity, as observed by Cesonia: 'Day by day I see everything in you that has the form of a man dying little by little.'[49]

If Helicon has not brought him the moon, it means that the absolute power he desires and the absolute fulfilment of 'desire' (perceived as an anthropological-transcendental and psychological category of unappeasable desire for the whole) will never be realized. The outcome is isolation in the total solitude of unbearable companionship with himself. In the last scene Caligula holds out his hands to the mirror, weeping and discovers with rage that he only encounters himself, a self that he has come to hate.

CALIGULA. [...] The impossible! I searched the limits of the world, the boundaries of my own self. I stretched out my hands. (*Screaming.*) I stretch my hands and it's you that I meet, you always before me, and I am filled with hatred for you).[50]

Caligula offers himself to death at the hands of the conspirators, not as a sacrifice of atonement prepared by a ritual, fruitful as an example in the history of humanity. Death is an instant that closes on the spite and amazement of his inability to have the moon. Whether the dominant motive is madness as a regression to childhood or the delusion of frustrated omnipotence, depending on the edition of the work, the knowledge evinced by the plot is the failure of the approach taken by Caligula in his challenge to and competition with the absurd. Camus's Caligula, though an 'intelligent tyrant' is unable to submit to living and growing with life.

The work, inspired by tragedy, embodied the failure of tragedy, above all because of the ideological elements: the indifference and interchangeability of values, the absolute insignificance, the negation of time, the randomness of death and isolation from the group. The work is also the failure of tragedy through the dissolution of the form into the grotesque and the parody.

Grotesque Tragedy

Camus is highly consistent in the invention of a form befitting the philosophical and poetic side of his work. A key element is the treatment of the subject in keeping with the ancient *topos* of the theatre within the theatre, or the *theatrum mundi*, giving a new twist to the traditional meaning.[51] It is naturally no longer the idea of the great theatre of the world in which God and man are represented as cooperating in the work of salvation and the free constitution of humanity in the creation and in history. It is rather the idea expressed in Shakespeare's *Macbeth*:

> Life's but a walking shadow, a poor player,
> That struts and frets his hour upon the stage
> And then is heard no more; it is a tale
> Told by an idiot, full of sound and fury,
> Signifying nothing.[52]

Awareness of the absurd induces Caligula to stage life, his own life, that of the state, of the city, as a comedy of masks, the masks of nothingness, a game that is resolved in the fleeting instant of the performance of the part. There are theatrical moments in the strict sense in the play, with an emphasis that is now choreutic, now ritual, now clownish or competitive: the imitation of Venus and the choral prayer, the dance of life like a shadow play and the poetry competition. But in reality the characters are acting all the time, and when Caligula exposes their pretence, his act is strongly destabilizing and may lead to their deaths. Sincerity is likewise a comedy, as in the dialogue between Cherea and Caligula, and even in the dialogue conducted on the razor's edge between Caligula and Scipio. Caligula is a great actor who performs in monologues, in dialogues recited with willing stooges, and in numbers in which he compels a chorus of cowards to dance to his command. He plays multiple roles: lover, artist, judge, executioner, god, destiny. The prop for his stage is the mirror.

Camus, here engaged in a philosophical theatre, a theatre of speech, in reality had in mind a theatre for great actors, for bodies that enact and reveal the knowledge and the truth of existence.⁵³ It takes a great actor to carry off the part of Caligula the actor. And this, too, is closely bound up with the theme of the absurd.

Caligula is wedded to the absurd. He is the supreme actor, one of the greatest personifications of the absurd condition, as stated in Camus's *Mythe de Sisyphe*. In this essay Camus presents the actor as a type of the absurd man together with the adventurer and the creator. He represents many lives, while being restricted to one, and tastes poetry without its bitterness, being a Proteus who is burnt up in the ephemera, leaving no trace.⁵⁴ A great talent to be many characters and none.

Another Way: From Cherea to Rieux

Human revolt 'au delà du nihilisme'

Riding the absurd, in the way that Caligula does, signifies, as we have seen, becoming a slave to death, submitting to inflict it on others and oneself. But Camus thought more deeply into the question and Caligula's way was definitely superseded by a different approach which has its highest expression in *La Peste*, published in 1947 and *L'homme révolté*, published in 1951.

Camus's argument is straightforward and of great human profundity: if one does not believe in anything and nothing makes sense, we cannot affirm any value. Everything is possible and nothing matters. The absurd produces the absurd conclusion that stoking the ovens or devoting ourselves to healing the lepers are equivalent in value. The law of the strongest will prevail; the world will be divided not into just and unjust but into masters and slaves: 'In this abyss of negation and nihilism, murder seems to occupy the privileged position.'⁵⁵

But if we take the logic of the absurd to its extreme, we have to admit that to keep up this desperate confrontation between human questioning and the silence of the world, to proclaim that life is absurd, the conscience has to be alive. In this way Camus raises his loud and solitary voice against the absolute nihilism which nourishes his and our time and whose most striking demonstration was provided by the Hitlerian apocalypse: 'Here suicide and murder are two aspects of a single system, the system of a misguided intelligence that prefers, to the suffering imposed by a limited situation, the dark victory in which heaven and earth are annihilated.'⁵⁶

The absurd is represented as only a starting point, the equivalent, in existence, of the methodical doubt of Descartes. The sense of the absurd is one among others. It is contradictory in itself, because it excludes value judgements while seeking to keep life, when living is a value judgement. The fact that it gave its colouring to many thoughts and actions between the two world wars only proves its power. It leaves us at an impasse, but like doubt it can guide a new search. This is revolt. The individual in revolt is the one who says no. There is a limit that cannot be passed. Revolt is not a selfish impulse. By opposing lies and oppression and defending the dignity common to all humanity, the individual surpasses selfhood for the sake of other. The absurd consciousness of the suffering individual grows into a collective movement, the adventure of all, with a role like that of the Cartesian *cogito*.

When in history a so-called revolution becomes, by the will to power, a mechanism of death and excess, then a new revolt in the name of restraint and life becomes sacred. With dictatorships and the follies of war still fresh in his memory, Camus suggests another line, which at that time went largely unheeded amid the fever of ideologies and conflicts, but which now proves to be a prophetic warning.

Viewed from our perspective, the tragic, without negating the absurd, discovers the potential that enables it to be presented again in modernity with its new kind of hero, worthy of its ancient greatness. It is not Caligula. If anyone, it is Rieux, the doctor who is the central character in *La Peste*. The absurd consciousness seeks a more constructive breakthrough, projection into meaning, while excluding the fideistic leap, just as it excludes a closed and limited entrenchment in the everyday. This is the way of Cherea, who kills Caligula for the sake of security, accepting a compromise which does not risk all, while repressing passion, the absurd and imagination. But Rieux does not. The lucidity of the intuition of the absurd is accompanied in him by passion and compassion for the human, for its concreteness and frailty.

The beleaguered city of Oran is the human condition into which the consciousness of the absurd suddenly bursts. It is implacable death, evil that afflicts with blind obtuseness, power that oppresses with rules and prohibitions, while the seduction of life persists with its scents and tastes, its sensuousness and love and promise of freedom.

The various reactions to the plague are so many metaphors that man's consciousness opposes to this awakening of the absurd. The most constructive is that of Rieux, with his mental clarity, his personal willingness to risk death, his selflessness, his sacrifice. Rieux resists evil steadily, stubbornly. He struggles against death, overcomes it and accepts his provisional victory. He fights in the trenches but with his eyes on the ground. While under the pressure of the emergency, he never ceases to inquire into the meaning of things, conversing with Tarrou and Paneloux at the height of the plague (Tarrou is a curious atheist traveller, who loves and describes with obsession the life of the city; Paneloux is an erudite and militant Jesuit who lives in Orano; both of them will die during the plague). At the same time he keeps fanaticism, bigotry and ideologies at arm's length and protests against them.

He accepts the burden of everyday life, but does not allow it to numb him and does not evade the radical question that continually resurfaces. In fact it is he who shows up Tarrou and Paneloux. Fideism and fatalism, fanaticism and renunciation: these are the extremes which Rieux shuns, upright and radical as the tragic hero, but more open to connection and responsive to the multiform attractions of living.

Chapter 6

DIANOETIC LAUGHTER IN TRAGEDY: ACCEPTING FINITUDE: *ENDGAME* BY SAMUEL BECKETT[1]

'He's crying. [...] Then he's living': Weeping and Life

Hamm wonders whether old Nagg is dead yet. Clov replies that he appears not to be and adds, 'He's crying.' Hamm replies, 'Then he's living. (*Pause.*) Did you ever have an instant of happiness?'[2]

In Beckett, as in the earliest perception of the tragic in the West, weeping is an inextricable part of human life, a sign of living. And yet, as Nell has observed in an earlier passage in the work: 'Nothing is funnier than unhappiness [...]. Yes, yes, it's the most comical thing in the world.'[3]

A refined lover of language and the startling syntheses of significance that it can evoke, Beckett plays on the ambiguity of 'funny', as both peculiar and comic, so giving us a glimpse of two different sets of implications. The tragedy of the human condition, arising out of the inescapable limit imposed by suffering, is both inexplicable and disturbing, yet it can be distanced and controlled by the comic vision and laughter.

We can take this as the starting point for exploring of one of the outstanding responses in the literature and theatre of the twentieth century to the central issue of tragedy, which Beckett embodied in all his works, but with the greatest complexity and incisiveness in *Endgame*, which he described as 'the favourite of my plays'.

The fruit of a lengthy, troubled gestation, the work was issued in 1957 in French by the Éditions de Minuit as *Fin de partie* and in English as *Endgame* in 1958 by Faber and Faber. As always, Beckett was responsible for producing the translation, with a number of variants, into his mother tongue. He also presented the work on the stage, first as assistant to the director and then with the memorable Berlin production which he directed at the Schiller Theater on 26 September 1967. In the creative process, the production and work on the text were closely integrated and gave Beckett a heightened awareness of the theatre's independence from literature and the specifics of writing directly for the stage.[4]

The play represents a small, emblematic human universe, which has reached its extreme point of crisis, on the threshold of departure or the end. This is the point from which the meaning of existence, if there is one, is best mastered. Hamm, Clov, Nagg and Nell represent three generations: father-master, servant-son, mother and father, the last two being the 'progenitors' immobilized in their ashbins. The setting of the play is an interior, bare and grey, with two windows set high up. A picture hangs with its face to the wall. There are two ashbins front left. Hamm is seated centre in an armchair on castors, covered with a white sheet. Clov is standing, his face 'very red'. The game is about to start again, like the moves in a game of chess, with two key pieces on the board, one of which puts the other in check. Miming the actions, Clov opens the curtains, removes the sheet from the armchair, lifts and then lowers the lids of the two ashbins, accompanying his mechanical gestures with brief bursts of laughter. He announces 'it's nearly finished', that he 'can't be punished any more', and goes into the kitchen to await Hamm's whistle.[5]

On awakening Hamm launches into his first bogus monologue and he too speaks of an end to suffering. He then summons Clov, announcing he is ready for bed again, but receives a rebuff. Then follows a dialogue between the two with repeated questions and answers, demands and threats. Their words and gestures are understated. Hamm is blind; Clov's legs are stiff so that he is unable to sit down. They bully and depend on each other, because only one has the combination to the cupboard and only the other can go to it. Outside the world drifts by: there is nothingness, a desert and leaden waves. Nagg and Nell emerge from their bins on their 'stumps' and the game becomes a foursome. Doting senilely, Nagg and Nell engage in a frustrated and pathetic dalliance, plead petulantly for sugar plums, turn angry and spiteful, and tell old stories that no longer elicit laughter. The ashbins are again closed, excluding the couple from the game which continues to be played out between Hamm and Clov.

The banal, repetitive dialogue conceals matters of great import: Hamm's fear of Clov, knowing he would kill him if he could; his will to power and, at the same time, his destructive pleasure at a world that is nearing its end: 'zero', 'corpsed', 'lead' – there is 'nothing on the horizon'.[6] From the dialogue there emerges the disquieting suspicion that they might 'mean something', the alarm that some form of life might survive, and the hilarious decision to suppress it in the form of the rat in the kitchen or the flea in Clov's pubic hair. There are affections and their surrogates, such as the toy dog, lacking a leg and sex organs. Dreams of love, escape and freedom are relegated to sleep. There is a need for pity and attempts at intimidation and blackmail. Guilty actions surface, such as Hamm's treatment of Mother Pegg, with Clov upbraiding him for letting her die of darkness. In the revised text we read, '"You know what she died of, Mother Pegg? Of darkness", Clov says'.[7] Old nightmares are nurtured, like Hamm's fondness for the mad painter obsessed with the end of the world.

Then their voices are raised in a routine of a different kind, though churned out in the same way at set times: a new chapter of Hamm's 'story' to be recounted to Nagg, who forms the audience, offering applause in return for a biscuit, and then the collective prayer that ends in blasphemy and negation, with Nagg's paternal curse on Hamm, brimming with biblical overtones.

We laboriously return to the usual dialogue and customary gestures, and learn in passing that Nell, who from the start had appeared distant and dreamy, has died quietly in her ashbin. Chills of cold and fear run through Clov and Hamm, with the circle of death tightening around the latter.

Holding the stage, as always, like a ham actor, Hamm launches into his speech with the words 'Me to play'.[8] Left alone, he plays his part, passing from one challenging rhetorical fragment to another: tears and laughter, the Gospel's new commandment of love, the beginning and the end, being there and not being there, the grains of sand and the heap of life.

Clov seems to emancipate himself, daring to present a series of refusals and acts of rebellion: no more painkiller, no more listening to stories he is weary of. He urges Hamm to think of his own misdeeds. Clov refuses to promise him burial, hits him over the head with the toy dog, and gives him some mischievous and alarming information: there is something out there that looks like a small boy, a possible sign of rebirth, intolerable to one like Hamm who wants everything to die with him. At this point, in the French original, Clov sings a mock love song, ending in a sneer.

Clov utters a brief, disenchanted monologue filled with confused accusations aimed at Hamm and all he stands for. Clov has been given faith, values, knowledge and great learning to cure those dying of their wounds, then all of a sudden the words are empty, they cannot say anything. But he is also playing and is making his preparations, as they say in theatrical parlance, for 'making an exit'.[9]

Hamm is left with the last monologue, the endgame, the last move to have done with losing. The stage directions describe his gestures: a line of verse that evokes Baudelaire, a brief narrative with pathetic, tear-jerking touches, a little philosophy on the great theme, always carefully calculated, of time and then nothingness.

Hamm covers his face with the old handkerchief-shroud of the opening scene, as Clov reappears in travelling clothes by the door, remaining motionless. The king is in checkmate. There are no more moves.

The Limit and the Evil of the World Disguised as a Minimalist Universe

This human universe, represented as a series of role plays or the moves in a game of chess, in keeping with Beckett's predilection for understatement and the principle of 'less is more', subtends, as we have seen, the major themes of the tragic and the limit. The limit is physical: it appears in the form of bodily mutilations. Hamm is blind and unmoving; Clov has stiff legs; Hamm's parents are mutilated, weak-sighted and hard of hearing. The limit takes the form of decay and is embodied in the signs of the passing of time.

The limit is psychic, emotional, cognitive. As in Lucky's famous monologue in *Waiting for Godot*, so in the monologues of Clov and Hamm, the words of man's wisdom, while drawing on higher ideas such as meaning and God, fail to endure. They turn to dust and crumble into insignificance. This foreshadows what Beckett later distilled as acquired knowledge. What is the word to a man who, he says, 'does not and cannot know'? The characters' memories are weak and intermittent. Affections cool. The mind that seeks to put the world into order through its stories is actually as self-referential and illusory as Hamm's stories and his dreams of escape, which are no more than fantasies that surface in his sleep. The limit lies in the situation in which humanity is placed: in the ark-bunker with its windows open onto a horizon over which life can disappear either as a result of humanity's violatory and destructive misdeeds or from some other cause impenetrable to mankind's limited understanding. The limit lies in death: death is the key word and the theme of all Beckett's plays. 'They give birth astride of a grave, the light gleams an instant, then it's night', says Pozzo in part 2 of *Waiting for Godot*.[10] The limit lies in the evil people inflict on each other in their relationships. If it is true that Beckett's focus is on the way people behave, it is likewise true that his basic question concerns being and time and that the mutual relations between people constitute a theme of his work which traverses not just the psychological, interpersonal plane, but also the anthropological and the ontological. On this level the limit therefore lies in humanity's misunderstanding of its own project for the dominion of nature and in the erroneous and culpable urge to tyrannize over our fellow men and women. These themes are respectively suggested and sustained by the biblical source of Genesis (which surfaces in Beckett's reading close to the time *Endgame* was composed), and by philosophical sources in Hegel and above all Sartre.[11]

Hamm embodies the figure of the overlord or king, though in decline, installed in an armchair on wheels as if enthroned. He is enclosed in his circle as a 'situated body' and in his absolute passion for absolute freedom and absolute control, frozen in separateness and 'being against' others, impulses which seem more primeval than the bond and the sense of 'being with' them, in a structural solitude that can only be embodied as conflict. Dispossession and submission, master and slave, are the dominant modes of relationship in the play, leading to alienation in the extreme forms of sadism and masochism. Subjugating others, enjoying seeing them suffer because of him, is a sign of power.[12] Hamm makes Clov his object-instrument, after demanding in an open contradiction that he freely acknowledge him as absolute master:

> But in this way the singularity is not made absolute; rather it is dissolved. The passion that traverses it is revealed as a 'useless passion'. Whatever path he takes is a dead end, into which consciousness is blocked in deadlock. The overlord is in check, because his totalising project can only be realized through the free recognition of the Other [...]. And the servant is in check, as his project of objectification can never be fully attained.[13]

Hamm embodies the figure of the overlord with all the concreteness of that theatrical figure, here and now, with features that can always be related to those of some ruling figure. (Beckett clearly had in mind some of the dictators in recent history and the 'enigma of consensus' by which they were surrounded.)[14] But Hamm also possesses the depth of a symbol that traverses the whole of humanity's history. He is gifted with culture and powers of expression, as we see from the surfacing of a whole tradition out of which his speech is woven; he possesses ideology and imagination. He governs the relations between the generations and the sexes, emblematically present in the four characters on stage. He has a strategy of power. He issues absurd orders and asks obsessive questions, is arrogant and contemptuous, displays bad faith and duplicity, blackmails others, utters threats, and demands affection and absolute loyalty.

Clov embodies his counterpart, the servant. As noted above, Clov has all the connotations of a servant: the rigid posture, the automatic and repeated gestures, the repressed anger that surfaces in the redness of his face. He is devoid of power, passion and affect, of impulses, imagination and creativity. He lacks words of his own. Like the squire in Bergman's film, *The Seventh Seal*, his point of view is a narrow, flat and bored realism, stripped of illusions. Clov cannot create anything, but only bring order by a meticulous and obsessive routine that prefigures the stillness of death:

CLOV, (*straightening up.*) I love order. It's my dream. A world where all would be silent and still, and each thing in its last place, under the last dust.[15]

While a variety of tones and flaunted emotions emerge from Hamm's speeches, expressed in a wide range of timbres and nuances, Clov's unvaryingly correct monotone expresses the aridity and flatness of a psyche frustrated in its development and stranded in the shallows of his twofold tie (servant-son) and his inability to rebel. His petty acts of revenge (refusing to give Hamm the painkiller), while struggling in vain to resist (his unwillingness to fetch the telescope), are interwoven with the leitmotif of his repeated threat, 'I'll leave you', which remains unfulfilled.[16]

Language has been inculcated in him. He has never harboured any illusions:

CLOV. Mean something! You and I, mean something! (*Brief laugh.*) Ah that's a good one![17]

His realm is the kitchen, his aspiration to eliminate all traces of life.

An analogous relationship links the father-master to the older generation, now awaiting death in the ashbins at the side of the stage. Nagg is the worthy begetter of this humanity, which is capable only of dominating or being dominated, which only knows the useful or the supposed useful and is on the point of regressing. Parodying the biblical patriarchs and Shakespeare's King Lear, Nagg curses and then retreats into weeping like a senile child, now alone and without authority.

Is this kind of attitude, which mortifies humanity and is an expression of evil, structural to human existence or is it the product of a local history and culture? Does the tragic consciousness that Beckett expresses, nurtured both by his highly sensitive observation of experience and reflections on philosophy and the scriptures, lead to a pessimistic and nihilistic position or an open position? These are the fundamental questions.

Once again we must clarify Beckett's meaning by unravelling a web of closely entwined strands. He interwove the psychological or psychoanalytic thread with the historical thread of a world overwhelmed by two world wars, the collapse of nineteenth-century civilization and totalitarian regimes, and then in the fifties and sixties suffering the nightmare of opposed blocs, the Cold War, and outbursts of racism and genocide. Beckett, like other artists and intellectuals, was obsessed by the idea of power that requires for its exercise the consensus of the enslaved, a reciprocal tie and personal loyalty capable of anything. Out of these two threads, in a closed circle of significances, he wove an anthropological and philosophical fabric.

> [*Endgame*] becomes a great suspended meditation on the problem of evil that has seeped into the 'creation', on the mode of relationship of person with person, with the world and with God. Evil contradicts and radically betrays the project embodied in the Judaeo-Christian tradition and a certain philosophical construct of the West, such as the strand related to rationalism, well known to Beckett, as it was devised by Descartes and Leibniz,

and with the idea of a supreme intelligence who is the reason for existence and order and disposes all things in the best possible way. The French text of *Endgame* alludes significantly to this promise betrayed.[18]

The same allusion emerges in the references to Genesis and Deuteronomy with regard to Moses (in the French edition). These are associated with the boy outside (who seems to be watching the house, but may be 'gazing at his navel') as an impossible or failed hope.[19] With Beckett's customary technique of dredging up allusions with distant associations – his use of pauses, irony, the retrieval of words deposited by past centuries – the plot unfolds in a decaying interior and rises to symbolize, in a striking synthesis, the raft sailing through history, the drifting ark, genesis and apocalypse.

Without depicting bloodshed, crimes, torture or sensational deaths, *Endgame* touches on all the phenomenology of the limit and of the evil associated with the tragic condition, through the fibres of banality and everyday life: physical evil, moral evil, ontological evil. Having already covered the physical limit above, I will now look at the moral and ontological limits.

Moral evil appears in the form of the disharmony which violence, selfishness and tyranny culpably introduce into the relations between individuals and the world. Of this the sadistic and destructive behaviour of Hamm, Clov and Nagg (essentially 'wicked men') are metaphors. Evil appears as the chaos which constantly threatens the world order, represented by the rising waters which are about to submerge the ark-bunker, like the grey desolation overspreading the splendours of creation – those described on the living page, enamelled with colours and filled with movement, in Genesis or exalted in wonder and gratitude in the *Confessions* of St Augustine, both works very much present to Beckett's mind.

Ontological evil appears in the irreducible disproportion between essence and being, the finiteness of the creature which finds its radical expression in the figure of death, a theme that significantly runs throughout the play, with the recurrence of the keywords 'death', 'dying', and their synonyms. It appears again in Clov's definition of mankind in Hamm's foreshadowing of his own death, the story of the crazy painter, the ironic deaths of the flea and the rat, and the silent death of the lyrical Nell.[20]

The phenomenology is wide ranging, but we have not yet touched on the ultimate reason for this ineluctable limit, the reason for the tragedy of life, which is defined and identified by Pozzo in the second half of *Waiting for Godot* as a brief light that glimmers for an instant before nightfall: 'They give birth astride of a grave.'

Beckett hides himself behind allusions, or rather he elicits responses to them, looks at them in their transparency and puts them to one side with the eye of the observer, or rather of the author who allows his creatures to act for themselves. With his habitual understatement, his habitual modesty and discretion, he does not suggest solutions or answers, because here more than ever man 'does not and cannot know', as Beckett often said. He cannot explain the irrational with the rational, he cannot with his local and limited gaze embrace the universe or grasp Being.

He allows the biblical hypothesis of the Fall to emerge as the start of a tale of betrayals by man and corruption.[21] He allows the hypothesis of a Christian promise of redemption to emerge in the image of the child; he brings out the idea of retributive justice which inflicts suffering in order to cleanse guilt.[22] He records the atheistic and nihilistic response which, through the negation of God, negates meaning and hypothesises absurdity; but he also gives a glimpse of the desolation after Auschwitz and the theme of God's silence, so crucial to his generation.[23]

Beckett is no moralist, and his theatre does not seek to teach or preach, but the great tragic theme of *responsibility* is very much on his mind. He feels its urgency with a prophetic insight which at the end of the fifties was still nurtured by the recent experiences of modern war, dictatorships and genocide, and terminated by the atom bomb. Then in the late sixties, at the time of the Berlin production of *Endgame* by Beckett himself, it was confirmed by the emergence of the superpower blocs and the technological threat to humanity's existence.

Here Beckett seems to have sensed what the philosopher Hans Jonas was soon to express systematically in his famous book on the *Imperative of Responsibility* (1979). But whereas Jonas presents a project for an ethical remedy, a regulatory framework, Beckett does not go beyond a lucid diagnosis in the form of a poetic image that raises the radical question. 'Prometheus unbound' endangers life itself, our own life and that of nature, present and future, for the first time in history. And yet, does it make sense to assert the need for the existence of life and nature? Or is the sceptical or nihilistic assumption valid? Better *noluntas*, better the *cupio dissolvi*.

Beckett does not offer solutions. Naturally the collapse of Hamm's small world in his refuge is complete, irredeemable and without a future. Outside the windows nature disappeared and the seeds don't sprout. The sea is leaden. Hamm and Clov assail any possible residual form of life, such as the flea.

CLOV. Looks like it (*He drops the tin and adjusts his trousers.*)
    Unless he's laying doggo.
HAMM. Laying! Lying you mean. Unless he's *lying* doggo.
CLOV. Ah? One says lying? One doesn't say laying?
HAMM. Use your head, can't you. If he was laying we'd be bitched.
    The universe is falling apart. 'To hell with the universe!'
    A boy glimpsed on the horizon arouses dismay as a 'potential procreator'.
    (CLOV *moves ladder nearer window, gets up on it, turns telescope on the without.*)
CLOV, (*Dismayed.*) Looks like a small boy!
CLOV, (*Sarcastic.*) A small... boy!
CLOV. I'll go and see. (*He gets down, drops the telescope, goes towards door, turns.*)
    I'll take the gaff.
    (*He looks for the gaff, sees it, picks it up, hastens towards door.*)
HAMM. No! (CLOV *halts.*)
CLOV. No? A potential procreator?

Laughing at Tragedy

The sage attitude that Beckett seems ultimately to recommend, given this lucid perception of the tragic, is not fierce rebellion in the tradition of heroic tragedy, grappling with an absolute which man presumes to represent to himself, with his weak perceptions and his poor language. This is no more than a storm in a teacup, Beckett implies, and naturally, 'There are no easy solutions.'[24]

Beckett, personally endowed with a fine sense of humour, uses it as a source of cognitive, dianoetic laughter, as a way of helping humanity kindle the light of intelligence and knowledge. It enabled him to hold a view of reality that serenely accepted finitude while knowing that the absolute is other than and inexpressible by human speech. A number of currents come together in this attitude, especially the philosophical tradition from Socrates to Kierkegaard and the theological tradition. They merge with the impressions left by the Protestant outlook, absorbed by Beckett in his youth, though abandoned in his subsequent detachment from all positive religion, and enriched by his readings of Augustine, 'who emphasized the absolute gratuitousness of God's saving initiative and slighted the significance and utility of mankind's efforts, its acts and speeches. Humanity's efforts are risible, if seen in relation to its actual power to save itself, to alter its structural condition in any way.'[25]

The tragic situation elicits laughter, which can range from irony to sarcasm and humour. At times it is detached, aggressive and destructive, at others sympathetic and compassionate. We laugh at times to vent the tension associated with the perception of an unpleasant and unavoidable situation, and at other times to downplay the drama or tone down something that is being taken too seriously. At times it is to demolish illusions and false beliefs, to present a different point of view, or to express disapproval, contempt or indignation. We laugh above all to achieve detachment, to clear the air or make the breakthrough onto a different plane.

This range is fully represented in *Endgame*. The techniques of comedy that Beckett deploys are many and sophisticated: incongruity, paradox, the mechanization of the body, repetitions and tics, the sudden emergence of vulgarity, repartee without logic, unexpected nonsense, general wackiness and contradictions, clowning, exaggeration, puns, the failure to comply with the normal rules of conversation, gags, and allusions to silent movies and comedy classics like Chaplin and Keaton.

Nell, the only female character in *Endgame*, is endowed with this resource of humour. As noted above, she appears to express the vision essentially most congenial to Beckett and the wisest attitude to life. She seems to foreshadow Winnie in Beckett's *Happy Days* (1961) and some of the women of his late period in the *dramaticules*. Shut up in her ashbin, like her old husband, she is now remote from the everyday sadomasochistic comedy characteristic of her little family universe and the human universe in general. She is already in another dimension, on the threshold of death, into which she slips during the course of the play, silently, without pathos, without tragedy, as many people die in real life.

The images that fill her mind on the threshold of death range either among distant memories, with the peaceful simplification of time, or into an unknown future. She no longer allows herself to be distracted by the petulant, blasphemous tales of her aged husband, who continues to tell his stories amid the indifference of others and of Nell herself. With the detachment of true humour, she again sees the deep water in the lake of her youth, so clear that one April morning she could see right to the bottom.

Then, with a rapid association of ideas, turning to Clov, she urges him to leave ('Desert!'). The verb is pregnant with meaning. It is an imperative that urges him to cut and run, to break the circle around him, and yet we also read in it the great theme of the desert. (The verb–noun homograph, as well as the covert association between 'water' and the word 'desert' may authorize the connection when reading Beckett, given his skill at playing with language. Moreover this is how Clov takes it, since he says: 'She told me to go away, into the desert.') It is the last word he utters in the play.[26]

As noted above, the desert is an ambivalent symbolic image. It is the site of primordial chaos, of barrenness and the ordeal (to which Israel is subjected in Exodus), a place of desolation as punishment, but it also has positive overtones, being associated with springs of water, manna and the law. Then it is a place of progressive idealization, a type of the monastic and mystical experience, of the inner emptiness which dispels the 'sounds of the world' and its encrustations as a prelude to an encounter with the absolute and the 'return'. An emblem of great richness in Beckett's work, the desert is not an abstract symbol but a physical perception, embodied in the concreteness of the increasingly bare set, in the icon of an inner experience leading to the threshold of death and rebirth, to what is either nothing or all things, a choice which Beckett leaves undecided.

Form without Drama

Given these philosophical premises, the dramatic form of tragedy no longer makes sense as a way to represent the tragic. Though pity and fear, the original cornerstones of this genre, remain (and they are explicitly mentioned many times in the lexicon of *Endgame*), other key elements are dispelled by some of Hamm's lines. The model for the play's form is furnished rather by music, painting, photography, the *tableau vivant*, mime and the game of chess. Set in a nontime and nonplace, what is performed on the stage is an unchanging situation without climax or resolution, peripeteia or catastrophe. There are no actions, only microactions repeated in gestures that are disconnected, slowed or convulsive. It is a play without heroes, with characters who are disintegrating, who cannot be related to a permanent and structured identity, who are dissociated by gestures unrelated to their words (reflected in Beckett's advice as director to the actors). They are eroded and declining. Their speech is never elevated, compelling, never rigorous in logic, rhythm or tension, but laconic. Their lines are brief; they speak by fits and starts and their words peter out in aberrant replies, stale repetitions or the weakness of a senile memory.

The final outcome is stillness and silence, prepared by the initial extended tableau and by an increasingly intensified interplay of pauses, skilfully scored by Beckett with his intimate understanding of music, an art with which he frequently established analogies in directing the actors. Music, so Schopenhauer claimed, was the most philosophical of the arts. He considered it the direct expression of that blind will to live which he saw as the *noumenon*, the ontological principle that explains phenomena, causing them to exist, suffer and subside like ripples on the surface of the water.

Music, technically understood, loved and philosophically filtered in this way, is the true substrate of this tragic meditation on existence.

Oedipus the King (*Edipo Re*) by Sophocles. Roberto Abbati and Cristina Cattellani in the parts of Oedipus and Jocasta, directed by Gigi Dall'Aglio. Production of the Compagnia del Collettivo, Teatro Due, Parma, 1986 (© 1986–2014 Maurizio Buscarino).

Ghosts (*Spettri*) by Henrik Ibsen, directed by Luca Ronconi, Spoleto, June 1982. (Photograph by Eugenio Napoli / Courtesy Teatro Stabile di Torino - Centro Studi.)

Ghosts (*Gengangere*) by Henrik Ibsen, directed by Alexander Mork Eiden, Oslo, National Theatre, August 2006. (Photograph by Marit Anna Evanger / Courtesy National Theatre, Oslo.)

Ghosts (*Gengangere*) by Henrik Ibsen, directed by Alexander Mork Eiclen, Oslo, National Theatre, August 2006. (Photograph by Marit Anna Evanger / Courtesy National Theatre, Oslo.)

Louis Jouvet and Monique Mélinand in *The Tidings Brought to Mary* (*L'Annonce faite à Marie*) by Paul Claudel, Paris, Théâtre de l'Athénée, June 1946 (© Studio Lipnitzki, Roger Viollet / Archivi Alinari, Florence).

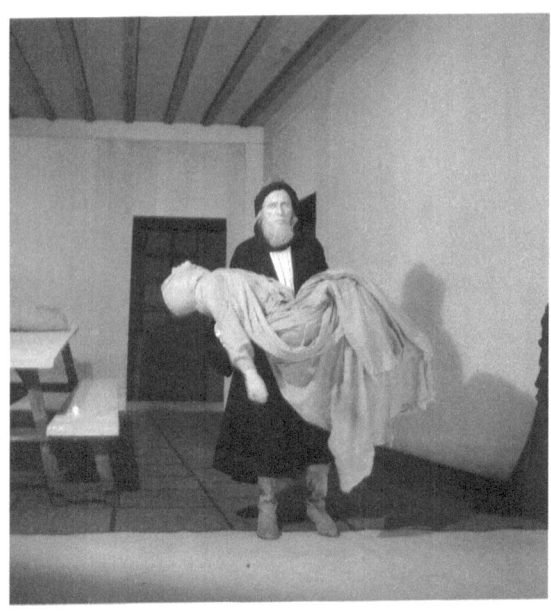

Mother Courage and Her Children (*Mutter Courage und ihre Kinder*) by Bertolt Brecht, directed by Bertold Brecht. On stage, Helene Weigel. Berlin, Berliner Ensemble, Deutsches Theater, 1951. (Photograph by Heiner Hill / Courtesy Bertolt Brecht Archiv.)

Mother Courage and Her Children (*Mutter Courage und ihre Kinder*) by Bertolt Brecht, directed by Bertold Brecht. On stage, Helene Weigel, Angelika Hurwicz, Werner Hinz, Ingo Osterloh. Berlin, Deutsches Theater, 1949. (Courtesy Bertolt Brecht Archiv.)

Germaine Montero and Jean Vilar in *Mother Courage and Her Children* by Bertolt Brecht, directed by Jean Vilar, Théâtre National Populaire, Festival de Suresnes, 1951 (© Studio Lipnitzki, Roger Viollet / Archivi Alinari, Florence).

Catherine Hiegel in *Mother Courage and Her Children*, directed by Jorge Lavelli, Paris, Comédie Française, 1998 (© Marc Enguerand).

Gérard Philipe and Michel Bouquet in *Caligula* by Albert Camus, directed by Paul Oettly, Paris, Théatre Hébertot, 1945 (© Roger Viollet / Archivi Alinari, Florence).

Carmelo Bene in *Caligula* (*Caligola*), directed by Alberto Ruggiero, Rome, Teatro delle Arti, October 1959. (Courtesy Museo Biblioteca dell'Attore, Genova, Fondo Gastone Bosio.)

Caligula by Albert Camus, directed by Youssef Chahine, Paris, Comédie Française, February 1992 (© Brigitte Enguerand).

Endgame (*Finale di partita*), directed by Carlo Cecchi, Florence, Teatro Niccolini, February 1995. (Photograph by Massimo Agus / Courtesy Massimo Agus.)

Franco Citti (Oedipus the wanderer), frame from the film *Oedipus Rex* (*Edipo re*) by Pier Paolo Pasolini, Italy, 1967 (© Reporters Associati, Rome).

Silvana Mangano and Franco Citti (Oedipus and Jocasta), frame from the film *Oedipus Rex* (*Edipo re*) by Pier Paolo Pasolini, Italy, 1967 (© Reporters Associati, Rome).

Franco Citti (Oedipus blind), frame from the film *Oedipus Rex* (*Edipo re*) by Pier Paolo Pasolini, Italy, 1967 (© Reporters Associati, Rome).

Umberto Ceriani and Marisa Minelli (Pylades and Electra) in *Pylades* (*Pilade*) by Pier Paolo Pasolini, directed by Lamberto Puggelli, Milan, Piccolo Teatro Studio, May 1989. (Photograph by Luigi Ciminaghi / Courtesy Piccolo Teatro di Milano.)

Pylades (*Pilade*) by Pier Paolo Pasolini (*The Pasolini Project*), directed by Adam Paolozza, Toronto, Canadian Stage: Spotlight Italy Festival, March 2011. (Photograph by Coleen MacPherson / Courtesy TheatreRUN.)

Michelle Smith (Athena) in *Pylades* (*Pilade*) by Pasolini (*The Pasolini Project*), directed by Adam Paolozza, Toronto, Canadian Stage: Spotlight. Italy Festival, March 2011. (Photograph by Erin MacPherson / Courtesy TheatreRUN.)

Akropolis, directed by Jerzy Grotowski, variant I; Teatr 13 Rzędów, Opole 1962. Maja Komorowska, Rena Mirecka, Zbigniew Cynkutis, Barbara Barska, Zygmunt Molik. (Photograph by the Teatr Laboratorium / Archiwum Instytutu Grotowskiego / Courtesy the Grotowski Institute.)

Akropolis, directed by Jerzy Grotowski, variant III; Teatr 13 Rzędów, Opole 1964. Zygmunt Molik, Rena Mirecka. (Photograph by the Teatr Laboratorium / Archiwum Instytutu Grotowskiego / Courtesy the Grotowski Institute.)

Akropolis, directed by Jerzy Grotowski, variant III; Teatr 13 Rzędów, Opole 1964. Zygmunt Molik, Ryszard Ciesiak, Mieczyslaw Janowski, Andrzej Bielski, Gaston Kulig, Rena Mirecka. (Photograph by the Teatr Laboratorium / Archiwum Instytutu Grotowskiego / courtesy the Grotowski Institute.)

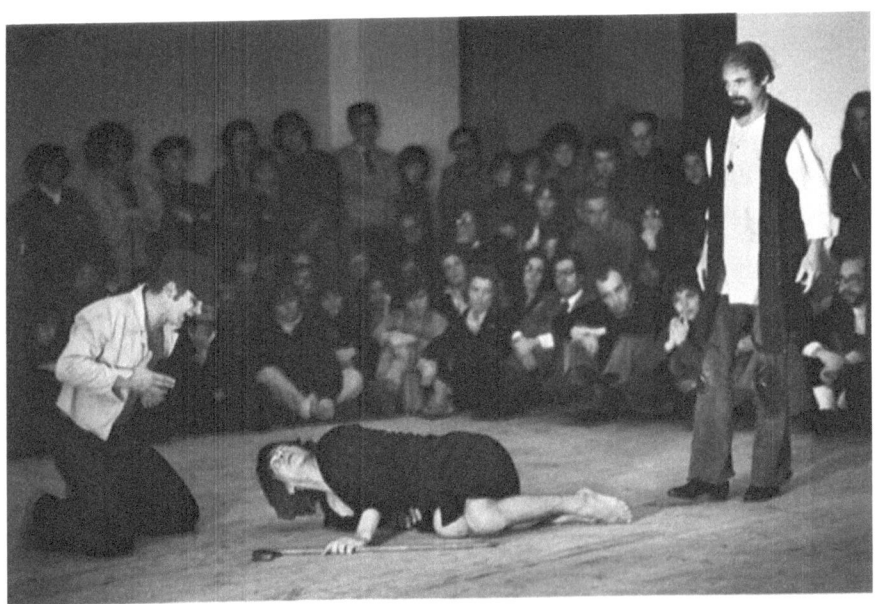

Apocalypsis cum figuris, directed by Jerzy Grotowski, Włochy, 1979. Stanislaw Ścierski, Ryszarcl Cieślak, Antoni Jahołkowski. (Photograph by Maurizio Buscarino / Courtesy Maurizio Buscarino).

Apocalypsis cum figuris, directed by Jerzy Grotowski, Włochy, 1979. Rena Mirecka, Zygmunt Molik, Antoni Jahołkowski, Stanislaw Ścierski, Zbigniew Cynkutis, Ryszard Cieślak. (Photograph by Maurizio Buscarino / Courtesy Maurizio Buscarino.)

Rwanda 94, directed by Jacques Delcuvellerie, Festival of Avignon, July 1999. (Photograph by Lou Hérion / Courtesy GROUPOV asbi - Centre Expérimental de Culture Active.)

Rwanda 94, directed by Jacques Delcuvellerie, Festival of Avignon, July 1999. (Photograph by Lou Hérion / Courtesy GROUPOV asbi - Centre Expérimental de Culture Active.)

Ruhe, conceived and directed by Josse de Pauw, Brussels, May 2007. (Photograph by Herman Sorgeloos / Courtesy Muziektheater Transparant.)

Ruhe, conceived and directed by Josse de Pauw, Brussels, May 2007. (Photograph by Herman Sorgeloos / Courtesy Muziektheater Transparent.)

The author with Ludwig Flaszen (founder with Jerzy Grotowski of the Teatr Laboratorium of Wrocław, Poland), Paris, summer 2012.

Chapter 7

THE ARROGANCE OF REASON AND THE 'DISAPPEARANCE OF THE FIREFLIES': *PILADE (PYLADES)* BY PIER PAOLO PASOLINI

The Idea of the Tragic: Between Structure of the Human and Historical Transformation

The idea of the tragic is elaborated with great intellectual commitment and elevated poetry in Pier Paolo Pasolini's writings for the stage. His work follows a distinctive and original path which we can rightly include in the map of fundamental twentieth-century developments in the genre.

In Pasolini it is not so much philosophical culture as literary (in this case ancient Greek drama) and anthropological culture that constitute the matrix of the work in consideration and provide the basic ideas with which the universal experiences of the limit and necessity are reinterpreted.[1] The tragic action is presented as an arrogant and absolute affirmation of one-dimensional man, that of abstract standardized reason, which overwhelms all individual differences, cultures and desires. But it also represents the other side: bloody revolution followed by solitude incapable of mediation and reciprocity.

The Theatre as 'Cultural Ritual'

In the mid-sixties, when the Italian avant-garde gathered at the Conference in Ivrea and the 'new theatre' was established in Europe by the journal *Nuovi Argomenti*, Pasolini launched a provocation, hotly controversial in its tones but prophetic in its lucidity: the 'Manifesto per un nuovo teatro'.[2] He had already produced his theatrical corpus.[3]

He envisaged the theatre of the new times as a *séance* (the French term seems accurate), a vigilant session of participation in a 'cultural ritual'. In his polemic against the moribund 'theatre of chat' (a ritual which he saw as the reflection of bourgeois culture) or the hysterical and mystifying 'theatre of the shout' (his swipe at the scandal mongering in which he saw bourgeois culture as still indulging), Pasolini envisaged 'the theatre of speech', intended for advanced cultural groups. It is evident that he thought, beyond the dated labels and classifications (which he did actually use), of a theatre in which everyone would seek for constructive and genuine moments of reflection, awareness and the development of cultural projects. He sought a theatre of ritual, of convocation – a strong, transforming experience of that incarnate consciousness that is the actor, the 'living vehicle', as Pasolini said, of the world and of that collective body or community that is the audience.[4]

Theatre as the Awareness and Pilot of Change

Theatre going is no longer a 'religious ritual' in the secular age (as our age is defined in the important book by the philosopher Charles Taylor),[5] no longer a 'social ritual', still less a 'ritual theatre', but a 'cultural ritual'.

It is a theatre without aestheticism, sophistication, hysteria or breakaways, produced by advanced intellectuals who accept it as a 'practical undertaking'. This expression, which almost evokes Benedetto Croce's distinctions between the various activities of the spirit and recalls the categories that left their mark on Pasolini's formation, distinguishes between territories of poetry and territories of practice. With a felicitous insight, it enhances the theatre's relation to practice, perception and physicality, and unites in a direct, stringent relationship the author, the actor, the 'living vehicle' and the audience, without any scenery, and with the performances not restricted to the canonical times and places but presented in workplaces, schools and cultural spaces. The themes peculiar to this theatre, says Pasolini (albeit somewhat reductively), 'may be typical of a lecture, an ideal political rally or a scientific debate'[6].

Pasolini sought new space for a different audience, and it is interesting to note in retrospect that the success of *Pylades* and the testing of the objectives of Pasolini's new theatre occurred above all in Italy in the nineties, after the phase of the official circuits, in the ambit of the social circuits and in synergy with projects/experiments of civil theatre, school theatre and research into expression, as can be seen by examining the work's stage history. As a form of commitment, growth, knowledge and design of the self, this theatre recalls the great theatre of Athenian democracy.

The inspiration for *Pylades* stemmed from the experience of the *Oresteia*. Pasolini's aesthetic sensibility, the efficacy of his poetic images, the depth of the human characters in his narrative and his directorial skill expressed in film enabled him to intuit that what appeared didactic, ideological, orotund and arid in the written pages of this play could acquire density, subtlety and human substance when it was embodied in the living body of the actor and the chorus, namely the public. It is in this reality that the cultural ritual is fulfilled. And it is in this concreteness of the word incarnate that the character, through the actor, manifests his 'style'. 'Style' is an emblematic word in Pasolini.

Today it is natural to associate Pasolini's intuition with the tendency peculiar to our own period towards the civil theatre – the theatre of narration, the theatre of performance – in which the naturalness of the living sign of the actor, embodied with his word incarnate and his gesture, governs (in the 'difference' of the stage, in flesh and blood) the flow of technology, affirms his sensibility and resists the anaesthetization, the technical administration, of his feeling.

Culture is the ambiance and the theme of this theatre. By this Pasolini means not erudition but the culture that is the object of knowledge of cultural anthropology and philosophical anthropology: the idea of the structure of the human, of its consciousness and its relationship with the world, inflected and objectified in historical institutions.

An Anthropological Key to *Pylades*

I have chosen *Pylades* as an emblematic work, a node in Pasolini's encounter with the original intuition of the tragic in ancient Greece and its embodiment in the modern consciousness and in modern forms of art. It has therefore to be analysed in its intertextual relationship, particularly with Pasolini's translation of the *Oresteia* (1960)[7] and the films *Oedipus Rex* (1967)[8] and *Notes for an African Oresteia* (1970).[9]

The modern reworking of a great text (the *Oresteia* of Aeschylus) and a founding myth of antiquity, written at the origins of Western theatre and in a phase of transition from the mythic-heroic phase to the legal-political phase, *Pylades* is firstly a play that speaks of theatrical culture and launches a signal of separation from what was called 'mass culture', as well as from realism, by that time the homologue of mass culture and its media. The realism that Pasolini had practiced in the fifties and early sixties – in the novels *Ragazzi di vita* (1956) and *Una vita violenta* (1959) or the films *Accattone* (1961), *La ricotta* (1962) and *Mamma Roma* (1962) – no longer struck him as capable of being truthful, unconventional or effective. So Pasolini chose to be 'difficult', not facilely denotative. He turned to the theatre as an art of difference, which here proceeded by mythologizing and transvaluing, in a process of symbolization, the allusions to his autobiography, the allusions to political events, the allusions to social reality and the reality relative to developments in culture.

Secondly, the text is the subject of the representation of a historical anthropology: the clash of personalities and the division of the story into a prologue and nine episodes are the mythical guise of a cultural revolution that took place in Italy and generally in Western Europe in the postwar period and were the prelude to a kind of alarming 'mutation'.

Thirdly, the text is the expression of the disquiet of the eye of the artist, in this case of the theatre artist, who descends as an anthropologist into a world that is not his, but which he loves and which fascinates him, even though he suffers from a hopeless distance and isolation. In this regard, Pasolini (who read, in the years when these authors became the bread and butter of European intellectuals, Ernesto De Martino, Lucien Levy Bruhl and Claude Lévi-Strauss, whom he refers to explicitly in his essays), shared the passion and the disquiet clearly expressed by Lévi-Strauss in *Tristes Tropiques* concerning the ability to authentically grasp and render a different world then disappearing, the irreversible drift of monoculture, the passion for man underlying every anthropological approach.[10]

Finally, the work is the representation of the theme of philosophical anthropology with which I am dealing in this book: that which investigates the tragic among the structures of the human. Pasolini discovers the modern version of the tragic in the hubris embodied in one of the dimensions of man: reason. It is personified in Athena, who comes to represent, in her excess and exclusivity, the antilogos; that is, not the logos in the sense of that which binds the living together, but arid, one-dimensional, manipulative, cynical, prevaricating reason, the modern face of power, today bound up with money and its unifying forces. In other words, this reason is the modern embodiment of the urge to power or of power that weighs on mankind as a fatality, seemingly irresistible as fate, when Western man constructs his history and determines its tragic nature. Though the destiny of man is tragic quite apart from this: the destiny of suffering and death is tragic.

We shall briefly review the story of *Pylades*. The work, in a prologue and nine episodes, begins with a puzzled reflection of the people of Argos. After the revolution that killed the tyrants, everything has returned to normality and oblivion. The chorus engages in self-criticism; it feels fearful, acknowledges its guilt in having accepted paternalistic powers or absolute powers as if they were imposed by a superior will above ordinary men. Now everyone is waiting for Orestes to find a solution. Will something change (prologue)?

In the heady air of the evening, Orestes, illuminated by Athena, has returned. Declared innocent by a court of men instituted by the youthful and modern goddess, he is ready to establish democracy in Argos, on the model Athens and well aware that the Erinyes, the goddesses of nightmares and fears, have been transformed into goddesses of courage and inspiration. Orestes clashes with Electra, the sister who clings to the past, the law of the tyrants (though she helped him to slay them), of the fathers and the fathers of the fathers. Pylades follows in silence. He seems absent, absorbed in something far away. The chorus is enthusiastic and enjoys the atmosphere of celebration and the innovations that are announced (episode 1).

In the renewed city, where business thrives and money accumulates, in front of the parliament a dismal announcement is unexpectedly made: some of the Eumenides are returning to sing their nightmares. Before the house of Electra they crouch like heaps of vipers. The chorus panics, feeling the threat of the past returning. Orestes is optimistic. Pylades is gloomy and pessimistic (episode 2).

Now it is clear that there is an irreducible conflict between Orestes and Pylades in the project for the city. Pylades is a threat; he has to be expelled. In the forum of the city a trial is held. The boyhood friend from the past has become 'the cause of the scandal', come to 'question the order, now sacred, / in which we live under the aegis of the purest divinity'. But who was Pylades? And who is Orestes? The debate begins: they are the opposite of each other, yet they are united in the root of understanding, of complicity, of their original symbiosis. Pylades, dark, is wholly withdrawn, bearing witness to a life that embodies 'fidelity, loyalty, / disinterestedness, passion'. Orestes, fair, is all glory, untiring action of progress, moving towards the future, which Pylades insinuates is actually movement towards the past. The Furies, who now again appear in the city, are the proof of this. The people show signs of resignation and foolishness. The chorus hastens to find Pylades guilty. It is suspected that he wishes to overthrow the city's institutions, that he brings destruction, unleashing the hungry, the old peasants, the new workers. There is no reason and no hope in him. The chorus-city needs more: a civic form of subjection and obedience, an unpretentiously humble and active life, a comprehensible and sustainable ideal (episode 3).

In the mountains Pylades' consciousness grows to its fullness. While the farmer swallows the soothing and paternalistic language of the Eumenides, Pylades feels even more of a misfit, without clear ideas. He dreamed he was poor, but the reality in which he lives is a constant disquiet, the disquiet of being excluded, not fitting in anywhere he goes. The Eumenides tempt him with their consolatory speech and promise: the fable of the future, as a utopia when all barriers will fall and reason and hope will emerge into an endless paradise. But it is the shadow of death that appears at the end in the eyes of the young people placed in the pillory (episode 4).

Pylades takes his decision: he descends from the mountains leading a mysterious army of peasants and some workmen recruited in the city. The chorus trembles, afraid that Orestes may throw away what he has built. The only way out is by civil war, in which Orestes and Electra, so attached to the past, are reconciled.

Orestes and Electra, urged on by the chorus (representing the people that count, the professionals), come to an agreement: not equality of power, which Electra desires, but the re-establishment of the cult of the Furies. Athena will stay in parliament, the Furies in the temple. Athena (who loves, fatuous as she is, puns, humour and deception, disguised as talk) prophesies a new revolution, not Pylades', but one that will be born in the heart of the old city. This will be accomplished by the city itself and Orestes.

The substance is what is seen in the humorous, macabre description: in an expanse of snow a pot boils, in which float the dismembered limbs of a young man. On the cover can be seen the sign of the cross (episode 5).

At the head of the army of revolutionaries, Pylades, moving from victory to victory, arrives before the walls. He is about to take the city, but once again he falls into crisis. There is an abyss between him and the people who follow him. His difference is evident. It is manifest in the gaze that those people turn on the city. Their gaze is pure, barbarian, virgin. They do not read anything in the city that can paralyse them, but his is a gaze filled with recollections, memories imprinted in him by the culture and history that he, an intellectual, has mastered. The city, adored and hostile, is afflicted by a deep-seated evil that does not diminish its beauty. But it will soon be a pile of rubble.

Orestes and Pylades face off. Orestes expresses his admiration for Pylades, who went away alone but now unmasks his illusion: he is an old man with the innocence of a boy. It was not he who was to make the revolution, but the city itself with its democratic principles and in the light of a new reality (episode 6).

There follows, near the cemetery of the city of Argos, an encounter between Pylades and Electra. In the silent atmosphere of his truce and surrender, Pylades is in the grip of turbulent feelings: a sense of death and a longing for love. Veiled in her mourning garments, Electra comes to perform the rites at the tomb of her parents. As if drawn out of themselves, the two kiss (episode 7).

In the eighth episode, the most tormented in Pasolini's text, events reach their climax. In the revolutionaries' camp, a boy messenger tells of the apparition of Athena in a great light and the announcement of a new revolution: the city would no longer be 'markets / built with kindness by the hands of builders', attached to the values of common sense, honour, foresight, dignity, devotion, modesty and religion. Another messenger announces that the city has actually failed to achieve what was expected: the invention of the beautiful flags of the revolution. A great procession enters, led triumphantly by Athena. Faced with a people uncertain but intoxicated with life, the procession of scientists, technicians, artists and politicians advances. The city has grown more than it has ever done in all the centuries of its past existence. Athena's miracles have begun. After driving out the Erinyes, Athena has opened the city gates to the Eumenides, who are now working on the people's hearts.

The field of revolutionary victory is emptied, silent, deserted. The novelty of life of the city has attracted the revolutionaries, who have gradually deserted. The old man is disenchanted: it was easy for them to defend themselves from the old Erinyes, who were the past, with all its darkness, but how can they defend themselves now from the new, brilliant, unpredictable Eumenides (episode 8)?

Withdrawing into the woods outside the city, Pylades is left alone with an old man and a boy, who fall asleep with the mountains and distant cities in their eyes. It is here in the city that the unity of the self is recomposed. The tragedy is about to end. There is something that Pylades does not understand, or does not yet understand. But he knows with certainty that reason was not his divinity. It was the divinity of Orestes. Pylades curses it, because it is only consolatory, a deception. Is his love for Electra all that is left to him?

But Pylades is lucid. He is capable of looking deep within himself. And he sees that when he heeded reason, the force that moved him was the same for him, too: to seize power. This is destiny. This is the worst of sins. Destiny and guilt. The story is not resolved. It remains suspended in 'a pure and simple uncertainty'. The work ends with a curse on reason and all its gods (episode 9).

In the dramatic mechanism of this emblematic work we can observe the process of opening up the text to the symbolic, which certainly in Pasolini falls well short of the metaphysical leap which the symbol, philosophically defined, can attain; but it is also true that it probes in depth and embodies the anthropological reflection that is celebrated in the agora of the theatrical gathering. Here I will seek to retrace the planes of this anthropological probing, the point of view from which Pasolini meditates on tragedy. I have identified at least four such planes.

Firstly *the plane of philosophical anthropology*, here identified with the relationship to the tragic: a fundamental structure of consciousness. The belief that tragedy is dead in contemporary dramaturgy is commonplace, as we have seen, after Steiner's celebrated study.[11] And it is true. It is repeated several times in this book, if we adhere to the formal model of a genre, but far from true if we begin with the distinction between tragic consciousness and the form of tragedy, and if in the analysis of dramatic and stage texts we place ourselves in the perspective of historical and philosophical anthropology and focus on the metamorphosis of forms. Pasolini himself stated that *Pylades* is a tragedy, placing the work in continuity with the *Oresteia*, and so naming it in the text.[12] But there is an anomaly compared to the tradition of the model. 'I should ask myself why, / if it was a tragedy / it does not close with new blood', Pylades reflects, ultimately unable to understand the suspended conclusion of his story.[13]

Of the structural elements of the tragedy, identified by Aristotle, there is the 'reversal' (for example of the Erinyes into the Eumenides, and vice versa, of one revolution into the other, in the lot of Pylades) and there is an irreducible conflict (between Athena and the other goddesses, between Orestes and Pylades, between the Furies and the Eumenides). But there does not appear to be evidence of an inevitable catastrophe. In reality this is manifested in a more subtle and dangerous way. It acts with more sophisticated weapons than the sword and is far more destructive, leading Pylades to the defeat of absolute solitude, as he retreats cursing and unheard. Pylades now 'sees' clearly, like the ancient hero, but unlike the ancient hero clarity stems from the exercise of his intelligence, which encompasses reason, but is not exhausted in it and is superior to it.

Apart from pointing out these analogies, the crucial question is: what is the necessary or even fatal limit with which the character Pylades comes into conflict and which is the driving force of the catastrophe? What is that connotation that structures the human but is manifested epochally, namely the connotation that combines philosophical anthropology and historical anthropology? It is a power which acts from within man, hypostatizing itself as a god and pouring itself onto the world, conforming the world to itself, in the objectivity of institutions and achievements. This power is reason, the discursive faculty, the practical, abstract guide, devoid of feeling, which has long since been separated from the wisdom of the logos, from the profound depth of true intelligence, which respects mystery, complexity and diversity. It has become cynical standardizing efficiency, insensibility and indifference. It is a faculty which, when raised to an absolute, has anaesthetized, frozen and distanced vigorous human richness in irony; it has diminished the logos, which in Greek tragedy was the elevated language of metaphor, of poetry, interwoven with music and dance in the recurrence of the Dionysian festival, when the city smelt the stench of the chthonic powers and the Dionysian seethed beneath the harmony of Apollonian forms.

Pasolini developed this notion of reason by his lucid, tenacious, prophetic observation of the contemporary anthropological and social reality and through philosophical culture and the abiding debate over reason, as well as through the debate in the sixties over the neo-Enlightenment positions encouraged by interest in the Frankfurt School. Defined in this way, reason is identified with the desire for power, exploitation and domination. It instrumentalizes value discourse while manipulating and disguising reality with reassuring and falsely comforting words. Its rational condescension conceals a harsh arrogance.

This is the new face of the goddess Athena, who assumes the features of an ancient destiny and acts like Ate, blinding humanity. It is an irresistible force which even threatens to subjugate Pylades, an unflagging drive that takes on different faces or different nuances and appearances in different periods and cultures. In this and other works, Pasolini was the prophet of this face underlying the present and destined to dominate in the immediate future. As I have said, this force also acts in the best of men: even Pylades recognizes the germ of it in himself. It paves the way for the catastrophe: the total solitude of Pylades, the apartheid to which he is subjected, the ruin of the fine promises of his youth in the 'humorous' image of the dismembered limbs of the young man, among which floats his prematurely castrated member, 'still immature but already strong', the 'timid and mature manhood' of that beautiful youth who attracted the poet so profoundly.

The metaphor is extended to represent the downfall of a culture and an idea of life. As Pasolini foresees, in a veritable prophecy, there is the prospect of absolute uniformity, which in man becomes conformity, massification and standardization, while in the relationship with nature it becomes, as we now know, suppression of biodiversity, of the life of the land and the variety of its seeds, the diversity and harmony of its species. The vestiges of this richness, created and accumulated through millennia, are evident in natural forms, as in those human faces which so fascinated Pasolini, because they were evocative of antiquity and innocence. The arrogance of reason, its presumption of being able to deal with everything, extends over all things with its stolidly ironic and consolatory smile, its claim to be capable of explaining and violating everything.

The characters are significant on all the above planes. Firstly there is Athena. She is assimilated to reason, a faculty born of modern humans, as Athena was born already fully formed. She does not lose her way in the darkness of the centuries. The places in which she manifests herself are the public relations between people who produce, trade, learn, compete and communicate. She knows nothing of the travail of birth in the flesh, nor of the flesh that grows and takes form from nothing and to nothing returns. She did not have a 'mother crazy or too humble', being 'a slave to the father, bloody tiger or obedient cow' (episode 1). 'She has no memories: / she only knows reality. / What she knows / the world is' (episode 1).[14] She has no links with the past, which weighs like a harsh legacy, like a nightmare. With light and ironic condescension she admits only the dreams by which she allows herself to be instrumentally assisted and supported: this is the meaning of the allegory of the Eumenides. The character, drawn from myth, becomes an allegory of a human faculty which gradually diverges from the 'logos' and is transformed into a cold operator who abstracts and flattens reality to the point of cynicism and domination.

ORESTES.
    A God enlightened me. […]
    She is called Athena. […]
    She is the last of the Gods. She was not born
    in ancient times, the story of her birth
    is not lost in the long night of centuries.
    She has come among us today, into the light.
    As if we conceived her ourselves…
    Her time is neither dawn nor dusk:
    but the heart of day, and her cult
    requires no sanctuaries, hidden in the fields, at the outskirts of the city:
    Instead her sacred places are the markets, the city centres,
    the banks, the schools, the stadiums, the city gates,
    the factories. The youth know her better than us.
    It's in the crowd and in the light that she shows herself. […]
    She's never known the waiting inside the viscera, […]
    She knows nothing of the calvary
    of a flesh that grows
    from nothing and takes the form
    of that which it must resemble: she never had
    a crazy mother, nor a humble one,
    a mother slave to the father, nor bloodthirsty tigress,
    nor obedient cow.
    She only had a father. […]
    She has no memories:
    she knows only what is *real*.[15]

She fosters and makes use of light, the superficial dreams of the Eumenides, into which she has transformed the Erinyes, the deep fears of mankind (those that speak of the mystery hidden in humanity, making it unknown to itself), a 'happy [...] madness' in which reason becomes a 'light dance'.[16] Then there is Orestes, the man who becomes an instrument of that reason from fideistic and opportunistic good faith.

Contrasting with these two figures are Electra and the Erinyes, who represent irrationality, fear, nightmare, conservatism at all costs, a morbid attachment to the past. In political terms they are meant as an allegory of absolutisms and fascisms, of counterrevolutions. The allegory is extended to indicate a form of government guided by this kind of reason: a moderate 'liberal democracy', then a capitalist democracy, with the lobbying power of businesses and technologies that pursue consumer uniformity. And here we are on another plane, that of historical anthropology: that human structure, reason absolutized, which pervades and accelerates a political and anthropological transition.

Pasolini alludes here to one strand in his work as writer, artist and polemicist, the revolution of the sixties. The transition is made from a peasant civilization to an industrial and urban civilization, the adoption of the American model, modernization of technology, capitalist levels of consumption, the free market. Civil society and party politics are pushed toward interclassism. The economic miracle of the late fifties and early sixties determines the rural exodus and the transformation of one Italy into another, affecting every aspect of life and culture through the model of consumer capitalism, which takes its driving force from America. It is also a generational shift, with the pressure of the baby-boom generation and a transition towards implacable secularization.[17]

The formation of a centre-left government in Italy, after an interval of 15 years, brought the Left back to power, based on a moderate reformist platform,[18] tamed by the criteria of rationality, efficiency and convergence, of which Pasolini presents an ironical image in the new army that peacefully invades the city:

MESSENGER.
>It was an army, carrying olive branches instead of weapons [...].
>Grace and authority walked together.
>It was Athena, that came out ahead, and behind her,
>carrying flowers from the fields, the Eumenides.
>Towards this triumphal invasion,
>the people, as always, were doubtful,
>drunk on life.
>But first the men of science, the inventors,
>the ones that create the means of work,
>those that transform daily life,
>improving day after day man in his nature;
>next, the men that express the life of others,
>in verse, in painting, in music;
>finally, guided by Orestes, those that, elected by the people,
>govern the city

> – came and united themselves in this procession. [...]
> ... a new life began. [...]
> the city grew
> more than it had ever grown in all the centuries
> of its existence. The work bore immediate fruit.
> Palaces, factories and bridges suddenly whitened,
> made of a new material, never seen before. [...]
> It appeared as though, more than a new idea of man,
> a new idea of *life*
> had entered into people's minds. [...]
> Athena had created a new city.[19]

In the new city there occurs something that, with a poetic-literary metaphor drawn from observation but also from the great literary influence of Dante,[20] Pasolini described 10 years later as the 'disappearance of the fireflies'.[21] The still vague feeling that disturbs Pylades (a character with autobiographical connotations), which paralyses him and eventually leaves him isolated, is then clarified: the cultural transition concealed a historical regression, a 'genocide'. 'So I saw "with my own senses" the compulsive power of consumerism to recreate and warp the consciousness of the Italian people, leading to an irreversible degradation.'[22]

It is a new revolution, a new fascism far worse than the historical one, Pasolini says, because whereas the earlier totalitarianism was unable to penetrate minds, this is pervasive – an anthropological disaster. Doesn't the tragedy of the apartheid of Pylades acquire an even more dramatic relevance for us now in this millennium and in our current crisis?

Pylades is an allegory of the man in crisis, of the intellectual who lives and suffers from the contradiction between the class to which he belongs, the high culture which he has absorbed, and the class of the dispossessed, the poor, which is not his but whose cause and archaic culture he embraces – their simple and innocent ideas, unrestrained and unveiled by the encrustations of secular discourse. Pylades is different. He is the unheard voice, put on trial and silenced.

Christian overtones, a secular Christianity, comprised wholly within human limits, are always present in Pasolini. It is the allegory of idealism that accepts no compromises, the projection of a gaze that rests lovingly on those people, on those young people whose tragic mutation in death it follows. The boy torn to pieces floating in the 'seething pot, [...] in an expanse of snow, between small blockhouses',[23] is the epilogue, narrated by Athena with macabre humour, to a theme that Pasolini had begun to explore a few years earlier, depicted in poems of love and truth. It appears in the faces and bodies of Riccetto and the other *Ragazzi di vita*, and the child who dies in the Tiber under the eyes of his helpless brothers. It appears again in the streetwise and already cynical boy Tommaso and his friends in *Una vita violenta*, in *Accattone*, and in Ettore, the son of *Mamma Roma*, all sacrificed by the 'dry godmother' death, which comes to them all with the increasingly explicit sign of Christ's Passion.

The Passion is present, through Bach, in the soundtrack and the final shot of *Accattone*, in a pose that has prompted some viewers to think of Mantegna, or the young man who dies on the cross at the end of *Mamma Roma*, the 'biel zuvinin' ('handsome youngster') from 'i dis robàs' (stolen days) in Pasolini's collection of poems *La meglio gioventù*.

ATHENA.

> In the murky water, between the clouds of smoke,
> I see the shape of a body: it is not an animal,
> a tiny sheep or a piglet; no, it is a little boy,
> it is a son, naked; his limbs
> have been amputated, and they float,
> restlessly, all mixed up together in the water.
> Now a foot emerges, the same foot that leapt joyfully –
> in the fields around his small city
> of mountain or plain – together with his school friends;
> now a tuft of hair surfaces, brown or blonde,
> I don't know, the colour is lost in the void; his tiny penis
> now surfaces, still unripe, but already strong
> – that is to say, it is his wretched mystery, the assurance
> of his timid and mature virility,
> so far from the tomb![24]

The political aspect of its significance lies in the socialist and partisan revolution, as Pasolini himself stated, representing total democracy in its radical formulation. In short, the allegorical meanings of the characters are thus distributed across the plane of psychological types, political choices, philosophical and anthropological categories and ideas, while the tragic nucleus identified above traverses all these planes. While the context that fostered the work of other authors of tragedy in the twentieth century was often their philosophical understanding and historical experience of the traumatic first half of the century, the context of Pasolini's thought is rather his political experience of the years of the 'strategy of tension' and the sociological and anthropological knowledge that was beginning to develop and provide the interpretive categories of the sixties. In the form of his representation of the tragic consciousness, with which we are here concerned, there is no catharsis, neither inner for the character nor outer for the audience, of which the chorus is the representative on stage. There is no equivalent in *Pylades* for the tranquillity and the intellectual and ethical accomplishment peculiar to the tradition of tragedy, which ratifies, through the sacrifice and sanction of the hero, a reconciliation of the conflict, the redressing of the balance and the restoration of order with an increase in collective experience, of the kind we find in the *Oresteia*.

In *Pylades*, the reign of uniform affluence and cynical and indifferent reason, which is established in the city and spreads false happiness, means an impoverishment of awareness and culture. The promise of youth, the memory of old age and the ideal and active energy of the intellectual are expelled from the city, embodied in the three characters who meet in the woods in the final episode, before Athena's mocking appearance. The craving for power that Pylades even finds in himself, concealed beneath a reason that becomes an alibi, would seem to be that fundamental structure that takes on the character of necessity, almost of inevitability or destiny. The standpoint of philosophical anthropology and historical-cultural anthropology enables Pasolini to grasp it in both its fundamental dimension as an inescapable drive and in the historical variations that appear in modernity as the distorted or even perverted absolutization of the rational. So too do the actors and the audience who participate, in the circle of the stage, in the cultural ritual. And the cultural ritual is not an anaesthetic, a cathartic restoration, but a vigilant and challenging experience pressing for change.

The Return of the Same, or Destiny and the March of History

To better understand Pasolini's reflection on the tragic embodied in this tragedy it is advisable to explore his films, particularly the works most closely linked to it: *Oedipus Rex* and *Notes for an African Oresteia*. These works extend and clarify the notion of destiny, but also partly resolve the impasse, the suspension on which *Pylades* closes.

Summing up, we can say that, assisted by ancient models and anthropological categories, Pasolini intuited that human existence has a structurally ineluctable limit: the condition of sorrow and death, but also an uncontrollable hubris that results in the desire for power. They emerge with different connotations and different co-responsibilities in the historical vicissitudes of humanity. Humans in history, while recognizing the inevitability of these background conditions, can plan resistance and progress. In short, in the inescapable horizon of the tragic there is space for the historical project responsibly embraced by humanity.

Oedipus Rex, a film chronologically close to Pasolini's theatrical period, is a meditation on destiny. The interest underlying the inspiration for the film and the rewriting of the myth through Pasolini's reading of Sophocles was not so much psychoanalytic (a concern with the themes of incest and patricide) or sociopolitical (the theme of revenge wreaked on the arrogance of power). Rather it was a philosophical and anthropological interest which sought to express the tragic sense. Pasolini himself explicitly said as much in the essay accompanying the screenplay.[25] The term 'tragedy' occurs repeatedly in the screenplay itself.[26] Grief and tears soon trouble the happiness of the brash young Oedipus, who has grown up in the court of Polybus and Merope. They undermine his confidence in his strength and superiority.

The film adheres to the themes of pity and terror. Inescapable fate manifests itself implacably. Even where a man's will or chance seem to be at work (the coin tossed at the fork in the road and chance revealing the milestone indicating Thebes), destiny is actually at work. Sounds and images evocative of weeping and death pervade the film; silences accompany long sequences, and though it is true that both are motivated 'realistically' by the situations or settings and times, one is immediately aware of a further significance: openness to the impending mystery, a truth that is emerging. It is the idea of the tragic as inescapable fate, very close to the ancient conception but without the assumption of a cosmos ordered by *dike*.[27] It is better to remain in ignorance of it all, says Jocasta. How terrible it is to know, Tiresias says; but a fury to know the truth takes possession of Oedipus, of mankind. It is true that scholarly adherence to the ideological framework of antiquity supports this interpretation, but the transposition of the core of the Oedipus story to different periods shows that Pasolini focuses on and tends to embrace this idea of the tragic as if it were still valid in modern times, in spite of assumptions about freedom and the modification of things stemming from Christian, Enlightenment and neo-Enlightenment culture.

The screenplay is divided into 48 sequences, including 6 set in the Italian town of Sacile in the thirties, 39 in ancient Greece, 1 in the piazza of a bourgeois city (Bologna), traversed by twenty freedmen, 1 in a modern industrial suburb, and the last in contemporary Sacile again. What unites them is Oedipus, passing through epochs and cultures; the link between them is the sound of the flute, the melody always obsessively the same, indicating the presence of the blind seer: at first it is Tiresias, then Oedipus himself is blinded, so as not to see, or see more deeply into the profound mystery of life in the abyss governed by fate. The links are the analogical images of transition from one age to another: the shot of the legs of the modern child grasped angrily by his father, a lieutenant of Sacile in the thirties, and the shot of the swollen, pierced feet of the infant Oedipus abandoned on Mount Cithaeron; the close-up of the gaze of the father, a lieutenant in the army of petit-bourgeois Italy, troubled by dark fear at the birth of the one who will steal his wife's love and life, and the fearful, threatening gaze of King Laius, who meets the young wanderer ready to contend the road with him and kill him; the figure of Angelo ('angel'), the messenger, the youth who accompanies Oedipus through the ages. There is no development, no progress, no advancement of knowledge which alters the radical human condition. Each phase repeats the same motif: 'The mysterious music of childhood – the prophetic love song – which is before and after destiny – the source of all things.'[28] Each phase returns to birth, from which everything begins on a journey that is actually 'a repetition, a return – an original stillness in the vain movement of time'.[29] There is a static, unmoving idea, or at least a cyclical time, fatalistic and ancient, behind this perception. Each age and culture analogically repeats the same story, a story that demands and deludes itself that it will achieve understanding:[30]

OEDIPUS. I want to know finally who I am! [...] I have to see clearly.[31]
OEDIPUS. Now everything is clear.[32]

But what is clarified is that everything is willed by fate and man sinks into the darkness of his visionary blindness, seeing the arrogance of his reason and his power crushed.

What distinguishes the story as told by Pasolini from Sophocles' *Oedipus* is not so much the prior events, which are recounted chronologically in the film, while in the Greek tragedy they emerge as a result of the investigation, nor is it the obvious transcoding from a purposeful verbal language, geared to simple staging and governed by precise conventions, to the visually rich and free language of film. It is the concentration of the struggle between two people, the man with himself, who in turn gazes at the only struggle that counts, between man with destiny, blind and ineluctable. This interpretation overshadows the dimension of the historical-political background of Sophocles' story of the city and the function of royalty in a dialectical relationship with the chorus-people. The film emphasizes the relationship with the mother, maternal love which becomes married love and again maternal in a tangled web associated with the origin, and a symbiosis that alludes to the close bond uniting all beings (each is father and brother of his children) in a common matrix and destiny. The times of the narrative are multiplied: from the less recent present to the archaic past, not in order to affirm a progression but the eternal recurrence of the same.

'Life ends where it begins': these words – which close the film on the images of the farmhouse to which the blind man, guided by Angelo, returns – contain the epitome of this vision. At its root certainly lies Pasolini's experience of a rural childhood in Friuli as expressed in his poetry, centred on the iterated theme of the immobility of time and the repetitiveness of peasant life. But it also stems, on the level of cultural achievements, from his scholarly knowledge of the Greek world through its literature[33] and his knowledge of anthropology – especially the structuralist approach, with its assumption, when confronted with the question 'What is man?', that all human phenomena, in their apparent diversity, can be reduced to a small number of intelligible principles or structures. Herein lies Pasolini's contradiction and his disquieting relationship with the tragic: his extraordinary civic passion, his rootedness in history and yet the irresistible fascination he feels for myth and what lies before and beyond history. Certainly some discomfort persists in him at the contradiction that we have already seen in the analysis of *Pylades*, and which determines his tendency to become paralysed and isolated in the awareness of the inability of the character, the author's alter ego, to change reality.

Humanity can do something. Confidence reappears in Pasolini's *Notes for an African Oresteia*, having gained in shrewdness from so much experience. *Pylades* ends with a suspension: the character retreats, withdraws into solitude accompanied by the youth and the old man, who fall asleep while his profound crisis is consummated. One is reminded of Jesus in the Garden of Gethsemane, in the consummation of his agony, when the disciples failed to watch with him. The transition from one world to another takes place in an aberrant fashion. The Furies have not really been converted into a fruitful and positive force; reason has shown its worst face. Modern Western culture has failed to adequately seize the promise of the ancient world. But the suspension did not satisfy Pasolini. His reflection on the tragic, the ancient (with its phase of greatest interest in Greek culture), on the journey through history, continued to stir his interest and he returned to it in this extraordinary film. The form is that of a film to be made, a work in progress, consistent with the idea of a process of transformation which occurs slowly, even in the permanence of an unchanging underlying structure, the tragic fact. It was filmed largely in Africa, in Tanzania, including Dar-es-Salaam and by Lake Tanganyika, in Uganda and partly in Italy, at the University in Rome, the setting for an interview with a group of African students. One scene is set in a recording studio with the group of the saxophonist Gato Barbieri, who accompanies two singers, Yvonne Murray and Archie Savage, as interpreters of the Cassandra episode in a free jazz piece. The core of the *Oresteia* of Aeschylus was the representation of the transition from an archaic tribal structure, dominated by the irrational, into a more modern, civic structure dominated by the equilibrium of reason through the aid of a goddess. This is exerted not from above but with the active engagement of other men, in which the Erinyes, the terrifying and irrational goddesses of remorse, are transformed into the beneficent goddesses of permanent tradition, sentiment and fertile imagination. Where can we look for a re-enactment of this process, given the betrayals of the West, if not in Africa, recently redeemed to freedom and moving towards democracy?

As Enrico Medda shrewdly observes,

> To Pasolini's eyes, Africa in the sixties appeared a privileged place, where the transition was taking place between a 'medieval' historical period and a 'democratic' period, a change that European cultures have already experienced, with the result that the contact with the ancient roots is being irretrievably lost. In Africa that transition is the theme of history today and the archaic magical-ritual culture is still present alongside modern rational culture, although in rapid decline. Hence it is only there that can one still pursue the dream of a vital synthesis between two civilizations, and rediscover an opportunity now irretrievably lost to Europeans.[34]

There it is possible to contain and control the irrational, integrating it with reason and, after discarding its destructive character, making it an 'active energy, a productive and fertile passion'.[35] This was Pasolini's inspiration.

Pasolini chose Tanzania probably because it is inhabited by the Wagogo and Masai ethnic groups, in which he glimpsed the roots of ancient tradition. Another reason was that the country was experimenting in those years with a nondoctrinaire, autochthonous socialism guided by Julius Nyerere, centred on the peasant world, valued in the community and defended from exploitation by the city. The policy of 'villagization' was opposed to the Western model of individualism and capitalism, and drew on the example and friendship of China.[36]

The theme of analogy returns to emphasize the eternal return of the same and the similarity of circumstances and paths in the slow flow of time in human history. The situations narrated by the *Oresteia* are transplanted to Africa in the sixties. Pasolini went to Tanzania and Uganda, to the shores of Lake Victoria and Lake Tanganyika, in search of suitable faces which the camera captures and surprises: Agamemnon, a regal old man or a Masai; Pylades, a young man with a thoughtful and intense expression; Clytemnestra, a rigid, strong young woman wearing a sinister black veil; Electra, a harsh, proud young girl, hardened by hatred, difficult to find among the cheerful young African women; Orestes, a young man who gazes into the distance. Then there is the chorus, representing the people: children roaming through the marketplace in a village under the harsh sun, young people, elegant or somewhat delinquent, girls at the factory gates, students. 'They say', relates Pasolini's voiceover, 'that precisely because they are so realistic, so real, they have within them the sacred and mythical moment that makes them say, for example, sentences like this: "God, if this is the Your name / if with this name you want me to invoke you, / I have weighed everything: / I know that only you / can truly melt / this nightmare that weighs on my heart."' Pasolini went to Africa (though he also went elsewhere: one sequence is filmed in Europe) to seek situations that could resemble that ancient story: the flashback about the war in Biafra (using terrible stock footage) evoking the Trojan War, the words of Cassandra, translated into English and sung by a singer accompanied by an African-American jazz musician (as in a 'tragic musical' says Pasolini in the voiceover, with that 'mystic, tragic quality typical of negro song'), evoking Cassandra's vision. The funeral rite on the grave of a family member near a hut evokes the encounter of brother and sister at Agamemnon's tomb. A judicial execution recalls the murder of Agamemnon, while the modern African city of Kampala evokes the developed world of Athens compared with the archaic world of Argos, while the courthouse in Dar-er-Salaam celebrates the advent of justice and democracy.

The ancient world of the Erinyes, the goddesses of atavistic, ancestral terror, is presented by means of a nonanthropomorphic figuration. It appears in the nonhuman aspects of the landscape with its loneliness, its monstrous forms, its profound and fearful silences, and the animals, such as the wounded lioness and the voices of the birds in the savannah. They are the goddesses of the animal age of mankind. This world appears in tattoos and in the hairstyles of the figures in the surviving tribal dance. The new world of the Eumenides, who coexist with and balance 'the gift of reason',[37] is present in the wedding party, the singing and the dancing women who are the custodians of the ancient yet domesticated spirit.

What is Pasolini trying to tell us here in relation to the suspension on which *Pylades* closed? The tragic remains the tragic. 'Nothing', says the poet's voiceover, 'is further away than these images from the idea that we commonly have of Greek classicism. Yet sorrow, death, mourning and tragedy are eternal and absolute elements that can easily link these intense contemporary images with the fantastic images of ancient Greek tragedy.' But in this ineluctable background is embedded the slow time of the life of humanity: people express their eagerness for the future and this eagerness is also a great 'patience'.[38] This is the film's last word. There is an inescapable resonance according to Aeschylus with *pati* (suffering) and with *pathei mathos* (learning from suffering). The tragic, according to the poet, does not erode or mortify history, but remains its underlying structure. Reason, interwoven with emotions, dreams and imagination, can foster the growth of a bright and harmonious humanity. *Pylades* ended with a curse against reason which had degenerated into cynicism, indifference and calculation.

After *Pylades*, *Notes for an African Oresteia* also remains suspended, but with greater confidence: Pasolini believed that he had found in a faraway culture and in the cinema anthropological redemption and an expressive form that could not come to him from preindustrial Western culture and the form of the theatre. The journey was and still is long and difficult, but Pasolini's gaze (obscured by his early death), as it dwells on the tangle of tragedy, history and anthropology, is an extremely lucid contribution to the issue that we are exploring in this book.

Chapter 8

THE APOCALYPSE OF A CIVILIZATION: FROM *AKROPOLIS* TO *APOCALYPSIS CUM FIGURIS* BY JERZY GROTOWSKI

A radical transformation in the theatrical representation of the tragic occurred in the late twentieth century, beginning in the sixties and growing out of the performance scene and avant-garde experiments. It launched a new course of the "living art" that characterized the last decades of the century and pioneered performative theatre, the modern version of the *ars una* by which the current emergence of the tragic consciousness will have to be explored.

Jerzy Grotowski, whose work I now intend to explore, was the great teacher and founder of the Teatr Laboratorium. Grotowski presented to the audience's vigilant consciousness the great myths that have fostered and formed Western man. They are traversed by a lucid and pitiless gaze which oscillates between apotheosis and derision, the only mode of confrontation, he declares, possible today.[1] Among these myths we can count tragedy as a genre that traditionally represents values such as heroism, the exaltation of sacrifice, the punishment of guilt and the acquisition of a knowledge which is fruitful for the community. But viewed through the lens of the century and its aberrations, these values seem to have been shattered.

While tragedy stands out against the backdrop of centuries of sacred history, in the two performances that I have chosen to analyse here (*Akropolis* and *Apocalypsis cum figuris*) we will see history and the sacred evoked through the characters of the classical muse, Clio, and the Saviour Christ, but inverted and overwhelmed. The tragic endures and manifests itself in all its naked clarity. There is a 'necessity' (the word recurs, as we shall see, explicitly in *Akropolis*) which dominates humanity. But in these works humanity is represented as following a dangerous course that leads past a point of no return, having ravaged an entire civilization and centuries of human construction.

As Ludwik Flaszen writes, Grotowski, in drawing inspiration from Wyspiański, seeks 'to represent the sum total of a civilization and test its values against the touchstone of contemporary experience', that of the later twentieth century, by raising the fundamental question: 'What happens to human nature when it faces total violence?'[2]

An Introductory Summary

Akropolis was inspired by the play of the same name by Stanisław Wyspiański, an exponent of Polish Romanticism. Jerzy Grotowski adapted it with the literary consultancy of

Ludwik Flaszen. It was the first of Grotowski's historic productions, in collaboration with József Szajna, who designed the costumes and props from his direct experience of concentration camps and was rightly acknowledged as co-creator. The sets were designed by Jerzy Gurawski.

The work had its official premiere on 20 October 1962. It also had a number of variants: two in 1962, three in 1964, 1965 and 1967. The first two were staged in Opole, at the Theatre of 13 Rows, as was the third, with Eugenio Barba and Ryszard Cieślak assisting in the direction. The fourth was staged after the group had moved to the bigger and more important university city of Wrocław, and the fifth when Grotowski's Laboratorium had altered its status and renamed itself the Institute for Research into Acting Method.[3] Further performances were presented in various European countries, Mexico and the United States.

I shall try to summarize, as far as possible, the play's development. For ease of exposition alone, I propose to subdivide it into sequences, though this may diminish the continuity and the hectic rhythm of the work's montage.[4] It lasts less than an hour and it is undoubtedly difficult to understand because of its density of significance and concentration of signs.

The stage space is a large room with chairs scattered about and flat steps set on several levels, with a large central box/trapdoor. The actors carry poor and shabby objects, which look as if they come from a junk shop: stovepipes, a wheelbarrow, a bathtub, nails, hammers. The actors and the audience, numbering no more than a few dozen, share the same space, in a relationship of closeness–estrangement. The actors perform in their midst. The audience is seated in front, behind and beside them.

Enter the Singer, who acts as coryphaeus and prologue. He carries a dummy made of old stockings stuffed with rags. He announces he will declaim the scenes of *Akropolis*, probably an allusion to the play by Wyspiański. The actors enter carrying their belongings, and mime the actions of a number of episodes (the angels on the sarcophagus of St Stanisław in Wawel Cathedral that come alive on Easter night, the love of Paris and Helen, Jacob's dream). The actions evoke an image of humanity's development, a life of war and herding in which the power of song is dominant. The actors wear sacking with two holes for the arms, caps and heavy shoes. The voices of the coryphaeus and the chorus of actors utter and iterate certain key lines: 'the cemetery of the tribes', 'our Acropolis', 'they have are gone up in spirals of smoke', scornfully emphasized and with Jewish intonations. The dummy, standing for the risen Christ, is thrown to the ground. The actor (Molik) takes a violin and strikes up 'Tango Milonga', the leitmotif of the play. The popular pre–World War II tune, written by two Polish Jews, Jerzy Petersburski and Andrzej Własta, appears to have been performed in some extermination camps. Here it is a signal, because the characters break off what they are doing and, stamping their clogs, hurry to continue the work of building the installation. The banging of a hammer on metal is heard (prologue).

The two angels (Cieślak and Jahołkowski) who support the sarcophagus – bearing with immense effort the weight of humanity on the command of a god who 'has not spared us pain' and is described as 'creator and executioner' – are released for a single hour of life from their burden. But first they describe the black and livid face, running with blood, of the dead Christ, the bowed head with black curls crowned with thorns. They hang the rag dummy on a taut rope. 'He died and the blood runs down from his hands and feet and face.' In these words there returns the motif of 'the spirals of smoke' (sequence 1).

A woman (Mirecka) engages in dialogue with the angels, sliding a piece of white tulle curtain between her fingers. She dreams of love, a man who will come to her, a dress woven with lilies, a garland of flowers of the kind brides wear to secure their wedding veil: its removal symbolizes the passage from virginity to their married state. Yet it is not the bridal veil that will cover her, but the funeral veil. Through the text repeatedly echo the lines: 'Love, love, love', 'Do not cry, do not curse', 'Forget', 'Do not remember anything', 'Do not complain, do not weep'. The violin melody spreads and then falls silent. Work on the installation made of stovepipes resumes with the sound of hammer blows. Again the song 'Tango Milonga' is played (second sequence).

The melody ceases. The two actors playing the angels hold hands with a third who is playing a woman (Paluchiewicz). The body is stiff and they throw it back and forth like an upright board. They are waking it up, tormenting it: they speak of happiness, of dawn, splendour and even oblivion. Then they cease to throw the rigid body back and forth and hang it on the wire, bending its knees. Again the rhythmic blows of the hammer ring out and again we hear the tune of 'Tango Milonga' (sequence 3).

When the tune stops an actress (Ścierski) is kneeling as if in prayer in a sheet metal bathtub that serves as an altar niche. She is Clio, the muse of history. She is joined by a young woman (Mirecka). She persuades Clio not to bother with history, so as not to be so sad. 'What do you care about the dirt of others? What do you care about the tears of others? What do you care about a torment that is now done with?' While speaking of redemption, of a God who will come in the guise of a king to bring redemption, resurrection and reward or punishment by weighing the fate of each in his scales, the girl forces Clio to make love and then slams her head on the bottom of the tub (sequence 4).

The long and highly articulated central sequence begins with Jacob (Molik). It evokes the first deception of Isaac by Jacob to extort the blessing owed to Esau, betrayed at the instigation of Rebecca. There follows Jacob's dream: he sees the angel and receives the ambiguous promise for his future. Then there is his sojourn with Laban, his love for Rachel, his deception by the substitution of Leah for his betrothed, and finally the challenge of Jacob, who wrestles with the angel.

The biblical episodes and passages in Wyspiański's play are concentrated into a few powerful images of ambivalent significance. Esau (Cieślak) alludes to the departure for the hunt that should herald his blessing, with the palms of his hands quivering on the line like a bird in flight or a man traversed by an electric shock. At the prediction that one day he will cast off the yoke from his shoulders he swears he will kill his brother and at the same time overturns the tin wheelbarrow in which his dying father Isaac is laid. Jacob is pursued and surrounded by the chorus of actors, who represent the angel of the Lord, each of whom whispers a line. Jacob leads the procession in his marriage to Rachel (Paluchieiwicz), while the chorus sings the ancient melody of a Polish wedding song. But Rachel is here a stovepipe decorated with a piece of tulle; the movements of the procession are those of the prisoners parading; the bell of the exposition of the Blessed Sacrament during the ritual is the chinking of the nails that one member of the chorus holds in his hand. The struggle between Jacob and the angel is the effort of the actor (Molik) as he hoists the wheelbarrow with the angel onto his shoulders and then rhythmically bangs its head on the floor as it hangs out of the wheelbarrow.

Meanwhile, the words fall thudding like stones. Here are a few excerpts:

ISAAC. My son!
ESAU. Here I am, Father!
ISAAC. You will go forth and multiply. You will be raised up and you will become the lord of lords.
JACOB. The time begins of the sacred signs, the time of the covenant of heaven and earth. Open, O doors of Zion. The doors are thrown open. The messengers come from the throne of God. They stand on the threshold, dressed in dalmatics, waving flags. And they halt and descend to the gates dressed in long robes.
JACOB. I have long awaited a sign from God, I have found it in your calling. [...]
RACHEL. I wanted to say I love you.
RACHEL. And I followed the flocks, and I saw a spring of water, and in it I saw the beauty of my face and a man bent behind me and looked at me from the depths of the water, an apparition. He will be my husband.
JACOB. You told me you would give me a great good, and my race would multiply as the sands of the sea that no one can count. [...]
Let go, do not challenge me [...] I will not utter the words of salvation, you liar, you are accursed.
I will challenge God with my strength. [...]
When I open my wings to the living bone of your sides, then you will know, blind to reason, my strength, and you will strike your knees by falling onto the living stones. You will know wisdom, which is lord of all creatures. Stop, I shall crush you with the punishment! You will feel your hand wither! [...]
Do not play with man's faith, you know he lives in grief. [...]
I will break you. [...]
Blood flows in streams, have mercy on the servant of God [...]. Say the word. Who are you? [...] Necessity [...] Necessity.

The acting is at times mechanical; the words are chanted, then shouted and then sung in harsh passages with interruptions, alienating all emotional participation. The sequence is interrupted several times by the notes of 'Tango Milonga', which marks the frenzied resumption of the work (sequence 5).

The sentinel (Jahołkowski) strikes a signal on the tube and the actors change their appearance by putting their hands inside their costumes, leaving empty holes in the sleeves, in imitation of the armless Greek statues that have come down to us. This marks the transition to the sequence with the heroes of the *Iliad* set in Troy. Paris (Cinkutis) and Helen (Ścierski) extol insatiable love, beauty, youth. Their words are accompanied by bursts of raucous, mocking laughter from the other actors. Hector (Cieślak) extols love of country and his desire to fight. Priam (Molik) and Hecuba (Paluchiewicz) speak mechanically of the brief life now past. Hecuba asks Cassandra (Mirecka) to foretell her fate. Cassandra's chanting voice rises high: 'Mother, I have fire on my brow, I feel the power of Apollo. Ah, Apollo, a burning arrow, a dart embedded in my breast! The vultures will croak on the ruins of the palace. And there will no longer be for you either daylight or sun, or sunrise, or the glow of red dawn, or the golden sunbeam.' The vulture created by the ensemble of the voices of the actors ranged in a row accompany Cassandra's last words with its sinister 'kra-kra-kra' (sequence 6).

There follows the summons to life of the last character: the singer (Molik), who has entered between two rows of players standing to attention. He climbs onto their shoulders and sits above on the arms of two actors standing together to form a seat. He immediately reveals he is David. He raises his song: 'God of my father Abraham and God of my father Isaac, I am king and ruler of my people, and I was a simple shepherd.' He recalls the feat of his victory over Goliath, the revelation of God's love, then his hatred of Saul:

I trembled at the thought. Will I be saved before quenching the fire of hatred? You commanded me to wait. I was exposed to the ridicule of the pillory, in the midst of those who insulted me. I trembled at the thought. Will I be saved before quenching the fire of hatred? You commanded me to wait and persevere in strength, and I was bowed under a great burden in the struggle and torment of a long night, before the fire of dawn. You said you would come, that you would give salvation by the Word, you would descend on the ruins, you would bring grace to us slaves, and you would put an end to the shame.

The setting slips into the atmosphere of the synagogue with the intonation of the recitation, the melody sung and the final *rejwach*, the noise that accompanies the Hasidic ceremonies, heightening the tension of the assembly (sequence 7).

In the next short sequence Aurora (Paluchiewicz) informs the singer (Molik) that a large crowd is waiting for the sound of his harp. They are gathered on the banks of the Jordan. 'Oh, hasten Risen One! Oh, come quickly, saviour of the people! [...] Have pity on the suffering of the people.' Then a voice from the chorus (Cieślak) calls him (sequence 8).

The procession of the actors begins, under the guidance of the singer. He first sings words to the tune of a Polish lullaby and a Polish Easter hymn. The words sung by the singer and chorus evoke the resurrection: 'Apollo, come, Apollo arise, for the Lord's Resurrection! [...] And the song went over the people, over the land, over the blood-soaked Polish soil, over the Acropolis, where the kings and their laws sleep. [...] I will wake the centuries for a single night. I am in the presence of God. God the living Word descended on the tombs. I have glorified him with choirs.'

While singing the last verse all the actors disappear one at a time into the box/trapdoor in the middle of the stage. When the last actor has disappeared, the singing stops and the wooden box is closed. A moment of silence follows, then a voice from inside the box utters the final words, reiterating those at the beginning and certainly evocative of the opening of Ecclesiastes: 'They have gone in spirals of smoke' (epilogue).

The Language of Nightmare

The construction of the signs, the interweaving of the various visual and auditory codes, and their montage are not realistic. The work is not meant to be a record of the concentration and extermination camps.[5] It is analogous to the materialization of a dream, a nightmare of the kind that comes when one is sleeping lightly, close to waking, or when slumber is troubled by anxiety.[6] The mechanisms that govern the images and sounds are close, for example, to those described by Freud: obsessive repetition, unnatural movements with a sense of helplessness, and especially condensation and displacement.[7] It is also analogous to memories and fantasies in a psychologically disturbed state, or a grotesque tale that seeks to express and give utterance, in utter weariness, to what is unendurable. Primo Levi has described these dynamics superbly.[8] These mechanisms intersect onstage in *Akropolis*. Hence the technique is not realistic in the sense of adopting a documentary approach to reality, but true in the sense of penetrating into the depths of an experience and a work of the mind.

All through the performance there arise decipherable elements of life in a concentration camp as residues connected with the metaphorical work of associations in dreams, reveries and memories, and the elaboration of the story. I list a few, drawing on both the script notes and memorials of the camps. 'Tango Milonga', played repeatedly by the actors, evokes the love of concert music in Nazi Germany and the songs that accompanied the marching of the poor wasted bodies to and from work. The puppet Christ, hung like a rag on the line, evokes the prisoners who flung themselves onto the wires of the electric fence or were thrown there out of pity when they reached the end of their tether. The banging of the hammer on sheet metal is the noise of work, but also a signal agreed between the prisoners. The frequent interruptions of the performance and the rushing to the tool chest recalls the rush to work in the camp when the order was given, with the threat of violence. The stiff gait is a puppet-like reminiscence of the pathetic march of prisoners returning from forced labour with sore feet in mismatched, inadequate, broken shoes and the noise of their clogs on the arid ground or the snow (one of the most poignant memories of all the survivors). The man, stiff as a plank, pushed from one to another recalls how the inmates treated their companions who risked falling asleep at roll call. The prisoner with his bruised throat evokes the violence inflicted by the kapos on their fellow prisoners. The wheelbarrow on the shoulders of Jacob evokes many moments. At work, if the mud was deep, the barrow would be hoisted onto a prisoner's shoulders. It would also be used to carry the prisoners who died at work to the mass grave. The movements of the angel and the blow it receives evoke the last spasms of life of those borne on the prisoners' shoulders and the final *coup de grâce* that put an end to their suffering or saved the other prisoners from getting into trouble.

The elements of waking and real life, though reduced to the elementary and inhuman level of pure survival, drown in metaphor. Around the simple individual elements found in all the codes of stagecraft are crystallized a plurality of significances peculiar to the symbolic set and a polyvalence of functions characteristic of the techniques of 'poor theatre' or the 'theatre laboratory'.

For example the performance space is also the Polish Acropolis (the Wawel of Krakow comprising the cathedral and the sixteenth-century building with its altar and tapestries, the epitome of Polish identity and civilization); it is the literary setting of Wyspiański's play, the concentration camp and the human world adrift before the extreme.[9] The great box/trapdoor in the centre of the stage is a basic element of the set as well as a construction facility for the absurd program of work at the camp and the crematorium, into which a race, a culture, will disappear – 'the cemetery of the tribes'. The costumes suggest the labour uniform (but poetically rethought and differing from the familiar striped garments), effacing individual differences and identities, with the humiliation of the naked body glimpsed through holes in the sacking and in the patches (another realistic feature recorded by the memorialists). The obsessive repetition of the word 'hair, hair, hair' alludes to the nostalgia of erotic pleasure experienced in freedom and the searing humiliation of heads shaven to disfigure the prisoners and for the sake of 'hygiene' (the fear of contagion from typhus), as well as the disgust and horror at its recycling into products manufactured in the factories of the Reich. The wheelbarrow is an instrument of work, a coffin, the burden of the supernatural and of *ananke* (when it hosts the angel during the struggle with Jacob), and a throne. The stovepipe becomes a bride on her wedding day in her life outside the camp; it is an instrument of work in the camp and the chimney of the crematorium that awaits them all. The final procession is the essence of condensation. As Flaszen observes perceptively,

> The Saviour is a headless, bluish, badly mauled corpse, horribly reminiscent of a miserable skeleton in the concentration camp. The Singer lifts his hands in a lyrical gesture, like a priest raising the chalice. The crowd stares religiously and follows the leader in a procession. They begin to sing a Christmas hymn in honour of the Saviour. The singing becomes louder, turns into an ecstatic lament torn by screams and hysterical laughter [...]. Intermittently, the procession stops and the crowd is quiet. Suddenly, the silence is shattered by the devout litanies of the Singer, and the crowd answers. In a supreme ecstasy, the procession reaches the end of its peregrination. The Singer lets out a pious yell, opens a hole in the box, and crawls into it, dragging after him the Saviour's corpse. The inmates follow him one by one, singing fanatically.[10]

Past, present and future are fused: traditional devotional processions overlap with the files of inmates going to work or roll call, the ranks of the newcomers destined for the crematorium. The god of the covenant in Genesis and the son of the promise of salvation all disappear into the trapdoor and are puffed out as smoke.

The montage follows a sequence featuring pieces of text and images taken from Wyspiański's text, used as the basis for the action; but it is then freed from it by following the laws of association in dreams and reveries of the living theatre.[11] The scenes unfold, rhythmically punctuated by the musical summons to labour in the workshop.

In Wyspiański's four-act play the poet imagines that on the night of the resurrection, the night of miracles according to popular tradition, a miracle occurs in Wawel Cathedral. The angels who laboriously support the precious tomb of St Stanisław, martyr and patron saint of Poland, are freed for a short while from their burden and return to life. With them gradually come to life the figures depicted in the tapestries on the walls. They narrate the events of biblical history and Greek epic: Cupid, Clio, Hector and Andromache, Jacob, Esau and David. The point of view is patriotic, expressing the cultural identity of a country humiliated, subjugated and divided. The montage presents the landscape in a succession of shifting temporal and spatial planes which in its day made the work enigmatic and difficult to perform.

Of great interest is the vocal, musical and audio scoring of the performance. The language (as Ludwik Flaszen helps me to understand) is an artificial Polish, which mingles the archaic and popular, with various assonances that allude to the meeting in the extermination camp of many languages ('the Babel of languages') and many nationalities ('the Cemetery of Tribes'), in which the Yiddish accent is dominant. Each vocal utterance is technically studied to extraordinary effect, using different resonators, such as the throat, and changing the timbre (from harsh to soft), the volume (from shout to whisper), the tone (from low to high) and the rhythm (from normal to chanted). The music, made up of songs and the violin melody of the Singer (whose mouth is rounded like one of many angelic singers in Italian paintings), is all produced on stage, mingling the dance rhythms of tango (which some say they heard in the concentration camps) and folk tunes adapted liturgically, with the words of Wyspiański's drama modulating into a song of the synagogue, then into a Polish lullaby and finally an Easter hymn. Prominent among the noises are the rhythmic stomping of clogs and the rhythmic metallic chinking of nails on metal pipes.

Our Acropolis: A Colossal Tragic Farce

Akropolis, as mentioned above, is a great meditation on the tragic in the mode and form pertinent to the historical moment and the culture in which it was conceived. The traditional elements of tragedy resurface in painful fragments: prologue, choruses, episodes, reversal, catastrophe, hubris and 'necessity', yet the overall picture is completely different.

First of all, Grotowski seeks to arouse neither terror nor pity nor empathy nor projection in accordance with the classical dynamics. There is no catharsis, because there is no order that ensures the expiation of guilt and no prospect of salvation or redemption.

The work aims to elicit a lucid awareness: firstly, of the destructive threat of humanity itself, to which it is led by the lust for power and violence raised to the threshold between life and death, the human and the nonhuman, life and survival; secondly, of the ease with which even one's most recent wrongs can be covered by oblivion and indifference;[12] and thirdly, of the role that the intellectual and the artist (meaning the man of the new theatre or the 'saint' as Grotowski describes him in his theory of theatre, referring to the idea of sacrifice and authenticity on the part of the actors) can play in the awakening of the moral and civil awareness of the individual and society. Given this point of view, we can clearly understand some expressive devices adopted in *Akropolis*. The first is the position of the small audience, spread across the middle of the set, separate from but in close proximity to the actors, who move behind as well as in front of them, creating uneasiness, embarrassment, surprise, a sense of distance, provocation and estrangement. The audience is given the feeling they have been summoned as witnesses. The emotional release of applause at the end would be totally out of place. There would be no sense in it and it is never offered.

Secondly there is the distinctive character of the movements of the actors, which embody pantomime techniques. Grotowski explains very clearly the antisentimental function of this device, which is also consistent with the lack of feeling peculiar to dream scenes:

> At times in *Akropolis* we tried to recover a human expression that would not be sentimental in the tragic situation of prisoners in an extermination camp. Playing this on certain emotional notes would have lacked modesty and proportion. So how could we find a physical expression that would be cold enough as a base? We took some elements of pantomime and changed them. This pantomime did not remain a classic pantomime. We kept the cold elements of pantomime. They were repeatedly transformed inwardly and violated by the living impulses of the actors [...] After the application of different types of plastic exercises from well-known systems, by Delsarte, Dalcroze and others, step by step we began to consider these exercises which are termed plastic as a "conjunctio oppositorum" between structure and spontaneity.[13]

Thirdly, this effect is enhanced by the device of facial masks. Slowiak and Cuesta express the significance of this technique used in performances:

> During early rehearsals, Grotowski realized that some of the actors easily slipped into an emotional attitude when confronted with the concentration camp material. [...] Grotowski [...] began to ask the actors to recreate facial masks based on photographs of actual concentration camp inmates. Grotowski guided the actors to select and freeze sneers, scowls, frowns, and other expressions. He sought expressions that connected as well to each actor's own personality and typical reactions [...] The actor's face stayed frozen in this mask throughout the performance, providing a strong emotional impact which transcended the obvious artificiality of the effect. [...] But each mask also was unique to the individual actor and mysteriously revealed something essential about each of the actors [...].[14]

The film *Akropolis*, directed by James MacTaggart, records them in a number of effective close-ups that may certainly correspond to some of the views of the audience magnetized by those face masks. All the individuals, all reciprocal communications, all exchanges with the outside (except for the automatism of the few unvarying operations of the completely anonymous camp) are dissolved and the faces speak only of the residual effort to survive in a world without a future, with vague memories of a past of values drowned in the reality of the camp, which has murdered all morality.[15] Each prisoner is cocooned in a lonely struggle for survival; no one has time, no one is patient, no one listens. Relationships are neither benign nor courteous.[16] People are crowded up against one another, and each remains just a lump of exhausted energy to be defended as long as possible. Characters are abstracted, distant, stoically resigned or already on the verge of madness, with crooked smiles frozen on their faces. A very beautiful touch in this respect is the almost sculpted physiognomies of the characters as they move in procession towards the box/trapdoor into which they will disappear.

There are no heroes or saints. That world is not divided here conventionally into good and bad. Dehumanization affects everyone in this order of things, in what Primo Levi described as a grotesque, sarcastic, colossal foolery.

What facets of the expression of the human face could be expressed by this humanity, whose body is razed to its zero point? This is effectively expressed by Borowski, whose work, as we have seen, Grotowski studied deeply.[17] Hence we understand the frequent disconnection between words and gestures, and certain proxemic devices such as the fact that the actors often do not look at each other, even when engaged in a dialogue. We understand the coherence of the gestures of aggression that seal many sequences: Clio's head is slammed against the bottom of the metal trough after what seems like an orgasm of love and the words of the promise ('When God comes dressed like a king, / his robe will be of gold / and a banner will be in his hands'). Esau tips up the wheelbarrow and ejects the body of the actor who plays Isaac. He announces he will kill his brother. Jacob squeezes Laban's throat so that his legs bend convulsively and he is speechless, so closing their patriarchal relationship with brutality. Jacob strikes Rachel with the spindle, the angel strikes the wheelbarrow near Jacob's head with his clogs, and Jacob slams the angel's head dangling out of the wheelbarrow against the floor. The relations between the characters of the mythical and literary tale become the aggressive relationships between prisoners. 'The protagonists cannot escape from each other', notes Flaszen.[18]

Akropolis is not an easy work. This is due not only to the difficulty of Wyspiański's original text, but also the difficulty of making visible and audible the tragically dangerous condition of liminality: between life and death (one might even say of dying rather than of death), between the human and the nonhuman, where the limit is transgressed both downwards (into the utter helplessness of the subhuman) and upwards into the supposed omnipotence of the superman, between rationality and absurdity. The outcome is a catastrophic withdrawal, not of a man or a culture, but of the point reached in the construction of humanity and its foundations. *Akropolis*, namely the Acropolis set in a concentration camp, represents all this.

The classical, biblical, Christian and Enlightenment foundations of civilization are overwhelmed. The morality of the church fathers, the anthropological and moral foundations resting on the Christian principle of love, as expressed by St Paul, are annulled.[19] The idea of the covenant between man and God in a project of salvation, established in Genesis, Psalms and the Gospels, is cancelled. The classical ideal of beauty and harmony is forgotten. The principles of the new order that emerged from the French Revolution (liberty, equality, fraternity and the declaration of human rights) are effaced. The great value of reason fostered by Enlightenment thought degenerates into a resource used to build a perfect organizational and technological machine to serve a nefarious purpose.

Towards the Tragedy of Apotheosis and Derision: A Laboratory for 'Poor Theatre'

There is nothing hazy, mystical or psychopathic in Grotowski's theatre, as many misguided critics have sought to maintain. There is only an idea of art and a method of theatrical work made up of intellectual rigour, authenticity and truth. It rests on a powerful theatrical culture which stems from the teaching of Stanislawski, and an anthropological and psychological culture supported by the extraordinary strength of the ties within the group.[20] Grotowski's theory of the theatre and his method of work are entirely coherent and almost rendered necessary by the embodiment of the tragic awareness that I have sketched above. This was to be fulfilled and radicalized in the last production of the Teatr Laboratorium before the new paratheatrical approach adopted by the group in the late sixties: *Apocalypsis cum figuris*.

Here I will briefly sum up its principles, rereading the famous words of Grotowski's *Towards a Poor Theatre* (1968), whose publication marked a turning point in the theatrical culture of the West. The words of the performance do not grow out of the text and move towards the stage, but grow out of the stage and become the text. Even when an existing text is adopted, as in *Akropolis*, it is used only after being edited and reduced dramaturgically by Grotowski, as suspended matter, a kind of summary script – not fixed but furnishing a basis for the actors' improvisations:

> We know that the text per se is not theatre, that it becomes theatre only through the actors' use of it – that is to say, thanks to intonations, to the association of sounds, to the musicality of the language.[21]
>
> My encounter with the text resembles my encounter with the actor and his with me. For both producer and actor, the author's text is a sort of scalpel enabling us to open ourselves, to transcend ourselves, to find what is hidden within us and to make the act of encountering the others.[22]

The essential core of the theatre is the actor, whose expressive potential is directly proportional to the acceptance of the poverty of the theatre and the renunciation of buildings, sets, greasepaint and lights, the effects of the rich theatre.

> The acceptance of poverty in the theatre, stripped of all that is not essential to it, revealed to us not only the backbone of the medium, but also the deep riches which lie in the very nature of the art form. Why are we concerned with art? To cross our frontiers, exceed our limitations, fill our emptiness – fulfill ourselves. This is not a condition but a process in which what is dark in us slowly becomes transparent. In this struggle with one's own truth, this effort to peel off the life-mask, the theatre, with its full-fleshed perceptivity, has always seemed to me a place of provocation.[23]

The actors work hard through vocal and physical training to free themselves from the clichés of everyday life and the conventional training of the academy, so as to attain their whole expressive potential. The director works to help the actors make the most of their resources, and they work together to fulfil the process of self-penetration. 'Ours is not a deductive method of collecting skills. Here everything is concentrated on the "ripening" of the actor which is expressed by tension towards the extreme, by a complete stripping down, by the laying bare of one's own intimacy – all without the least trace of egotism or self-enjoyment.'[24]

There is a close struggle between the actor and the 'suspended matter' as the starting point. The descent from the present situation to the roots is profound and free, from the extreme of apotheosis to the extreme of derision, and so draws on the truth of the actor's being, and of being with connecting: 'The actor is reborn – not only as an actor but as a man – and with him, I am reborn. It is a clumsy way of expressing it, but what is achieved is a total acceptance of one human being by another.'[25]

The montage of the actions, determined by Grotowski, and the never definitive form of the performance attain its end when the actor, who has been defined as 'holy', engages in a 'gift of the self', in a 'total, absolute act',[26] and is ready for the other essential moment, so that there is theatre: the direct relation with the audience – an elite, not of money or social status, but special in its readiness for an intense, testimonial, transforming, experience of ritual (another term used by Grotowski with a precise anthropological understanding, and again often misunderstood by critics). All this was to be clarified in his subsequent production, but it is already foreshadowed in *Akropolis*.

This theatre is contemporary because 'it confronts our very roots with our current behaviour and stereotypes, and in this way shows us our "today" in perspective with "yesterday", and our "yesterday" with "today"'.[27] This enables us to understand that such a rigorous and lucid approach could hardly evade the question about humans' fundamental awareness of the tragic, which continually recurs, like the continual return of the clash between man and his project with the limit and the liminal. By this path tragedy entered the modern form of stage performance, with Grotowski as its pioneer and *Apocalypsis cum figuris* as a mature form that has been used around the world as a model of method and an example of the depth of significance that the theatre can achieve today.

Apocalypsis cum figuris is an emblematic work in the elevation of the idea it embodies and the strength of its cultural provocation, in the writing technique, not derived from a dramatic text, and in the expression of a method that has served as a model for drama in recent decades. I am referring particularly to the vast and widespread sphere of 'grassroots theatre' or the so-called 'third theatre' which proliferated in Europe and America in the 1970s, but also the extensive renewal of actor training and the modes of constructing the spectacle.

If we retrace the etymology of the ancient term (*apocalypsis*) which Grotowski inserted into the title of the Teatr Laboratorium's last stage production, we find a lucid key to the whole operation. *Apocalypse* alludes to a kind of writing typical of Jewish and early Christian literature in the first centuries after Christ (in particular the book composed by St John the Evangelist and forming part of the canon, the books which the church accepts as inspired by God), containing awesome and terrifying 'revelations'. The term comes from the Greek *apokalypto* (to discover, reveal, unveil). Taken metaphorically it has come to indicate 'ruinous catastrophe, the end of the world'.[28] With its twofold significance, the title guides the audience towards a possible twofold approach to the interpretation of the work, on the existential level and the metatheatrical level. The revelations which the work contains relate to man's existence and the plane of the conception of the theatre. The first of these themes is the revelation of the suffering of the one who seeks to save humanity, vilified and expelled from the human community, the tragedy of the authentic individual who is unable to make mankind accept sincerity and freedom. The second theme is the revelation of the need to refound the theatre and the inevitable failure of the inauthentic, but it is also the declaration of a Utopia which, in order to plumb the depths, cannot emerge from the institution while awaiting a 'Second Coming'. *Apocalypsis cum figuris*, with a bold and analogical evocation, is akin to the Revelation of St John, the vision of what could be in the future.

One of the great theatrical productions of the twentieth century, *Apocalypsis cum figuris*, was first presented at Wrocław in 1968 and then repeated periodically for about twelve years, even after the group had already abandoned the theatre in the strict sense. It was profoundly altered between 1971 and 1973 as part of an intense revision of post-theatrical forms carried out by the Grotowski group. It was taken around the world as an image and record of a creative effort, unique in the twentieth-century history of the form, and of an exemplary group which by that time had moved on to other things. The relationship of intimacy with the audience-participants in a rite was intensified, its visual sign made even starker. The light was dimmed and the contrast with the darkness accentuated.[29]

A new method of constructing the text

The text was built up for performance through discussions between the group of actors, led by Grotowski and with the support of the literary director Flaszen, who focused on a suspended subject: the image of the Simpleton and the Second Coming, taken from the ancient Slavic tradition. There are strong echoes of this theme in Russian literature, especially Dostoevsky, and Johannine theology. The theatre laboratory in Wrocław had already drawn on the Gospel of John and Dostoevsky.

The genesis of the production, which lasted nearly three years, was complex and indirect, and it is probably impossible for an outside observer to reconstruct the precise paths it followed, as Kumiega points out.[30] What is certain, however, is that this writing for the stage marks a radical development in the twentieth century and the future of the theatre in general. While in Grotowski's earlier productions a dramatic text had always been the source of a creative path (which, while unravelling freely, at least began with the distribution of roles to serve as starting points), this time there was no real textual foundation for the performance.[31] Outstanding skill in improvisation developed during long hours of training was therefore the basis of the creative work.[32] Bodies were to be 'used' on stage before words. As Grotowski recounts, 'In *Apocalypsis* we departed from literature. It was not a montage of texts. It was something we arrived at during rehearsals, through flashes of revelation, through improvisations. We had material for twenty hours in the end. Out of that we had to construct something which would have its own energy, like a stream. It was only then that we turned to the text, to speech.'[33]

From the point of view of the director, *Apocalypsis* marked a significant change that foreshadowed the transition to Grotowski's paratheatrical phase. As Flaszen recalls: 'In the course of *Apocalypsis*, Grotowski discovered another way of work and who he was in the work. The basic method of his activity was no longer the instruction of the actors, but rather expectation. He sat silently, waiting, hour after hour. This was a great change, because previously he really was a dictator. At that point there was no more theatre, because theatre to some extent requires dictatorship, manipulation.'[34]

The story that grew out of this long process of development is well known: a small company, weighed down and dulled by sleep following a night of partying and orgying, bears the marks of what has passed: sweat, semen, wine and garments that distinguish their identities and their social roles.

One, with a tipsy idea, leads the group to engage in a theatrical game: to represent the old stories of the innocent who redeems mankind and the Second Coming of Christ. Through a game that is often cruel, mingling desecration with apotheosis, the members of the group are given the scriptural names which best seem to suit the way they are and behave today: Simon Peter, Mary Magdalene, John, Lazarus, Judas and the Innocent (called the Dark One, like the garments he wears, being given a black overcoat to cover his naked body and a stick to hold in his hand). But he is also the Simpleton, the village idiot, who cannot see the world as others do.[35] The situations and words are modelled on episodes and words stored in the cultural memory. Everyday language slips into the language of scripture and literature. The verbal segment of the scenario is made up of quotations from the Gospels of John, Luke and Matthew, from Revelation, the biblical books of Job, the Psalms, the Song of Songs, from Dostoevsky's *The Brothers Karamazov*, from Eliot's *Ash Wednesday* and *The Waste Land*, and from poems by Simone Weil.

Weaving back and forth between their present roles and the ancient characters (evoked by the biblical tradition), between name/social mask, archetype, everyday situation and mythical situation, the former partygoers begin individually to try to absorb the characters of those earlier figures, pushing each other into their situations and discovering resemblances in themselves. All through their actions runs an unconscious logic, as explained by a programme distributed during events at the 1975 biennale, which drives the individuals, their masks and their roles to gravitate automatically, in moments of truth, towards the same mythical patterns.

The attempt to bring out the truth, to turn the mocking and cruel game into conversion and sanctification, is a failure. The efforts and self-sacrifice of the Simpleton lead to his humiliation. In the end Simon Peter, in the words of Dostoevsky's Grand Inquisitor against the returned Christ, casts out the innocent one: 'Go and never return.' The group has expelled the Dark One, the Simpleton, the Innocent.

An article by Ludwik Flaszen (published in Italy in 1980 but which appeared in Poland in 1967) explained the reasons for this choice and method.[36] The centre of interest is the theatre as art, not the theatre as entertainment or amusement. As an art the theatre has a discipline, principles, a subject matter and a specific content. But its traditional image was dissolved in the fifties. Authors like Beckett have disintegrated the theatrical language by taking it to its logical consequences, to silence and immobility, to the empty stage. On the other hand, in a world that changes and undermines the traditional communities, the past is also the time of the great rituals, ceremonies and festivals. Flaszen writes:

> What is it beyond an aesthetic, beyond an entertainment? Theatre will become a hobby for a lonely madman. Becoming aware, therefore, of a lonely madman's situation

may result in the pathos of authenticity. When the time for great festive ceremonies, bacchanalia and mysteries, rallies and carnivals is over, theatre can finally become a place for concentrated seclusion. [...] In poor theatre, the world is constructed solely from the actor's impulses and reactions. We don't multiply effects; on the contrary, we eliminate them. If the theatre today is Job deprived of any legacy, let it at least learn a lesson from Job's condition.[37]

To create the theatre, we have said, Grotowski had to go beyond literature. 'The true object of the theatre, its specific score, inaccessible to other branches of the arts, is [...] the score of human impulses and reactions. The psychic process expressed through the bodily and vocal reactions of the living organism.'[38] This enables us to understand the starting point for the construction of the verbal and scenic score: the suspended matter taken from the group, with the function of a myth which they have to measure themselves against by drawing on their great cultural tradition. The theatre makes its poverty a strength, one that is capable of revealing the condition of humanity, at the point it has reached in its project.

The introductory programme notes prepared by the Centro di Ricerca per il Teatro in Milan indicate that the names of the characters evoke basic associations in the common language: Simon Peter and John are popular names everywhere; Judas is the name and epithet of a traitor; Mary Magdalene is commonly identified with a lost woman; in Polish Lazarus is an insult to indicate a weakling. The associations cluster together as the action develops. The names are distributed by a Simon Peter of today, who attributes to himself the function of the first apostle. The investitures take place in the second scene. The role of the Saviour passes from someone who could play the part of Lazarus (and then actually does) to the Simpleton. His name in Polish evokes the innocent, the naïf, the idiot who lives outside the conventions; the muddler, the man possessed of a demon in the Slav tradition: an object of mockery and terror, but also a superstitious revelation of holiness in the peasant world.

There is a correspondence between the performance and the Gospel account of Jesus, but we are not presented with a dramatization of that account. We are presented with a bodily struggle with a textual myth, a crucial text that has forged the essential imagination and marked the consciousness of a culture. The relation to it is of apotheosis and derision, attraction and repulsion. The sign that results from it is ambiguous. The situation from which the story starts is relevant to the present and it is only gradually that it establishes an analogy with the events narrated in the Gospel. These men of today slip into the names, attributes and circumstances of those other men. People naturally gravitate towards myth at moments of truth. The stories of today and of all time are modelled on the ancient founding history.

The succession of events is not determined by the Gospel sequence but by the logic of the group and the associations that gradually arise between the situations and passages of scripture and literature.[39] The humdrum, everyday, contemporary situation slides into the mythical, symbolic situation. Everyday objects acquire the depth of symbol through analogies with the objects of the scriptural or literary narrative. Hence the party evokes the ritual festival; the festive dinner evokes the *agape*, the Last Supper; the bread placed on the napkin (as a synecdoche of the tablecloth) evokes the food of the *agape* – the sacrificial victim, the food of life. The bread, a sign of life, is wounded by the knife, crumbled and thrown like a weapon, a projectile. It is eaten, introjected like a sacred body, or scattered in pieces like the good seed that is cast away. The lascivious act of drinking sperm has connotations of an inverted Eucharist: blasphemous and at the same time symbolically taken to extremes of signification, the drinking of the lifeblood. The tangle of meanings and their condensation into a single gesture, performed with marked brutality, affects the image of the knife stuck in the bread, while John moves his whole body, quivering and jerking. It contains an allusion to the sexual act and the transport of love, but also to being wounded to death and the deep wound inflicted by the Saviour's love.

The girl/Mary Magdalene who washes the feet of Lazarus is superimposed on the Gospel scene of Mary Magdalene washing and anointing the feet of Jesus. Lazarus, lying down, forms the figure of a cross. The invitation to lunch resolves into the refusal of the call from Jesus. The sequence of the Simpleton – who goes down on his knees in suffering, crouching and reviled, and beats three times on the stage with his hands – is the evocation and figure of the ritual 'Passion', analogous to that of the *Via Crucis*. The Simpleton's stick pointed at Peter's heart introduces the passage from Dostoevsky and the theme of the Second Coming in a world that does not want the Saviour and refuses to acknowledge him.

The line interweaving apotheosis and profanation includes the image of Lazarus, who 'drinks' the blood from the wounded side and simultaneously seems to eat the flesh of the Simpleton. This fuses references to the Eucharist under both kinds (as in the Orthodox tradition) and the Gospel passage which states that blood and water flowed from Christ's side. The orgiastic dancing, laughter and drunkenness of the party allude to the primal ritual dance around the victim, the liberating laughter and the mocking of Christ.

The scene of the young man and the girl who look on, giving rise to a succession of actions, including the formation of the wedding party, recalls the wedding at Cana and the religious procession. The hoax of the man who pretends to be dead and covers his face with a white handkerchief is a travesty of a raucous wake, which elicits the severe intervention of the Simpleton, armed with a stick, and the conversion of the scene into an evocation of the resurrection of Lazarus. The procession around the tablecloth with the bread resting on it passes through a number of different representations: the Wedding at Cana, the Eucharist, the difficult acceptance of the Simpleton in the procession of humanity on its journey. The dance of the Simpleton recalls the dance of the fool and the Feast of Fools, but also the archetype of the Slavic and Orthodox tradition of the fool of God. The members of the group, one at a time, recognize and elect Peter, but it is the Simpleton who raises him on his shoulders, carries him and runs alone. The simple bears the burden of the powerful. He is the true free and liberating person. The powerful is powerful in his name. The simplest carries the powerful on his shoulders. It is again a highly effective symbolic condensation.

The love sequence foreshadows Jesus' predilection for women. The Simpleton bowed over Mary Magdalene's lap evokes the symbolism of the pietà. The Simpleton, bizarrely pulling the black jacket over his head, poses as a pilgrim, a friar travelling the earth. Then in the grand finale, the group gathers around the candles with intense concentration, bleating and singing ironically; draped around the Simpleton's neck, the scarf looks like a shroud. Tired and sweaty the Simpleton falls to the ground: the symbol of death on the cross. In their robes the group run round him three times waving white towels. It is a penitential procession, the procession of the monks and the adoration of Jesus. The great confrontation between Peter and the Simpleton, modelled on the episode of the Grand Inquisitor, closes on an invincible pessimism. The world is desolate and abandoned.

The words needed to express these situations are modelled on scriptural and literary texts, with a movement made natural by a culture's familiarity with those voices, which are part of the imagination. The construction of the text ranges across various sources, from the icon of Christ the Saviour derived from 'the great code' of the Bible down to contemporary literature. We can review them in the order in which each text surfaces.

The first line of the text of the production is taken from the Gospel of John. It is at the centre of the inspiration of Grotowski and his group and forms a core from which radiates the movement of exploration, reflection, testing and challenge, through constant cross-references, from ancient to modern, to the promise and hope of the salvation of man. The verses in question are 6:53–6, sung in Spanish by Mary Magdalene, and repeated at the same time, translated into Polish, by John. The interlacing of the voices and the multiplication of languages are signs that the promise is repeated to all corners of the earth and penetrates into all cultures.

The opening of the text immediately focuses on the religious significance of Jesus' life, then associated with the Simpleton, which is the fundamental aspect of the fourth Gospel, the most spiritual of all. He re-establishes the community by renewing the bond between God and humanity, offering himself as the bread of life, even as life itself:

> Verily, verily, I say unto you, except ye eat the flesh of the Son of man, and drink his blood, ye have no life in you.
>
> Whoso eateth my flesh, and drinketh my blood, hath eternal life; and I will raise him up at the last day.
>
> For my flesh is meat indeed, and my blood is drink indeed.
>
> He that eateth my flesh, and drinketh my blood, dwelleth in me, and I in him.[40]

The metaphor is reinforced, later, with another association (Jesus as the door of the sheepfold), following the words of Judas which give rise to the parable.[41] The strand taken from John culminates with the evocation of the 'sign' of victory over death, the recapitulation of salvation: the resurrection of Lazarus. The Simpleton, in a clear, calm voice, speaks to Lazarus, 'Lazarus, come forth!'[42]

The call of the investiture of Peter by Jesus for the foundation of his church is attributed to the character of Judas, who utters, in the presence of Peter and the Simpleton, standing in a triangle, the evangelical formula:

> So when they had dined, Jesus saith to Simon Peter, Simon, son of Jonas, lovest thou me more than these? He saith unto him, Yea, Lord; thou knowest that I love thee. He saith unto him, Feed my lambs.

He saith to him again the second time, Simon, son of Jonas, lovest thou me? He saith unto him, Yea, Lord; thou knowest that I love thee. He saith unto him, Feed my sheep.[43]

The borrowings from the fourth Gospel close with two extensive quotations from Chapter 13, in which Jesus washes Peter's feet, indicating the mysterious nature of the sign which Peter will only later be able to understand, announcing Peter's betrayal and Jesus' departure to a place where Peter will not be able to follow until later. These interlacing themes, consequential to the whole theme outlined above and the overall montage of the sources, touch on the purification from guilt of the man who accepts cleansing and the man who does not accept and betrays; and it touches on the crux of the witness to martyrdom.

The passage runs as follows: Peter turns and walks toward the Simpleton, who is seated, and asks, 'Lord, dost thou wash my feet?' The Simpleton replies, 'What I do thou knowest not now; but thou shalt know hereafter.' Peter kneels down, sets his candles on the stage next to the Simpleton, who touches the fire of the candles with his hand and says to Peter, looking at him, 'Ye are clean, but not all. Now I tell you before it come, that, when it is come to pass, ye may believe that I am he. One of you shall betray me.' The Simpleton lights a candle, gets up, touches the flame with his fingers to extinguish it and marks the forehead of Peter. Judas says in a tone of surprise, 'Lord, and I?' Peter says to Judas, 'Judas Iscariot, Simon's son.' The Simpleton says, 'Little children, yet a little while I am with you. Ye shall seek me: and as I said unto the Jews, Whither I go, ye cannot come.' Peter asks, 'Lord, whither goest thou?' The Simpleton replies, 'Whither I go, thou canst not follow me now; but thou shalt follow me afterwards.'[44]

One of the key texts in the whole montage is introduced by a few verses from an old Polish hymn on the theme of man's unbridled freedom as the cause of his suffering: the Grand Inquisitor chapter from book 5, part 2 of *The Brothers Karamazov*. The complex tale and argument that Ivan recounts to Alyosha is summed up in short lines adapted from the text. The first is placed in the mouth of Peter, who says sternly,

> Twenty centuries have already passed when he promised to return and establish his kingdom. It has been already twenty centuries since his prophet wrote that he would come soon. Not even the Son knows the day and the hour, but only the heavenly father. But humanity awaits him with the same faith as before and with the same hope. And with even greater faith, because heaven has ceased to give pledges to man. Believe what your heart says, heaven no longer gives pledges.

Judas ironically recalls the parable of the guests' refusal of the invitation to the Lord's banquet, then Peter continues:

> Man was created rebellious. Can rebels perhaps be happy? You were warned. You had no lack of warnings and advice, but you did not heed them. You rejected the only way by which you could make men happy. Fortunately, by going away, you returned matters to our own hands. By your word you ensured, you gave us the right to bind and loose, and you can hardly think you can take back this right. So why did you come to trouble us?

As for the Simpleton, who is squatting, touching the floor with his face and hands, Peter continues:

> The intelligent and terrifying spirit, the spirit of self-destruction and nonbeing, the great spirit spoke to you in the wilderness. Did he tempt you? Wasn't this what happened? But was it perhaps possible to say something more real than what he revealed to you with his three proposals, which in books are called temptations and which you disdained? Yet if there ever was on earth a true and wonderful miracle, it was on that day, the day of the three temptations! The miracle consisted precisely in the formulation of those three proposals.

Then, only after some stage business consisting only of actions performed by the Simpleton, Mary Magdalene and Lazarus, and after a sort of mime of the three falls of the *Via Crucis* which Peter performs, he continues:

> Decide for yourself: who was right, you or the one you were talking to? Think back to the first proposal. If not the words, the sense was this: 'You want to go into the world and you are going empty-handed, with the promise of a freedom that they, in their simplicity and their innate disorder, cannot even conceive, for which they feel fear and terror because nothing has ever been more unbearable than freedom for man and for human society. Do you see rather these stones, in this bare and burning desert? Turn them into bread and mankind will come after you docile and grateful like sheep, though eternally afraid that you might withdraw your hand and leave them without your bread.'

The same text provides the closing words of the performance: 'Go, and never return.'

It should be said, incidentally, that Dostoevsky not only provides an indispensable frame of reference for the European cultural awareness, but offers a much-frequented reservoir of texts and situations that have nurtured the theatre in the late twentieth century and the early years of the new millennium.[45] It must also be said that what appears contradictory is actually revelatory of a new and far more significant development. Dostoevsky had a true aversion to the theatre, but as illusion, as artifice, according to the canons of much nineteenth-century theatrical practice. But he actually had the theatre in his blood: as a form of exploration of the self and the overt staging of the innermost self of the character-performer; as dialogue, a dialectic of objectified positions in the midst of the world and life; and as free and open engagement, assumption-profanation of the great founding myths of European culture. (Mikhail Bakhtin termed this dialectic the 'polyphonic novel'. It can perhaps be retraced to the original performative quality of Dostoevsky's work.)[46]

The high literary source is interwoven with an old Polish hymn reiterating the theme of human suffering and freedom:

> The Lord, creator of heaven,
> hangs on the cross.

> He has to bewail human sins.
> Ah, ah, for my unbridled freedom,
> Ah, ah, for my unbridled freedom
> The man suffers and dies.

The third source that enters into the construction of the text is again evangelical, being the Gospel of Luke 14:16–21: the parable of the great supper. Many of the guests decline the invitation of the lord and are replaced by the outcasts of society. The passage, summed up in two lines, is recounted with an ironic smile and a provocative air by Judas:

> A certain man made a great supper, and bade many, and sent his servant at supper time to say to them that were bidden, Come, for all things are now ready. And they all with one consent began to make excuses. The first said unto him, I have bought a piece of ground, and I must needs go and see it: I pray thee have me excused. [Judas stops, takes a jump, then comes back before Peter, and continues:] And another said, I have married a wife, and therefore I cannot come. So that servant came, and showed his lord these things. Then the master of the house being angry said to his servant, Go out quickly into the streets and lanes of the city, and bring in hither the poor, and the maimed, and the halt, and the blind.

It is again a passage from Luke (12:22–3) which underscores and seals the admonition of the Grand Inquisitor, evoked by Peter, that man is not in favour of liberty but material goods: 'Take no thought for your life, what ye shall eat; neither for the body, what ye shall put on. The life is more than meat, and the body is more than raiment.' The play of associations and the thematic development leads to the elevated religious poetry of Eliot's poem *Ash Wednesday*. The Simpleton attracts the attention of the group by twice raising his voice, with a growing tension, to stop the flow of arrogant refusals of men by reciting the verses on detachment, the invocation of redemption, mercy and caring.

The passages which appear in the text are as follows, interspersed with the quotations from Dostoevsky, Luke and Matthew noted above. The first is an abbreviation of the first section:

> Because I do not hope to turn again
> Because I do not hope
> Because I do not hope to turn
> Desiring this man's gift and that man's scope
> I no longer strive to strive towards such things
> (Why should the aged eagle stretch its wings?)
> Why should I mourn
> The vanished power of the usual reign?
> Because I do not hope to know again
> The infirm glory of the positive hour
> Because I do not think

Because I know I shall not know
The one veritable transitory power
Because I cannot drink
There, where trees flower, and springs flow, for there is nothing again
Because I know that time is always time
And place is always and only place
And what is actual is actual only for one time
And only for one place [...]
Because I do not hope to turn again
Let these words answer
For what is done, not to be done again
May the judgement not be too heavy upon us
Because these wings are no longer wings to fly
But merely vans to beat the air
The air which is now thoroughly small and dry
Smaller and dryer than the will
Teach us to care.[47]

Quoted in the text of *Apocalypsis* and spliced with allusions from other sources, the passage from Eliot undergoes a twist of meaning, in keeping with the character who utters it and with the sense of the whole. The reference to God and the Miserere ('And pray to God to have mercy on us') present in Eliot's poem are omitted.[48] Also omitted is the prayer formulated in the words of the Hail Mary ('Pray for us sinners now and at the hour of our death. Pray for us now and at the hour of our death').[49] It expresses a premonition of imminent defeat, the powerlessness of an eagle that once soared as testimony to elevation and freedom but is now unable to fly, its wings no more than feathers to beat the empty air with, in disappointment with a world that has proved meagre and irredeemable.

But the vision of Grotowski's text is not so much that of the journey of the self with itself, as in Eliot's poem, towards the conquest of a mystical union, but the relation with the group to the world, which, as we shall see, will cast him out. The objective is to raise up and free a world that does not desire to be raised and freed, in a more deeply anthropological, moral and religious sense.

The same lines are followed in the second quotation from Eliot, a selection and slight adaptation of the fourth section:

Who walked between the violet and the violet
Who walked between
The various ranks of varied green
Going in white and blue, in Mary's colour,
Talking of trivial things
In ignorance and knowledge of eternal dolour
Who moved among the others as they walked,
Who then made strong the fountains and made fresh the springs [...]

> Redeem the time, redeem the dream
> The token of the word unheard, unspoken
> [in] this [our] exile.⁵⁰

Eliot, on the basis of Dante, St Paul and the Salve Regina, imagines the garden and the lady who walks through it 'between the violet and the violet', making it the symbol of the invisible good, sought through the attempted dispossession of the self. But the poet's wholly inner vision is reduced to a struggle between the Simpleton and the world/gang who resist redemption. They are deaf to the promise made at the time when the story takes place, the time of his 'exile'.

The third sampling from *Ash Wednesday* is a group of verses in the sixth section, spoken calmly by the Simpleton:

> Although I do not hope to turn
> Wavering between the profit and the loss
> In this brief transit where the dreams cross
> The dreamcrossed twilight between birth and dying
> (Bless me father)
> though I do not wish to wish these things [...]
> This is the time of tension [...]
> The place of solitude where three dreams cross [...]
> But when the voices shaken from the yew-tree drift away
> Let the other yew be shaken and reply.
> Blessed sister, holy mother, spirit of the fountain, spirit of the garden,
> Suffer us not to mock ourselves with falsehood.

Here we have another twist of significance. The inspiration of the poet focuses on submission to God and prayer, evoking the *terzina* from Dante's *Paradise* (3, 96–8) that begins with the verse in the poem, 'And in His will is our peace'. But the character of the Simpleton moves the point of view onto the anthropological and ethical plane of the actor's work, to the lie that does not prevail, to inauthenticity.

It is again the Simpleton, as if inspired, with eyes closed, who elicits the themes of memory and forgetfulness, drawn from the second canto:

> Lady, three white leopards sat under a juniper
> In the cool of the day, fed to satiation
> Of my arms and my heart and my liver
> and how
> Was contained in the round hole in my skull.
> God said
> These bones live? Live
> These bones? And all that had been contained
> In the bones (which were already dry) said chirping [...]
> There is no life in them. [...]

And God said:
Prophesy to the wind, the wind just because
The wind will listen only [...]
Lady of silences
Quiet and distraught
Worn and more integrated
Rose Memory
Rose of forgetfulness [...]
After the torment [...]
Language without words [...]
Grace to the Mother
For the Garden.

The transposition to the second last passage in the second section of Eliot's *Ash Wednesday* brings out the poet's theme of the death of the old man, symbolized by the bones left by three white leopards, which the Simpleton still hopes to raise to life ('Shall these bones live?'). But then the gaze is turned away from this world and from the people who reject the word as too arduous. The right time and place are not here. The dramatist gives the Simpleton the verses from the fifth section of Eliot's poem, uttered in an increasingly clear voice, speaking from the ground where he lies stretched out as if crucified. He speaks the verses of the Word that can no longer resonate in this place:

If the lost word is lost, if the spent word is spent
If the unheard, unspoken
Word is unspoken, unheard;
Still is the unspoken word, the Word unheard,
The Word without a word, [...]
O my people...
Where shall the word be found, where will the word
Resound? Not here. [...]
The right time and the right place are not here
No place of grace for those who avoid the face
No time to rejoice for those who walk among noise and deny the voice
Will the veiled sister pray for
Those who walk in darkness, who chose thee and oppose thee,
Those who are torn on the horn between season and season [...]
power and power.

The dramatist continues, interpolating and varying Eliot's text in the lines of the production which, in translation, read as follows:

For those that love each other in the desert, in the garden
In the desert of desire
Spitting from their mouth a withered seed.

In the montage of texts, the last quotation from Eliot's poem, interspersed with a few verses in liturgical Latin, is united directly with the passage from Dostoevsky's *Brothers Karamazov*, in which the attempt of the Simpleton-Christ of the Second Coming to recreate the relationship between man and his high vocation shatter against the connivance between the ambitions of power with the most cowardly and wretched part of mankind. In short, it heralds failure.[51]

There follow further biblical and liturgical sources. Peter and then John evoke passages reminiscent of the funeral liturgy, respectively of the *Ordo sepeliendi parvulos* and the *Exsequiarum ordo seu ritus completus sepeliendi adultos*, the first of which draws on Psalm 23. Mary Magdalene (and at one point Lazarus) expresses herself through images of beauty and love from the Song of Songs. Lazarus, and also Judas for a few lines, quotes fragments from the Book of Job and from Dostoevsky. Each character draws in memory on the immortal words suited to their characterization and the archetype associated with them. So it is in the case of John and the Apocalypse (i.e., the Book of Revelation), a text that could hardly have been omitted since it appears in the title.

One passage, freely translated from Simone Weil's *Supernatural Knowledge*, is placed in the mouth of John, who speaks it in a desperate voice. It introduces the theme of doubt, that God 'does not love me', and yet there is a persistent return to the thought that 'in spite of everything he loves me', in two segments mounted antiphrastically, with the opposed gestures of an embrace and lashes. The passage also introduces the theme of unfulfilled promise, of abandonment, the paralysing doubt that leads to the decision to depart. John, after his struggle with the Simpleton, goes away rapidly with a gesture similar to that which Peter later addresses to the Simpleton himself in the finale. There remains the 'decayed house' of Eliot's poem.

Following the thread of the quotations, mounted on the imagery, the whole plot unfolds and attains clarity as the conclusion draws closer. Christ comes among humanity in the figure of the Simpleton. With all the strength of his provocation he presses on the others, even striking them violently, to awaken recognition and be readmitted to their lives. But even the most willing of those who hear him, those who have known and loved him before and who have even sought his love and guidance, remain deaf and blind, enclosed in doubt, and eventually abandon him.

There is no better way to give expression to this situation than the page by Simone Weil, found loose in one of her notebooks and placed in the prologue to *La connaissance surnaturelle*, the title given by those who published the work posthumously in the collection *Espoir*, edited by Albert Camus. To Grotowski and his group Weil was an important point of reference in the guiding principles of her life and work. She was the spirit of truth, or as Camus said, 'la folie de vérité' (the madness of truth); the spirit of poverty, seen as a necessary path of access to true freedom; adherence to the spirit of Christianity outside the restrictions of institutions and the monopolies of the truth peculiar to dogmatism; an extreme rigour, without the slightest weakness or illusion or well-meant untruth –which ultimately led to her death.[52] A meeting of souls that was inevitable: Weil and the modern theatre artist with the most stringent profile in ethical terms, the most rigorous work, and a burning hunger for the absolute which (as evidenced by Flaszen) devoured him.

The passage of Weil that inspired the group narrates an encounter with the divine in the context of a place and a concrete, everyday situation. John begins to speak, his eyes closed and arms outstretched toward the Simpleton, who is lying in front of him:

> He came into my room and said: poor thing who understands nothing, knows nothing. Come with me, I'll teach you what you do not even expect. I went out and followed him up to the attic. There, through an open window, we could see the whole city, some wooden scaffolding and the river, where some ships were unloading their cargoes. We were alone. From a cupboard he took some bread which we shared. That bread really tasted of bread. Never ate such good bread ever since. He promised to teach me, but didn't teach me anything. One day he told me: 'Now go away.'

Meanwhile the Simpleton has stood up and is right in front of John, who goes on: 'I never went looking for him. I realized he had come to me by mistake.' At this point, the Simpleton begins to strike John hard on the back and very angrily. John keeps speaking calmly out loud: 'My place is here in this attic. Wherever he is, in a jail cell, in a station waiting room, anywhere, but not in this attic.'

John jumps a couple of times, then kneels down and caresses Simpleton's feet with his hands: 'Sometimes I can't help repeating, with fear and remorse, little by little, everything he said. But how can I remember him. He won't say anything any more, because he isn't here now. I know quite well he doesn't love me, how could he love me?'

The Simpleton kneels in front of John, who embraces him. Then suddenly the Simpleton gets up and starts to flog John's back. In a desperate voice John says, 'But inside me there are a few crumbs of myself, and at the bottom of my soul I'm trembling with fear, which cannot exclude the thought that despite everything he loves me.' John gets up and goes away quickly.

With an utterance that is at first slow and then gradually becomes more rapid, the Simpleton again draws from Eliot's *Gerontion* words that are interwoven with Dostoevsky's and lead to the final bleak conclusion: 'My house is a decayed house [...]. I that was near your heart was removed therefrom [...]. I have lost my passion [...] I have lost my sight, smell, hearing, taste and touch. How should I use it for your closer contact?'

The Lamentations of Jeremiah, including the liturgy, offer the last song of the Simpleton words that evoke the apocalyptic image of the fate of the world, symbolized by Jerusalem, and the last prayer and exhortation that remain unheeded, until the final expulsion:

> Cogitavit Dominus dissipare
> Murum Filiae Syon
> Tetendit funiculum suum, et
> Non avertit manum suam a
> Perditione luxitque antemurale
> Et murus pariter dissipatus est.
> Sederunt in terra conticuerunt
> Senes Filiae Syon
> Consperserunt cinere capita

Sua accinti sunt ciliciis
Abiecerunt in terram capita
Sua virgines Jerusale.
Defecerunt prae lacrimis
Oculi mei, conturbata
Sunt viscera mea, effusum est
In terra iecur meum super
Contritionem filiae populi mei
Cum deficeret parvulus et
Lactens in plateis oppidi.
Jerusale, Jerusale
Convertere ad Dominum
Deum tuum.[53]

(The Lord hath cast off his altar, he hath abhorred his sanctuary, he hath given up into the hand of the enemy the walls of her palaces; they have made a noise in the house of the Lord, as in the day of a solemn feast [...]. The elders of the daughter of Zion sit upon the ground, and keep silence: they have cast up dust upon their heads; they have girded themselves with sackcloth; the virgins of Jerusalem hang down their heads to the ground. Mine eyes do fail with tears, my bowels are troubled, my liver is poured upon the earth, for the destruction of the daughter of my people; because the children and the sucklings swoon in the streets of the city.)[54]

The Simpleton-Christ Theme, or the Challenge of Freedom: The Expulsion

We come now to the significance, the great epic theme, on which the text, so innovatively constructed, turns. It is focused on the guiding image of the Innocent, the Simpleton, the figure of the *Christus patiens*, and the challenge which he issues to humanity, urging it to choose a free and authentic life. The challenge has been disregarded and gradually expelled from the dulled consciences of mankind and its institutions, primarily the church, symbolized by Peter, anxious to consolidate his power and satisfy human needs on a low and unproblematic level.

The core of the performance is the game played between the Simpleton and Peter in two sequences, the central one and the dramatic finale. The head of the village and the village idiot, or the idiot Peter and Christ, are isolated in the darkness of the stage, lit only by candles, as the noise of life with all the other actors falls silent. Dostoevsky, Simone Weil, Eliot and Jeremiah lend them the high notes of their speeches, which resound disquietingly amid the general tone of irony and blasphemy.

The scene explores the universal and epochal theme of freedom in its embodiment as inner freedom, religious, social and political freedom, and freedom as the constitutive datum of mankind, the foundation of Christian anthropology. Metatheatrically, it also embodies the liberation of the actors from the clichés of their craft and the subject to be performed. In the individual and collective memory, it touches on the great traditional archetypes, and is distilled into the splendour of the Grand Inquisitor in *The Brothers Karamazov*.[55]

The hallmarks of the Simpleton, in the actor Ryszard Cieślak's interpretation, were extraordinary intensity and depth of emotion. The poverty and density of his interpretation combined memories of the Christological iconography of suffering in great paintings and the popular Polish tradition,[56] the features of the 'fool of God', and Dostoevsky's two Christlike characters – Prince Myshkin (of *The Idiot*)[57] and Alyosha, the youngest of the Karamazov brothers. By following the line of an internal intertextuality, it also comprised the humiliation and patience of the victims in *Akropolis* with the transfiguration of *The Constant Prince*.[58] Hence the 'myth' revisited between fascination and repulsion, sought and rejected, posed the question of what has happened, in the contemporary world, to the early Christianity which confronted humanity with its challenge to freedom and authenticity.

The text, in the complexity of the highly condensed dramatic writing, traverses all the planes of the problem, as it appeared to the consciousness of the Polish group at a crucial and transitional phase in the history of a man, a country, a culture, an institution, a faith, and a form of art: namely Jerzy Grotowski, Poland, the West, the church, Christianity and the theatre.

The sign of Christ, in relation to the theme of freedom, involves first of all the plane of inwardness. The action unfolds in expressive ideograms, in an interplay of encounters and clashes, seductions and rejections, which link the former partygoers (and their roles) to the names and figures of myth, to each other and to the catalytic figure of the Simpleton-Christ. It functions (to use a Jungian term bound up with Grotowski's formation) as a 'process of individuation'.[59] It entails the liberation of the possibilities of the self, assimilating its repressed contents, relating the individual's social mask or crystallized identity to the structures of 'myth', set freely in play in relation to the founding 'myth', which may be accepted or rejected. Acceptance means spontaneously consenting to be inwardly free, free in 'detachment', by embracing the model of Christ's rejection of the temptations (which is also Eliot's great theme).

On a second level the theme of freedom involves the plane of history. The setting in which the production developed (before becoming for a decade the visiting card of the group, after leaving the theatre as an institution) was the plight of Poland, its recent history confined between two despotisms, its proud people offended by the cynicism of a politics which never respected its identity, its independence and its rights, a land violated by the death camps and forced to become an instrument of the Final Solution. Also significant was the plight of the church, with its strength, its ancient, burning faith, its deep roots in the nation's life, the energy of its pastors (its primate Cardinal Wyszynski, Archbishop of Krakow, and Karol Wojtyla), the strength, suffering and sacrifices (even to martyrdom) of its clergy, and its resistance to the attempts to decapitate the church (during the Nazi era) and then to silence it (under communism). The Polish church, the true frame of reference and custodian of the Polish identity (first during the German occupation and then during the 'limited sovereignty' of the people's democracy), was inevitably a crucial focus for reflection and inspiration to the artist and the intellectual of the Teatr Laboratorium in the dialectic between the spiritual call of original, evangelical Christianity, and the everyday engagement of a temporal organization forced to cope with a hostile power – the central Vatican diplomacy.[60]

It is true that Grotowski's physiognomy seems essentially apolitical, but it is also true that he was involved in the hopes and actions of the 1956 'Polish October', in the movement of intellectuals and the brief season when the press and clubs were a laboratory for ideas previously considered subversive. And it is evident that he must have been influenced not just by the end of the illusions nurtured by the period that began with the 22nd Congress of the Communist Party of the Soviet Union (1961) and ended with the fall of Khrushchev, announced on 15 October 1964. At Wrocław, where the theatre had moved from the town of Opole (60 miles from Auschwitz), the great theme of freedom was catalysed in the modes of work of the theatre actor and the creation of the sign.

The sign that was to be imprinted in the imagination of the audiences who, in small groups, in a relationship of intimacy and intense participation, would encounter it all over the world, was the *Figura Christi* of *The Constant Prince* and the Simpleton in *Apocalypsis cum figuris*. Hence two other planes for the interpretation of the guiding image: the *Figura Christi* and the theme of freedom. One is the freedom to compare and choose the foundation of meaning. The parable of the 'Second Coming' as a 'modern Passion' brings back into play, as at the origin (where, as we read in the Gospel, Jesus came among men, but they knew him not), the free embrace of the difficult core of Christianity: the relationship with God the Father who loves mankind and sends his son to redeem it, accepting even ingratitude, suffering and the humiliation of the death sentence. This love is objectified in the theatre through the metaphor of the physical love of the Simpleton and Mary Magdalene (following the model of the Song of Songs). The purpose, as Jennifer Kumiega effectively points out, is 'to bring us momentarily in contact with the deepest levels within ourselves, deeper than those engaged within the order of forms, through incarnate mythic confrontation. If we succeed, through the shock of exposure, in touching those depths, we are changed for ever.'[61]

Finally, one level in the work of the Teatr Laboratorium acquires primary importance and becomes the basis and a metaphor for all others: in theatre the players may function as a microcell that can experiment, even in extreme and radical ways, possibilities and projects not found in actual life. The microcell works in a free and safe space, protected by its boundaries.

This is the level of the freedom of the actor, achieved by probing the depths through the laboratory method. Kumiega clarifies this point. The work is only created through improvisation and is configured as a network, as we have seen, of interlacing stories, starting from literature, religion, poetry and fiction, developed through the rehearsals and the result of the reduction of a quantity of material lasting many hours to the duration of about one hour. The basic work of Grotowski, who had previously been highly active, a director who kept control in his own hands, was now to watch and wait in tense silence for the actors to find their personal 'total act', their own motifs, expressed in a terse and intense language, in which the writing was pared away stringently and combined with the greatest possible density of meaning. It should be borne in mind that

Beckett had produced his major works not many years before this. The performance is stark and wholly resolved into the psychophysical unity of the actor. In the laboratory method the actor's skin, nerves, muscles, brain cells and voice become the exclusive field of experience, offering (in the gift of relationship with the audience) a course of liberation of the self and of striving towards the 'absolute' (freed from constraints and clichés), towards the true act.

A Provisional Epilogue

BETWEEN THE EXPERIENCE AND THE REPRESENTATION OF THE TRAGIC: TOWARDS A PERFORMATIVE THEATRE

Endless Horrors in Stage Scripts from the End of the Century: The Representation of Planned Genocide[1]

I close this study with a provisional epilogue, which offers a glimpse at tragic dramaturgy in the last decades of the century (to which I plan to devote a future study) within the radical renewal of Western theatre since the late sixties.

It takes the form of an advance on two fronts. The first is thematic, it is the subject of this book taken to its extreme, the greatest and undoubtedly the most hateful transgression of the limit in this century: genocide, of which we saw a memorable anticipation in Grotowski's *Akropolis*. The second concerns the form and theory of theatre.

I will briefly examine two texts for the stage that are extraordinary in their lucidity, emotional impact, effectiveness and originality of form: *Rwanda 94* and *Ruhe*. They are both Belgian productions, one from the French-speaking region and the other the Flemish. They are writings for the stage which did not originate from a dramatic text, in keeping with a custom widespread in this period. They are profoundly and dramatically concerned with eternal and unresolved questions about the structures of human and social coexistence. They foreground the two nuclei of tragedy: the transgression of the limit, including the most extreme and unimaginable excesses, and the irreducible conflict that pits one person against another, going to the extreme of murdering opposition groups identified by unfounded theories of ethnic identity and race.

They again confront and question the traditional effect of catharsis attributed to tragedy, embedding it in a social drama that does not seek to tranquilize and soothe, but to arouse a rationally vigilant alarm, an awareness, and an experience of ritual transformation. Above all, they again dramatically present the theme of evil and the burden of human responsibility in the tragedy of existence.

They belong to an area of the theatre that characterized the last years of the century and the early years of the new millennium in which we live and in which we will now have to find the current embodiment of the tragic, its conscience and its alarm. It is a theatre that I shall call performative and that many scholars authoritatively call 'postdramatic'.[2] The term *performative* may seem tautological, because every theatre is properly performative, being not a literary genre but an event acted on a stage before an audience. Here, however, it indicates a specific strand of postmodernity.

Of its salient characteristics, we can say that it is not a theatre of texts and literature grounded in philosophy, like that dealt with in this book. On the plane of the composition presented on the stage, it rests on a *plateau à habiter*, as the French say, in which arts, languages and materials are interwoven into a total equivalence in the construction of signs and meanings, even down to the possible rejection of the theatrical 'aura' and the acceptance of the everyday, of ugliness and of poor materials. It oscillates between the greatest possible sparseness, in keeping with Beckett's and Grotowski's stripping of the stage, and the greatest possible deployment of multiple languages and expressive materials. On the plane of the construction of the performance onstage, it often follows the method of the workshop, of collective construction, or the construction of the sign modelled on the concrete reality of the performer. In its relation with its public, it focuses on the intensity of the relationship and the search for various forms, some even provocatively involving the audience in what happens on the stage.

Essential to this type of theatre is the focus on the performance of the actors or the author-actors. The performative value of their work becomes all the more intense because what the actors say and do is credible – not separate or split off from the person of the actor in the flesh. The actors are not only signs that allude to something else, allegorically, but presences heavily involved in what they represent and present. What the actors say and do cannot be separated from what they are. This implication makes them credible. What the actor says and does gains force from their experience made tangible.

All this brings us back to Utopia and Artaud's prophecy, which the theatre is gradually interpreting and translating into reality. It is at the heart of a culture, a tissue of ideas that have a living force,[3] culture in action, not petrified, capable of grasping life profoundly and renewing it, causing 'les plus mystérieuses altérations' (the most mysterious alterations), of which St Augustine speaks pejoratively, and which Artaud turns into positive values.[4] It restores the spirit to the source of its conflict, to the terrifying revelation of evil.[5] It serves not the abstract and disembodied word, but physical, concrete language, occupying the stage in everything that can be materially expressed and that is directed primarily to the senses, 'poésie dans l'espace' (poetry in space).[6]

'The theatre should also be regarded as the Double, not of this direct and everyday reality, of which it has gradually been reduced to a mere inert copy, equally vain and cloying, but of a different reality, dangerous and typical, whose Principles, like dolphins, when they have shown their heads, plunge back into the darkness of the waters.'

This deals with principles embodied in the times of history that are 'the materialization or rather the externalization of some kind of essential drama, which in a certain sense contains both the basic principles, multiple and unique, of any drama.' It was in this way that I have decided to interpret the tragic in the history of European drama of the twentieth century. Certainly it is a theatre of cruelty, not necessarily of blood, but of a violent and implacable rigour with which to see into the depths of reality, because 'we are not free. And the heavens may still fall on our heads.'[7]

Rwanda 94

Rwanda 94 grew out of an idea by Jacques Delcuvellerie and was produced under his direction by the Belgian Groupov troupe, founded by Delcuvellerie as an ensemble of artists possessing different skills and of different nationalities.[8] The work was inspired by the massacres in Rwanda between 7 April and 2 July 1994: the genocide of the Rwandan Tutsi, meticulously planned over a long period, and which eliminated 80 per cent of the total Tutsi population of 1,250,000.[9] The genocide was triggered by the assassination of President Juvénal Habyarimana, whose plane was shot down. It was conducted with unprecedented cruelty and a highly decentralized organization through the broad involvement and consensus of the Hutu population, incited to hatred by the ruling class and representatives of the institutions.[10]

I shall now examine the structure of the work.

Part 1: Itsembabwoko (Genocide)

The stage is almost empty. The backdrop represents a red mud wall evoking the earth of Rwanda, marked with a black stain, as of a wounded land. In the middle of the stage in front of it is a chair. On the right are the music stands and instruments of a small band.

Prélude 1

La mort ne veut pas de moi (Death does not want me)

The musicians enter and take their places. A Rwandan woman, simply dressed in Western garments, takes her place on the chair in the middle, calm and composed. The band strikes up a tune – almost of lament in the notes of the violin and piano. When the music falls silent, the woman begins to speak, at first in Rwandan and then in French, calmly and clearly, only occasionally interrupted by her tears, which she dries with dignity, saying, 'Excusez-moi'. Her testimony lasts forty minutes. She is not an actress. She is Yolande Mukagasana, a survivor of the Rwandan genocide.[11] She recounts six weeks of her life during the genocide: her normal life in Kigali as a wife, the mother of three children, the head nurse at her clinic, respected for the treatment she had given to many people. She relates the sudden change after the official order to kill the Tutsi, no longer spoken of as human beings but 'snakes' or 'cockroaches'. She relates the manhunts, the killing of her husband and children, her helplessness, fear, betrayal and total humiliation, the murderous folly and cruelty described as 'travail civique' (civic work), the nightmare of the machetes and her outrage: 'I wanted the sun to shine on this country. I wanted everything for it.' She relates how she escaped, her urge to bear witness and her pity. 'I want to arouse neither fear not pity. I want to bear witness. Simply to bear witness. Those men who subjected me to the worst sufferings, I neither hate nor despise them. I even pity them.'[12]

Mutunge (Mutungo)

The music resumes. The Rwandan cantor Muyango sings of the desolation of the country with the words of a song composed in 1966 which bears witness to the pogroms of 1959.

Le choeur des morts (The chorus of the dead)

The European orchestra joins the voice of the cantor. A number of Rwandan actors move among the audience and speak of death, their own deaths, of rape, mutilation, sudden deaths, of lingering, excruciating deaths and unavailing resistance. This is a chorus of the dead. At the end of their account, they join the first witness, who remains on stage: 'I am dead; they have killed me. / I do not sleep. I am not at peace.'[13]

Part 2: Mwaramutse (morning greeting: As-tu passé la nuit? – Have you passed the night?)

The red mud wall opens to reveal a large screen. Across it passes a stream of TV images from the media in different languages: a boxing match, a papal message about abortion, a speech by President Mitterrand, a pilgrimage to Mecca, a Beijing opera. At a table below the screen are the fashionable journalist Bee Bee Bee and her Portuguese colleague Paolo Dos Santos. Strange electronic phantoms speaking a strange language disturb the images: a black woman, a man and a child. The Rwandan linguist Kamali and a noted special correspondent, Colette Bagimont, who is familiar with the situation in Africa, are invited to decipher the strange images and the strange language, whose obsessive admonitions and disquieting faces are troubling the normal indiscriminate stream of TV pictures. The phantoms speak of the tortures and death they have suffered, but they also voice their anger, their need for justice, to call what has happened by its true name: genocide. The TV presenter has to change course. Colette Bagimont warns: 'The dead, among other things, can no longer stand imprecise language, without victims and without executioners. A "tragedy", you know? If someone says tragedy they mean fate, inescapable destiny. The apparition comes to insist strongly on the right word for the crime: genocide.'[14] Where are the great criminals, the instigators and their European associates? The dead ask why they are dead. 'Never again' are empty words if we fail to reflect on 'why'.

Bee Bee Bee, at first irritated, is now convinced. She will organize a major television special to impartially examine the causes of the disaster.

Part 3: La litany des questions (The litany of questions)

The chorus of the dead returns to the scene: three men simply dressed and two women in traditional clothes, unmoving, drawn up in a row behind the music stands. Before them, seated on the same chair as Yolande, reflecting a growing awareness, is the TV journalist. Muyango sings. The litany of questions begins, divided into seven sections, asked by five members of the chorus of the dead, punctuated by the anaphora 'Diront-ils' (They will say), 'Parleront-ils' (They will speak), and introduced by a refrain that warns against the mystification of the information supplied by the media:

> Look at them, but beware:
> These devices that spread
> information,
> It is they that infect
> hearts
> And defile minds.
> A cunning hyena starts
> to low
> as if it was a cow.
> We are in their
> Lair.
> Please be watchful.[15]

The voices of the chorus represent the million cries that hang over the hills of Rwanda, awaiting redress and justice and still not at peace. Will they tell the media what was left unsaid? About the incitement to hatred by RTLM, the Rwandan broadcaster which accompanied the slaughter? The duplicity, the collusion, the calculated negligence of the United Nations? The events of 1959, the revolt of a Hutu elite against a Tutsi elite and the *volte-face* by the Church? The responsibility of the colonists in introducing racial divisions on the basis of fanciful origins (the Batutsi as a Hamitic race, 'une race de seigneurs, les Juifs de l'Afrique' [A master race, the Jews of Africa])[16] and schematic identificatory features, when they actually spoke the same language, had the same God and the same culture, and there was not even a word for race or ethnicity, only clan (*ubwoko*)? The responsibility, the connivance, of the Church and the wickedness of some of its members? The profanation of mourning by which the dead were denied burial and their remains violated?

Part 4: Ubwoko (Clan)

Prélude 2

The chorus of the dead now occupies the stage. Seated on a row of chairs, the chorus follows the progress of the journalist in her imaginary investigation as she seeks to understand, and it intervenes with increasing frequency. A woman in the chorus presents the clue. The reason lies in the keyword 'ubwoko', repeated several times. It means clan, not ethnicity or race. It comes dripping with decades of ignorance, deceit, exploitation, hatred, shame, exile and bloodshed.

Nécessité du savoir (Need to know)

The journalist's awareness is then gradually raised in stages. The first is the meeting with Jacob, a Jewish cabinetmaker who lost his family in the death camps in Poland.

The meeting takes place at a table in the bar of the Hôtel Intercontinental. He trusts Bee Bee Bee, who strikes him as sincerely wanting to understand and he senses that she feels the burden of responsibility, despite representing the media and the entertainment industry and being accustomed to a kind of 'impartiality' that is ultimately blind. Now she knows that 'la vérité a besoin du désir de la vérité' (truth needs the desire for truth)[17] and those who do not want to know preach caution, are suspicious of exaggeration and tend towards denial. The journalist shows him something shocking: a French news programme broadcast a year before the genocide. The president of the Human Rights League of France, on returning from Rwanda, had warned: serious violations are being passed off as ethnic conflicts. In reality they are politically organized in preparation for genocide. Something could have been done. Nothing was.

Where are the seeds of this genocide? In the colonial period. Bee Bee Bee's investigation continues.

Ubwoko (Clan)

The journalist accompanies Jacob to a conference where a lucid speaker, calm and knowledgeable, replies to the journalist's basic question, 'Hutu, qu'est-ce que cela signifie; Tutsi, qu'est-ce que cela signifie?' (Hutu, what does this mean; Tutsi, what does this mean?)[18] with an explanation lasting about an hour.

The terms refer to what is conventionally called the issue of ethnicity in Rwanda. But when the Belgian administration required ID cards to specific the ethnicity of their bearers in 1931, it was realized that the Rwandan language, though rich, lacked the term. At this point there was a semantic shift: *ubwoko*, meaning clan, was used to indicate ethnicity. There was no justification in recognizing ethnic differences in a nation that shared the same language, territory and religion. Differences in identity bound up with physical appearance were wholly relative. Their ancient hatred was a European extrapolation of the theory of Hamitic invasion, which was erroneous, firstly because it asserted the natural superiority of the Tutsi and then justified their oppression as foreigners. The differences in functions and wealth had already disappeared at the time of the genocide.

What was the role of the Europeans and what responsibilities do they bear? They organized Rwandan society as bipolar, having established the two categories of identity as separate races. In this way they helped foment enduring hatred between them, first by favouring the Tutsi, then by supporting the Hutu elite in the repression of the Tutsi, and above all completely effaced the culture of all the colonized peoples. Finally, under their guardianship, they guided a revolution in 1959 which, under the banner of ethnic democracy, led to the genocide of the Tutsis. This is the essence of the speaker's explanation given to the journalist and her Jewish companion.

Naho se bene wacu? (Et les gens de chez nous? – And what about our people?)

The chorus returns. The traditional guitar accompanies a chant composed and performed by Massamba. With the constant presence of Bee Bee Bee, the chorus of the dead raises urgent, insistent questions. What are the responsibilities of the Rwandans? Among them was cast the seed of hatred and shame that numbed their consciences, inverting the commandment not to kill, fuelling the criminal logic which produced the plans for the genocidal machinery. The responsibility rests on the heads of the 'ethnic republic'.

Si c'est un homme… (If this is a man…)

The scene cuts to a small and simple stage set representing Jacob's home. The journalist and Jacob sit facing each other. One of the members of the chorus of the dead has followed them in silence and rests a hand in sympathy on his shoulder as he speaks: a profound bond. What passes through the mind of a man who murders his neighbour, one to whom he was close until the day before? To explain, Jacob tells his story. After escaping death with his brother and returning to Poland, he saw his brother himself brutally killed together with other Jewish survivors by an enraged mob who accused them of stealing children and committing human sacrifice. Calumnies crept into people's brains. People were no longer people but rats, vermin. They had to be done away with, just as one might do away with a virus or a worm. She, too, the intelligent Bee Bee Bee, has given credence to sly calumnies. The hyenas.

Voulez-vous chanter avec moi? (Would you like to sing with me?)

Three hyena-headed men make their entry, preceded by Colette Bagimont. They make their well-meaning speeches: the anarchy after the end of the colonies, the clean hands of France, the far more complicated question of responsibility for the genocide. But the journalist no longer falls for this and refuses to associate herself with their song, sung with masks in their hands in a circle of light. The hyenas exit with animal-like movements.

Amararo (La veillée – The wake)

While images of ancient Rwanda are projected on the screen, the choristers enter playing ancestral rhythms on drums. The musicians urge vigilance. The men advance with ceremonial spears.

Les trois visions de Madame Bee Bee Bee (The three visions of Madame Bee Bee Bee)

The chorus of the dead exits singing, leaving the journalist Bee Bee Bee onstage. Jacob enters and relates that she has had three visions which have increased her eagerness to understand and have begun to disturb her superiors. The three visions pass before our eyes, interpreted by the actors of the chorus. The first represents the procession on Golgotha. The holy women, St John and the Virgin Mary bear in her arms a black Christ crowned with thorns, who will be beheaded, while a well-known bishop, who played an important role in the events of 1959, in the form of a giant bird of prey, offers his dubious justifications. The second is a famous UN general, active in Rwanda in 1994, with a wolf's head. Against the backdrop of Niagara Falls, whose beautiful noise covers all the world's cries of pain, he sheds crocodile tears and justifies his failure to intervene by taking refuge behind the fact he never received the necessary orders. The third represents the 'Hamletic' appearance of the 'thing', the ghost of the father (Mitterand) to his son. Weighty accusations, says his son, have been made about the connivance of his father, who seeks to justify himself with various evasions, while anger mounts among the Rwandan women. Who taught the murderers how to kill? Who protected the murderers?

Façon de fabriquer (Building method)

The journalist seems to have completed her work. Her understanding is mature, her planned broadcast is ready, but the officials have misgivings. Is her programme information or something else? And what is that 'silence d'éternité' at the opening, lasting eight minutes, in which images of genocide flow across the screen, broken only by an extract from the RTLM radio broadcast: 'In fact all the Tutsis will perish; / they will disappear from this country. [...] Because they are being killed like rats.'[19]

À travers nous l'humanité (Through us humanity)

Jacob announces: Bee Bee Bee never broadcast her programme. The chorus of the dead, having watched the whole of the previous scene, now advances to the audience: 'Through us, humanity / looks on you sorrowfully. [...] Forever we are this accusing cloud. / It is for eternity that we, the dead, demand our due. [...] I am not at peace.'[20]

Part 5: *La cantate de Bisesero (The cantata of Bisesero)*

This is the last scene of the performance. The orchestra is in the middle of the stage, while the African and European actors are behind the music stands. The coryphaeus and the voices of the individual singer-witnesses alternate, preceded by a prologue and followed by an epilogue, through all the phases of the event evoked: the resistance of Bisesero. A refrain accompanies each of the phases (the phases are: the exodus to Bisesero, the resistance, the massacre, the agony, the French soldiers):

> On the hills of Muyira
> Covered with forests and bushes
> Before the genocide there lived
> Large numbers of strong men.
> MUYIRA MUYIRA MUYIRA MUYIRA MUYIRA
> MUYIRA MUYIRA MUYIRA MUYIRA MUYIRA
> Between the bushes and the forests
> On the hill of Muyira
> There is a handful of men
> A handful of men
> That now die of sadness.
> MUYIRA MUYIRA MUYIRA MUYIRA MUYIRA
> MUYIRA MUYIRA MUYIRA MUYIRA MUYIRA.[21]

The music and the light fade on the long list of the names of the dead of Bisesero, like the long list of Jewish children constantly repeated at the Holocaust Memorial in Jerusalem.

The tragic condition and evil

The tragic is the presence, as inescapable as it is mysterious at its root, of the evil in man dramatically and inevitably brought to the self-awareness of contemporaries in the twentieth century by genocide. The question of the substance of evil, its origin and its causes, remain inexplicable to reason. Evil is absolute contradiction. As the contemporary philosopher Virgilio Melchiorre rightly says: 'Understanding means finding an explanation, bringing out a meaning or an essential structure of meaning. But how to make sense of the irrational? Of nonsense? Finding a meaning in this case would amount to not recognizing the irrationality of evil, not believing that evil produces the contradiction of affirming and willing not-being as being.'[22] The reality of evil is as undeniable as it is incomprehensible, 'a body foreign to the eidetic of humanity', as Ricoeur puts it.[23]

The question which closes *Rwanda 94* – 'Why?' – remains unanswered. Significantly it rings out at the end against the silence.

If our point of view were political alone (the director stated it was one of his primary intentions), seeking to bring out the responsibilities of the West in setting in motion and sustaining the genocidal machinery, there would be an answer and the construction of the stage text expresses it unhesitatingly. But the signs say something else: the symbolic depth of the characters (the mother, the chorus of the dead, the black Christ beheaded), the Rwandan song, the Western music, the silences, the image of the wounded red earth, the composure of the gestures, the slow rhythm, the proxemics and the intensity of the whole – all these face the audience with a final question which has a very different significance. The layers of significance – psychological, historical-political, anthropological-philosophical-religious – are respectively concentrated principally around three nuclei: the testimony of the mother who has survived, the lecture, the procession and chorus.

How can it happen that neighbours you have lived with until recently on normal, everyday terms are transformed almost overnight into cold-blooded murderers? How is it that normal, good workers and family men become accomplices and perpetrators of massacres planned and orchestrated on the technological level appropriate to them, whether wielding machetes or more sophisticated weapons? How does the unspeakable enter the ordinary?

Shock underlies Yolande's grief. In the audience's distracted or numbed consciousness, it cannot prevent echoes surfacing of the writings, studies and discussions centred on the issue of genocide in recent decades. The enemy is constructed as a phantom.[24] It is constructed by means of a disturbed imagination, fuelled by historical references with no real basis in fact, handed down and orally elaborated and made more acute by the custom of threatening and insulting each other in drunken and aggressive play. Verbalization in terms of 'us' and 'them' does the rest.

Hatred gradually creeps in, but even hatred may be unnecessary to prompt some people to pass from words to deeds. The transition occurs when the potential murderers, feeling they are part of a group that shields and conceals them, are brought together in a task assigned by a leader, a party, an ideology that provides the justification and ensures impunity, and when some event triggers fear and disturbs the social equilibrium. (For the Hutus the event was the shooting down of President Habyarimana's plane together with the spectre of poverty and the scarcity of land for all.) At this point the scapegoat mechanism comes into play. Violence is wreaked against the constructed enemy; the order is simply to kill.[25] But a wide range of different drives and motives are at work in individuals: self-preservation when faced with threats of punishment for failing to carry out an order, the will to power, exhibitionism, paranoid and psychopathic impulses; sexual drives combined with the urge to humiliate and inflict suffering; sadism and vengefulness; compensation for an inferiority complex towards those who are more attractive, wealthier, more refined or elegant; resentment, greed, the exaltation of being able to do without God himself (or, conversely, the desire to earn praise); devotion towards leaders; ambition or frustration; a sense of invulnerability through power over the lives of others; and finally madness. Common to most of the assassins are the interests of poor people, such as the appropriation of possessions shared out after the licensed looting (a few cows, a piece of land, corrugated iron for roofing, electric appliances and so forth). Then there is the propaganda that dehumanizes the other, whom the disturbed imagination is indoctrinated to despise as no longer human but simply vermin to be removed from the earth: *concrelats* (cockroaches), rats and snakes.

There is a second level of analysis. How can a political strategy make use of such an extreme instrument as genocide? The text of the drama is, as we have seen, exhaustive in its treatment of this factor.

Finally, what is the ultimate root of an extreme and recurrent evil of this kind? It returns at an advanced phase of human progress and reveals that the 'project' of humanity (whether viewed in theological or anthropological terms or as part of a programme of evolution) is still at a backward stage and exposed to the continual risk of recidivism.

History is fused with the myth of origins: Cain kills Abel. 'I know that God alone can understand what we did', says one witness quoted in the book by Jean Hatzfeld.[26] But another says, 'God was silent and churches stank of corpses that had been left in them.'[27] The long silence that descends on the last scene of *Rwanda 94* says this and again raises the question of tragedy and the ineluctability of evil within the limit of human being.

From the form of the tragedy to a new dramaturgy of truth, between testimony and ritual

As we have seen, the structure of the performance is atypical: a montage of sequences in a nonchronological, polymorphic sequence, which mingles an eye-witness monologue with the drama dialogued in conversation, the lecture, the dream sequence with grotesque masks and music hall tunes, oratorio, the chanted ritual of the wake, a musical sequence, audio-visual sequences, a ritual procession and the *tombeau* in the final 'Cantate de Bisesero'.

The verbal text, like many dramatic works in recent decades, is not dramatic in origin but constructed out of a multitude of materials drawn from documentary fiction, historical works and journalism, literature and liturgy.[28] In the process of signification, it is intrinsically interwoven with other stage codes. The restrained set represents, in an image on the backdrop, the earth with a material energy, as in painting, the work of Alberto Burri for example. Above all the music fuses the African and Western traditions. The drums, the *enganga* (a Rwandan zither), Muyango's song, in addition to expressing the emotions of the ritual, form a sort of musical stage set which is more effective than any documentary image. The score composed by Garrett List was created in part as a result of a lengthy stay in Rwanda. It seeks to express the contrast, as the musician himself declares, between the beauty of the land of a thousand hills and such great horror. The alternation of periods of silence and sound helps the audience concentrate and raises their consciousness. Outstanding moments of great intensity are the 'Litany of Questions' and the 'Cantata of Bisesero', in which the repetition of the name of the hill of resistance and death, Muyira, offers a sort of dignified burial for those who had none. As Jacques Delcuvellerie himself noted, the play creates 'a close symbiosis between text, play and music, tending not in the least towards opera, but rather towards ancient tragedy'.[29]

The appeal to the spirit and form of tragedy arises spontaneously. A sensitive critic such as Georges Banu grasped this immediately, writing that *Rwanda 94* regains the tragic form, not by an archaeological process but through direct quotations. In fact one is inevitably led to think of the Greek audiences who watched *The Persians* by Aeschylus for the first time. Representing a world driven to the utmost bounds of grief inevitably takes the work towards the tragic form. Banu adds that evil leads us to the origins and that the violence of man against man recalls that unique choral expression whose source is Athens. The elements that elicit it are the presence of the chorus, songs and music, and the frontality of the fixed backdrop. Banu also observes that addressing the public directly, as in the Greek world, is an evocation of society. When it is necessary to warn the world about the unthinkable there is no room for reticence or secrets: the horror is stated openly.[30]

But the return to this form and above all the horizon of thought which underlays it, discussed in the introduction to this book, is insufficient and if prevalent could be misleading. The perception of impending evil, the unavoidable limits of man today, as never before, and the rise of the new questioning of it in the past century clashes with answers and explanations that never appear definitive, being based on ideologies, philosophies, beliefs inherited and reinstated by our extraordinarily receptive and omnivorous contemporaneity. The path briefly explored in this book has sought to demonstrate this.

The tragic consciousness emerges here in a highly complex theatrical experiment. Its crux is the relationship between reality and representation, between truth and fiction, a crucial nucleus which the history of the theatre in the twentieth century debated widely, with the work of Grotowski marking a watershed and the practice of the performers as a field of investigation and outstanding achievement. The theatre needs truth.

Rwanda 94 goes so far as to stage the actual testimony of a Tutsi mother who escaped when her children and her husband were killed, and who still remembers the aggression suffered by her mother and herself as a child during a pogrom. The words she utters are her own, taken from her book, selected by the group and herself, but interwoven with other memories, like that of her mother. She is not an actress and is not acting. But, says Decuvellerie incisively: 'She moves on a knife edge. [...] There are no suggestions of charm or spontaneous aberrations, and we feel this: the fact that she is not an actress and that this is an artful form. She is what she says but she "plays" the part of herself. She is performed in this performance.'[31]

An urgent need for truth does not fear to live with a horizon of performance. In fact it is the depth and intensity of the symbolic impact of the performance that enable it to avoid the risk of the continuous flow of information or the TV reality show. Doing wrong or suffering it, the direct testimony of having done wrong or having suffered it, may slide into indifference, the *basso continuo* of a medium that churns out everything, trivializing and justifying it. The performance isolates the fact and makes it stand out, inscribing it in a set of signs that give it a depth of analogy and meaning, and converts indifference into fear, shame, indignation and understanding.

Yolande Mukagasana is also Andromache, Atossa and Hecuba. She is Dante's Francesca, who is 'like one who weeps and speaks'.[32] She is the Mater Dolorosa of the crucifixion and the pietà. She is Bertolt Brecht's Mother Courage but also evokes Paul Claudel's Violaine (both these works are in Decuvellerie's repertoire).

The true Rwandan mother appears at the end of our path of analysis. Therefore she naturally evokes other mother characters we have met: Mrs Alving, Mara/Violaine, Christine Mannon, Mother Courage, Cesonia (Caligula's loving mother), and Nell. Though we have registered the distance from the sacred, the great core of the foundation of the genre, in our reflections on the tragic and the dramatic transformation of tragedy in the twentieth century, I feel it is true that the recurrent archetype of the mother restores the sacred by a different path, through the indissoluble and ambivalent bond with the origin.

The forms of the theatre and the forms of ritual and social practice, tragedy, ritual weeping, the epic-political theatre, the trial, converge in a choral meditation that seeks the meaning of the self and of one's life with others in the sense of the tragic.[33]

Ruhe: Silence and Peace

What drives the ordinary person to be voluntarily complicit with the evil which insinuates itself into reality, subverts its order, stops the movement towards harmony and human development? How can one stoop to make a pact with the Devil without realizing it, or else being fully aware and yet allowing oneself to be led astray? The question is certainly bound up with the insoluble problem of the foundations of evil and its contradictions, the radical nature of the tragic.

Here I wish to evoke, to convey the final sense of this whole essay, a very beautiful, powerful and poignant performance produced by the Muziektheater Transparant of Antwerp. It premiered at the Kunsten Festival des Arts in Brussels on 10 May 2007, and was then repeated in many cities, including Paris, as part of the Festival d'automne 2007 (where I saw it), with the dramaturgy and direction of Josse De Pauw and the participation of the Collegium Vocale de Gent.

The first of the above questions underlay this production, which we can describe as a dramatic concert, based on the combination of a number of Schubert's Lieder with monologues woven out of the 1967 book *De SS'ers*. In it Armando and Hans Sleutelaar brought together eight interviews with anonymous Dutch citizens, seven men and one woman, who were German collaborators in World War II. The men fought on the Eastern front, the woman worked in a German hospital.

Some ordinary chairs are arranged without any apparent order in a bare space. (I saw the production in the former convent where the Maison de l'Architecture was installed in Paris.) Members of the audience enter and take their seats. In a few minutes the singers of the noted vocal ensemble, seated amid the audience on similar chairs, stand up and begin the Lieder, which is sung a capella. They fall silent and sit down again. An actor and actress, also seated in the audience, wearing normal clothes, stand up by turns and recite their monologues, facing the public, often embarrassingly close and questioning. Each could seamlessly take the place of the other. They speak, explaining what they felt at the time. They feel no remorse. They do not deny their past. It is as if they are still unaware: a common humanity, very common, which can only present justifications after the fact.

The woman, the talented Carly Wijs, reveals what motivated her. She was young when she began working in a particularly pleasant hospital, north of Berlin, reserved for members of the SS units who arrived mutilated by the war. She had ended up there because she was a good linguist. The work satisfied her fine sense of pity, her powers of female consolation and her need to use her abilities. She felt fulfilled; she felt she was *someone*. Her vanity at the privilege of coming into contact even once with those who counted (whether Hitler or Himmler), at being able to say that she had found them kind or mean, as others could never have done, tickled her conceit. She was excited and even proud of her closeness to the outstanding heroism shown by the victims of mutilation, endured with incredible courage and even ostentation (such as the pilot who had lost his legs and nose while struggling out of a burning plane). She has not yet understood what happened next. She only knows she spent nine months in prison.

The man (the gifted Josse De Pauw, Tom Jansen and Dirk Roofthooft alternated in this role) also presents his reasons. He was a farmer and joined the party to escape from poverty and get a job. Then he was convinced that the fascists were more serious than the socialists in their opposition to capitalism and he wanted to be completely consistent in his beliefs. He became a captain. In the party he felt he belonged and counted. In the army he felt the pride of the German soldier: no tenderness, no failure. At the front, when attacking in terrible hand-to-hand combat, he experienced a headiness, like being high on drugs, which he found it difficult to do without. It would be followed by the strangeness of indifference and normality ('But an hour after the attack I would eat').[34] As a soldier he was always excited by a sense of superiority: 'I find military life wonderful. The whole military set-up is great in itself. What an army can do! The mass! In the SS we were always superior to the enemy, you know? We were always superior.'[35] Of course he also had misgivings: all those wounds, all those hardships in the mud of the trenches, and for what? War. As for the Jews, he couldn't say: he wasn't mixed up in the business when it was going on. Later there was propaganda which confused matters. What he knows is that he does not agree with anti-Semitism and the Final Solution, but certainly races are races and a system can make mistakes. Yet he remains a National Socialist: 'You can't just wipe out a quarter of your life.'[36]

The audience is uncomfortable, embarrassed. They would prefer not to have anything in common with these people, yet they feel the boundary line in behaviour is not always clear, that the sound and the sense of those words is not new and not alien to them. Their simplifications are passed off as common sense, false bonhomie, bad faith, stupidity, vanity and illusion. The facile acceptance of ideologies, the inability or refusal to raise one's gaze toward the broader horizon and complexity, suffice to create a consensus that conceals, as we saw in the case of *Rwanda 94*, many other covert motives. There are dissonant notes in the world of humanity.

With a leap onto a different plane the audience is transported to another horizon, which opens up and troubles the mind: the music of Schubert's *Lieder*.[37] They speak of the harmonies of voices and elements of nature and the universe, they speak of ideal faces and dreams, of quiet valleys, animal myths, but also of storms that threaten, roaring winds and burning deserts, of vultures suddenly attacking, of wild beasts that use force and cunning, of wine and love but also death. Evil is always lurking. Humanity seeks peace:

> Ruhe, schönstes Glück der erde,
> Ruhe, senke segnend dich herab,
> dass es stille in uns werde,
> wie in Blumen ruht ein Grab. [...]
> Ruhe, deinen Frieden gib der Erde,
> deinen Balsam geuss herab,
> dass geheit die Seele werde,
> sich erhebend aus dem Grab.[38]

> (Peace, the supreme happiness of the earth,
> peace, call down a blessing on us,
> that silence may be in us,
> as a grave sleeps
> beneath flowers. [...]
> Grant your peace to the earth,
> pour your soothing balm over it,
> so that the soul may be healed
> and rise above the grave.)

The words and notes of Schubert's *Lied*, slow, melancholy and solemn, spread above all this harshness. But if the word 'Ruhe', spoken or sung, bespeaks peace and silence, shouted harshly it is an imperative that the actor, the captain who was a Nazi collaborator, barks out like a threatening military order. There is also ambiguity in the beauty. 'Nous devons être nos propres sentinelles' (We have to be our own sentinels), says the director Josse De Pauw. Oedipus has not yet ceased to see and humanity still knows not what it does.

I will stop here; however, further exploration of the works from the last decades of the century could enrich and extend these first reflections.

It is said that the effect of time is the opposite of that of space, in which things become more indistinct as they recede from us. But with the passing of time things gain in clarity. In a century like the twentieth, traversed by unfathomable mysteries which defy explanation by the most diverse ideologies, history is projected into a very long period of comprehension and conversion. The imperatives that humanity finds or sets itself, when faced with the inescapable limits, are continually under threat, especially the imperative not to repeat those errors. For this reason the space offered by the theatre has a particular importance in the twentieth century and for the twentieth century. This brings us back to the origins of Greek tragedy – a religious, philosophical, poetic and political theatre – to the striving to understand and master the mystery of mankind, its unfathomable capacity for good and evil.

More than any other means of communication and expression, in the century of communication the theatre is the place for meeting and sharing experiences that bring to life texts made to live by the people who, in the here and now, present them and embody them concretely in themselves and to themselves, in the chorus. The growing understanding, necessarily only intellectual, of facts which become gradually remote in time is accompanied in the theatre by an immediacy, a freshness, even a physical closeness, the communion of an experience which is of today and is repeated anew in every performance, in which the individual stakes his or her whole being on every occasion.

A real group is convened around the millennial ritual of collective meditation on the philosophical and existential questions that traverse the darkness of human life, resting on an ancient insight that has come down through the centuries and still concerns us with ever greater urgency. In the era of the virtual and secularism, the audience's experience, physically present in live theatre and compelled to reflect in depth on a reality that the media continually and rapidly presents to their eyes, is 'necessary', as Peter Brook saw.[39] In the modern scheme of things, to which, however, it belongs wholly, it makes a difference.

Tragedy was born in our cultural tradition as a meditation on fate, on necessity, which looms above human freedom. The gift of freedom that Christianity promised man has not resulted in man enabling good to triumph. The current forms of the tragic and of tragedy arise out of the misuse of freedom. This, in extreme synthesis, is the discourse of *Akropolis* and *Apocalypsis cum figuris*, as well as the theme of this book. The image of the rag dummy of Christ placed in the cremation oven by the prisoners in the camp is fused with the image of Christ returned and forever expelled from the horizon of mankind. Is this the denial of a great project for mankind?

Appendix

CHRONOLOGY OF PRODUCTIONS

This appendix, which includes entries on the composition, publication and reception in the theatre of the texts analysed, has been prepared in collaboration with Maria-Rita Gaito. The chronology includes a selection of productions limited to the twentieth century, with some exceptions justified by references in the analysis. The sources used are largely from newspaper clippings, press releases, posters and other archival materials. We have preferred to leave them in their original form, however variable, unorganized and often incomplete, deeming them useful to the reader.

The appendix seeks to convey an idea of the resonance of the reflection on the tragic in individual texts examined, and their concrete life on stage, before a wide range of different audiences. Obviously it offers merely quantitative data related to a history of interpretation and reception that goes beyond the limits of this book. It may suggest further points of interest and approaches to study.

Gengangere

(It. *Spettri*, Fr. *Les revenants*, Eng. *Ghosts*, Ger. *Gespenster*)

Composed in Rome and Sorrento during the summer of 1881. The first notes probably date back to the winter of that year. The first version, lost, was made in June and the second in October. The work was published in December 1881. Among the principal Italian translations of recent decades I can recommend those by Piero Monaci (Milan: Rizzoli, 1954); Anita Rho (Turin: Einaudi, 1959; 1976; 1981); Alfhild Motzfeldt Tidemand-Johannessen, authorized by the Ibsen estate (Milan: Mursia 1962–85); Roberto Alonge (Milan: Mondadori, 1988); Claudio Magris (Milan: Garzanti 1995, 2006); and Roberto Alonge and Franco Perrelli (Milan: Rizzoli, 2008), from which I quote. This last has been republished with variations that I have indicated in the notes, in Henrik Ibsen, Drammi moderni, edited by R. Alonge (Milan: Radici BUR, 2009). Notable among French translations are those by Terje Sinding (Paris: Imprimerie Nationale, 2003) and Régis Boyer (Paris: Gallimard, 2006). Notable among the English translations is the one by James McFarlane (Oxford: Oxford University Press, 1961). Notable among the German translations is that by Egon Gerlach (Stuttgart: Reclam, 1968 and subsequent editions).

Productions

20 May 1882
Cast: Helen Alving – H. von Bluhme; Oswald, Pastor Manders and Regina Engstrand – Norwegian and Danish nonprofessional actors. World premiere in Chicago, Aurora Turner Hall.

22 August 1883
Swedish version by F. Hedberg (Gengångare); director: A. Lindberg; production: August Lindbergs Sällskap. Cast: Helen Alving – H. Winterhjelm; A. Oswald – Lindberg; Pastor Manders – G. A. Ranft; Engstrand – K. Axelsson; Regina Engstrand – A. Rustan. Helsingborg, Hälsingborg Stads Teater.

27 September 1883
Swedish version by E. Hwasser; director: G. Fredrikson; production: Kungliga Dramatiska Teatern. Cast: Helen Alving – E. Hwasser; Oswald – G. Törnquist; Pastor Manders – A. Elrnlund; Engstrand – F. Thegerström; Regina Engstrand – G. Ulff. Stockholm, Kungliga Dramatiska Teatern.

20 April 1885
Swedish version; production: Nya Teatern/Svenska Teatern. Cast: Helen Alving – I. Reis; Oswald – H. Bang; Pastor Manders – H. Agardh; Engstrand – A. Arppe; Regina Engstrand – H. Bruno. Helsinki, Nya Teatern.

14 April 1886
German version by M. von Borch. Cast: Helen Alving – Hausen; Oswald – Wendt; Pastor Manders – W. Hellmuth-Bräm; Engstrand – J. Krägel; Regina Engstrand – Weigel. First private performance in Germany at Augsburg in the presence of the author, Augsburger Stadt-Theater.

21 December 1886
German version. Cast: Helen Alving – M. Berg; Oswald – A. Barthel; Pastor Manders – M. Grube; Engstrand – C. Weiser; Regina Engstrand – C. Schwarz. Performed at Meiningen, in the presence of the author, Herzogliches Hoftheater.

9 January 1887
German version; director: A. Anno. Cast: Helen Alving – C. Frohn; Oswald – E. Wallner; Pastor Manders – E. Reicher; Engstrand – L. Würmburg; Regina Engstrand – H. Schüle. Performed in Berlin in the presence of the author, Residenz-Theater.

29 September 1889
German version by M. von Borch; director: H. Meery; production: Freie Bühne (Lessing-Theater). Cast: Helen Alving – M. von Bűlow-Schanzer; Oswald – E. Robert; Pastor

Manders – A. Kraußneck; Engstrand – T. Lobe; Regina Engstrand – A. Sorma. Berlin, Lessing-Theater.

30 May 1890
French version by R. Darzens; production: Compagnie du Théâtre Libre. Cast: Helen Alving – Barny; Oswald – A. Antoine; Pastor Manders – Arquillière; Engstrand – Janvier; Regina Engstrand – L. Colas/Ms. Nau. Paris, Théâtre Libre.

13 March 1891
English version by W. Archer; production: The Independent Theatre. Cast: Helen Alving – A. Austin Wright; Oswald – F. Lindo; Pastor Manders – L. Outram; Engstrand – S. Howard; Regina Engstrand – E. Kenward. London, Royalty Theatre.

22 February 1892
Italian version by E. Polese and P. Rindler; production: Compagnia Giovan Battista Marini. Cast: Helen Alving – V. Marini; Oswald – E. Zacconi; Pastor Manders – L. Pilotto; Engstrand – O. Calabresti; Regina Engstrand – E. Saporetti-Sichel/A. Moro-Pilotto. Milan, Teatro Manzoni.

19 November 1892
Italian version; production: Compagnia Grisanti-Micheluzzi. Cast: Oswald – A. Grisanti, with: E. Micheluzzi; E. Treves; M. Borisi Micheluzzi; G. De Santis; C. Grisanti; M. Grisanti. Como, Teatro Cressoni.

5 March 1900
Director: B. Bjørnson; sets: J. Wang; production: Nationaltheatret. Cast: Helen Alving – T. Hansson/S. Reimers; Oswald – H. Christensen; Pastor Manders – O. Voss/H. Stormoen; Engstrand – J. Selmer/G. Thomassen; Regina Engstrand – R. Wettergreen/J. Voss. Kristiania (Oslo), Nationaltheatret.

21 April 1900
German version; director: E. Lessing; production: Deutsches Theater. Cast: Helen Alving – L. Dumont; Oswald – R. Rittner; Pastor Manders – E. Reicher; Engstrand – M. Reinhardt; Regina Engstrand – E. Lehmann. Berlin, Deutsches Theater.

25 January 1903
Italian version; director: E. Zacconi; production: Compagnia Ermete Zacconi. Cast: Helen Alving – A. Moro-Pilotto; Oswald – E. Zacconi; Pastor Manders – E. Dominici; Engstrand – A. Rossi; Regina Engstrand – I. Cristina. Florence, Teatro Niccolini.

26 January 1903
English version; director: G. Fawcett; production: George Fawcett Company. Cast: Helen Alving – M. Shaw; Oswald – F. Lewis; Pastor Manders – M. Wilkinson; Engstrand – C. A. Gay; Regina Engstrand – V. Kline. New York, Manhattan Theatre.

29 January 1903
Danish version; director: J. Nielsen; production: Det Kongelige Teater. Cast: Helen Alving – B. Hennings; Oswald – N. Neiiendam; Pastor Manders – P. Jerndorff; Engstrand – E. Reumert; Regina Engstrand – E. Sinding. Copenhagen, Det Kongelige Teater.

24 November 1903
Italian version; production: Drammatica Compagnia Italiana director: Vittorio Farinati. Cast: Helen Alving – R. Venturini; Oswald – V. Farinati; Pastor Manders – I. Marchetti; Engstrand – F. Marchetti; Regina Engstrand – D. Giorgi. Naples, Teatro Fiorentini.

5 December 1903
French version by R. Darzens; production: Théâtre Antoine. Cast: Helen Alving – Grumbach; Oswald – A. Antoine; Pastor Manders – Mosnier; Engstrand – Signoret; Regina Engstrand – L. Colas/J. Lion. Paris, Théâtre Antoine.

31 March 1905
Russian version by A. Hansen and P. Hansen; director: K. Stanislavsky; sets: V. Simov; production: MXAT (Moscow Art Theatre). Cast: Helen Alving – M. Savitskaya; Oswald – I. Moskvin; Pastor Manders – V. Kaćalov; Engstrand – A. Višnevsky; Regina Engstrand – O. Knipper. Moscow, MXAT.

1 May 1906
Italian version; production: Drammatica Compagnia Italiana del Cav. Uff. Gustavo Salvini. Cast: Helen Alving – G. Aliprandi; Oswald – G. Salvini; Pastor Manders – G. Maione Diaz; Engstrand – C. Aureli; Regina Engstrand – I. Salvini. Como, Teatro Cressoni.

8 November 1906
German version; director: M. Reinhardt; sets: E. Munch; production: Deutsches Theater, Kammerspiele Berlin. Cast: Helen Alving – A. Sorma; Oswald – A. Moissi; Pastor Manders – F. Kayßler; Engstrand – M. Reinhardt; Regina Engstrand – L. Höflich. Berlin, Kammerspiele Berlin.

12 January 1912
Japanese version by O. Mori; director: K. Osanai; sets: K. Kajita; production: Engeki Doshikai. Cast: Helen Alving – H. Kitamura; Oswald – S. Kitamura; Pastor Manders – E. Tanaka; Engstrand – S. Kamiyama; Regina Engstrand – H. Azuma. Tokyo, Yurakuza Theatre.

18 June 1922
Italian version; director: A. Ninchi; production: Compagnia Annibale Ninchi. Cast: Helen Alving – L. Torri; Oswald – A. Ninchi; Pastor Manders – G. Lacchini; Engstrand – G. Barnabo; Regina Engstrand – L. Piacentini. Rome, Teatro Argentina.

APPENDIX

18 October 1922
Italian version; production: Compagnia Eleonora Duse. Cast: Helen Alving – E. Duse; Oswald – M. Benassi; Pastor Manders – C. Bertramo; Engstrand – A. Martelli; Regina Engstrand – L. Carrara. Trieste, Teatro Verdi.

30 December 1922
Italian version; director: A. De Sanctis; production: Compagnia Alfredo De Sanctis. Cast: Helen Alving – E. Berti Masi/I. Colonnello; Oswald – A. De Sanctis; Pastor Manders – A. Valenti; Engstrand – L. Lambertini; Regina Engstrand – R. Masi/G. Dondy. Rome, Teatro Argentina.

12 June 1923
Italian version; director: E. Duse; sets: Stroppa; production: Compagnia Eleonora Duse. Cast: Helen Alving – E. Duse; Oswald M, Benassi; Pastor Manders – C. Bertramo/L. Orlandini; Engstrand – C. Galvani; Regina Engstrand – L. Carrara/M. Morino/J. Morino. Oxford, New Oxford Theatre.

26 March 1928
French version; director: G. Pitoëff; sets: G. Pitoëff; production: Compagnie Pitoëff. Cast: Helen Alving – G. Prozor; Oswald – G. Pitoëff; Pastor Manders – H. Gaultier; Engstrand – J. Hort; Regina Engstrand – L. Pitoëff. Paris, Théâtre des Mathurins.

4 April 1929
Italian version; director: E. Zacconi; production: Compagnia Drammatica Italiana Ermete Zacconi. Cast: Helen Alving – I. Cristina; Oswald – E. Zacconi; Pastor Manders – C. Tamberlani; Engstrand – A. Contardi; Regina Engstrand – E. W. Tettoni. Rome, Teatro Argentina.

13 November 1934
Italian version; production: Compagnia Alessandro Moissi-Vanda Capodaglio. Cast: Helen Alving – V. Capodaglio; Oswald – A. Moissi; Pastor Manders – P. Campa; Engstrand – G. Miotti; Regina Engstrand – M. Fabbri. Rome, Teatro Argentina.

14 May 1949
Italian version; director: R. Ricci; production: Teatro Stabile Eliseo di Roma. Cast: Helen Alving – E. Magni; Oswald – R. Ricci; Pastor Manders – G. Oppi; Engstrand – G. Piamonti; Regina Engstrand – L. Angeleri. Rome, Teatro Eliseo.

27 July 1956
Italian version by G. Puccini and L. Lucignani; director: L. Lucignani; sets: G. Polidori. Cast: Helen Alving – E. Albani; Oswald – E. Giovampietro; Pastor Manders – A. Foà; Engstrand – R. Giangrande; Regina Engstrand – L. Alfonsi. Casamicciola.

12 November 1958
English version by N. Ginsbury; director: J. Fernald; sets and costumes: N. Hobson; production: The Old Vic Company. Cast: Helen Alving – F. Robson; Oswald – R. Lewis; Pastor Manders – M. Hordern/D. Wolfit; Engstrand – E. Thorndike/D. Thorndike; Regina Engstrand – A. Iddon. London, The Old Vic.

9 January 1959
Italian version by N. Zoja; director: M. Ferrero; sets and costumes: E. Frigerio; production: Compagnia Proclemer-Albertazzi. Cast: Helen Alving – A. Proclemer; Oswald – G. Albertazzi; Pastor Manders – T. Bianchi/G. Mauri; Engstrand – G. Galavotti; Regina Engstrand – E. Albertini. Milan, Teatro Odeon.

14 June 1967
English version by W. Archer; director: A. Bridges; scenography: J. Herbert; production: Royal Shakespeare Company. Cast: Helen Alving – P. Ashcroft; Oswald – J. Castle/M. Jayston; Pastor Manders – D. Waller; Engstrand – C. Rose; Regina Engstrand – C. Ashcroft/N. Pyne. London, Aldwych Theatre.

8 April 1973
Polish version by I. Suesser; director: H. Baranowski; sets: J. Juk Kowarski; production: Teatr Polski. Cast: Helen Alving – E. Studencka-Kłosowicz; Oswald – W. Rudzki; Pastor Manders – C. Stopka; Engstrand – A. Krajewicz; Regina Engstrand – M. Chruścielówna. Bydgoszcz, Teatr Polski.

25 October 1975
Italian version by C. Magris; director: E. Fenoglio; sets and costumes: M. Giorsi; production: Compagnia Brignone-Pagliai. Cast: Helen Alving – L. Brignone; Oswald – U. Pagliai; Pastor Manders – R. Giovampietro; Engstrand – G. Becherelli; Regina Engstrand – P. Gassman. Bari, Teatro Piccinni.

12 January 1982
Italian version; director: N. Sanchini; sets: U. Martinelli; production: Compagnia Teatro Club Rigorista. Cast: Helen Alving – G. Martinelli; Oswald – J. Baiocchi; Pastor Manders – N. Sanchini; Engstrand – R. Cucciolla; Regina Engstrand – A. Sessa. Sorrento, Teatro Tasso.

26 June 1982
Italian version; director: L. Ronconi; sets: M. Garbuglia; production: Luca Ronconi Produzioni Teatrali. Cast: Helen Alving – M. Fabbri; Oswald – M. Avogadro; Pastor Manders – W. Bentivegna; Engstrand – P. di Iorio; Regina Engstrand – G. Zamparini. Spoleto, XXV Festival dei Due Mondi, former church of San Nicolò.

20 February 1985
Italian version by G. Lavia; director and sets: G. Lavia; production: Teatro Stabile Eliseo di Roma. Cast: Helen Alving – V. Fortunato; Oswald – G. Lavia; Pastor Manders –

U. Ceriani; Engstrand – P. Triestino; Regina Engstrand – M. Guerritore. Pisa, Teatro Verdi.

May 14 1985
Italian version based on an essay by R. Alonge; director: B. Navello; sets: P. Bregni; production: Teatro Stabile d'Abruzzo. Cast: Helen Alving – C. Scarpitta; Oswald – E. Schilton; Pastor Manders – L. Virgilio; Engstrand – B. Alessandra; Regina Engstrand – C. Vertova. L'Aquila, Teatro Stabile dell'Aquila.

2 October 1986
English version by P. Watts; director: D. Thacker; sets: S. Keegan; production: The Young Vic. Cast: Helen Alving – V. Redgrave; Oswald – A. Dunbar; Pastor Manders – T. Wilkinson; Engstrand – P. Theedom; Regina Engstrand – A. Wray/E. Matheson. London, The Young Vic.

6 March 1987
Italian version by R. Alonge; director: F. Branciaroli; sets and costumes: A. Buti; production: Teatro de Gli Incamminati. Cast: Helen Alving – V. Fortunato; Oswald – F. Branciaroli; Pastor Manders – G. Fortebraccio; Engstrand – E. Florio; Regina Engstrand – O. Notati. Monza, Teatro Villoresi.

28 February 1991
Italian version by L. Chiavarelli and O. Jo Norbye; director: W. Manfrè; sets: T. Stefanucci; production: Compagnia del Teatro Ghione. Cast: Helen Alving – I. Ghione; Oswald – S. Onofri; Pastor Manders – C. Simoni; Engstrand – R. Rossi; Regina Engstrand – M. Piana. Rome, Teatro Ghione.

9 February 1993
Italian version by M. Podestà; director: G. Bosetti; sets and costumes: M. A. Giuri; production: Teatro Stabile del Veneto. Cast: Helen Alving – M. Bonfigli; Oswald – S. Romano; Pastor Manders – G. Bosetti; Engstrand – M. Loreto; Regina Engstrand – R. Del Greco. Milan, Teatro Nuovo.

24 February 1998
Italian version by R. and G. de Monticelli; director: G. de Monticelli; sets and costumes: G. Gregori; production: Teatro Stabile Eliseo di Roma. Cast: Helen Alving – R. Falk; Oswald – R. Sturno; Pastor Manders – F. Graziosi; Engstrand – I. Petruzzi; Regina Engstrand – M. Richeldi. Rome, Piccolo Eliseo.

5 November 1998
French version by P. A. Evensen and O. Werner; Director: O. Werner; sets: P. Miesch; costumes: C. Mateos; production: Les Gémeaux, Scène Nationale. Cast: Helen Alving – E. Scob; Osvald – M. Quidu; Il pastore Manders – P. Bonke; Engstrand – A. Trétout; Regina Engstrand – S. Schwartzbrod. Sceaux (Île-de-France), Grand Théâtre.

27 July 2000
Director: F. Balestra; sets: P. Portoghesi; production Bottega San Lazzaro di Salerno, Ass. Amici del teatro di Norcia. Cast: Helen Alving – E. Gardini; Osvald – L. Amato; Il pastore Manders – F. Temperini; Engstrand – S. Somma; Regina Engstrand – B. Mautino. Amalfi, Teatro La Darsena, Ibsenfestival.

30 January 2001
Italian version and director: C. Lievi; sets: C. Antal; costumes: L. Perego; production: CTB Teatro Stabile di Brescia. Cast: Helen Alving – F. Nuti; Oswald – F. Migliaccio; Pastor Manders – G. C. Dettori; Engstrand – M. Toloni; Regina Engstrand – S. Toffolatti. Brescia, Teatro Sociale di Brescia.

17 November 2004
Italian version by A. Rho; Director: M. Castri; sets and costumes: C. Calvaresi; production: Teatro Biondo Stabile di Palermo. Cast: Helen Alving – I. Occhini / V. Moriconi; Oswald – P. Corallo; Pastor Manders – L. Virgilio; Engstrand – A. Salaroli; Regina Engstrand – I. Petris. Palermo, Teatro Biondo.

8 January 2008
Italian version by C. Magris; director: L Loris; sets: D. Gardinazzi; costumes: N. Ceccolini; production: Teatro Out Off. Cast: Helen Alving – E. Callegari; Oswald – M. Sala; Pastor Manders – A. Zanoletti; Engstrand – M. Greco; Regina Engstrand – S. Ugomari Di Blas. Milan, Teatro Out Off.

1 September 2008
Version in Farsi by M. Hadi; director and sets: S. M. Hosseini; production: Mordad Theatre Group Teheran. Cast: Helen Alving – F. Shiva; Oswald – A. Hushyar; Pastor Manders – S. Shahir; Engstrand – K. Hashemi; Regina Engstrand – M. Mahmodzadeh. Oslo, Nationaltheatret, The Ibsen Stage Festival 2008.

6 October 2011
Italian version by C. Perrelli and dramaturgy by L. Russo; director: C. Pezzoli; sets: G. Andrico; costumes: R. Monti; production: Teatro Stabile di Bolzano. Cast: Helen Alving – P. Milani; Oswald – F. Paravidino; Pastor Manders – C. Simoni; Engstrand – A. Battain; Regina Engstrand – V. Brusaferro; Bolzano, Teatro Comunale.

9 March 2012
Reduction by F. Hirsch; director: D. Bösch; sets and costumes: P. Bannwart; production: Burgtheater (Akademietheater). Cast: Helen Alving – K. Dene; Oswald – M. Meyer; Pastor Manders – M. Schwab; Engstrand – J. Krisch; Regina Engstrand – L. Amuat. Vienna, Akademietheater.

L'annonce faite à Marie

(It. *L'annuncio a Maria*, Eng. *The Tidings Brought to Mary*, Ger. *Verkündigung Mariä*)

Composition, based on *La jeune fille Violaine* (in the two forms of 1892 and 1901), appears to have been begun in 1909. The work was published in the December 1911 and January, March and April 1912 editions of the *Nouvelle Revue Française*. It was then issued in 1940 by Éditions Gallimard, with the addition of a variant for the stage. In 1948 the definitive stage text was published, dedicated to Jacques Hébertot. Notable among the translations into Italian are that by Francesco Casnati published in 1912 (Milan: Vita e Pensiero, 1931) and that by Giuliano Vigini of the same version (Milan: Vita e Pensiero, 1993), into English that by Louise Morgan Sill (London: Chatto & Windus, 1916), and into German that by Jacob Hegner (Bonn: Buchgemeinde, 1930).

Productions

20 December 1912
Director: A. Lugné-Poe; sets: J. Variot; costumes: C. Betout; production: Théâtre de l'Oeuvre. Cast: Violaine Vercors – L. Lara; Jacques Hury – R. Karl; Pierre de Craon – V. Magnat; Anne Vercors – A. Lugné-Poe; The Mother – Mme Franconi; Mara – M. Frappa. World première in Paris, Théâtre de l'Oeuvre.

5 October 1913
German version by J. Hegner; director: P. Claudel, W. Dohrn, A. von Salzmann; sets: A. von Salzmann; production: Institut d'Art d'Hellerau. Cast: Violäne (Violaine Vercors) – E. Martersteig; Jakobäus (Jacques Hury) – W. Lotz; Peter von Ulm (Pierre de Craon) – K. Ebert; Andreas Gradherz (Anne Vercors) – B. Decarli; The Mother – L. Hohorst; Mara – M. Dietrich. Hellerau, Institut d'Art d'Hellerau.

10 June 1917
English version by L. Morgan Sill; production/direction: Pioneer Players. London, Strand Theatre.

8 February 1918
German version; director: H. Ihering; sets: Hoenig; production: Wiener Volksbühne. Cast: Violäne (Violaine Vercors) – A. Straub; Jakobäus (Jacques Hury) – W. Momber; Peter von Ulm (Pierre de Craon) – F. Kortner; Mara – L. Karoly. Vienna, Wiener Volksbühne.

28 October 1919
German version; director: Révy; production: Zürcher Kammerspiele. Cast: Violäne (Violaine Vercors) – Clarens; Jakobäus (Jacques Hury) – Hess; Peter von Ulm (Pierre de Craon) – Rainer; Andreas Gradherz (Anne Vercors) – Hardt; Mara – Kinz. Zurich, Zürcher Kammerspiele.

2 May 1921
Director: G. Baty and F. Gémier; sets: G. Baty; production: Compagnons de la Chimère. Cast: Violaine Vercors – E. Francis; Jacques Hury – C. Dullin; Pierre de Craon – H. Rollan; Anne Vercors – Lugné-Poe; Mara – Mme Geoffroy. Paris, Comédie Montaigne.

22 December 1927
German version; director: P. Legband; sets: H. Jűrgens; production: Theater der Stadt Mönchengladbach. Cast: Violäne (Violaine Vercors) – E. Mendelssohn; Jakobäus (Jacques Hury) – R. Greving; Peter von Ulm (Pierre de Craon) – V. Soetbeer; Andreas Gradherz (Anne Vercors) – H. Brackebusch; The Mother – H. Westphal; Mara – H. Reiß. Munich, Theater der Stadt.

26 January 1933
Italian version by U. Nanni; director: G. Tumiati; sets and costumes: B. Tumiati; production: Teatro Manzoni. Cast: Violaine Vercors – W. Bernini; Jacques Hury – Boari; Pierre de Craon – G. Cimara; Anne Vercors – G. Tumiati; The Mother – Belsani; Mara – L. Paoli. Milan, Teatro Manzoni.

19 June 1942
Director: L. Jouvet; sets: C. Bérard and E. Anahory; costumes: C. Bérard and A.-I. Carcano; music: R. Massarani; production: Theatro municipal do Rio de Janeiro. Cast: Violaine Vercors – M. Ozeray; Jacques Hury – R. Outin; Pierre de Craon – S. Audel; Anne Vercors – L. Jouvet; Mara – Wanda. Rio de Janeiro, Theatro Municipal.

12 May 1944
Director: P. Bertin; sets and costumes: E. Labisse; music: M. Scibor; production: Compagnie du Regain. Cast: Violaine Vercors – H. Sauvaneix; Pierre de Craon – J. H. Chambois; Anne Vercors – G. Vitray; Mara – G. Bray. Lyon, Théâtre des Célestins.

11 June 1946
Director: L. Jouvet; sets: E. Anahory and C. Bérard; costumes: A. I. Carcano and C. Bérard; music: R. Massarani; production: L. Jouvet. Cast: Violaine Vercors – M. Mélinand; Jacques Hury – L. Lapara; Pierre de Craon – J. Dalmairi; Anne Vercors – L. Jouvet; Mara – Wanda. Paris, Théâtre de l'Athénée.

12 March 1948
Director: J. Vernier, P. Claudel and E. Francis; music: M. Scibor; production: Jacques Hébertot. Cast: Violaine Vercors – H. Sauvaneix; Pierre de Craon – C. Nissar; Anne Vercors – J. Hervé. Paris, Théâtre Hébertot; toured Italy with performances in Rome, Florence and other town in April 1950.

4 March 1953
Italian version; director: A. Ori; sets: M. Rovida; production: Compagnia del Teatro delle Arti di Firenze. Cast: I. Alfaro, A. Bonari, M. Fossi, M. Mazzucchelli, M. Fabbri, V. Benincasa. Florence, Teatro Rondò di Bacco.

17 February 1955
Director: J. Bertheau and P. Claudel; sets and costumes: G. Wakhévitch; music: M. Scibor; production: Théâtre de l'Oeuvre. Cast: Violaine Vercors – E. Bertrand; Jacques Hury – A. Falcon; Pierre de Craon – Deiber; Anne Vercors – J. Jonnel; The Mother – L. Noro; Mara – D. Noël. Paris, Comédie Française.

25 November 1956
Italian version by E. Pisoni; director: C. Lari; sets: L. Carminati; costumes: E. Ciuti; production: Teatro Sant'Erasmo. Cast: Violaine Vercors – L. Ferro; Jacques Hury – G. Bartolucci; Pierre de Craon – G. Mantesi; Anne Vercors – C. Polacco; Mara – M. Fabbri. Milan, Teatro Sant'Erasmo.

21 January 1961
Director: P. Franck; sets: P. Simonini; costumes: M. H. Dasté; music: M. Scibor; production: Théâtre de l'Oeuvre. Cast: Violaine Vercors – D. Delorme; Jacques Hury – A. Oumansky; Pierre de Craon – A. Taffin; Anne Vercors – M. Etcheverry; Mara – L. Bellon. Paris, Théâtre de l'Oeuvre.

19 March 1962
Director: E. Franck; sets: P. Simonini; costumes: M. H. Dasté; music: M. Scibor; production: Théâtre de l'Oeuvre. Cast: Violain e Vercors – D. Delorme; Jacques Hury – R. Rodier; Pierre de Craon – J. Harden; Anne Vercors – M. Etcheverry; The mother – G. Delbat; Mara – L. Bellon. London, Piccadilly Theatre, French Theatre Festival.

13 August 1966
Director: G. Mairesse; costumes: G. P. H. De Montfaucon, N. Picart; music: M. Scibor; production: G. Mairesse. Cast: Violaine Vercors – A. Morot-Sir; Jacques Hury – G. Bellec; Pierre de Craon – G. Mairesse; Anne Vercors – C. Beautheac; The Mother – J. Moresco; Mara – M. Schiltz. Josselin, Festival de Josselin.

30 October 1970
Director: P. Franck; sets and costumes: P. Simonini; music: R. Rossellini; production: G. Mairesse. Cast: Violaine Vercors – E. Manchet; Jacques Hury – C. Burles; Pierre de Craon – J. P. Laffage; Anne Vercors – J. Haas; The Mother – B. Monmart; Mara – C. Stutzmann. Paris, Opéra-Comique; on tour to the Teatro San Carlo in Naples, then La Fenice in Venice from April 1973.

6 May 1971
Italian version by E. Casnati; director: E. Piccoli; sets and costumes: L. Crippa; production: Compagnia Gli Associati. Cast: Violaine Vercors – I. Meda; Jacques Hury – A. Terrani; Pierre de Craon F. Ferri; Anne Vercors – U. Bologna; The Mother – R. Centa; Mara – B. Tellah. Milan, Teatro San Babila.

5 February 1974
Director: J. Térensier; sets and costumes: G. Wakhévitch; production: ACT. Cast: Violaine Vercors – M. Rayer; Jacques Hury – C. Buhr; Pierre de Craon – J. Le Carpentier; Anne Vercors – R. Party; The Mother – N. Nattier; Mara – H. Merian. Paris, Théâtre de l'ACT.

8 April 1979
Director: B. Boy; production: Compagnie du Trèfle. Cast: Violaine Vercors B. Boy; Jacques Hury – C. Larry; Pierre de Craon – J. Pisigo; Anne Vercors – S. Martin; The Mother – C. Narovitch; Mara – D. Charbonnier. Château de Lourmarin.

17 February 1988
Director: J. P. Rossfelder; sets: M. Trembleau; costumes: A. Berger; production: Théâtre de la Fontanelle, CAC de Sceaux, Jeune Théâtre National, Théâtre 14 Jean-Marie Serreau. Cast: Violaine Vercors – C. Benamou; Jacques Hury – X. Brière; Pierre de Craon – D. Znyk; Anne Vercors – M. Etcheverry; The Mother – J. Boulva; Mara – F. Lefebvre des Noëttes. Paris, Théâtre 14.

11 September 1991
Director: P. Adrien; sets and costumes: P. Dios; production: ARRT Philippe Adrien. Cast: Violaine Vercors – B. Delavaux; Jacques Hury – J. Gamblin; Pierre de Craon – A. Macé; Anne Vercors – J. P. Bagot; The Mother – A. Mercier; Mara – H. Lapiower. Paris, Théâtre de la Tempête.

22 August 1995
Italian version by A. Syxty and D. Rondoni; director: A. Syxty; sets and costumes: A. Zaccheria and Y. Matoga Katarzyna; production: Teatro dell'Arca. Cast: Violaine Vercors – R. Boscolo; Jacques Hury – A. Soffiantini; Pierre de Craon – F. Palmieri; Anne Vercors – S. Braschi; The Mother – F. Martins; Mara – E. Mazzoni. San Marino, Teatro Dogana.

16 September 1998 (*La jeune fille Violaine*)
Director: M. Hermès; sets: T. Leproust; costumes: C. Masson; production: Théâtre de la Huchette. Cast: Violaine Vercors – M. Cuvelier; Jacques Hury – B. Bollet; Pierre de Craon – D. Sarky; Anne Vercors – B. Jousset; The Mother – C. Day; Mara – O. Roire. Paris, Théâtre de la Huchette.

24 February 1999
Director: D. Goudet; sets and costumes: D. Goudet and A. Ogier; production: La Compagnie Théâtrale Francophone. Cast: M. Daube, J. J. Forbin, J. Grange, A. Martirossian, O. Waibel, T. Weller. Paris, crypt of the Church of Saint-Sulpice.

8 November 2001
Director: M. Jocelyn; sets: A. Lagarde; costumes: Z. Koscianski; production: Atelier du Rhin (Centre Dramatique Régional d'Alsace, Colmar), l'Athénée Théâtre Louis-Jouvet. Cast: Violaine Vercors – C. Morrison; Jacques Hury – H. Gaboriau; Pierre de Craon – B. Pesenti; Anne Vercors – L. Astier; The Mother – P. Verdeil; Mara – M. É. Pourtois; Colmar, Théâtre Municipal.

2 October 2005
Director: C. Schiaretti; sets: R. de Fontainieu; costumes: T. Welchlin; production: Théâtre National Populaire, Villeurbanne, les Gémeaux (Sceaux, Hauts-de-Seine). Cast: Violaine Vercors – J. Brouaye; Jacques Hury – O. Borle; Pierre de Craon – S. Maggiani; Anne Vercors – A. Falcon; The Mother – A. Benoit; Mara – L. Besson. Villeurbanne, Théâtre National Populaire.

13 June 2006 (*Violaine* from *The Tidings Brought to Mary*)
Reduction by A. Syxty and D. Rondoni; Director: F. Palmieri; revisitation for two voices of the production by A. Syxty (1995) with video inserts from the television version from three years later; production: Elsinor. Milan, Teatro Stabile di Innovazione. Cast: R. Boscolo (Violaine) and F. Palmeri. Milan, Teatro Sala Fontana.

15 July 2008
Director: C. Perton; sets: C. Perton and C. Fenouillat; costumes: A. Wassev; production: Comédie de Valence, CDN Drôme Ardèche, with the participation of the ENSATT. Cast: Violaine Vercors – J. Delfau; Jacques Hury – H. Gaboriau; Pierre de Craon – V. Garanger; Anne Vercors – A. Marcon; The Mother – C. Cohendy; Mara – H. Viviès. Alba-la-Romaine, Théâtre antique.

Mourning Becomes Electra

(It. *Il lutto si addice ad Elettra*, Fr. *Le deuil sied à Électre*, Ger. *Trauer muss Elektra tragen*)
Composition was begun in October 1929. The first draft was completed in February 1930, the second in July 1931. The final draft was completed in the following months and published by Liveright in New York in 1931. Notable among the translations is the Italian version by Bruno Fonzi (Turin: Einaudi, 1962 and subsequent editions), the French version by Jacqueline Antrusseau and Maurice Goldring (Paris: l'Arche, 1965) and that by Louis-Charles Sirjacq (Paris: l'Arche, 2001), and the German version by Michael Walter (Frankfurt: Fischer-Taschenbuch, 1990).

Productions

26 October 1931
Director: P. Moeller; sets and costumes: R. E. Jones; production: Guild Theatre. Cast: Seth Beckwith – A. Hughes; Christine Mannon – A. Nazimova; Lavinia Mannon – A. Brady; Peter Niles – P. Foster; Hazel Niles – M. Arbenz; Adam Brant – T. Chalmers; Ezra Mannon – L. Baker; Orin Mannon – E. Larimore. World premiere in New York, Guild Theatre.

28 March 1941
Italian version by A. Moltedo; director: G. Pacuvio; sets to sketches by: E. Prampolini; costumes: E. Calderini; production: Compagnia del Teatro delle Arti director: Anton Giulio Bragaglia. Cast: Seth Beckwith – G. Dolfini; Christine Mannon – L. Braccini; Lavinia Mannon – D. Torrieri; Peter Niles – A. Varelli; Hazel Niles – T. Farnesi; Adam Brant – F. Diaz; Ezra Mannon – S. Randone; Orin Mannon – S. Randone; a singer – G. Giachetti. Rome, Teatro delle Arti.

15 December 1945
Italian version, director: G. Strehler; sets: G. Ratto and Fornasetti; production: Compagnia Benassi-Torrieri. Cast: Seth Beckwith – A. Ortolani; Christine Mannon – C. Gheraldi; Lavinia Mannon – D. Torrieri. Peter Niles – L. Severini; Hazel Niles – A. Brandimarte; Adam Brant – G. Oppi; Ezra Mannon – M. Benassi; Orin Mannon – M. Benassi; a singer – T. Bianchi. Milan, Teatro Odeon.

18 January 1947
French version by P. Blanchart; director: M. Jamois; sets: E. Hervier; costumes: O. Choumansky; production: Marguerite Jamois. Cast: Christine Mannon – V. Tessier; Lavinia Mannon – M. Jamois; Orin Mannon – A. Cuny. Paris, Théâtre Montparnasse.

17 March 1967
(Opera) Composer: M. D. Levy; conductor: Z. Mehta; production: Metropolitan Opera House. Cast: Christine Mannon – M. Collier; Lavinia Mannon – E. Lear; Peter Niles – R. Bottcher; Hazel Niles – L. Sukis; Adam Brant – S. Milnes; Ezra Mannon – J. Macurdy; Orin Mannon – J. Reardon. New York, Metropolitan Opera House.

Summer 1971
Director: M. Kahn; sets: W. Ritman; costumes: J. Greenwood; production: Joseph Verner Reed. Cast: Seth Beckwith – M. Cooper; Christine Mannon – S. Thompson; Lavinia Mannon – J. Alexander; Peter Niles – R. Stattel; Hazel Niles – M. Anderman; Adam Brant – R. Cooper; Ezra Mannon – L. Richardson; Orin Mannon – P. Thompson. Stratford, American Shakespeare Festival Theatre.

15 November 1972
Director: T. Mann; sets: M. L. Eck; costumes: N. Taylor; production: Circle in the Square. Cast: Seth Beckwith – W. Hickey; Christine Mannon – C. Dewhurst; Lavinia

Mannon – P. Payton-Wright; Peter Niles – Ryland; Hazel Niles – L. Richards; Adam Brant – A. Mixon; Ezra Mannon – D. Davis; Orin Mannon – S. McHattie. New York, Circle in the Square, Joseph E. Levine Theatre.

1982–83
Italian version, director and sets: G. Cavarretta; costumes: G. Stancanelli; production: Gruppo Teatrale II Canovaccio. Cast: S. Pizzurro, G. Silvestri, C. Menconi Orsini, A. Boari, A. Pizzurro. Bologna, Teatro Dehon.

6 March 1989
Italian version by I. Ghione; director: E. Fenoglio; sets and costumes: T. Stefanucci, production: Compagnia del Teatro Ghione. Cast: Seth Beckwith – A. Bufi Landi; Christine Mannon – E. Valente; Lavinia Mannon – I. Ghione; Peter Niles – F. Sciacca; Hazel Niles – G. Saitta; Adam Brant – D. Mazzoli; Ezra Mannon – G. Musy; Orin Mannon – L. Loddi. Rome, Teatro Ghione.

20 February 1997
Italian version by C. Garboli and G. Amitrano; director: L. Ronconi; sets: M. Palli; costumes: M. Canonero; production: Teatro di Genova, Teatro di Roma, in collaboration with the Teatro Stabile di Parma. Cast: Seth Beckwith – M. Fabbri; Christine Mannon – M. Melato; Lavinia Mannon – E. Pozzi; Peter Niles – R. Bini; Hazel Niles – V. Milillo; Adam Brant – R. Alpi; Ezra Mannon – M. Popolizio; Orin Mannon – M. Popolizio. Rome, Teatro Argentina.

14 November 1999 (*Le deuil sied à Electre*)
Director: J.-L. Martinelli; translation: L.-C. Sirjacq; sets: R. Caussanel; costumes: P. Dutertre; production: Théâtre National de Strasbourg. Cast: Seth Beckwith – R. Sassi; Christine Mannon – C. Gagnieux; Lavinia Mannon – S. Milhaud; Peter Niles – E. Caruso; Hazel Niles – A. Rouillier; Adam Brant – L. Diquero; Ezra Mannon – B. Freyd; Orin Mannon – A. Fromager; Strasbourg, Théâtre National de Strasbourg. Performed on 26 and 27 November at the Piccolo Teatro di Milano (Teatro Strehler) at the Festival del Teatro d'Europa.

17 November 2003
Director: H. Davies; sets; B. Crowley; production: Royal National Theatre, London. Cast: Seth Beckwith – C. Peters; Christine Mannon – H. Mirren; Lavinia Mannon – E. Best; Peter Niles – D. Rowan; Hazel Niles – R. Johnson; Adam Brant – P. McGann; Ezra Mannon – T. Pigott-Smith; Orin Mannon – P. Hilton. London, Lyttleton, National Theatre.

21 September 2011
Reduction: G. Edelstein; director: T. Douglas; sets: T. Morrison; costumes: S. Jones; production: Remy Bumppo Theatre Company, Chicago. Cast: Seth Beckwith – V. G. Carey; Christine Mannon – A. Armour; Lavinia Mannon – K. Brennan; Peter

Niles – L. Daigle; Hazel Niles – S. Chavera; Adam Brant – N. Sandys; Ezra Mannon – D. Darlow; Orin Mannon – S. Stangland; Chicago, Greenhouse Theater Center.

2 October 2011 (*The Cursed* – based on *Mourning Becomes Electra*)
Director: A. Areima; sets and costumes: K. Daujotaite; production: OKT/Vilnius City Theatre: Cast: T. Vaskeviciute, T. Gryn, D. Stubraite, A. Dapsys, D. Gavenonis, S. Sipaitis, D. Ciunis, I. Patkauskaite. Vilnius, Theatre Arena, Vilnius International Theatre Festival Sirenos 2011.

Mutter Courage und ihre Kinder

(It. *Madre Courage e i suoi figli*, Fr. *Mère Courage et ses enfants*, Eng. *Mother Courage and Her Children*)
    The composition and revision of the text with variants essentially passed through three phases: the 1939 draft, the acting script of 1941 and the draft of 1950 with alterations that passed into the version published in 1950. Note the edition published in Bertolt Brecht, *Werke*, *Stücke* 6, edited by Klaus Detlef Muller (Berlin/Weimar/Frankfurt, 1989). Quotations in English are from the translation by B. Brecht, *Mother Courage and Her Children*, edited and introduced by John Willett and Ralph Manheim, translated by John Willett (London: Methuen Drama, 1986), also containing translations of the important notes of the Couragemodell. In Italian note the translation by Ruth Leise and Franco Fortini, partly revised by Consolina Vigliero, in an edition with parallel text published by Einaudi (Turin, 2000). In French note the translation by Benno Besson and Geneviève Serreau in the series Théâtre National Populaire, Collection de répertoire, no. 2 (Paris: l'Arche, 1952 and subsequent editions).

Productions

19 April 1941
Director: L. Lindtberg; sets: T. Otto; music: P. Burkhard; production: Schauspielhaus Zürich. Cast: Mother Courage – T. Giehse; Eilif – W. Langhoff; Swiss Cheese – K. Paryla; Kattrin – E. Pesch. World premiere in Zurich, Schauspielhaus Zürich.

11 January 1949
Director: B. Brecht and E. Engel; sets and costumes: T. Otto and H. Kilger; music: P. Dessau; production: Deutsches Theater. Cast: Mother Courage – E. Weigel; Eilif – E. Kahler; Swiss Cheese – J. Teege; Kattrin – A. Hurwicz. Berlin, Deutsches Theater.

8 October 1950
Director: B. Brecht; sets: T. Otto; production: Münchner Kammerspiele. Cast: Mother Courage – T. Giehse; Eilif – H. C. Blech; Swiss Cheese – K. Lieffen; Kattrin – E. Wilhelmi. Munich, Münchner Kammerspielen.

11 September 1951
Director: B. Brecht and E. Engel; sets and costumes: T. Otto and H. Kilger; production: Berliner Ensemble. Cast: Mother Courage – H. Weigel; Eilif – E. Kahler; Swiss Cheese – J. Teege; Kattrin – A. Hurwicz. Berlin, Deutsches Theater.

18 November 1951
French version by G. Serreau and B. Besson; director: J. Vilar; sets and costumes: E. Pignon; music: P. Dessau; production: Théâtre National Populaire. Cast: Mother Courage – G. Montero; Eilif – G. Philipe; Swiss Cheese – J. Négroni; Kattrin – F. Spira. Festival de Suresnes, Théâtre de la Cité Jardins.

4 November 1952
Italian version by F. Grani and F. Candia; director: L. Lucignani; sets: T. Otto and E. Laurenti; costumes: R. Guttuso; music: P. Dessau; production: Compagnia del Teatro dei Satiri. Cast: Mother Courage – C. Gheraldi; Eilif – R. Giovampietro; Swiss Cheese – M. Maldesi; Kattrin – F. Maresa. Rome, Teatro dei Satiri.

July 1955
English version; director: J. Littlewood; sets: J. Bury; production: Theatre Workshop Company. Cast: Mother Courage – J. Littlewood. Barnstaple, Devon Arts Festival.

18 July 1959
French version by G. Serreau and B. Besson; director: J. Vilar; sets: J. Le Marquet; costumes: E. Pignon; music: P. Dessau; production: Théâtre National Populaire. Cast: Mother Courage – G. Montero; Eilif – J. P. Darras; Swiss Cheese – Y. Gasc; Kattrin – C. Minazzoli. Avignon, Palais des Papes.

20 February 1960
Director: E. Piscator; sets: E. Graler; music: P. Dessau; production: Kassel, Staatstheater. Cast: Mother Courage – R. Mosch. Kassel, Staatstheater.

28 March 1963
English version by E. Bentley; director: J. Robbins; sets: M. Cho Lee; costumes: Motley; music: P. Dessau; Production: C. Crawford and J. Robbins, Cast: Mother Courage – A. Bancroft; Eilif – C. Bromberg; Swiss Cheese – J. Catusi; Kattrin – Z. Lampert. New York, Martin Beck Theatre.

25 November 1964
Director: P. Palitzsch; sets and costumes: FI. Schneider; music: P. Dessau; production: Bühnen der Stadt. Cast: Mother Courage – U. von Reibnitz; Eilif – P. Lieck; Swiss Cheese – J. Rickert; Kattrin – A. Schmid. Cologne, Bühnen der Stadt.

26 March 1969
French version by G. Serreau and B. Besson; director: J. Tasso; sets and costumes: R. Deville; music: P. Dessau; production: Agence Littéraire et Artistique Parisienne Société des Spectacles Lumbroso. Cast: Mother Courage – M. Casarès; Eilif – J. de Coninck; Swiss Cheese – Valardy; Kattrin – D. Labourier. Paris, Bobino Music Hall.

11 March 1970
Italian version by E. Filippini; director: L. Squarzina; sets and costumes: G. Padovani; music: P. Dessau; production: Teatro Genovese. Cast: Mother Courage – L. Volonghi; Eilif – O. Antonutti; Swiss Cheese – G. Zanetti; Kattrin – L. Morlacchi. Genoa, Teatro Genovese.

6 October 1971
Czech version; director: J. Kacér; sets: J. Svoboda; costumes: Z. Seydl; music: P. Dessau; production: Narodni Divadlo, National Theater of Prague. Cast: Mother Courage – D. Medricka. Venice, XXX Festival della Prosa.

27 April 1981
Director: A. Kirchner; sets: M. Eggmann; costumes: G. Schlinkert; music: P. Dessau; production: Schauspielhaus Bochum. Cast: Mother Courage – K. Dene. Bochum, Schauspielhaus Bochum.

6 February 1986
Castillian version by A. Buero Vallejo; director: L. Pasqual; sets and costumes: F. Puigserver; production: Madrid, Centro Dramatico Nacional. Cast: Mother Courage – R. M. Sarda; Eilif – J. A. Gallego; Swiss Cheese – V. Diez; Kattrin – V. Peña. Madrid, Teatro Nacional María Guerrero.

27 September 1988
Italian version and Director by: P. Billi and D. Marconcini, in collaboration with R. Molinari; sets: C. Angelini and L. Pari; music: P. Dessau; production: Pontedera Teatro. Cast: Mother Courage – M. D'amburgo and the Compagnia del Maggio di Buti. Pontedera, Festival d'Autunno; Buti, Teatro Francesco di Bartolo.

4 May 1990
English version; director: P. Prowse; sets: P. Prowse; production: Citizens' Company. Cast: Mother Courage – G. Jackson. Glasgow, Citizens' Theatre.

30 November 1991
Italian version by R. Leiser and F. Fortini; director: A. Calenda; sets: N. Rubertelli; costumes: G. Schlinkert; music: P. Dessau; production: Teatro d'Arte. Cast: Mother Courage – P. Degli Esposti; Eilif – G. Cirilli; Swiss Cheese – D. Perugini; Kattrin – L. Marzotto. Cesena, Teatro Bonci.

APPENDIX

9 March 1995
French version by G. Serreau and B. Besson; director: J. Savary; sets and costumes: E. Toffolutti; music: P. Dessau; production: Théâtre National de Chaillot. Cast: Mother Courage – K. Thalbach; Eilif – N. von Tempelhoff; Swiss Cheese – B. Utzerath; Kattrin – A. Thalbach. Paris, Théâtre National de Chaillot.

19 October 1995
Luganda version by J. Bewulira-Wandera (*Maama Nalukalala Ne'zzadde Lye*); director: J. Collins and J. Kaahwa; sets: M. Mpyangu and M. Pavelka; production: Uganda National Theatre, Theatre Guild and The Royal Court Theatre in London. Cast: Mother Courage – R. Mbowa. Kampala, National Theatre.

27 June 1996
Italian version by R. Leiser and F. Fortini (Madre Coraggio di Sarajevo); staged reading conceived by G. Strehler and curated by C. Battistoni; sets and costumes: L. Damiani; music: P. Dessau; production: Piccolo Teatro di Milano. Cast: Mother Courage – G. Lazzarini; Eilif – S. Leone; M. Ovadia and the TheaterOrchestra, the pupils of the Scuola di Teatro del Piccolo; Palermo, via d'Amelio.

24 October 1998
French version by E. Guillevic; director: J. Lavelli; sets: A. Pace; costumes: D. Borg; music: P. Dessau; production: J.-P. Miquel. Cast: Mother Courage – C. Hiegel; Eilif – C. Gonon; Swiss Cheese – E. Génovèse; Kattrin – C. Samie. Paris, Comédie Française.

19 October 2002
Italian version by S. Vertone; director: M. Sciaccaluga; sets: M. Langhoff; costumes: G. Fiorato; music: P. Dessau, C. Boccadoro; production: Teatro Stabile di Genova. Cast: Mother Courage – M. Melato; Eilif – G. Sciortino; Swiss Cheese – E. Paci; Kattrin – A. Comes. Genoa, Teatro della Corte.

12 January 2006
Italian version by R. Menin and dramaturgy by I. Burton; director: R. Carsen; sets: R. Boruzescu; costumes: M. Boruzescu; the 'Song of Mother Courage' by P. Dessau arranged by Marlene Kuntz; production: Piccolo Teatro di Milano – Teatro d'Europa. Cast: Mother Courage – M. Crippa; Eilif – T. Minniti; Swiss Cheese – A. Onofrietti; Kattrin – S. Guliotis. Milan, Teatro Strehler.

8 August 2006
English version by T. Kushner; director: G. C. Wolfe; sets: R. Hernández; costumes: M. Draghici; music: J. Tesori; production: Public Theater, New York. Cast: Mother Courage – M. Streep; Eilif – F. Weller; Swiss Cheese – G. Arend; Kattrin – A. Wailes. New York, Public Theater at the Delacorte Theater, Central Park.

25 January 2008
Italian version by R. Menin and dramaturgy by A. Tarantino; director: C. Pezzoli; sets: B. Buonincontri; costumes: G. Falaschi; music: P. Scialò; production: Gli Ipocriti – Nuovo Teatro, Napoli. Cast: Mother Courage – I. Danieli; Eilif – M. Cremon; Swiss Cheese – Y. Shi; Kattrin – X. Bevitori. Lucca, Teatro del Giglio.

4 March 2008
French version by G. Serreau and B. Besson; director: A.-M. Lazarini; sets: F. Cabanat; costumes: D. Bourde; music: P. Dessau; production: Compagnie Les Athévains. Cast: Mother Courage – S. Herbert; Eilif – D. Fernandez; Swiss Cheese – H. Fontaine; Kattrin – J. d'Aleazzo. Paris, Théâtre Artistic Athévains.

5 October 2012
Performance on the occasion of Maribor European Capital of Cultural 2012; produced by the Ana Monro Theatre (Slovenian street theatre company).

Caligula

(It. *Caligola*)

Composition began in 1937 and was completed in 1941, but the play remained unpublished. Camus then produced a new version, which was published by Gallimard in 1944, first together with *Le Malentendu* and then separately. The final edition was published by Gallimard in a volume entitled '*Le Malentendu' suivi de 'Caligula'* in the Blanche series of 1958. The drafts mentioned can now be read in: Albert Camus, *Oeuvres complètes*, edited by J. Lévi-Valensi (Paris: Gallimard, 2006). Among the translations, note the Italian version by Franco Cuomo based on the 1941 draft and used in the 1983 production, published by Bompiani; in English note the translation by Stuart Gilbert published in London in 1947 by H. Hamilton and inserted in the *Collected Plays*, published by H. Hamilton in 1965, and the new translation by David Greig (London: Faber, 2003); in German note the translation by Guido G. Meister (Berlin: Volk und Welt, 1990).

Productions

27 June 1945
Director: G. Firmy (pseudonym of Giorgio Strehler); sets: G. Firmy; costumes: Kaiser; production: Compagnie des Masques. Cast: Caligula – C. Maritz; Cesonia – B. Galland. World premiere in Geneva, Théâtre de la Comédie.

26 September 1945
Director: P. Oettly; sets: L. Miquel; costumes: M. Viton; production: Jacques Hébertot. Cast: Caligula – G, Philipe; Cesonia – M. Lion; Scipio – M. Bouquet. World premiere in Paris, Théâtre Hébertot.

5 January 1946
Italian version by C. Vico Lodovici; director: G. Strehler; sets and costumes: G. Strehler; production: Compagnia Renzo Ricci. Cast: – R. Ricci; Cesonia – E. Magni; Scipio – G. Strehler. Florence, Teatro della Pergola.

29 November 1946
Director: I. Bergman; sets: C.-J. Ström; production: Stora scenen, Göteborgs Stadsteater. Cast: Caligula – A. Ek; Cesonia – I. Borthen; Scipio – F. Sundquist; Göteborg, Göteborgs Stadsteater.

6 October 1950
Director: P. Oettly; production: J. Hébertot. Cast: Caligula – M. Herbault; Cesonia – J. Moresco; Scipio – M. Lesage. Paris, Theatre Hébertot.

June 1957
Director: A. Camus. Cast: Caligula – M. Auclair; Cesonia – M. Jamois; Angers, Festival of Angers.

10 February 1958
Director: A. Camus; sets and costumes: M. Juncar; production: Elvie Popesco and Hubert de Malet. Cast: Caligula – J. P. Jorris; Cesonia – H. Bossis; Scipio – D. Manuel. Paris, Nouveau Théâtre.

October 1959
Italian version by C. Bene and A. Ruggiero; director: A. Ruggiero, sets and costumes: T. Vossbeg. Cast: Caligula – C. Bene; Cesonia – F. Milanta; Scipio – A. Salines. Rome, Teatro delle Arti; repeated in Genoa: director: C. Bene, Teatro Politeama, May 1961.

29 November 1961
German version by G. G. Meister; director: W. Dueggelin; sets and costumes: J. Zimmermann; production: Kurt Hirschfeld. Cast: Caligula – P. Arens; Cesonia – H. Mikulicz; Scipio – R. Scheibli; Zurich, Schauspielhaus Zürich.

24 July 1962
Arabic version by H. Zmerli; director: A. Ben Ayed; sets and costumes: L. Ben Abdallah and S. Puck; production: Second International Festival of Carthage (Tunisia).

17 September 1970
Italian version by N. Chiaromonte; director: G. Sbragia; sets: G. Polidori; costumes: M. d'Andrea; production: Compagnia Gli Associati. Cast: Caligula – G. Sbragia; Cesonia – V. Fortunato; Scipio – G. Giuliano. Vicenza, Teatro Olimpico, XXV Ciclo di Spettacoli Classici.

18 September 1971
Director: G. Vitaly; sets and costumes: O. Gustin; production: Tréteau de Paris. Cast: Caligula – J. P. Leroux; Cesonia – J. Drancourt; Scipio – B. Develdere. Paris, Théâtre La Bruyère.

3 February 1981
Director: P. Guinand; sets: S. Marzolff; costumes: D. Puisais and S. Marzolff; production: Jeune Théâtre National. Cast: Caligula – A. Recoing; Cesonia – D. Reymond. Paris, Odéon Théâtre de l'Europe.

24 November 1983
Italian version by F. Cuomo; director: M. Scaparro: sets: R. Francia; costumes: E. Luzzati; production: Teatro di Roma. Cast: Caligula – P. Micol; Cesonia – C. Giannotti; Scipio – M. Toccacelli. Rome, Teatro Argentina.

2 October 1990
Italian version by E. Capriolo; director: C. Martin; sets: A Chiesa; costumes: J. Perez and Solo/Sybilla; production: CRT di Milan and Diputación di Saragozza. Cast: Caligula – G. Battiston. Milan, Salone CRT.

Autumn 1991
Director: J. Rosny; production: Théâtre 14 Jean Marie Serrau. Cast: Caligula – E. Decharte; Cesonia – P. Roberts; Scipio – M. Roze. Paris, Théâtre 14 Jean Marie Serrau.

15 February 1992
Director: Y. Chahine; sets: F. Darne; costumes: J. P. Delifer; production: Comédie Française. Cast: Caligula – J.-Y. Dubois; Cesonia – M. Chevalier; Scipio – L. Dadi. Paris, Comédie Française.

18 October 1993
Italian version by E Cuomo; director: M. Lucchesi; sets: S. Tramonti; costumes: S. Benelli; production: Osi 85. Cast: Caligula – C. Liberati; Cesonia – B. Moratti; Scipio – L. Loris. Rome, Teatro Nazionale.

12 February 1997
Italian version by F. Cuomo; director: E. De Capitani; sets and costumes: C. Sala; production: Teatridithalia. Cast: Caligula – F. Bruni; Cesonia – L. Maglietta; Scipio – M. Giovara. Milan, Teatro di Portaromana.

2 May 2001
Italian version by F. Cuomo; director: C. d'Elia; sets: F. Palla; costumes: C. d'Elia; production: Compagnia Teatri Possibili. Cast: Caligula – A. Astorri / C. d'Elia; Cesonia – G. Rossi / L. Ferrari; Scipio – M. Cacciola / S. Annoni / A. Tibaldi / A. Tibaldi. Milan, Teatro Libero.

4 March 2003
Director: C. Longhi; sets: G. Andrico; costumes: G. Sbicca, S. Valsecchi; production: Teatro de gli Incamminati. Cast: Caligula – F. Branciaroli; Cesonia – G. Zamparini; Scipio – T. Cardarelli. Padua, Teatro Verdi.

APPENDIX   185

24 January 2006
Director: C. Berling; sets: C. Fenouillat; costumes: S. Skinazi; production: Théâtre de l'Atelier, Paris. Cast: Caligula – C. Berling; Cesonia – A. Val d'Or; Scipio – A. Toth / A. Gillet. Paris, Théâtre de l'Atelier.

22 August 2010 (*Caligola e la luna*)
Director: O. Cenci; sets and costumes: M. Gasperoni; production: Made Officina Creativa. Cast: Caligula – S. Pesce; Cesonia – B. Mautino; Scipio – D. Nigrelli. Rimini, *Meeting per l'amicizia fra i popoli* (Meeting for friendship among peoples), 2010.

4 November 2010
Director: S. Olivié-Bisson; sets: G. Vafias; costumes: R. M. Melka; production: l'Avant-Seine Théâtre de Colombes; Caligula – B. Putzulu; Cesonia – C. Paoli; Scipio – M. Mikolajczak. Colombes, l'Avant-Seine théâtre de Colombes.

1 July 2011
Director: E. Nekrosius; sets: M. Nekrosius; costumes: N. Gultiaeva; production: Teatro Statale delle Nazioni di Mosca; Caligula – Y. Mironov; Cesonia – M. Mironova; Scipio – Y. Tkachuk. Tivoli, International Festival of Villa Adriana. European premiere.

1 October 2011
Italian version by R. Reim; director: P. Micol; sets: A. Santarelli; costumes: A. Carota; production: Compagnia Teatro Zeta, Teatro della Cometa. Cast: Caligula – M. Morgese; Cesonia – M. L. Gorga; Scipio – G. Merolli. Rome, Teatro della Cometa.

Fin de partie

(It. *Finale di partita*, Eng. *Endgame*, Ger. *Endspiel*)
Composition begun in 1955. The first draft was completed in 1956, the second in 1957. The work was published in Paris by Les Éditions de Minuit in 1957; in English translated as *Endgame* (New York: Grove Press, 1958; London: Faber and Faber, 1958). The Italian translation, published by Einaudi in Teatro (1961), is by Carlo Fruttero. The translation was revised and republished in the volume *Teatro completo: Drammi, sceneggiatura, radiodrammi, pièces televisive*, presented and annotated by P. Bertinetti (Turin: Einaudi-Gallimard, 1994). In German note the version by Elmar Tophoven (Frankfurt: Suhrkamp, 1960 and subsequent editions).

Productions

3 April 1957
Director: R. Blin; production: Royal Court Theatre. Cast: Clov – J. Martin; Hamm – R. Blin; Nell – C. Tsingos; Nagg – G. Adet. World premiere in French in London, Royal Court Theatre.

26 April 1957
Director: R. Blin; sets and costumes: J. Nöel; production: Jacques Hébertot. Cast: Clov – J. Martin; Hamm – R. Blin; Nell – G. de France; Nagg – G. Adet. Paris, Théâtre des Champs Elysées.

30 September 1957
German version; director: H. Bauer. Cast: Clov – R. Schmitt; Hamm – B. Minetti; Nell – E. Ehser; Nagg – W. Stock. Berlin, Schlosspark.

28 January 1958
English version; director: A. Schneider; sets: D. Hays; production: N. Behn. Cast: Clov – A. Epstein; Hamm – L. Rawlins; Nell – N. Westman; Nagg – P. J. Kelly. New York, Cherry Lane Theatre.

3 July 1958
Director: R. Blin; production: Théâtre d'Aujourd'hui. Cast: Clov – J. Martin; Hamm – R. Blin; Nell – G. de France, A. Reicher; Nagg – G. Adet. Venice, Teatro del Ridotto, Festival della Prosa.

8 September 1958
Italian version by L. Candoni (Il gioco è alla fine); director: A. Camilleri; sets and costumes: T. Vossberg; production: Teatro dei Satiri. Cast: Clov – G. Rocchetti; Hamnz – M. Chiocchio; Nell – M. Piergiovanni; Nagg – M. Milita. Rome, Teatro dei Satiri.

28 October 1958
English version; director: G. Devine; sets: J. Herbert; production: Royal Court Theatre. Cast: Clov – J. MacGowran; Hamm – G. Devine; Nell – F. Cuka; Nagg – R. Golden. London, Royal Court Theatre.

19 February 1959
Director: C. Apothéloz; sets: A. Abplanalp; production: Compagnie Tréteaux des Faux-Nez. Cast: Clov – P. Boulanger; Hamm – A. Abplanalp; Nell – J. Burnard; Nagg – B. Arczynski. Milan, Teatro Gerolamo.

25 May 1959
Italian version (Il gioco è alla fine); director: A. Trionfo; sets and costumes: L. Crippa; production: La Borsa di Arlecchino. Cast: Clov – P. Poli; Hamm – V. Ferro; Nell – T. Zaffra; Nagg – E. Poggi. Genoa, La Borsa di Arlecchino.

November 1962
Italian version; director: G. Montemagno; sets and costumes: M. Glaviano; production: Club Mirage Teatro dei 172. Cast: Clov – G. Meli; Hamm – A. Marsala; Nell – G. Savoja; Nagg – P. Taranto. Palermo, Club Mirage Teatro dei 172.

APPENDIX

4 February 1963
Italian version; director: C. Quartucci; sets and costumes: C. Quartucci; production: Compagnia Teatro della Ripresa. Cast: Clov – L. De Bernardinis; Hamm – R. Sudano; Nell – A. D'Offizi; Nagg – C. Cimieri. Rome, Teatro Ateneo.

8 June 1963
Director: J.-P. Laruy; sets: C. Perset; production: Jeune Théâtre Compagnie Régnier-Laruy. Cast: Clov – J.-P. Laruy; Hamm – C. La Hire; Nell – F. Linet; Nagg – G. Régnier. Paris, Hôtel de Sully.

20 February 1964
Director: M. Blake (with the assistance of Samuel Beckett); production: Studio Champs-Elysées. Cast: Clov – J. MacGowran; Hamm – P. Magee; Nell – E Hale; Nagg – S. Bromley. Paris, Studio Champs-Élysées.

12 May 1966
Italian version; director: M. Mezzadri; sets: R. Borsoni; costumes: M. Mezzadri; production: Compagnia della Loggetta. Cast: Clov – R. Borsoni; Hamm – A. Engheben; Nell – M. Germano; Nagg – G. Germi; Brescia, Teatro della Loggetta.

26 September 1967
German version; director: S. Beckett; sets: Matias; production: Schiller-Theater Werkstatt. Cast: Clov – H. Bollman; Hamm – E. Schröder; Nell – G. Genest; Nagg – W. Stock. Berlin, Schiller-Theater Werkstatt.

29 April 1968
Director: R. Blin; sets and costumes: Matias; production: Théâtre Alpha 347. Cast: Clov – A. Julien; Hamm – R. Blin; Nell – G. Defrance; Nagg – G. Adet. Paris, Théâtre Alpha 347.

20 March 1970
Italian version; director: G. Sepe; sets and costumes: A. Mariani; production: Compagnia Teatro La Comunità Centro Teatrale Affratellamento. Cast: Clov – G. Sepe; Hamm – E. De Marco; Nell – L. Mezzabotta; Nagg – P. Vegliante. Rome, Teatro di via Stamira.

15 May 1971
Italian version by C. Fruttero; director and sets: R. Sudano; production: Compagnia Teatro Stabile di Torino. Cast: Clov – F. Ferrarone; Hamm – R. Sudano; Nell – A. D'Offizi; Nagg – A. Esposito. Borgo San Dalmazzo (Turin), Salone della Pro Loco.

3 April 1974
Italian version; director: M. Mattia Giorgetti; sets: L. Luzzati; production: La Contemporanea del Centro Attori di Milano. Cast: Clov – S. Masieri; Hamm – M. Craig; Nell – R. Genia; Nagg – E Ponzoni. Milan, Teatro dell'Arte.

9 April 1975
Director: P. Lefebvre; sets: J. M. Quesne; production: Compagnie du Parnasse. Cast: Clov – P. Lefebvre; Hamm – M. Darrière; Nell – J. Quentin; Nagg – C. Pelissier. Paris, Studio-Théâtre 14.

15 February 1977
Italian version; director: R. Sudano; production: Cooperativa Gruppo Quattro Cantoni. Cast: Clov – F. Ferrarone; Hamm – R. Sudano; Nell – A. D'Offizi; Nagg – A. di Stasio. Milan, Salone Pier Lombardo.

4 October 1977
Italian version; director: E.M. Caserta; production: Teatro Laboratorio di Verona. Cast: Clov – T. Giuliani; Hamm – G. Giuffrida; Nell – S. Bonomi; Nagg – R. Dalle Pezze. Verona, Teatro Laboratorio.

26 May 1980
English version; director: S. Beckett; production: The San Quentin Drama Workshop. Cast: Clov – B. Thorpe; Hamm – R. Cluchey; Nell – T. Garcia Suro; Nagg – A. Mandell. Dublin, Peacock Theatre.

14 October 1980
Director: G. Rétoré; sets and costumes: C. Lemaire; production: Théâtre de l'Est Parisien. Cast: Clov – M. Robin; Hamm – P. Dux; Nell – G. Casadesus; Nagg – A. Reybaz. Paris, Théâtre de l'Est Parisien.

24 February 1982
Italian version by C. Fruttero; director: W. Pagliaro; sets and costumes: U. Bertacca; production: ATER-Emilia Romagna Teatro. Cast: Clov – G. Dettori; Hamm – G. Santuccio; Nell – R. Bassani; Nagg – L. Ottoni; Bologna, Teatro Testoni.

24 January 1984
Italian version by C. Fruttero; director: M. Santella; sets and costumes: M. L. Santella and M. Santella; production: Nuovo Teatro Contro di Napoli. Cast: Clov – F. Bovicelli/ C. di Maio; Hamm – R. Crescenzi; Nell – J. Carola; Nagg – R. Piscopo. Rome, Teatro in Trastevere.

19 October 1986
Italian version by C. Fruttero; director: G. Di Leva; sets: G. Marotta; costumes: E. Coveri; production: Teatro Regionale Toscano. Cast: Clov – R. Rascel; Hamm – W. Chiari; Nell – R. Neri; Nagg – M. Pachi. Florence, Teatro Nuovo Variety.

November 1990
Italian version; director: G. Leonetti; production: Teatro Instabile. Cast: Clov – S. Ricci; Hamm – J. Baiocchi; Nell – M. Micheli; Nagg – W. Tulli. Rome, Teatro dell'Orologio.

15 November 1990
Italian version; director: A. Santagata; production: Katzenmacher-Santagata and Morganti. Cast: Clov – A. Santagata; Hamm – C. Morganti; Nell – F. Pistoni; Nagg – C. Gradilone. Milan, Teatro Arsenale.

23 March 1992
Director: G. Rossi. Cast: G. Rossi; D. Gandini; A. Latorre; D. Inzaghi. Milan, Teatro Olmetto.

14 April 1992
Italian version by C. Fruttero; director: F. Tiezzi; sets: P. P. Bisleri; costumes: G. Buzzi; production: CTB-I Magazzini. Cast: Clov – G. Varetto; Hamm – V. Gazzolo; Nell – E. Villagrossi; Nagg – P. Ricchi. Brescia, Teatro Santa Chiara.

21 April 1992
Director: M. Perriera; sets: E. Venezia; costumes: L. Ricca. Cast: Clov – S. Barone; Hamm – E. Cucinotti; Nell – G. Liberati; Nagg – G. Borruso. Palermo, Teatro Teatès.

7 February 1995
Italian version by C. Cecchi; director: C. Cecchi; sets and costumes: T. Maselli; production: Teatro Stabile di Firenze. Cast: Clov – V. Binasco; Hamm – C. Cecchi; Nell – D. Piperno; Nagg – A. Cirillo. Florence, Teatro Niccolini.

25 July 1995
Director: J. Jouanneau; sets: J. Gabel; costumes: J. Gonzalez; production: Théâtre Vidy (Lausanne), Theater am Turm (Frankfurt). Cast: Clov – D. Bennent; Hamm – H. Bennent; Nell – M. Mossé; Nagg, – J. C. Grenier; Avignon, Cloître des Carmes.

23 October 1996
Director: A. Delcampe; sets: G. C. François; costumes: E. Mannini; production: Atelier théâtral de Louvain-la-Neuve. Cast: Clov – Rufus; Hamm – M. Bouquet; Nell; J. Carré; Nagg – M. Cuvelier. Louvain-la-Neuve, Théâtre Jean Vilar.

9 January 1998
Version in Calabrian dialect by J. Trumper (*U juocu sta' finisciennu*); director and sets: G. Cauteruccio; production: Compagnia Krypton. Cast: Clov – F. Cauteruccio; Hamm – G. Cauteruccio; Nell – L. Marchianò; Nagg – A. Russo. Scandicci (Florence), Teatro Studio.

3 March 1999
Director: P. Chabert and S. Solov; sets: G. Poitoux; production: L. Berthommé and C. Le Guillochet. Cast: Clov – H. Pillsbury; Hamm – P. Chabert; Nell – S. Solov; Nagg – W. Kleinertz. Paris, Le Lucernaire.

27 November 2002
Director, sets and costumes by P. Carriglio; production: Teatro Biondo Stabile di Palermo. Cast: Clov – U. Cantone; Hamm – G. P. Poddighe; Nell – F. Scaldati; Nagg – G. Cucinella. Palermo, Teatro Biondo.

18 November 2003
Version by C. Fruttero; director: L. Loris; sets: D. Gardinazzi; costumes: N. Ceccolini; production: Teatro Out Off. Cast: Clov – A. Genovesi; Hamm – P. Pierobon; Nell – Elena Arcuri; Nagg – G. Minneci. Milan, Teatro Out Off.

18 February 2006
Version by C. Fruttero; Director: F. Branciaroli; sets and costumes: M. Palli; production: Teatro de Gli Incamminati. Cast: Clov – T. Cardarelli; Hamm – F. Branciaroli; Nell – L. Ragni; Nagg – A. Albertin. Brescia, Teatro Sociale di Brescia.

19 April 2006
Director: C. Sturridge; sets: E. Diss; costumes: C. Walter; production: Beckett Centenary Festival – Barbican International Theatre Events (Bite 06) and The Gate Theatre, Dublin. Cast: Clov – P. Dinklage; Hamm – K. Cranham; Nell – G. Hale; Nagg – T. Hickey. London, Barbican Theatre, Beckett Centenary Festival 2006.

28 September 2006
Director : B. Levy; sets: G. Lichtner; costumes: E. Pavanel; production: Compagnie Lire aux éclats and Scène nationale de Sénart. Cast: Clov – G. Arbona; Hamm – T. Bosc; Nell – M.-F. Audollent; Nagg – G. Ser. Paris, Théâtre de l'Athénée, Festival Paris Beckett 2006–07.

23 May 2008
Director: P. Di Marca; sets and costumes: L. Taravella; production: Compagnia del Meta-Teatro. Cast: Clov – L. Lodoli; Hamm – P. Di Marca; Nell and Nagg (recorded voices). Rome, Atelier Meta-Teatro.

30 March 2010
Version by C. Fruttero; director: M. Castri; sets and costumes: M. Balò; production: Emilia Romagna Teatro Fondazione, Teatro di Roma, Teatro Metastasio Stabile della Toscana. Cast: Clov – M. Dapcevic; Hamm – V. Franceschi; Nell – D. Hobel; Nagg – A. G. Peligra. Modena, Teatro delle Passioni.

Akropolis

Inspired by the work of Stanisław Wyspiański, performed for the first time at the Teatr Laboratorium of the '13 Rows' ('13 Rzędòw') on 10 October 1962, the production was directed by Jerzy Grotowski in collaboration with Jòzef Szajna, who was responsible for the sets, costumes and props.

The production underwent numerous changes in the following months and years. On each first night audiences were told which version was to be performed. The differences were significant.

The cast of the first version was: Maja Komorowska, Rena Mirecka, Zygmunt Molik, Zbigniew Cynkutis, Antoni Jahołkowski, Ryszard Cieślak, Andrzej Bielski (Ewa Lubowiecka also took part in rehearsals). The second version was presented on 24 November 1962: Maja Komorowska was replaced by Maciej Prus. The first night of the third version was presented on 10 June 1964 (Zbigniew Cynkutis and Maciej Prus were replaced by Mieczysław Janowski and Gaston Kulig), while the fourth version was presented for the first time on 16 January 1965, at the new auditorium in Wrocław. The fifth version (the best known), with the participation of Zygmunt Molik (Jacob, Harp Player), Rena Mirecka (Rebecca, Cassandra), Antoni Jahołkowski (Izaak, Guardian), Ryszard Cieślak (sometimes replaced by Czeslaw Wojtała – Esau, Hector), Zbigniew Cynkutis (Laban, Paris), Stanisław Ścierski (Clio, Helena) and Andrzej Paluchiewicz, was staged for the first time on 17 May 1967 in Wrocław and later, on tour abroad in this order: Amsterdam (18–19 June 1967), Utrecht (20 June 1967), The Hague (21–22 June 1967), Rotterdam (23–24 June 1967), Brussels (26–28 June 1967), Edinburgh (22–30 August 1968), Paris (24 September–26 October 1968), Aix-en-Provence (4–26 November 1968), and New York (4–15 November 1969). This same version was filmed in the period from 27 October to 2 November 1968 for US television. (The film was produced by James MacTaggart and was introduced by Peter Brook.)

Apart from the performances at Opole, the first and second versions were presented at Wrocław (12–14 November 1962), Poznań (16–19 November 1962), Złoty Stok (4 December 1962), Gliwice (6–7 December 1962), Katowice (9–11 December 1962), Łódź (20 February–3 March 1963, and Kraków (9–15 May 1963). The fourth was staged at Kłodzko (18 June 1965).

Apocalypsis cum figuris

Production by the Teatr Laboratorium; directed by Jerzy Grotowski. It was also his last production. Subject and director: Jerzy Grotowski; co-director: Ryszard Cieślak; assistant director: Stanisław Ścierski. Costumes: Waldemar Krygier. Cast: Antoni Jahołkowski (Simon Peter), Ryszard Cieślak (Ciemny, the Simpleton), Zygmunt Molik (Judas), Zbigniew Cynkutis (Lazarus), Elizabeth Albahaca / Rena Mirecka (Mary Magdalene), Stanisław Ścierski (John).

The first performance, closed to the public, was presented on 19 July 1968, while the official premiere took place on 11 February 1969. The creative process accompanying the play was very long and elaborate down to its last performance in Wrocław on 11 May 1980.

Apart from being performed at the Teatr Laboratorium, it was presented in London (18–22 September 1969), New York (18–26 November and 10–15 December 1969), Holstebro (26 August–12 September 1971), Warsaw (22 September–10 October 1971), Munich (22 August–4 September 1972), Philadelphia (10–25 September 1973), Paris (12–18 November 1973), Sydney (4 April–18 May 1974), Venice (as part of the Biennale,

27–29 September, 3–5 October, 9–12 October, 15–17 October, 20–22 October, 25–27 October 1975), Gdańsk (6–18 October 1978), Milan (27, 28, 31 January, 1, 4, 5 February 1979), Pontedera (24–25 and 29–30 June 1979), Rome (4–7 December 1979), and Genoa (18–20, 22 and 23 January). In time the work increasingly moved away from the experiments of its director and became the property of the theatre group which produced it on national and international tours without Grotowski being present. This happened with the *Pół wieku po Reducie* (Half a century after Reduta) project, which included *Apocalypsis cum figuris* in selected Polish cities. The death of Antoni Jahołkowski put an end to the productions.

Ermanno Olmi directed the film version made for Italian television in 1979.

Pylades

Pier Paolo Pasolini wrote *Pylades* in 1966, published in *Nuovi argomenti* in 1967. But this tragedy had five subsequent versions and finally was republished posthumously by Garzanti in 1977. The edition I refer to is Pier Paolo Pasolini, *Tutte le opere: Teatro* (Milan: Arnoldo Mondadori Editore, I Meridiani, 2001), edited by Walter Siti and Silvia De Laude. The text has been translated into French by Michèle Fabien and Titina Maselli (Paris: Actes Sud, 1990); into English by Adam Paolozza and Coleen MacPherson for the play and workshop the Pasolini Project, TheatreRUN 2009, Canadian Stage Festival of Ideas and Creation 2010, and Canadian Stage's Spotlight Italy Festival. Then we have a German translation by Heinz Riedt (Frankfurt: Fischer, 1984) and another in Croatian by Ivica Buljan and Mani Gotovac (Zagreb: Italian Institute of Culture, 1998).

Productions

29 August 1969
Directed by G. Cutrufelli; sets: G. Sivieri; costumes: N. Sivieri; production: Compagnia Siciliana del Teatro Nazionale. Cast: Pylades – A. Ninchi; Electra – C. Giannotti; Orestes – A. Ninchi; Athena – W. Vismara; Shepherd / Farmer – C. Valli. First performance: Taormina, Teatro Greco.

18 July 1981
Directed by M. Freni; costumes: I. Stefanucci; production: E. P. T. di Benevento, Compagnia del Teatro di Tradizione. Cast: Pylades – L. Mezzanotte; Electra – I. di Benedetto; Orestes – F. Interlenghi; Shepherd / Farmer – M. Maranzana; Benevento, Teatro Romano.

23 April 1983
Directed by G. Pelucchi; sets and costumes: C. Belotti; production: Compagnia Il Capannone. Cast: C. Belotti, N. Carra, B. Gervasoni, M. Foresti, N. Foresti, L. Mazzola. Castelli Calepio (Bergamo), Cine-T. di Tagliuno.

25 June 1985
Directed by J. Kühnel; translation: von H. Riedt; sets: L. Dransfeld; production: Neue Studiobühne der Uni Siegen. Cast: Pylades – J. Kühnel; Electra – C. Schadt-Krämer; Orestes – J. Hütterott; Athena – L. Georg-Shirley; Shepherd / farmer – H. Gietz. Siegen, Kleine Theater Lohkasten.

11 May 1989
Directed by L. Puggelli; sets and costumes: L. Spinatelli; production: Piccolo Teatro di Milano. Cast: Prologue and one of the Eumenides – R. De Carmine; Pylades U. Ceriani; Electra – M. Minelli; Orestes – M. Foschi; Athena – S. Marcomeni. Milan, Piccolo Teatro Studio.

1 June 1993
Directed by L. Ronconi; sets: C. Giammello; costumes: A. Danon; production: Workshop performance of the School of Teatro Stabile Torino. Cast: Pylades – C. M. Giammarini; Electra – C. Panti Liberovici; Orestes – G. Lupano; Athena – E. Urban; Farmer / Messenger – M. Mecca. Turin, Castello di Rivoli.

12 March 1993 (*Pasolini viaggio in Grecia*)
Directed by M. Avogadro; dramaturgy and music by F. De Melis; production: Compagnia del Minotauro. Cast: Pylades – R. Girone; Orestes – P. Mannoni; G. Bisogno, M. Donadoni, D. Margherita. Venice, Teatro Fondamenta Nuove.

1 February 1994 (by Aeschylus, Pasolini, Ritsos)
Directed by S. Nordey; translation: M. Fabien and T. Maselli; production: Compagnia Nordey / TGP / Centre National Dramatique et Chorégraphique / Le Quartz de Brest / Le maillon – Centre Culturel de Strasbourg and Jeune Théâtre National. Cast: Prologue – V. Nordey; Pylades – J. C. Dumay; Electra – V. Lang; Orestes – S. Nordey. Brest, Le Quartz.

11 April 1996
Directed by F. Piacentini; production: Associazione Proteo. Cast: F. Piacentini, V. Piacentini, D. Genazzani, F. Fiesoli, A. Venturini. Sassari, Teatro Civico.

23 July 1998
Directed by I. Buljan; translation: I. Buljan and M. Gotovac; sets: R. Somek; costumes: I. Popovič; production: Teatar &TD (Zagreb) in collaboration with Mittelfest, Festival Internazionale Eurokaz, Artcarnuntum, Italian Institute of Culture, Zagreb. Cast: S. Bulič, I. Cremona, D. Despot, N. Dorčič, with the voice of D. Vejzovič; Mittelfest, Piazza Duomo-Cividale dei Friuli. The performance was preceded by *Scene da Pilade*, a reading of some scenes of the essay by the Scuola del Teatro Stabile di Torino, directed by L. Ronconi (1993) and filmed by M. Avogadro with E. Russo, D. Salvo, F. Gagliardi.

10 October 1998
Directed by G. Argirò; production: Laboratorio Dialoghi itineranti del tragico contemporaneo. Cast: M. G. Comunale, N. Arcangeli, V. Menna, R. Pappadà, C. Pieroni, A. Radici. Rome, Piazza Santa Maria Consolatrice.

7 December 1999
Directed by V. Cantoni; production: Gibus Teatro. Cast: A. Piccirillo, A. Putignano, A. Carlucci, F. Carbone, G. Romoli, L. Gionfrida. Bologna, Pavese Café Teatro.

17 December 1999
Directed by D. Polidoro; sets: Brunetti Filipponi Associati; costumes: F. M. Tulli; production: Accademia Nazionale d'Arte Drammatica Silvio d'Amico, Villaggio Globale, Associazione Rom 'Unirsi'. Cast: Pylades – M. Foschi; Electra – C. Visca and A. Presepi; Orestes – A. Trapani; Athena – B. Ciampaglia; Farmer / Messenger: R. Mantovani. Rome, Centro Sociale Villaggio Globale, ex Mattatoio – Campo Boario.

6 March 2001
Directed and sets by: J. Roman; translation: M. Fabien and T. Maselli; production: Narration & Cie. Cast: Pylades – S. Duprez; Electra – B. Schmucki; Orestes – S. Palese; Athena – D. Favre-Bulle; Boy – G. Dagon. Geneva, Théâtre du Grütli.

1 August 2001
Directed by M. Gagliardo; sets: C. Gai; costumes: M. Nateri; production: Sirio Sardegna Teatro. Cast: T. Petilli, G. Vacca, S. Dattena, N. Ebau, A. Tedde, M. Cirina. Cagliari, Teatro Comunale all'Aperto.

7 May 2002
Directed by A. Latella; sets: S. Cangini, A. Bartolini; costumes: C. Da Rold; production: Teatro Out Off. Cast: Pylades – M. Foschi; Electra – C. Spanò; Orestes – R. Tedesco; Shepherd / Farmer – M. Caccia. Milan, Teatro Out Off.

15 June 2004 (*Studio dal Pilade di Pier Paolo Pasolini*)
Directed by A. Pizzech; production: Il Cantiere Teatrale 2004. Cast: Pylades – D. Cecchi; F. Anelli, J. Bandecchi, A. Casarosa, C. Cavallini, M. Coli. Cascina (Pisa), Ridotto del Teatro Politeama.

24 February 2004
Directed by A. Meunier; translation: M. Fabien and T. Maselli; sets: E. Clolus; costumes: S. Heurlin; marionette: B. Vantusso; production: Le Granit / Maison de la Culture d'Amiens / La Comédie de Reims / Le Forum de Blanc-Mesnil / Compagnie de la Mauvaise Graine. Cast: Pylades – A. Brugière; Electra – C. Coustillac; Eumenides – A. C. Chagrot; Athena – J. Schuller. Paris, Théâtre Paris Villette.

9 July 2004
Directed by G. Ascari; sets: MRA+; production: La Zattera. Cast: M. Pintus, M. Ferrari, L. Sovieni, A. Spettoli, M. Del Nero, G. Bortoli. San Giovanni di Concordia (Modena), Festa d'Estate.

1 May 2005 (*Pylades von Pier Paolo Pasolini*)
Directed by M. Lex; translation: von H. Riedt; dramaturgy: A. Zimmermann; sets: T. Tesche; costumes: M. Liechti; production: Luzerner Theater. Cast: Pylades – P. Waros; Electra – K. Romig; Orestes – M. Metten; Athena – A. Schweitzer. Lucerne, Luzemer Theater.

24 September 2006
Directed by A. Paciotto; translation: I. Buljan; dramaturgy: J. Ćirilov; sets: M. David; costumes: S. Kovačević; production: National Theater of Uzice, Offucina Eclectic Arts. Cast: V. Prelić, I. Borojević, I. Kovačević, T. Jovanović, B. Zdravković, T. Trifunović. Bitef, Belgrade, Zvezdara Teatar.

18 February 2008 (*Des Batailles, d'après Pylade de Pier Paolo Pasolini et al.*)
Directed by O. Coulon-Jablonka; dramaturgy: O. Coulon-Jablonka and E. Gollac; sets: M. Dupuy; costumes: C. Brisson; production: Cie Moukden Théâtre / l'Echangeur-Cie Public Chéri / Théâtre de l'Université Paul Valéry-La Vignette Montpellier. Cast: J. Boris, V. Carette, F. Cheippe, P. Déaux, J.-M. Layer, G. Riant; Bagnelet, Théâtre de l'Echangeur.

2009–2011 (*The Pasolini Project*)
Directed by A. Paolozza; translation: A. Paolozza, C. MacPherson; dramaturgy: C. MacPherson; production: TheatreRUN. Cast: Pylades – D. Watson; Electra – M. Calderon; Orestes – J. Dezotti; Athena – M. Smith; Shepherd / Farmer – F. Fabbri; Toronto, TheatreRUN 2009, Canadian Stage Festival of Ideas and Creation 2010, Canadian Stage's Spotlight Italy Festival 2011.

4 June 2010
Directed by L. Gousseau and S. Siré; translation: M. Fabien and T. Maselli; dramaturgy: T. Taconet; sets: D. Payen; costumes: M. Luçon; production: Societas Péridurale / Carthago Delenda Est / Maison du Comédien-Maria Casarès (Alloue) / Festival Premiers Actes (Munster) / Théâtre & Publics (Liège). Cast: Pylades – A. Chéron; Electra – J. Nathan; Orestes – L. Gousseau; Athena – M. Luçon; Shepherd / Farmer – Jacques Bruckmann. Brussels, Carthago Delenda Est.

7 October 2010
Directed by B. Venturi; sets and costumes: L. Frongia; production: TSI La Fabbrica dell'Attore and La Nuova Complesso Camerata. Cast: Pylades – O. Braghieri; Electra / Eumenides / Athena – M. Kustermann; Orestes – A. Piovanelli; Boy – S. Porcu. Rome, Teatro Vascello.

25 August–18 September 2011 (workshop performance)
Directed by L. Ronconi; production: Centro Teatrale Santacristina, Accademia Nazionale d'Arte Drammatica 'Silvio D'Amico'. Cast: 16 young graduates from the Accademia Nazionale d'Arte Drammatica alternating in the different parts. Gubbio, Rehearsal room of Centro Teatrale Santacristina.

Rwanda 94

Devised by Marie-France Collard, Jacques Delcuvellerie, Yolande Mukagasana, Jean-Marie Piemme, with contributions to the dramaturgy by Dorcy Rugamba and Tharcisse Kalisa Rugano. Directed by Jacques Delcuvellerie with images by Marie-France Collard; music composed and orchestra conducted by Garrett List; songs by Jean-Marie Muyango. Cast: Yolande Mukagasana, Nathalie Cornet, Ansou Diedhiou, Stéphane Fauville, René Hainaux, Clotilde K. Kabale, Carole Karemera, Francine Landrain, Majyambere Massamba, Diogène Ntarindwa, Maurice Sévenant, Alexandre Trocki. Musicians: Manuela Bucher (viola), Geneviève Foccroule/Stéphanie Mouton (piano), Vincent Jacquemin (clarinet), Véronique Lierneux (violin), Marie-Eve Ronveaux (cello). Singers: Christine Schaller, Véronique Sonck. Sets: Johan Daenen. Costumes: Greta Goiris. Masks/marionettes: Johan Daenen, Greta Goiris, Françoise Joset, Marta Ricart Buxo. Lights: Marc Defrise. Video director: Fred Op de Beeck.

A production by Groupov, an ensemble of artists of different disciplines and different nationalities founded in 1980 on the initiative of the director Jacques Delcuvellerie, who was born in France and lives and works in Belgium. Co-production by the Théâtre de la Place, Théâtre National de la Communauté Wallonie Bruxelles/Brussels 2000, Ville Européenne de la Culture. Production in French lasting some six hours.

Productions

1999: Festival of Avignon (21–26 July)

2000: Brussels (20–25 March); Villeneuve-d'Ascq (27–29 April); Cherbourg/Octeville (9 May); Marseille, as part of the International Theatre Institute, sponsored by UNESCO's Utopia Project (16 May); Bonn (22–23 June); Limoges (20–30 September); Calais (8–9 December).

2001: Paris/Rungis (19–26 January); Mouscron (20 February); Braine-Le-Compte (8 March); Geneva (15–17 March); Mons (28 March); Rouen (10–11 May); Guadalupe (24–25 May); Montreal as part of the Festival de Théâtre des Amériques (1–3 June); Québec City (7 June).

2002: Angoulême (22 and 24 February, 1 and 3 March); Sartrouville (9 and 10 March); Angers (22 and 23 March); Louvain-la-Neuve (17–21 April); La Roche-sur-Yon (27 April);

Brussels (7–11 May); Cavaillon (18 May); Amiens (25 and 26 May); Udine, Mittelfest (28 July); Paris, Festival des Cultures Urbaines (9–11 November).

2004: Butare (6 and 7 April); Kigali (11–14 April); Bisesero (18 April); Palermo (12 September); Turin (18 September); Rome (24–26 September); Milan (2–3 October); Reggio Emilia (9–10 October).

The last performances of the production by the Théâtre de la Place in Liège were given in April 2005.

Ruhe

Devised and directed by Josse De Pauw; musical director: Christoph Siebert; music: Franz Schubert and Annelies Van Parys; text: Armando and Hans Sleutelaar, adapted by Josse De Pauw and Tom Jansen. Cast (two for each performance): Josse De Pauw, Tom Jansen, Dirk Roofthooft, Carly Wijs. Choir of the Collegium Vocale Gent.

2007: Brussels (9–12 May); Goes (1–8 September); Paris (25–30 September); Munich (22–23 November); Berlin (24–25 November).

2008: Eindhoven (17 January); Bruges (18 January); Rotterdam (20 January); Hasselt (21 January); Antwerp (23 January); Tiburg (January 24); Breda (27 January); Stavanger (9–11 February); Edinburgh Festival (21 August).

2010: Sydney Festival, Muziektheater Transparant, The Great Hall, Sydney University (25–29 January).

NOTES

Introduction   The Tragic, Tragedy and the Idea of the Limit

1   Søren Kierkegaard, *Either/Or*, trans. by Howard V. Hong and Edna H. Hong (Princeton: Princeton University Press, 1988), I: 139 (137–64; original edition 'Det antike Tragiskes Reflex i det moderne Tragiske', in *Enten-Eller*, Samlede Vaerker, Kyldendel, 1962, II).
2   George Steiner, *The Death of Tragedy* (London: Faber and Faber, 1961).
3   For an introductory outline, see Rebecca Bushnell, ed., *A Companion to Tragedy* (Oxford: Blackwell, 2005).
4   Péter Szondi, *Essay on the Tragic* (Palo Alto: Stanford University Press, 2002). On the whole question, see also Annamaria Cascetta, ed., *Il tragico: Filosofi a confronto* (Milan: Vita e Pensiero, 1988); Sergio Givone, *Disincanto del mondo e pensiero tragico* (Milan: Mondadori, 1988); William Storm, *After Dionysos: A Theory of the Tragic* (Ithaca: Cornell University Press, 1998); Miguel de Beistegui and Simone Sparks, *Philosophy and Tragedy* (London/New York: Routledge, 2000); Gianluca Garelli, ed., *Filosofie del tragico* (Milan: Bruno Mondatori, 2001); Terry Eagleton, *Sweet Violence: The Idea of the Tragic* (Oxford: Blackwell, 2003); Livio Bottani, *Il tragico e la filosofia* (Vercelli: Mercurio, 2008); Joaquin Esteban Ortega, ed., *Cultura contemporanea y pensamiento trágico* (Valladolid: Uemc, 2009); Carlo Gentili and Gianluca Garelli, *Il tragico* (Bologna: Il Mulino, 2010); Julian Young, *Philosophy of Tragedy* (Cambridge: Cambridge University Press, 2013).
5   *The Death of Tragedy*: George Steiner's thesis, which has found some supporters, is that after Racine there is no longer any tragedy in European literature and that rationalism, scientism and secular metaphysics have banished the tragic consciousness by their optimism. *La métamorphose de la tragedie*: In J. Omesco's study (Vendôme: Presses Universitaires de France, 1978), he argues that, though it is true that tragedy in its classical form has disappeared, it does not mean that the modern consciousness is incapable of finding tragic expression elsewhere.
6   I refer here to the book *Modern Tragedy*, full of fine insights and moral passion, published in 1966 and now available in the Broadview Encore Edition (Toronto, 2006), with a critical introduction by Pamela McCallum. Williams describes it as an 'unusual book' in terms of the academic conventions. 'To begin a discussion of modern tragedy with the modern experiences that most of us call tragic, and to try to relate these to tragic literature and theory, can provoke literal amazement' (34). 'It is to look, critically and historically, at works and ideas which have certain evident links, and which are associated in our minds by a single and powerful word. It is, above all, to see these works and ideas in their immediate contexts, as well as in their historical continuity and to examine their place and function in relation to other works and ideas, and to the variety of actual experience' (38). Williams's point of view is historical and almost sociological: 'The tragic meaning is always both culturally and historically conditioned […]. The real action embodies the particular meaning, and all that is common, in the works we call tragedies, is the dramatization of a particular and grievous disorder and its resolution' (76). Disorder is vengeance, ambition, pride, coldness, lust, jealousy, disobedience, rebellion defined within a particular culture and tradition, reaching all the way to social disorder with its revolutionary impulses and with the curbs that the postrevolutionary institutions will place on them.
7   Friedrich Wilhelm Joseph Schelling, Georg Wilhelm Friedrich Hegel, Arthur Schopenhauer, Søren Kierkegaard, Friedrich Wilhelm Nietzsche.

8   It is worth recalling the important names in the twentieth-century debate on the theme: Simmel, Miguel de Unamuno, Scheler, Walter Benjamin, Albert Camus, Franz Rosenzwig, René Girard, Hans Georg Gadamer, Hannah Arendt, Hans Robert Jauss, Emanuele Severino, Remo Cantoni, Luigi Pareyson, Martha C. Nussbaum.
9   A significant study of this point was made by Virgilio Melchiorre, *Saggi su Kierkegaard* (Genoa: Marietti, 1987). He reads Kierkegaard's reflection on the tragic consciousness as the basis for the Danish philosopher's whole aesthetic-ethical-religious system. Kierkegaard writes principally about the tragic in the essay, collected in *Either/Or*, 'Ancient Drama Reflected in the Modern', in the letters to the reader Frater Taciturnus included in *Stages on Life's Way*, and in some passages of *Fear and Trembling*.
10 Daniel Greenspan, in his book *The Passion of Infinity: Kierkegaard, Aristotle and Rebirth of Tragedy* (Berlin/New York: Walter de Gruyter, 2008), recalls in this respect the invitation of Roland Barthes to return to Kierkegaard: 'His essays invite a return to Kierkegaard as the first philosophical thinker to interrogate rational Enlightenment culture in terms of this challenge that the violence of divine madness once raised in the schoolhouse of philosophy. The irruption of the mystery and unstable emotion surrounding *daimōn* returns in Kierkegaard as an essential component of his critique of both philosophies of immanence and depressed cultures of reflection in need of a tragic blow and healing'.
11 'In the background of the philosophy of the ancient tragedy, *physis* is the transgression of the limit of what is right in the grand scheme of the cosmos, where each entity has its allotted place governed by fate. Note the famous fragment of Anaximander. I quote from the English translation of Kathleen Freeman: 'The Non-Limited is the original material of existing things; further, the source from which existing things derive their existence is also that to which they return at their destruction, according to necessity; for they give justice and make reparation to one another for their injustice, according to the arrangement of Time.' *Ancilla to the Pre-Socratic Philosophers: A Complete Translation of Fragments in Diels, Fragmente der Vorsokratiker* (Cambridge, MA: Harvard University Press, 1996), 19.
12 See Eric J. Hobsbawm, *Age of Extremes: The Short Twentieth Century 1914–1991* (London: Michael Joseph, 1994).
13 'χο. [...] ποῖ δῆτα κρανεῖ, ποῖ καταλήξει / μετακοιμισθὲν μένος ἄτης' (*Choëforoe*, vv. 1075–6). The quotations are from the following editions: Aeschylus, *The Oresteia of Aeschylus (Agamemnon, Choëforoe, Eumenides)*, trans. Lewis Campbell (London: Methuen, 1893); Sophocles, *The Seven Plays in English Verse*, trans. Lewis Campbell (Oxford: Oxford University Press, 1906).
14 'χο. [...] μί τὸ δυσσεβὲς γαρ ἔργον / μετὰ μὲν πλείονα τίκτει, / σφετέρᾳ δ'εἰκότα γέννᾳ' (*Agamemnon*, vv. 758–60).
15 'κα. [...] ἰὼ βρότεια πράγματ' εὐτυχοῦντα μὲν / σκιᾷ τις ἂν πρέψειεν, εἰ δὲ δυστυχῇ, / βολαῖς ὑγρώσσων σπόγγος ὤλεσεν γραφήν' (*Agamemnon*, vv. 1327–9).
16 'αν. [...] οὐδὲ σθένειν τοσοῦτον ᾠόμην τὰ σά / κηρύγμαθ' ὥστ'ἄγραπτα κἀσφαλῆ θεῶν / νόμιμα δύνασθαι θνητὸν ὀνθ' ὑπερδραμεῖν. / Οὐ γάρ τι νῦν γε κἀχθές, ἀλλ'ἀεί ποτε / ζῇ ταῦτα, κοὐδεὶς οἶδεν ἐξ ὅτου 'φάνη' (*Antigone*, vv. 453–7).
17 'CHORUS. [...] Evil oft seemeth goodness to the mind / An angry God doth blind (ἄταν). / Few are the days that such as he / May live untroubled of calamity' (*Antigone*, v.951).
18 'ἀλλ' ἁ μοιριδία τις / δύνασις δεινά' (*Antigone*, vv. 951–2).
19 'ἀνάγκηι δ' οὐχὶ δυσμαχητέον' (*Antigone*, v. 1106).
20 On Sophocles, see Charles Segal, *Sophocles' Tragic World: Divinity, Nature, Society* (Cambridge, MA/London: Harvard University Press, 1995).
21 'ΙΣ. περισσὰ πράσσειν οὐκ ἔχει νοῦν οὐδένα' (*Antigone*, v. 68).
22 See vv. 309, 480, 482 and the verb καλλύνειν in v. 496.
23 'ὕβρις φυτεύει τύραννον ὕβρις, εἰ / πολλῶν ὑπερπλησθῇ μάταν, / ἃ μὴ πίκαιρα μηδὲ συμφέροντα, / ἀκρότατα γεῖσ' ἀναβᾶσ' / ἀπότομον ὤρουσεν εἰς ἀνάγκαν' (Pride breeds the tyrant: monstrous birth! / Insolent Pride, if idly nursed / On timeless surfeit, plenty

accursed, / Spurning the lowlier tract of Earth / Mounts to her pinnacle, – then falls, / Dashed headlong down sheer mountain walls / To dark Necessity's deep ground) (*King Oedipus*, vv. 873–7).
24 *Mythe et tragédie en Grèce ancienne* (Paris: Éditions La Découverte, 1986, 1995, 2001). A reissue of the François Maspero edition of 1972.
25 'L'homme est "père" de ses actes quand ils trouvent "en lui" leur principe, *arche*, leur cause efficiente, mais cette causalité interne ne se définit que de façon purement négative' (ibid., 61).
26 *Poetics*, trans. Samuel Henry Butcher (London: Macmillan, 1898), 1453a.
27 'δύσμαχα δ'εστί κρῖναι' (*Agamemnon*, v. 1561).
28 *Antigone*, v. 367.
29 *Time in Greek Tragedy* (Ithaca: Cornell University Press, 1996); original: *La tragédie grecque* (Paris: Presses Universitaires de France, 1968).
30 On the relationship between the tragic and suffering see Aldo Magris, 'Il tragico nei filosofi antichi', *Annuario di filosofia* 1 (1985) and Salvatore Natoli, *L'esperienza del dolore* (Milan: Feltrinelli, 1986).
31 Diego Lanza, *La disciplina dell'emozione: Un'introduzione alla tragedia greca* (Milan: Il Saggiatore, 1997); Aristotele, *Poetica*, introduction and notes by Diego Lanza (Milan: Rizzoli, 1987).
32 Vincenzo Di Benedetto, 'Pianto e catarsi nella tragedia greca', in *Sulle orme dell'antico: La tragedia greca e la scena contemporanea*, ed. Annamaria Cascetta (Milan: Vita e Pensiero, 1991), 13–43.
33 Vincenzo Di Benedetto, introduction to *Orestea*, by Eschilo (Milano: Rizzoli 1995, 17).
34 On these topics see Antonio Gibelli, *La fabbrica della guerra: La grande guerra e le trasformazioni del mondo mentale* (Turin: Bollati Boringhieri, 1991); Eric J. Leed, *No Man's Land: Combat and Identity in World War I* (Cambridge: Cambridge University Press, 1979); Enzo Traverso, *A ferro e fuoco: La guerra civile europea 1914–1945* (Bologna: Il Mulino, 2007).
35 See Hannah Arendt, *Eichmann in Jerusalem: A Report on the Banality of Evil* (New York: Penguin, 2006).

Chapter 1   Hubris and Guilt: *Gegangere (Ghosts)* by Henrik Ibsen

1 The reference to Kierkegaard may provide a clue to Ibsen's source for the idea of the violated servant (which is also part of his youthful biography). Kierkegaard's mother may also have been violated, as Jean Brun notes in his *Introduction* to Søren Kierkegaard, *Oeuvres completes* (Paris: Éditions de l'Orante, 1970), III: xxi.
2 Note here in particular the observations by Roberto Alonge, *Ibsen: L'opera e la fortuna scenica* (Florence: Le Lettere, 1995).
3 Virgilio Melchiorre, 'La coscienza tragica', in *Saggi su Kierkegaard* (Genoa: Marietti, 1987), 30.
4 Harold Noreng, Knut Hofland and Kristin Natvig, eds, *A Concordance of the Poetry and Plays of Henrik Ibsen with References to the Centennial Edition*, 6 vols (Oslo: University Library, 1993). The first volume records that 'angst. subst. c.' occurs 100 times. In particular, in *Gengangere* 'angst' is found in the dialogues: Osvald/Alving (2.109), Osvald/Alving (2.109), Alving/Osvald (2.109), Alving/Osvald (2.109), Osvald/Alving (3.120), Osvald/Alving (3.130); 'anguste' occurs in the dialogues: Alving/Osvald (3.126), Osvald/Alving (3.126), Alving/Osvald (3.126), Osvald/Alving (3.126), Osvald/Alving (3.128), Osvald/Alving (3.128); 'angst' occurs in the stage directions at 3.120.
5 Kierkegaard refers to the Biblical passages Ex 20:5 and Dt 5:9, which is also the model for Ibsen's famous saying, in Virgilio Melchiorre, 'La coscienza tragica', in *Saggi su Kierkegaard*.
6 Søren Kierkegaard, *Either/Or*, trans. by Howard V. Hong and Edna H. Hong (Princeton: Princeton University Press, 1988), I: 341 (*Enten-Eller: Et Livs-Fragment*, I, Copenhagen, 1843).
7 Among only the most recent contributions, the following are notable: Terje Sinding, 'Les revenants: Une tragédie?' in *Théâtre et destin: Sofocle, Shakespeare, Racine, Ibsen*, ed. Jean Bessière (Paris: Honoré Champion Éditeur, 1997), 118–48; Astrid Saether, ed., *Ibsen, Tragedy, and the Tragic: Ibsen Conference in Athens 2002, 30 November–4 December*, Acta Ibseniana (Oslo: Centre for Ibsen Studies, University of Oslo, 2003). See also the synthesis that draws on the important

previous studies by Régis Boyer, in the introduction to Ibsen, *Théâtre* (Paris: Gallimard, 2006), which states that Ibsen's strange creatures need to be grasped 'dans la dialectique bien luthérienne du péché et de la mort, ou de la faute et de sa sanction' (xii), and stresses the tragic *Weltanschauung* centered on the notion of destiny, which in *Ghosts* is linked to the theme of heredity, partly following the vogue of the day. But, 'si hérédité et destin s'identifient, c'est bien parce qu'ils sont réunis par une dimension sacrée [...]. On pourrait tout aussi bien parler de la mort qui règne dans toutes ces pièces avec une sorte de souveraineté tranquille' (xxx–xxxi). Among Boyer's previous studies, see: 'Mesure et démesure: les ressorts du tragique chez Ibsen', in *Théâtre, tragique et modernité en Europe (XIX et XX siècles)*, ed. Muriel Lazzarini-Dossin (Brussels: Archives et Musée de la littérature / Peter Lang, 2004), 87–100; and the special edition of *Europe* which he edited, dedicated to the playwright, no. 840 (April 1999).

8 The introduction to the proceedings of the Athens conference states, 'In the drafts for *A Doll's House* (1879) Ibsen comments upon the need for a reinvention of the tragic genre. In *Notes for the Tragedy of Modern Times*, he writes, "The catastrophe approaches, ineluctably, inevitably. Despair, resistance, defeat"' (*Ibsen, Tragedy, and the Tragic*, 3).

9 On the life of Ibsen, see Michael Meyer, *Henrik Ibsen: A Biography*, 3 vols (New York: MacDonald, 1967; Doubleday, 1971); Robert Ferguson, *Henrik Ibsen: A New Biography* (London: Richard Coen Books, 1996).

10 Franco Perrelli, *Henrik Ibsen: Un profilo* (Bari: Edizioni di Pagina, 2006), 130. See also, for the sources, *The Cambridge Companion to Ibsen*, ed. J. McFarlane (Cambridge: Cambridge University Press, 1994).

11 In the decade between 1872 and 1882 Nietzsche published *The Birth of Tragedy*, *Untimely Meditations*, *Human, All Too Human*, *The Dawn* and *The Gay Science* (original titles: *Die Geburt der Tragödie*, *Unzeitgemässe Betrachtungen*, *Menschliches, Allzumenschliches*, *Morgenröte* and *Die fröhliche Wissenschaft*). In the 1870s he lived and taught in Germany. In the same years Ibsen lived in Germany, staying in Dresden and Munich, where he loved being in the thick of things.

12 In the above introduction, Régis Boyer, recalling Ibsen's youthful sympathies for the European revolutionaries, observes: 'Il récusait la "bonne" société "aux coeurs vides et aux bourses pleines", le sabre, la rosette et le goupillon, l'Église et ses attitudes de façade, le christianisme ostentatoire, tout un luthéranisme qui avait confondu une fois pour toutes la religion avec la morale et la morale avec la sexualité. Il faut relire sous cet angle *Les Soutiens de la société* [...] des sépulcres blanchis ces grandes sociétés d'aujourd'hui' (xxii–xxiii).

13 The original text can be read in volume 9 of the complete works: Henrik Ibsen, *Samlede Verker (Hundreårsuntgave)*, ed. Francis Bull, Halvdan Koht and Didrik Arup Seip, 21 vols (Oslo: Gyldendal, 1928–58). A rigorous and effective French translation is in Henrik Ibsen, *Théâtre*, ed. Régis Boyer (Paris: Gallimard, 2006). The edition used here is Henrik Ibsen, *Ghosts* in *The Collected Works of Henrik Ibsen*, revised and ed. William Archer, vol. 7, trans. Charles Archer (New York: Charles Scribner, 1911).

14 Alonge, *Ibsen*.

15 337. As follows in the original: 'FRU ALVING. Måtte gå her uden at ha' noget livsformål; han havde bare et embede. Ikke øjne noget arbejde, som han kunde kaste sig over med hele sit sind; – han havde bare forretninger. Ikke eje en eneste kammerat, som var mægtig at føle hvad livsglæde er for noget; bare dagdrivere og svirebrødre –' (*Samlede Verker*, vol. 9 (from which the quotations below also come), act 3, 122).

16 253. 'OSVALD. Nej; ved De, når og hvor jeg har truffet usædeligheden i kunstnerkredsene? PASTOR MANDERS. Nej, Gud være lovet! OSVALD. Nå, da skal jeg tillade mig at sige det. Jeg har truffet den når en og anden af vore mønstergyldige ægtemænd og familjefædre kom derned for at se sig om en smule på egen hånd – og så gjorde kunstnerne den ære at opsøge dem i deres tarvelige knejper. Da kunde vi få vide besked. De herrer vidste at fortælle os både om steder og om ting, som vi aldrig havde drømt om' (act 1, 75–6).

17 252.

18 250. 'OSVALD Jeg har aldrig mærket noget særlig vildt ved de folks samliv. [...] Men aldrig har jeg der hørt et anstødeligt ord, og endnu mindre har jeg været vidne til noget, som kunde kaldes usædeligt' (act 1, 75).
19 317. 'OSVALD Ja, det er bare det jeg mener, at her læres folk op til at tro, at arbejdet er en forbandelse og en syndestraf, og at livet er noget jammerligt noget, som vi er bedst tjent med at komme ud af jo før jo heller. FRU ALVING. En jammerdal, ja. Og det gør vi det da også ærligt og redeligt til. OSVALD. Men sligt noget vil menneskene ikke vide af derude. Der er ingen der, som rigtig tror på den slags lærdomme længer' (act 2, 112).
20 245. 'PASTOR MANDERS. Da Osvald kom der i døren med piben i munden, var det som jeg så hans far lyslevende. OSVALD. Nej virkelig? FRU ALVING. Å, hvor kan De dog sige det! Osvald slægter jo mig på' (act 1, 72).
21 Alonge, *Ibsen*, 48.
22 280. 'FRU ALVING [...] Jeg er ræd og sky, fordi der sidder i mig noget af dette gengangeragtige, som jeg aldrig rigtig kan bli' kvit. PASTOR MANDERS. Hvad var det De kaldte det? FRU ALVING. Gengangeragtigt. Da jeg hørte Regine og Osvald derinde, var det som jeg så gengangere for mig. Men jeg tror næsten, vi er gengangere allesammen, pastor Manders. Det er ikke bare det, vi har arvet fra far og mor, som går igen i os. Det er alleslags gamle afdøde meninger og alskens gammel afdød tro og sligt noget. Det er ikke levende i os; men det sidder i alligevel og vi kan ikke bli' det kvit. Bare jeg tar en avis og læser i, er det ligesom jeg så gengangere smyge imellem linjerne. Der må leve gengangere hele landet udover. Der må være så tykt af dem som sand, synes jeg. Og så er vi så gudsjammerlig lysrædde allesammen' (act 2, 92).
23 In this respect, an interesting production was presented by the young director Alexander Mørk-Linden at the Ibsen Festivalen in Oslo during the summer of 2006, featuring Anne Marit Jacobsen (Mrs Alving), Ole Johan Skjelbred (Oswald), Bjørn Sundquist (Pastor Manders), Trond Braemar (Engstrand) and Andrea Bræin Hovig (Regina). Underlying the interpretation was the question of the young to the older: what world have you made for us? Oswald and Regina, the former open and generous, the latter calculating and somewhat cynical, are both penalized by a selfish and dissipated generation, slaves to respectability and bourgeois comforts or money-grubbing prudence. The one is doomed to the inertness of a death in life; the other at the mercy of the vulgarity of money. This treatment reflects an emerging trend which also reinterprets the classics and certainly has its outstanding model in Peter Brook's *Tragédie d'Hamlet*.
24 299. 'OSVALD (krammer en avis). Jeg synes, det måtte næsten være det samme for dig, enten jeg var til eller ikke. [...] (standser ved fru Alving). Mor, må jeg få lov at sidde i sofaen hos dig? FRU ALVING (gør plads for ham). Ja, kom du, min kære gut' (act 2, 102–3).
25 299. 'FRU ALVING. Min ulykkelige gut! Hvorledes er dette forfærdelige kommet over dig? OSVALD (sætter sig atter oprejst). Ja, det er just det, jeg umulig kan fatte og begribe. Jeg har aldrig ført noget stormende liv. Ikke i nogen henseende, Det skal du ikke tro om mig, mor! Det har jeg aldrig gjort. FRU ALVING. Det tror jeg heller ikke, Osvald. OSVALD. Og så kommer dette over mig alligevel! Denne forfærdelige ulykke!' (act 2, 104).
26 306, 312. 'OSVALD. Sæt dig ikke imod det, mor. Vær nu snil! Jeg må ha' noget at skylle alle disse nagende tankerne ned med. [...] Jeg kan ikke gå her og bære al denne sjælekval alene. [...] Men det er alle kvalerne, naget, angeren, – og så den store dødelige angst. Å – denne forfærdelige angst! FRU ALVING (går efter ham). Angst? Hvilken angst? Hvad mener du?' (act 2, 107 ff.).
27 318. 'OSVALD. Derfor er jeg ræd for at bli' her hjemme hos dig. FRU ALVING. Ræd? Hvad er det du er ræd for her hos mig? OSVALD. Jeg er ræd for, at alt det, som er oppe i mig, vilde arte ud i styghed her. FRU ALVING. (ser fast på ham). Tror du, det vilde ske? OSVALD. Jeg véd det så visst. Lev det samme liv herhjemme, som derude, og det blir dog ikke det samme liv.' (act 2, 112).
28 The term money (*penge*) and related concepts are a key part of Ibsen's vocabulary. It recurs insistently in *Ghosts*, as revealed in the *Concordances*. Volume 4 records six occurrence of

'penge' (Regine/Engstrand, 1.57; Osvald/Manders, 1.75; Alving/Manders, 1.84; Alving/Manders, 2.87; Manders/Engstrand, 2.98; Manders/Engstrand, 2.98); one occurrence of 'penger' (Engstrand/Regine, 1.56); one occurrence of 'pengerne' (Engstrand/Regine, 1.56); one of 'penges' (Mendes/Alving, 2.88); five of 'pengene' (Regine/Engstrand, 1.57; Manders/Alving, 1.66; Engstrand/Manders, 2.98; Engstrand/Manders, 2.100; Regine/Alving, 3.124).

29 273. 'PASTOR MANDERS [...] Hvor stort var det beløb, pigen havde at råde over? FRU ALVING. Det var tre hundrede specier. PASTOR MANDERS. Ja, tænke sig bare, – for lumpne tre hundrede specier at gå hen og la' sig ægtevie til en falden kvinde!' (act 2, 88).

30 255. 'PASTOR MANDERS. Det er just den rette oprørsånd at kræve lykken her i livet. Hvad ret har vi mennesker til lykken? Nej, vi skal gøre vor pligt, frue! Og Deres pligt var at holde fast ved den mand, som De engang havde valgt og til hvem De var knyttet ved hellige bånd. FRU ALVING. De ved godt, hvad slags liv Alving førte i den tid; hvilke udskejelser han gjorde sig skyldig i. PASTOR MANDERS. Jeg ved såre vel, hvilke rygter der gik om ham; og jeg er den, som mindst af alle billiger hans vandel i ungdomsårene, såfremt rygterne medførte sandhed. Men en hustru er ikke sat til at være sin husbonds dommer. Det havde været Deres skyldighed med ydmygt sind at bære det kors, som en højere vilje havde eragtet tjenligt for Dem. Men i det sted afkaster De i oprørskhed korset, forlader den snublende, som De skulde have støttet, går hen og sætter Deres gode navn og rygte på spil, og – er nær ved at forspilde andres rygte ovenikøbet' (act 1, 77–8).

31 210. 'ENGSTRAND Jøss' som du snakker, Regine. (halter et par skridt frem i stuen.) Men det var det, jeg vilde sige – [...] Ja, for vi mennesker er skrøbelige, barnet mit – [...] Ja, men det var jo bare når jeg var på en kant – hm. Fristelserne er mangfoldige i denne verden, Regine' (act 1, 53 ff.).

32 294. 'ENGSTRAND. Jeg synes ligesom det, ja. Og så farvel, frue, og tak for her; og ta' rigtig godt vare på Regine for mig. (visker en tåre af øjet.) Salig Johannes barn – hm, det er underligt med det – men det er lige rakt som hun var vokset fast til hjerterødderne mine. Ja-mænd er det så, ja. (Han hilser og går ud gennem døren.)' (act 2, 100).

33 91.

34 331. 'ENGSTRAND. Jakob Engstrand er som en redningens engel at lignes ved, han, herr pastor! PASTOR MANDERS. Nej, nej, dette kan jeg tilforladelig ikke modtage. ENGSTRAND. Å, det blir nu så alligevel. Jeg véd en, som har taget skylden på sig for andre engang før, jeg' (act 3, 119).

35 325. 'ENGSTRAND. (kommer gennem forstuen). Herr pastor –! PASTOR MANDERS. (vender sig forskrækket). Er De efter mig her også! ENGSTRAND. Ja, jeg må Gu' døde mig –! Å, Jøss da! Men dette her er så fælt, herr pastor! PASTOR MANDERS. (går frem og tilbage). Desværre, desværre! REGINE. Hvad er det for noget? ENGSTRAND. Å, det kom af denne her andagten, ser du. (sagte.) Nu har vi gøken, barnet mit! (højt.) Og så at jeg skal være skyld i, at pastor Manders blev skyld i sligt noget!' (AIII, 116).

36 264–7. 'FRU ALVING. Jeg vilde ikke, at Osvald, min egen gut, skulde ta' nogetsomhelst i arv efter sin far. [...] Min søn skal ha' alting fra mig, skal han. [...] Men så er også dette lange stygge komediespil tilende. Fra iovermorgen af skal det være for mig, som om den døde aldrig havde levet i dette hus. Her skal ingen anden være, end min gut og hans mor' (act 1, 84–5).

37 303–4. 'OSVALD. [...] Og så sa' den gamle cyniker – (knytter hånden.) Å – ! FRU ALVING. Hvad sa' han? OSVALD. Han sa': fædrenes synder hjemsøges på børnene' (act 2, 105).

38 Dante, *Dante's Inferno: The Italian Text with a Translation into English Triple Rhyme*, trans. Laurence Binyon (London: Macmillan, 1933), 29.

39 'On pourrait pourtant parler du prophétisme d'Ibsen. Il aura vécu l'une de ces époques de transition où le monde bascule, où le passé dévoile sa caducité, où, de manière plus positive, la crainte de l'avenir désarçonne. Ce n'est pas vrai seulement de la petite Norvège qui est en train de changer de statut ou des lettres du Nord en pleine mutation. L'Occident tout entier chavire' (Régis Boyer, *Introduction* to Ibsen, *Théâtre*, xxv).

40 It is common knowledge that the atom bomb was likened to the sun and that Ibsen's compatriot Alfred Nobel invented dynamite in 1867 and in 1887 ballistite, which was heavily used in both world wars.
41 322.
42 246. 'OSVALD. Ja. Jeg var ganske liden dengang. Og så husker jeg, jeg kom op på kammeret til far en aften, han var så glad og lystig. FRU ALVING. Å, du husker ingenting fra de år. [...] Kære, det er bare noget Osvald har drømt' (act 1, 72–3).
43 349–56. 'FRU ALVING. Barnet har sin mor til at pleje sig. [...] OSVALD. Ja, lad os håbe på det. Og lad os så leve sammen så længe vi kan. Tak, mor. [...] FRU ALVING [...] Alt, hvad du peger på, skal du få, som dengang du var et lidet barn. – OSVALD (sidder ubevægelig som før og siger): Solen. – Solen' (act 3, 128 ff.).
44 225–6 'REGINE. Ja, det kan så være, men alligevel –. Ja, hvis det var i et godt hus og hos en rigtig reel herre – PASTOR MANDERS. Men, min kære Regine – REGINE. – en, som jeg kunde nære hengivenhed for og se op til og være ligesom i datters sted – PASTOR MANDERS. Ja, men mit kære gode barn –' (act 1, 61).
45 260. 'PASTOR MANDERS. (sagte og usikkert). Helene – skal dette være en bebrejdelse, så vil jeg be' Dem overveje – FRU ALVING. – de hensyn, De skyldte Deres stilling; ja. Og så at jeg var en bortløben hustru. Man kan aldrig være tilbageholdende nok lige over for slige hensynsløse fruentimmer. PASTOR MANDERS. Kære – fru Alving, dette er en så umådelig overdrivelse –' (act 1, 80).

Chapter 2   Eve Becomes Mary: *L'annonce faite à Marie* (*The Tidings Brought to Mary*) by Paul Claudel

1 For a general introduction to Claudel's work, see Annie-Marie Hubat-Blanc, *Paul Claudel* (Paris: Bertrand Lacoste, 1994) and Marie-Anne Lescourret, *Claudel* (Paris: Flammarion, 2003).
2 I discuss this topic in the chapter 'Murder in the Cathedral di Thomas E. Eliot: Il martirio per un testo simbolico fra poesia e liturgia', in Annamaria Cascetta, *La Passione dell'uomo: Voci dal teatro europeo del Novecento* (Rome: Edizioni Studium, 2006), 47–77, in the volumes dedicated to *Invito alla lettura di Testori* (Milan: Mursia, 1983; 1995).
3 The edition P. Claudel, *Théâtre: Édition revue et augmentée, textes et notices établis par Jacques Madaule et Jacques Petit*, 2 vols (Paris: Gallimard, vol. 1, 1967; vol. 2, 1971) contains the different versions of the text. In particular, volume 2 (henceforth simply *Théâtre*) contains the *Première version* (1912, 11–114), the 'variante pour la scène' of act 4 (1938, 115–29) and the 'version définitive pour la scène' (1948, 215). In English, only the 1912 edition is available. The passages quoted come from the translation by Louise Morgan Sill, *The Tidings Brought to Mary* (New Haven: Yale University Press, 1916) (hereafter *Tidings*).
4 *Tidings*, 62.
5 *Tidings*, 63. 'O ma fiancée, à travers les branches en fleur, salut!' (*Théâtre*, 94).
6 *Tidings*, 139. 'Mais que c'est bon aussi de mourir! / Alors que c'est bien fini et que s'étend sur nous peu à peu / l'obscurcissement comme d'un ombrage très obscur' (*Théâtre*, 95).
7 *Tidings*, 171. 'Les trois notes comme un sacrifice ineffable sont recueillies dans le sein de la Vierge sans péché' (*Théâtre*, 114).
8 *Théâtre*, 1382.
9 *Théâtre*, 208 (my translation).
10 *Théâtre*, 211–12 (my translation).
11 *Tidings*, 13–14. 'VIOLAINE. Et baisez pour moi ma soeur Justice. PIERRE DE CRAON. *(La regardant soudain et comme frappé d'une idée.)* Est-ce tout ce que vous avez à me donner pour elle? un peu d'or retiré de Votre doigt? VIOLAINE. Cela ne suffit-il pas à payer une petite pierre? PIERRE DE CRAON. Mais Justice est une grande pierre elle-même. VIOLAINE. *(riant)* Je ne suis pas de la même

carrière. PIERRE DE CRAON. Celle qu'il faut à la base n'est point celle qu'il faut pour le faîte' (Prologo) (*Théâtre*, 19).

12 Act 4, scene 3. *Théâtre*, 88: 'VIOLAINE. Ah, il était si triste et j'étais si heureuse!'

13 Pirandello too, though representing suffering as unendowed with meaning, evoked leprosy as a flower in his well-known one-act play *The Man with the Flower in His Mouth* (original title: *L'uomo dal fiore in bocca*).

14 The motif of the earth is related to the poet's life, the landscape of his beloved home, which he describes as a sea of emerald and fire, a plain of gold across which move the shadows of the glittering clouds.

15 Act 3, scene 1 (*Théâtre*, 68). The expression returns in the famous conclusion of the *Journal d'un curé de campagne* by Bernanos: 'Tout est grâce'.

16 Act 4, scene 3 (*Tidings*, 137). 'VIOLAINE. Il est fini, qu'est-ce que ça fait? On ne t'a point promis le bonheur. Travaille, c'est tout ce qu'on te demande' (*Théâtre*, 94).

17 Act 4, scene 3 (*Tidings*, 131–2). 'VIOLAINE. Il est trop dur de souffrir et de ne savoir à quoi bon. / Mais ce que d'autres ne savent pas, je l'ai appris et je veux que tu le saches avec moi. / [...] Tout ce qui doit périr, c'est cela qui est malade, et tout cela qui ne doit pas périr, / C'est cela qui souffre. / Heureux celui qui souffre et qui sait à quoi bon' (*Théâtre*, 89).

18 For a treatment of this delicate question the reader is referred to Cristiano Grottanelli, *Il sacrificio* (Bari: Laterza, 1999); Marco Rizzi, 'La vita del Cristiano come "sacrificio" tra Giustino e Clemente Alessandrino', *Annali di Scienze Religiose* 7 (2002): 15–28.

19 Quoted in Anne Ubersfeld, *Paul Claudel: Poète du XX siècle* (Arles: Actes Sud-Papiers, 2005).

20 Lk 1:26–38; Lk 1:39–55.

21 Mt 27:57–1; Mk 15:42–7; Lk 23:50–56; Jn 19:38–42.

22 Note the expression from act 1, scene 3: 'Il est un temps de prendre et un temps de laisser prendre' / 'There is a time to take and a time to let take' (*Théâtre*, 37; *Tidings*, 44).

23 It also encourages comparisons of poetic effect. For example, the comparison in act 4, scene 5 of the churches that Pierre de Craon builds to the 'Ten Wise Virgins whose oil is never exhausted, and who compose a vessel of prayers!' (159; 'Dix Vierges Sages dont l'huile ne s'éteint pas, et compose un vase de prières', *Théâtre*, 107).

24 '...deux textes écrits par Dieu, l'un est la Bible, l'autre est le monde, l'immense cercle de la Création'. Anne Ubersfeld, *Paul Claudel*, 265.

25 For a fuller treatment, see P. Ouvrard, *Aux sources de Paul Claudel: Littérature et foi; L'œuvre littéraire de Paul Claudel à la lumière de trois mystères chrétiens; La Création, la Communion des Saints, la Rédemption* (Laval: Siloë, 1994); J. Houriez, *L'inspiration scripturaire dans le théâtre et la poésie de Paul Claudel: Premières œuvres*, 2 vols. (Paris: Belles Lettres, 1996); and J. Houriez, *L'inspiration scripturaire dans le théâtre et la poésie de Paul Claudel: Les œuvres de la maturité* (Paris: Belles Lettres, 1998).

26 'Il ne faut pas lire la Bible, il faut l'écouter.' He continues: 'La prophétie pour *l'entendre* avec notre intelligence, il nous faut l'entendre avec nos oreilles. Elle devrait presque nous être présentée comme la partition d'un chanteur. Il n'y a pas d'esprit sans respiration et l'entrecoupement des verses nous donne le sentiment d'une haleine plus profonde. Sous l'écriture qui congèle la pensée pour en faire une espèce de plaque homogène il y a la voix, sous la voix il y a la pensée, et sous la pensée il y a l'émotion [...]. La voix du prophète, interrompue et nourrie par les silences, se fait entendre à nous avec d'innombrables variations d'intensité, de rapidité et de timbre. Tantôt hymne, tantôt récit, tantôt réquisitoire et plaidoyer.' (To *comprehend* the prophecy with our intelligence, we have to comprehend it with our ears. It should almost be presented to us like a score for a singer. There is no mind without the breathing and intervals of verses to give us the feeling of a deeper breathing. Beneath the writing that freezes the thought into a kind of homogeneous inscription, there is the voice, beneath the voice there is the thought, and beneath the thought there is feeling [...]. The voice of the prophet, interrupted and nurtured by silence, makes itself understood by us with endless variations of intensity, rapidity and timbre. At times a hymn, at times a tale, and at times an indictment

and a plea.) Paul Claudel's writings on the Bible are collected in: *Le poëte et la Bible*, vol. 1, *1910–1946*, vol. 2, *1945–1955* (Paris: Gallimard, 1998; 2004). (The quotation comes from vol. 2, 1225–6).

27 This involved endowing 'le catholicisme d'un mode de pensée synthétique et unificateur, capable d'articuler la foi et la raison, de délimiter le domaine de Dieu et de César, de fonder le rôle social de la religion'. Claude Prudhomme, 'Léon XIII et la Curie romaine à l'époque de Rerum Novarum', *Rerum Novarum: Écriture, contenu et réception d'une encyclique* (Rome: École Française de Rome, 1997), 30.

28 See the correspondence between them in 'Mémoires de Paul Claudel', *Revue des Sciences Humaines* 279, no. 3 (2005): 207–31. As the epigraph to his work *Antimoderne*, Maritain took a verse from Claudel's Third Grand Ode: 'Qui ne croit plus en Dieu, il ne croit plus en l'Être et qui hait l'Être, il hait sa propre existence. Seigneur je vous ai trouvé.' (Whoever no longer believes in God, no longer believes in Being, and whoever hates Being hates his own life. Lord I have found you.)

29 A rigorous and recent summary of this idea can be usefully read in Alessandro Ghisalberti, 'Tommaso D'Aquino', *Enciclopedia filosofica*, vol. 11 (Milan: Bompiani, 2006), 11655–91.

30 Consider the thread of analogy running through *The Tidings Brought to Mary*, which binds natural father/father-farmer who makes the earth fruitful/father-builder who builds the house of God/God the father and creator and saviour; or the call of Violaine and her 'conception'/the annunciation to Mary and the conception in the Holy Spirit; or again the farewell of the dying 'martyr'/the angel's greeting to the Virgin.

31 On Claudel's version of the *Oresteia*, see P. Alexandre, *Traduction et création chez Paul Claudel: L'Orestie* (Paris: Honoré Champion, 1997).

32 'Je crois que l'élément essentiel est moins le sens que l'intonation [...]. Il n'est nullement nécessaire que le public comprenne le sens de chaque phrase. Parfois un chuchotement mystérieux sera suffisant' (*Théâtre*, vol. 1, 1322).

33 'On dirait que le poète a hâte de reprendre ce long cri devant une tombe mal ferme, qui, à vrai dire, est tout le drame, l'étonnement devant la mort et le mal' (ibid., 1324).

34 See *Claudel homme de théâtre: Correspondances avec Copeau, Dullin, Juvet*, ed. H. Micciollo and J. Petit (Paris: Gallimard, 1966).

35 Prologue, 22–3. 'PIERRE DE CRAON. J'emporte votre anneau. / Et de ce petit cercle je vais faire une semence d'or! [...] / L'âme de Violaine, mon enfant, en qui mon cœur se complaît. [...] / Mais celle que je vais faire sera sous sa propre ombre comme de l'or condensé et comme une pyxide pleine de manne!' (*Théâtre*, 25).

36 On this topic see Monique Parent, 'Les éléments lyriques dans *L'annonce faite à Marie*', *Revue d'histoire du théâtre* 3 (1968).

37 Act 1, scene 3, (*Tidings*, 53). 'Prenez place tous! Une dernière fois je vous partagerai le pain' (*Théâtre*, 42).

38 Claudel offers numerous useful observations which have been collected in the volume *Mes idées sur le Théâtre* (Paris: Gallimard, 1966). A useful study is Alain Beretta, *La vie scénique d'une pièce de théâtre: L'annonce faite à Marie de Paul Claudel (1912–1995)* (Nancy: University of Nancy, 1996).

39 For a good introduction to the question and a fuller treatment see: Giuseppe Bernardelli, *Metrica francese. Fondamenti teorici e lineamenti storici* (Brescia: Editrice La Scuola, 1989).

40 *Théâtre*, 65. Here and in the following quotations the text quotes from the original and only appends the translation in the notes because of the obvious need to present the observations on the phonic aspect of the text in the original. 'ANOTHER WOMAN. 'Tis Christmas Day that our King Charles comes back to get hi'self crowned. ANOTHER. 'Tis a village girl, sent by God, Who brings him back to his own. ANOTHER. Jeanne, they call her! ANOTHER. The maid! ANOTHER. Who was born on Twelfth Night! ANOTHER. Who drove the English away from Orleans when they besieged it! ANOTHER WORKMAN. And who's goin' to drive 'em all out of France too, all of

'em! Amen. ANOTHER WORKMAN. *(humming)* Noel! Cock-a-doodle-doo! Noel! Noel come again! Rrrr! How cauld it be!' (*Tidings*, 90–91).
41 *Théâtre*, 75. 'You saw me kiss that leper, Mara? Ah the chalice of sorrow is deep, / And who once sets his lip to it can never withdraw it again of his own free will!' (*Tidings*, 107).
42 *Théâtre*, 76. 'No! No! No! You shall never trick me with your nunnish rigmaroles! / No! I shall never be silenced! / The milk that burns my breast cries out like the blood of Abel! / Have I got fifty children to tear out of my body? have I got fifty souls to tear out of my soul?/ Do you know what it is to be rent in two in order to bring into the world this little wrailing creature. / And the midwife told me I should have no more children. / But if I had a hundred children it would not be my little Aubaine' (*Tidings*, 108–9).

Chapter 3   The School of Hatred: *Mourning Becomes Electra* by Eugene O'Neill

1 A useful outline of the general context of the American theatre will be found in Don B. Wilmeth and Christopher Bigsby, eds, *The Cambridge History of American Theatre*, 3 vols (Cambridge: Cambridge University Press, 1998–2000); and, in Italian, Sergio Perosa, *Storia del teatro americano* (Milan: Bompiani, 1982).
2 On the dramaturgy of O'Neill, see Chaman Ahuja, *Tragedy, Modern Temper and O'Neill* (Atlantic Highlands, NJ: Humanities Press, 1983); Travis Bogard, *Contour in Time: The Plays of Eugene O'Neill* (Oxford: Oxford University Press, 1972; revised edition 1988); Arthur Gelb and Barbara Gelb, *O'Neill* (New York: Harper and Row, 1962; 1987); Chandreshwar Prasat Sinha, *Eugene O'Neill's Tragic Vision* (Atlantic Highlands, NJ: Humanities Press, 1981); William W. Demastes, *Theatre of Chaos* (Cambridge/New York: Cambridge University Press, 1998).
3 *Homecoming*, act 1. *Mourning Becomes Electra* (New York: Liveright, 1931) (hereafter *Electra*), 22.
4 *Homecoming*, act 1 (*Electra*, 26).
5 *The Haunted*, act 4 (*Electra*, 248).
6 *The Haunted*, act 4 (*Electra*, 256).
7 *The Haunted*, act 3 (*Electra*, 233).
8 *The Haunted*, act 4 (*Electra*, 256).
9 *Homecoming*, act 3 (*Electra*, 82).
10 *The Haunted*, act 4 (*Electra*, 218).
11 *Homecoming*, act 3 (*Electra*, 71).
12 *Homecoming*, act 1 (*Electra*, 28).
13 *Homecoming*, act 1 (*Electra*, 86).
14 *The Haunted*, act 4 (*Electra*, 247).
15 *Homecoming*, act 2 (*Electra*, 51).
16 *Homecoming*, act 3 (*Electra*, 76).
17 *The Hunted*, act 2 (*Electra*, 127).
18 See *The Hunted*, act 1 (*Electra*, 110).
19 *Homecoming*, act 3 (*Electra*, 82).
20 *The Hunted*, act 1 (*Electra*, 126).
21 *The Hunted*, act 2 (*Electra*, 123).
22 I will here briefly outline the question of the Oedipus complex, as summed up by Freud in *The Interpretation of Dreams, Totem and Taboo: Introduction to Psychoanalysis, Dostoevsky and Parricide* (see *The Standard Edition of the Complete Psychological Works of Sigmund Freud*, ed. J. Strachey [London: Vintage Press, 1953–74]). According to Freud, in the Oedipus legend and Sophocles' play it is not the tragedy of fate that strikes modern man so much as the degree to which his destiny could also be our own, and the secret content of the legend: perhaps all of us are destined to direct our first sexual impulse towards the mother (through the original contact with the breast, which becomes the first love object) and our first hatred and desire for violence against the father. Not everyone, however, becomes psychoneurotic, namely unable to detach these

impulses from their primary object. However, these impulses, though suppressed, remain present. This is the typical attitude of the male child to his parents and is the nuclear complex of neuroses. But the child's emotional attitude is ambivalent: the rivalry with the father gives rise to hatred of the father, but the child also feels tenderness and admiration for the same person. The conditions of the Oedipus complex have given rise, in the anthropology and psychology of peoples, to totemic systems with the twin taboos against killing the totem and having sex with a woman belonging to the same totem, and the immense sense of guilt that Freud believed to underlie morality and religion. These ideas should not be underestimated: they circulated widely in the early decades of the century and provided many artists and writers with something they could cling to when they had abandoned religion but not the religious sensibility and impulse. This was the case with O'Neill.

As for female sexuality and the onset of the related complexes (those that Jung called the Electra complex, emphasizing the analogy between the sexes), Freud explored this in, among other works, *Female Sexuality* (1931), *New Introductory Lectures on Psychoanalysis* (1933) and *Outline of Psychoanalysis* (1940). Female sexuality was seen as being analogous, though with obvious variations, to the dynamic described for males: attachment to the father and the urge to eliminate the mother as unnecessary and take her place. But Freud stresses that the strong dependence of the female on the father is the legacy of an equally strong attachment to the mother, the first love object, since the initial conditions are the same for all children, being then followed by a change in the sex of the object with the focus moving to the man-father. In the woman's subsequent development (relevant to the analysis of this text) she turns to the father as the object of her love and so establishes the female form of the Oedipus complex. The attachment to the mother tends to disappear, even though it is the earliest bond and so very deep, but it also has an ambivalent character, since a daughter often intuits her mother's unconscious hostility or is eclipsed by the arrival of a younger sibling. The daughter abandons the mother as love object and replaces her with her father through identification with the mother. This bond now takes the place of her former attachment to her mother. The daughter seeks to replicate her mother's relationship to her father and therefore hates her with feelings of jealousy and humiliation. Children have great difficulty in forgiving a mother's neglect. The place of the child's unfaithful mother can be taken by a sister as a love object. These subterranean incestuous choices, favoured by cohabitation, produce strict cultural prohibitions on incest.

23 'I have only read two books of Freud's, "Totem and Taboo" and "Beyond the Pleasure Principle". The book that interested me the most of all those of the Freudian school is Jung's "Psychology of the Unconscious" which I read many years ago. If I have been influenced unconsciously it must have been by this book more than any other psychological work.' Letter to Martha Carolyn Sparrow, 13 October 1929, quoted by Egil Törnquist, *O'Neill's Philosophical And Literary Paragons*, in Michael Manheim, ed., *The Cambridge Companion to Eugene O'Neill* (Cambridge: Cambridge University Press, 1998), 22.

24 Freud dealt with the death wish in *Beyond the Pleasure Principle*, which, as we have seen, O'Neill said he had read. Written in 1920, it was supported by clinical experience and his reading of works such as the philosophy of Schopenhauer. Freud argues that in the psyche there exists a powerful but nonexclusive tendency towards the pleasure principle. This is countered by other forces and circumstances. Under the influence of the drives (inescapable elementary pressures) of self-preservation of the ego it is replaced by the reality principle, which delays the satisfaction of pleasures. This is a source of regret to which is added another source of sorrow, one in which repression transforms a possibility of pleasure by keeping it at a lower level of psychic development, depriving it of the possibility of fulfilment and experiencing as a disorder the fact that the drives subsequently resurface, because repression is relaxed for various reasons, and achieve a direct or vicarious satisfaction. The compulsion to repeat unpleasant experiences, however, suggests that the regulatory principle of mental life is not

pleasure alone. From this it follows that drives have a conservative and regressive tendency aimed at restoring original states. Freud thus hypothesizes a dual presence in the psyche: the life instincts and the death instincts which drive life towards nothingness. Moreover, Freud observes, it is an experiential fact that every living thing dies for internal reasons and that death is the goal of all living things. 'Many of us will also find it hard', he writes, 'to abandon our belief that in man himself there dwells an impulse towards perfection, which has brought him to his present heights of intellectual prowess and ethical sublimation, and from which it might be expected that his development into superman will be ensured. But I do not believe in the existence of such an inner impulse, and I see no way of preserving this pleasing illusion' (*Beyond the Pleasure Principle* [*Jenseits des Lustprinzips*], trans. C. J. M. Hubback [London: International Psychoanalytical Association, 1922]), 20.

25 *The World as Will and Representation* (*Die Welt als Wille und Vorstellung*) was strongly influential on the irrationalist thought of the nineteenth and twentieth centuries and was widely read in the early decades of the twentieth, when it was felt to closely match the historical and individual disillusionment of the age and reveal the contradictions between the selfish, brutal impulses that actually drove events and the profession of moral standards and ideals.

26 The metaphor of calm at sea, the vanishing of the ripples of the waves in the surface of the water, which Schopenhauer evokes, is combined with O'Neill's biographical experience as a sailor for a short period in youth, and passes into the characters. Think of Captain Adam Brant's dreams of the South Seas. The reader is referred above all to the confession that Edmund makes to his father in *Long Day's Journey into Night*.

Chapter 4   The Destiny of Man Is Man: *Mutter Courage und ihre Kinder* (*Mother Courage and Her Children*) by Bertolt Brecht

1 In the immense bibliography on Brecht the following are notable: Hannah Arendt, *Benjamin, Brecht: Zwei Essays* (Munich: Piper, 1971); F. Ewen, *Bertolt Brecht: His Life, His Art and His Times* (New York: Citadel Press, 1967); Hans Mayer, *Brecht* (Frankfurt: Suhrkamp Verlag, 1996); Jan Needle and Peter Thomson, *Brecht* (Oxford: Basil Blackwell, 1981); Peter Thomson and Glendir Sacks, eds, *The Cambridge Companion to Brecht* (Cambridge: Cambridge University Press, 1994); Pia Kleber and Colin Visser, eds, *Re-interpreting Brecht: His Influence on Contemporary Drama and Film* (Cambridge: Cambridge University Press, 1990); Cesare Molinari, *Bertolt Brecht* (Rome-Bari: Laterza 1996); Claudio Meldolesi and Laura Olivi, *Brecht regista: Memorie dal Berliner Ensemble* (Bologna: Il Mulino, 1989).

2 See the notes to *Ascesa e rovina della città di Mahagonny*, in Bertolt Brecht, *Scritti teatrali*, vol. 3: *Note ai drammi e alle regie* (Turin: Einaudi, 1962; 1975); or ed. *Schriften zum Theater*, vol. 2 (Frankfurt: Suhrkamp Verlag, 1957).

3 This pleasure was not extinguished or darkened even on the verge of death and after many troubles: 'When in my white room at the Charité / I woke towards morning / And heard the blackbird, I understood / Better. Already for some time / I had lost all fear of death / [...] Now / I managed to enjoy / The song of every blackbird after me too.' (Als ich im weissen Krankenzimmer der Charité / Auf wachte gegen Morgen zu / Und eine Amsel hörte, wusste ich / Es besser. Schon seit geraumer Zeit / Hatte ich keine Todesfurcht mehr / [...] Jetzt / Gelang es mir, mich zu freuen / Alles Amselgesanges nach mir auch.) Bertolt Brecht, *Poems 1913–1956* (London: Methuen, 1956) (hereafter *Poems*), 451–2.

4 For the analysis and quotations see *Mutter Courage und ihre Kinder*, in Bertolt Brecht, *Werke*, ed. Klaus-Detlef Müller, vol. 4 (Frankfurt: Suhrkamp Verlag, 1989). The Italian edition is *Madre Courage e i suoi figli*, with parallel text edited by Consolina Vigliero (Turin: Einaudi, 2000), which prints the translation by Ruth Leise and Franco Fortini, partly revised and adapted to the needs of the parallel text by the editor (hereafter *Madre Courage*). The English translation quoted is Bertolt Brecht, *Mother Courage and Her Children*, ed. and intro. John Willett and Ralph Manheim, trans. John Willett (London: Methuen Drama, 1986) (hereafter *Mother Courage*).

5 For the very extensive interdisciplinary bibliography, I will only list texts that I have found particularly useful in my studies: Luigi Bonanate, *La guerra* (Rome-Bari: Laterza, 1998); John Keegan, *The Mask of the Command* (New York: Viking, 1987); Georg Lachmann Mosse, *The Nationalization of the Masses: Political Symbolism and Mass Movements in Germany from the Napoleonic Wars through the Third Reich* (New York: H. Fertig, 1975; Alessandro Roncaglia, *La ricchezza delle idee: Storia del pensiero economico* (Rome-Bari: Editori Laterza, 2003); Barbara W. Tuchman, *The Proud Tower* (London: Macmillan, 1966).
6 'Bad Time for Poetry' (Schlechte Zeit für Lyrik), in *Poems*, 330–31. 'In mir streiten sich / Die Begeisterung über den blühenden Apfelbaum / Und das Entsetzen über die Reden des Anstreichers. / Aber nur das zweite / Drängt mich zum Schreibtisch.'
7 'Deutschland', in *Poems*, 218.
8 *War Primer* (*Kriegsfibel*), trans. and ed. John Willett (London: Libris, 1998), 26. 'Such nicht mehr, Frau: du wirst sie nicht mehr finden! / Doch auch das Schicksal, Frau, beschuldige nicht! / Die dunklen Mächte, Frau, die dich da schinden / Sie haben Name, Anschrift und Gesicht. This is one of the epigrams commenting on a photograph, in this case of Berlin homes destroyed by British bombs in World War II.' A woman who has survived is searching among the rubble.
9 The responsibility attributed to Clausewitz for the spread of the mentality of World War I or world carnage is well known. He distinguished 'absolute war' (i.e., total obedience and self-sacrifice, total devotion to duty unto death in the cannon's mouth) from 'real war' (which prompts the soldier to escape and commit acts of cowardice while bringing commerce to the battlefield). This contradiction failed to assess the sources of the difference between the ethos of civil society from the ethos of the regiment, and failed to foresee that the idea of war as a continuation of politics by other means would prove the bankruptcy of politics.
10 'When once our body's eaten up / With an exhausted heart in it / The army spits our skin and bones out / Into cold and shallow pits. / And with our body hard from rain / And with our heart all scarred by ice / And with our blood-stained empty hands we / Come grinning into your paradise' (Wenn unser Leib zerfressen ist / Mit einem matten Herzen drin / Speit die Armee einst unser Haut und Knochen / In kalte flache Löcher hin / Und mit dem Leib, von Regen hart/ Und mit dem Herz, versehrt von Heis / Und mit den blutbefleckten leeren Händen / So kommen wir grinsend in euer Paradeis) ('Song of the Dead Soldier' [Gesang des Soldaten der Roten Armee], *Poems*, 23).
11 See 'Legend of the Unknown Soldier beneath the Triumphal Arch' (Gedicht vom Unbekannten Soldaten unter dem Triumphbogen), in *Poems*, 122–3.
12 The *German War Primer* (*Deutsche Kriegsfibel*) has many verses on this theme: 'War grows from their peace / Like son from his mother. / He bears / Her frightful features' (Der Krieg wächst aus ihrem Frieden / Wie der Sohn aus der Mutter / Er trägt / Ihre schrecklichen Züge); 'When the leaders speak of peace / The common folk know / That war is coming' (Wenn die Oberen von Frieden reden / Weiss das gemeine Volk / Dass es Krieg gibt) (*Poems*, 288–9).
13 'And what did the soldier's widow receive / From the frozen country of Russia?/ From Russia she received the widow's veil. / That's what she received from Russia' (Und was bekam des Soldaten Weib / Aus dem kalten Russenland? / Aus Russland bekam sie den Witwenschleier / Zu der Totenfeier den Witwenschleier / Das bekam sie aus Russenland). 'What Did the Soldier's Wife Receive?' (Und was bekam des Soldaten Weib?), in *Selected Poems of Bertolt Brecht*, trans. and intro. Hoffman Reynolds Hays (New York: Mariner Books, 1971), 161.
14 'In den Weiden am Sund / Ruft in diesen Frühjahrsnächten oft das Käuzlein. / Nacht dem Aberglauben der Bauern / Setz das Käuzlein die Menschen davon in Kenntnis / Dass sie nicht lang leben. Mich / Der ich weiss, dass ich die Wahrheit gesagt habe / Über die Herrschenden, braucht der Totenvogel davon / Nicht erst in Kenntnis zu setzen' ('Fruhling 1938', in *Poems*, 303–4).
15 Brecht, *War Primer*, 33.

16 Brecht, *War Primer*, 40. 'Als wir uns sahn – 's war alles schnell vorbei – / Ich lächle und die beiden lächeln wieder. / So lächelten wir erstmal alle drei, / Dann zielte einer, und ich schoss ihn nieder'.
17 The door opens onto nothingness ('nur ins Nichts'): ('And so I said: drop it! / Like smoke twisting grey / Into ever colder coldness you'll / Blow away'). 'The Song of the Smoke' (Das Lied vom Rauch), in Ralph Mannheim and John Willett, eds, *Bertolt Brecht: Poems and Songs from the Plays* (London: Methuen, 1992), 155–6.
18 In the 'Hymn to God' (Hymne an Gott) Brecht speaks, drawing on religious imagery, of a God who reigns eternal and invisible, radiant and cruel on the infinite plane, indifferent to obscure deaths (*Poems*, 9).
19 'Outside this planet, I thought, there is nothing / so desolate' (Ausser diesem Stern, dachte ich, ist nichts und er / Ist so verwüstet. / Er allein ist unsere Zuflucht und die / Siehht so aus). Untitled fragment in *Bertolt Brecht Gesammelte Werke*, vol. 8 (*Gedichte* 1) (Berlin: Suhrkamp Verlag, 1976), 202.
20 See the poems: 'Christmas Legend' (Weinachtslegende), in *Poems*, 99; and 'The Good Night' (Die Gute Nacht), in *Poems*, 130.
21 See the fine poem 'Christus vor dem Hohen Rat' (Christ before the Sanhedrin), in *Bertolt Brecht Gesammelte Werke*, vol. 10 (*Gedichte* 3) (Berlin: Suhrkamp Verlag, 1967), 63–4.
22 'Das Frühjahr kommt! Wach auf, du Christ! / Der Schnee schmilzt weg! Die Toten ruhn! / Und was noch nicht gestorben ist / Das macht sich auf die Socken nun.' Bertolt Brecht, *Collected Plays*, ed. Ralph Manheim and John Willett (New York: Vintage Plays, 1972), V, 120.
23 See Cicely Veronica Wedgwood, *The Thirty Years War* (London: Pimlico, 1992).
24 See the statements in Henry Kamen, *The Iron Century: Social Change in Counter-Reformation Europe 1550–1660* (London: Weidenfeld and Nicolson, 1971).
25 Ibid., 124.
26 Ibid., 134. And if there is an economic advantage, power is ready to find any excuse, as the Cook observes: 'Course the king took a serious view when anybody didn't want to be free' (Freilich, wenn einer nicht hat frei werden wolln, hat der König keinen Spass gekannt') (*Mother Courage*, 27).
27 Rv 6; Ez 14:21; Jer 14:12; Jer 15:2–3.
28 *The Life of Courage: The Notorious Thief, Whore and Vagabond* (*Trutz Simplex: Oder Ausführliche und wunderseltzame Lebensbeschreibung Der Ertzbetrügerin und Landstörtzerin Courasche*), translated with an introduction and chronology by Mike Mitchell (Sawtry: Dedalus, 2001).
29 'Stern is the on-look of necessity. / Not without shudder may a human hand / Grasp the mysterious urn of destiny. / My deed was mine, remaining in my bosom; / Once suffered to escape from its safe corner / Within the heart, its nursery and birthplace, / Sent forth into the foreign, it belongs / Forever to those sly malicious powers / Whom never art of man conciliated.' *Wallenstein: The Death of Wallenstein*, trans. Samuel Taylor Coleridge (London: Longman, 1800), act 1, scene 4.
30 *Mater Dolorosa* belongs to the iconography of the Passion of Christ and traditional sacred theatre.
31 The work is interwoven with biblical references, like much of great European literary culture. Most are from the Gospels and elicit the human story of Christ as the innocent victim of power. But the allusions are generally of an antiphrastic stylistic type which create an ironic and sarcastic reversal, raising critical alarm and emphasizing the critical distance of the world from the Gospels, being the residue of imagery that was once familiar and emerges in the language automatically, or as a professional jargon in the character of the Chaplain. Following the editions of the Italian text used, which identified them, the following allusions are notable: Genesis: Esau and Jacob (25:24–34; *Madre Courage*, 14–15); John (19:26–7) and the whole translation of the *Mater Dolorosa*, Pater Noster (*Madre Courage*, 56–7); Beatitudes: 'Blessed are the peacemakers' (Matthew 5:9; *Madre Courage*, 62–3); Revelations: the allusion

to Babylon (17:1–18; *Madre Courage*, 64–5); Matthew: the miracle of the multiplication of the loaves (14:15–21; *Madre Courage*, 38–39), 'Inasmuch as ye have done it unto one of the least of these my brethren, ye have done it unto me' (25:40; *Madre Courage*, 38–41), 'Of the abundance of the heart his mouth speaketh' (12:34; *Madre Courage*, 68–9), Jesus on Olivet (26:31–46; *Madre Courage*, 88–9); Luke: the stone begins to speak (19:40; *Madre Courage*, 176–7).

32 'MOTHER COURAGE. Business folk. (*Sings*.) […] O Captains how can you make them face it – / Marching to death without a brew (Geschäftsleut. (*Singt*.) […] Ihr Hauptleut, eure Leu marschieren / Euch ohne Wurst nicht in den Tod) (*Mother Courage*, 4).

33 'MUTTER COURAGE. […] Er verging wie der Rauch, und die Wärme ging auch / Denn es wärmten sie nicht seine Taten' (*Mother Courage*, 19).

34 *Madre Courage*, 64.

35 'MUTTER COURAGE. Holla, nehmts mich mit! / […] Mit seinem Glück, seiner Gefahre / Der Krieg, er zieht sich etwas hin. / […] Jedoch vielleicht geschehn noch Wunder: / Der Feldzug ist noch nicht zu End! / Das Frühjahr kommt! Wach auf, du Christ! / Der Schnee schmilzt weg! Die Toten ruhn! / Und was noch nicht gestorben ist / Das macht sich auf die Socken nun' (*Mother Courage*, 88).

36 *Mother Courage*, 185.

37 *Brecht, Collected Plays*, V, 161

38 A good English translation can be found in Brecht, *Collected Plays*, V,. The Italian reader can find a good selection in Bertolt Brecht, *Theaterarbeit*, (Milan: Il Saggiatore, 1969).

39 It was first drafted on the basis of the Berlin premiere at the Deutsches Theater, directed by Brecht and Erich Hengel, supplemented with further ideas after a new production in Munich in 1950. It was first published in the volume *Theaterarbeit* in 1952 after the reorganization of the work at the Berliner Ensemble in 1951, with Helene Weigel. In 1956, the texts of the model book were revised and a final selection of photos was made. It was published in 1958, two years after Brecht's death. Controversy was aroused by the 'normative' character of Brecht's model book. Brecht said that it was intended to prevent a resurgence of conventionality, disguised as creative freedom, that it was not meant to hamper creative thinking but foster it, and that the goal was not to replace but stimulate artistic creativity. What mattered was to provide a guide to solutions already found to certain problems and to reflect on these same problems.

Chapter 5   The Tragic and the Absurd: *Caligula* by Albert Camus

1 See: Anne Marie Amiot, *Nature et fonction du lyrisme de Caligula dans la redéfinition de la tragédie moderne*, in *Camus et le lyrisme: Actes du colloque tenu à Beauvais en 1996*, ed. Jacqueline Lévi-Valensi and Agnès Spiquel (Paris: Sedes, 1997); 'Violence as Tragic Farce in Camus's Caligula', in *Violence in Drama*, ed. James Redmond (Cambridge: Cambridge University Press, 1991); Pierre Louis Rey, preface to Albert Camus, *Caligula*, ed. Pierre Louis Rey (Paris: Gallimard, 1993); Paul Ginestier, *La Pensée de Camus* (Paris: Bordas, 1979); and Jeanyves Guérin and Madeleine Vallette-Fondo, 'Caligula, ou la nécessité du roman pour dire le totalitarisme', in *Pour un humanisme romanesque: Mélanges offerts à Jacqueline Lévi-Valensi*, ed. Gilles Philippe and Agnés Spiquel (Paris: Sedes, 1999).

2 *Oeuvres complètes*, vol. 2, *1944–1948* (hereafter *Oeuvres* 2), édition publiée sous la direction de Jacqueline Lévi-Valensi (Paris: Gallimard, 2006), 812. A historical summary can be found in Sophie Bastien, *Caligula et Camus: Interférences transhistoriques* (Amsterdam: Rodopi, 2006); a reconstruction of the genesis of the first version has been produced by Albert James Arnold, 'Caligula, texte établi d'après la dactylographie de février 1941', *Cahiers Albert Camus*, no. 4 (Paris: Gallimard, 1984). The French edition from which I quote, for both the 1941 and 1958 versions, is that contained in *Oeuvres complètes*, vol. 1, *1931–1944* (hereafter *Oeuvres* 1), édition publiée sous la direction de Jacqueline Lévi-Valensi (Paris: Gallimard, 2006), 323–442.

3 *Oeuvres* 1, 971.

4 *'Caligula' version 1941 suivi de la poetique du premier Caligula* (Paris: Gallimard, 1984).
5 Olivier Todd, *Albert Camus: Une vie* (Paris: Gallimard, 1996), 47.
6 'Noces à Tipasa', in *Oeuvres* 1, 105; 'Les ruines couvertes de fleurs et la lumière à gros bouillons dans les amas de pierre'.
7 'Le vent à Djémila', in *Oeuvres* 1, 111; '[…] sentiers parmi les restes des maisons, grandes rues dallées sous les colonnes luisantes, forum immense entre l'arc de triomphe et le temple'. This and the other text cited above, collected under the title *Noces*, were written between 1936 and 1937.
8 *Oeuvres* 1, 113; 'un goût de la mort qui nous était commun'.
9 For an interesting account of the repertoire see the 'Notice', in *Oeuvres* 1 and the chapter 'Fauteuils 156 et 157', in Todd, *Albert Camus*, 120–133.
10 Todd, *Albert Camus*, 99; 'Toute une création à faire, tangible, faite de poutres et de tréteaux, de pots de colle et de contacts électriques – ça pour commencer – et là dessus organiser des hommes, les animer construire des théories artistiques en pensant qu'il faut convoquer les pompiers – et une fois tout lancé, tout animé, faire arriver le tout jusqu'à la représentation, secouer les dégoûtés, les plaisanter, croire à tout ça qui sera donné et joué en une soirée et dont il ne restera rien le lendemain sinon la nécessité de balayer et de faire des comptes. Je ne connais pas d'expérience plus exaltante.'
11 'Le théâtre est un art de chair, qui donne à des corps vivants, le soin de traduire ses leçons, un art un même temps grossier et subtil, une entente exceptionnelle des mouvements, de la voix et des lumières. Mais il est aussi la plus conventionnel des arts, tout entier dans cette complicité de l'acteur et du spectateur qui apportent un consentement mutuel et tacite à la même illusion. C'est ainsi que, d'une part, le théâtre sert naturellement les grands sentiments simples et ardents, autour desquels tourne le destin de l'homme (et ceux-là seulement): amour, désir, ambition, religion. Mais, d'autre part, il satisfait au besoin d'une construction qui est naturel à l'artiste. Cette opposition fait le théâtre, le rend propre à servir la vie et à toucher les hommes. Le Théâtre de l'Équipe instituera cette opposition, c'est-à-dire qu'il demandera aux œuvres la vérité et la simplicité, la violence dans les sentiments et la cruauté dans l'action.' (The theatre is an art of the flesh, which gives living bodies the task of embodying its lessons, an art at once coarse and subtle, an exceptional unison of movements, voice and lights. But it is also the most conventional of arts, existing wholly in this complicity between actor and audience, who give mutual and tacit consent to the same illusion. Thus it is that on the one hand the theatre naturally presents large simple and ardent feelings, on which turns the destiny of humanity (and those alone): love, desire, ambition, religion. But, on the other hand it satisfies the need for a construction that comes naturally to the artist. This opposition makes the theatre, enabling it to serve life and stir people. The Théâtre de l'Équipe [Team Theatre] will institute this opposition, namely that it will ask plays for truth and simplicity, violence in feelings and cruelty in action). *Manifeste du Théâtre de l'Équipe*, in *Oeuvres* 1, 814–15; 1438–41.
12 See Fernande Bartfeld, *L'Effet tragique: Essai sur le tragique dans l'œuvre de Camus* (Paris: Slatkine, 1988).
13 'Carnets 1935–1948, Cahier 1 (mai 1935–septembre 1937)', in *Oeuvres* 2, 800.
14 *Oeuvres* 2, 920.
15 Albert Camus, *The Myth of Sisyphus*, trans. Justin O'Brien (New York: Vintage International, 1991), 21 (original edition: *Le mythe de Sisyphe*, Paris: Gallimard, 1942).
16 'But what is absurd is the confrontation of this irrational and the wild longing for clarity whose call echoes in the human heart' (ibid., 21).
17 Ibid., 28.
18 'A step lower and strangeness creeps in: perceiving that the world is "dense", sensing to what a degree a stone is foreign and irreducible to us, with what intensity nature or a landscape can negate us. At the heart of all beauty lies something inhuman, and these hills, the softness of the sky, the outline of these trees at this very minute lose the illusory meaning with which we had

clothed them [...]. The world evades us because it becomes itself again. That stage scenery masked by habit becomes again what it is. It withdraws at a distance from us. [...] Just one thing: that denseness and that strangeness of the world is the absurd' (ibid., 14).

19 'What, in fact, is the Absurd Man? He who, without negating it, does nothing for the eternal. Not that nostalgia is foreign to him. But he prefers his courage and his reasoning. The first teaches him to live without appeal and to get along with what he has; the second informs him of his limits. Assured of his temporally limited freedom, of his revolt devoid of future, and of his mortal consciousness, he lives out his adventure within the span of his lifetime' (ibid., 66).

20 *The Rebel: An Essay on Man in Revolt*, trans. A. Bower (New York: Vintage International, 1992), 41 (original edition: *L'homme révolté*, Paris: Gallimard, 1951).

21 *The Myth of Sisyphus*, 123.

22 'Letters to a German Friend: Second Letter', in *Resistance, Rebellion and Death* (New York: Alfred A. Knopf, 1961, translated from the French by Justin O'Brien), 14.

23 'Letters to a German Friend: Fourth Letter' (ibid., 22).

24 'où elle marchait si justement que le balancement de ces épaules suivait pour moi la ligne des collines à l'horizon' (*Oeuvres* 1, 393; where she worked so precisely that the rocking of the shoulders followed me to the line of hills on the horizon).

25 'Des soirs comme ce soir, devant ce ciel plein de l'huile brillante et douce des étoiles, comment ne pas défaillir devant ce que mon amour a de pur et de dévorant?' (*Oeuvres* 1, 400).

26 'L'éxécution soulage et délivre. [...] On est coupable parce qu'on est sujet de Caligula. Donc tout le monde est coupable. D'où il ressort que tout le monde meurt. C'est une question de temps et de patience' (*Oeuvres* 1, 410).

27 'J'ai simplement compris qu'il n'y a qu'une façon de s'égaler aux dieux: il suffit d'être aussi cruel qu'eux. (*Furieux*.) Dans mes nuits sans sommeil, vois-tu, j'ai rencontré le destin. Tu ne peux pas savoir comme il a l'air bête. Et monotone: il n'a qu'un visage. Du genre implacable, tu sais. Rien n'est plus facile à imiter' (*Oeuvres* 1, 421).

28 'Pourquoi d'ailleurs Hélicon ne t'apporterait – il pas la lune? Peut-être est-il possible de la pêcher au fond d'un puits et de la ramener dans un filet miroitant, toute gluante d'algues et d'eau, comme un poisson pâle et gonflé, sorti des profondeurs. Pourquoi pas, Caligula?' (*Oeuvres* 1, 423–4).

29 *Oeuvres* 1, 437.

30 *Oevres* 1, 439.

31 *Oeuvres* 1, 441.

32 *Oeuvres* 1, 376; 'Méprise l'esclave, Cherea! Il est au-dessus de ta vertu puisqu'il peut encore aimer ce maître misérable qu'il défendra contre vos nobles mensonges, vos bouches perjures'.

33 'CHEREA. Non, Scipion, il t'a désespéré. Et désespérer une jeune âme est un crime qui passe tous ceux qu'il a commis jusqu'ici' (*Oeuvres* 1, 372).

34 *Oeuvres* 1, 427; '(*Avec un accent furieux*.) La logique, Caligula, il faut poursuivre la logique. Le pouvoir jusqu'au bout, l'abandon jusqu'au bout. Non, on ne revient pas en arrière et il faut aller jusqu'à la consommation!'

35 *Oeuvres* 1, 367.

36 'Διὸ καὶ φιλοσοφώτερον καὶ σπουδαιότερον ποίησις ιστορίας εστίν' (Aristotle, *Poetics*, 9, 51b).

37 Camus read *De vita Caesarum* in Latin and the French translation by Henri Ailloud, published by Belles Lettres in 1931. He also read Cassius Dio's *Historia Romana* (Book 59), the Jewish authors Philo of Alexandria and Josephus Flavius.

38 Aristotle, *Poetics*, 9, 51b.

39 Jean Grenier, *Albert Camus: Souvenirs* (Paris: Gallimard, 1968).

40 'À travers Suétone, Caligula m'était apparu comme un tyran *intelligent*, dont les mobiles semblaient à la fois singuliers et profonds. En particulier, il est le seul, à ma connaissance, à avoir *tourné en dérision le pouvoir lui-même*.' ('Through Suetonius, Caligula appeared to me as an intelligent tyrant, whose motives seemed both singular and profound. In particular, he was

the only one, to my knowledge, who derided the power itself.') 'Programme pour le Nouveau Théâtre', cited by Sophie Bastien, *Caligula et Camus*, 26.

41 The modern historian Aloys Winterling frames the historical question clearly in *Caligula: Eine Biographie* (Munich: Verlag C. H. Beck, 2003); English translation: *Caligula: A Biography* (Berkeley/Los Angeles: University of California Press, 2005). The divine honours paid to Caligula, and which he did not refuse, but manoeuvred with cynical sarcasm and which in the provinces were demonstrations of loyalty to Rome by the ruling classes, did not really signify that his rule was based on the cult of the sovereign. Another interesting study of the emperor is by Anthony Barrett, *Caligula: The Corruption of Power* (New Haven/London: Yale University Press, 1990).

42 The study by Winterling cited in the previous note is enlightening in this regard. Despite the apparent contradictions, quirks and excesses of Caligula's life, it identifies a lucid design: the liquidation of the Augustan paradox of the co-presence of an aristocratic republic and of monarchical absolutism, the transformation of an explicit absolute monarchy into the paradoxical and dangerous role of emperor in a republican state, the development of a new approach to 'double' communication long affirmed in relations with the Senate. In this respect Caligula attributed to the adulatory statements of the senators a sincerity that they could not deny and forced them to accept their consequences when taken literally. By taking them seriously he unmasked them as falsehoods; by demanding a behaviour corresponding to their flattery he humiliated and destroyed his interlocutors, while also preparing his own destruction perpetrated through conspiracies until the final one. Hence calculation and lucidity lay underlay his eccentricities; bewilderment, extreme humiliation, culminating in the mockery of the horse honoured and made a candidate for the consulship, to show that it was the emperor alone who decided everything. Discredit, ridicule, repression, an escalation of suspicion and cruelty – Camus did not have the instruments for an advanced underlying historical analysis, but he showed a unique insight in grasping the tyrant's tragic, absurd and extraordinarily 'logical truth'.

43 1958 edition, act 4, scene 14 (*Oeuvres* 1, 387); 'J'ai peur. [...] La peur non plus ne dure pas. Je vais retrouver ce grand vide où le cœur s'apaise.'

44 1941 edition, act 3, scene 2 (*Oeuvres* 1, 421).

45 1958 edition, act 3, scene 2 (*Oeuvres* 1, 362); 'CALIGULA. [...] Si j'exerce ce pouvoir, c'est par compensation. SCIPION. À quoi? CALIGULA. À la bêtise et à la haine des dieux.'

46 1941 edition, act 1, scene 7: 'si le Trésor a de l'importance, alors la vie humaine n'en a pas' (*Oeuvres* 1, 396).

47 See the masquerade in Act 3 or the appearance of Caligula in Act 4 as a dancer who mimes the dance of appearances accompanied by cymbals.

48 1958 edition, act 4, scene 14 (*Oeuvres* 1, 386); 'Mais aujourd'hui, me voilà encore plus libre qu'il y a des années, libéré que je suis du souvenir et de l'illusion.'

49 1958 edition, act 4, scene 13 (*Oeuvres* 1, 385); 'Tous les jours, je vois mourir un peu plus en toi ce qui a figure d'homme.'

50 1958 edition, act 4, scene 14 (*Oeuvres* 1, 387); 'L'impossible! Je l'ai cherché aux limites du monde, aux confins de moi-même. J'ai tendu mes mains. (*Criant.*) Je tends mes mains et c'est toi que je rencontre, toujours toi en face de moi, et je suis pour toi plein de haine.'

51 In the relatively restricted bibliography on Camus's plays (compared with that for the fiction), this aspect has been studied effectively by Raymond Gay-Crosier, 'Caligula ou le paradoxe du comédien absurde', in *Albert Camus et le théâtre: Actes du colloqui tenu à Amiens en 1988*, ed. Jacqueline Lévi-Valensi (Paris: Imec, 1992), 19–28; and by Sophie Bastien in *Caligula et Camus*.

52 Act 5, scene 5.

53 In Paris, contacts with the milieu of Merleau-Ponty and Sartre's transcendental phenomenology seem to have strengthened Camus's natural propensity to value corporeality in the process of knowledge.

NOTES 217

54 We can again listen to Camus's words: 'The actor will leave us at best a photograph, but nothing of what he was, his actions and his silences, rapid breathing, or the sigh of love, will come to us. [...] The actor has three hours to be Iago or Alcestis, Phaedra or Gloucester. During this brief glimpse, he makes them to be born or die within fifty square feet of planking. Never the absurd has been explained so well for so long either. As a summary of the most revealing of the wonderful lives you could want, the destiny of the unique and complete that grow and fall between the same walls and in a few hours?' (*The Myth of Sisyphus*, 272).
55 *The Rebel*, 5.
56 Ibid., 7.

Chapter 6   Dianoetic Laughter in Tragedy: Accepting Finitude: *Endgame* by Samuel Beckett

1 This chapter draws generally, but adapted to the specific perspective of this book, on a fuller treatment published earlier, to which readers are referred for further study and a detailed bibliography: Annamaria Cascetta, *Il tragico e l'umorismo: Studio sulla drammaturgia di Samuel Beckett* (Florence: Le Lettere, 2000). Readers should also consult the seminal biography of Beckett by James Knowlson, *Damned to Fame: The Life of Samuel Beckett* (London: Bloomsbury, 1996); the *Grove Companion to Samuel Beckett: A Reader's Guide to His Work, Life and Thought*, ed. Chris J. Ackerley and Stanley E. Gontarski (New York: Grove Press, 2004); and some useful more recent volumes: Ronan McDonald, *Tragedy and Irish Literature: Singe, O'Casey, Beckett* (New York: Palgrave Macmillan, 2002); the *Cambridge Introduction to Samuel Beckett*, ed. Ronan McDonald (Cambridge: Cambridge University Press, 2007); and *Samuel Beckett's Endgame*, ed. Mark S. Byron (Amsterdam/New York: Rodopi, 2007). For a study of *Endgame* an essential work is the collection *The Theatrical Notebooks of Samuel Beckett*, ed. James Knowlson, vol. 2: *Endgame*, ed. Stanley E. Gontarski, revised text with introduction and notes (London: Faber and Faber, 1992). The edition quoted from here is *Endgame*, edited with a preface by Ronan McDonald (New York: Faber and Faber, 2009).
2 *Endgame*, 38.
3 *Endgame*, 14.
4 Of this production there remain the director's notes and the diary of rehearsals kept by Michael Haerdter. The combination of this experience with a subsequent production in 1980 gave rise to the 'revised text' cited above, edited by Stanley E. Gontarski in the series *The Theatrical Notebooks of Samuel Beckett*. For bibliographical references and details of the history of the text see my book cited above, in particular pages 78–9 and 126.
5 *Endgame*, 6.
6 *Endgame*, 20–21.
7 *The Theatrical Notebooks of Samuel Beckett*, 38.
8 *Endgame*, 41. The English text emphasizes the endgame in chess rather than the metatheatrical dimension. The French text simply has 'À moi': *Fin de partie* (Paris: Les Editions de Minuit, 1957), 91.
9 *Endgame*, 48.
10 Samuel Becket, *Waiting for Godot*, with a revised text, edited with an introduction and notes by Dougald McMillan and James Knowlson (New York: Bloom's Literary Criticism, 1993), 81; *En attendant Godot* (Paris: Les Éditions de Minuit, 1952), 126.
11 In those years Sartre was influential in the Parisian milieu and French culture. The servant-master theme was, as is well known, developed in *L'être et le néant* (Paris: Gallimard, 1943).
12 'HAMM. I've made you suffer too much. (*Pause.*) Haven't I? CLOV. It's not that. HAMM, (*shocked.*) I haven't made you suffer too much? CLOV. Yes! HAMM, (*relieved.*) Ah you gave me a fright! (*Pause. Coldly.*) Forgive me. (*Pause. Louder.*) I said, Forgive me' (*Endgame*, 8).
13 Cascetta, *Il tragico e l'umorismo*, 83.
14 Significantly Beckett has Clov say, 'Do this, do that, and I do it. I never refuse. Why?' (*Endgame*, 27).

15 35.
16 See Cascetta, *Il tragico e l'umorismo*, 84–5.
17 *Endgame*, 22.
18 Cascetta, *Il tragico e l'umorismo*, 88.
19 'HAMM. La pierre levée. (*Un temps.*) Ta vue s'améliore. (*Un temps.*) Il regarde la maison sans doute, avec les yeux de Moïse mourant. CLOV. Non. HAMM. Qu'est-ce qu'il regarde? CLOV, (*avec violence.*) Je ne sais pas ce qu'il regarde! (*Il braque la lunette. Un temps. Il baisse la lunette, se tourne vers Hamm.*) Son nombril. Enfin par là. (*Un temps.*)' (104).
20 See Cascetta, *Il tragico e l'umorismo*, 89.
21 'And God looked upon the earth, and, behold, it was corrupt; for all flesh had corrupted his way upon the earth' (Gn 6:12).
22 'CLOV, (*as before.*) I say to myself – sometimes, Clov, you must learn to suffer better than that if you want them to weary of punishing you' (*Endgame*, 48).
23 'NAGG, (*clasping his hands, closing his eyes, in a gabble.*) Our Father which art – HAMM. Silence! In silence! Where are your manners? (*Pause.*) Off we go. (*Attitudes of prayer. Silence. Abandoning his attitude, discouraged.*) Well? CLOV, (*abandoning his attitude.*) What a hope! And you? HAMM. Sweet damn all! (*To Nagg.*) And you? NAGG. Wait! (*Pause. Abandoning his attitude.*) Nothing doing! HAMM. The bastard!! He doesn't exist. CLOV. Not yet. NAGG. Me sugar-plum! HAMM. There are no more sugar plums!' (*Endgame*, 34).
24 James Knowlson, *Damned to Fame* (London: Bloomsbury, 1996), 477.
25 Cascetta, *Il tragico e l'umorismo*, 12.
26 The quotations are on 39 of the French text and 17 of the English.

Chapter 7   The Arrogance of Reason and the 'Disappearance of the Fireflies': *Pilade* (*Pylades*) by Pier Paolo Pasolini

1 Pasolini wrote *Pylades* in 1966. It was published in *Nuovi argomenti*, n.s., 7–8 (July–December 1967) and was republished posthumously in a nondefinitive version by Garzanti in 1977. There exist five texts of the tragedy. The edition I refer to is Pier Paolo Pasolini, *Tutte le opere: Teatro*, ed. Walter Siti and Silvia De Laude (Milan: Arnoldo Mondadori Editore, I Meridiani, 2001), and is based on the Mondadori edition called 'E', to which the reader is referred for further philological details. It is preserved in Rome: Biblioteca Nazionale Vittorio Emanuele, 1565/4 and is a photocopy of *Nuovi Argomenti* bearing handwritten corrections made by the author at different times. There is a translation of the text into French by Michèle Fabien and Titina Maselli (Paris: Actes Sud, 1990), republished in Pier Paolo Pasolini, *Théâtre* (Arles: Actes Sud, 1995), which the quotations are taken from. The English translation (from which the quotations are taken) was made by Adam Paolozza and Coleen MacPherson for the play and workshop *The Pasolini Project*, TheatreRUN 2009, Canadian Stage Festival of Ideas and Creation 2010, and Canadian Stage's Spotlight Italy Festival 2011.
2 The manifesto was published in *Nuovi argomenti*, n. s., 9 (January–March 1968).
3 Namely: *I Turcs tal Friul, Orgia, Affabulazione, Porcile, Calderòn, Bestia da Stile*, and he had translated the *Oresteia* of Aeschylus. What led Pasolini almost naturally to the theatre? Apart from the theoretical observations presented in this paragraph, naturally it was the attraction of the body, the awareness that the most intense level of communication is that between bodies. Then there was his love of the spoken word, sound, orality, rooted in physicality. Pasolini experienced the exciting and engaging aspect of orality in the Friulian peasant world, then in the *borgate* (suburbs) of Rome, which had developed their own language. Sergio Citti was his living dictionary. But to the theatre, apart from the emphasis on speech, he also brought his figurative taste, in which he was educated by the great critic Roberto Longhi, a professor of art during his years in Bologna, and his mythologizing tendency which developed after his first realist phase.

On Pasolini's plays I will confine myself to listing the following studies: Franca Angelini, *Pasolini e lo spettacolo* (Rome: Bulzoni, 2000); Stefano Casi, *I teatri di Pasolini*, introduction by Luca Ronconi (Milan: Ubulibri, 2005). A useful overview of this work in Pasolini's biography is provided by: Barth David Schwartz, *Pasolini Requiem* (New York: Pantheon Books, 1992).

4 Pier Paolo Pasolini, 'Manifesto per un nuovo teatro', *Nuovi Argomenti*, n.s. (January–March 1968) (my translation), 8–19.
5 Charles Taylor, *A Secular Age* (Cambridge: Belknap Press of Harvard University Press, 2007).
6 Pasolini, *Affabulazione, Pilade* (Milan: Garzanti, 1977), 145–6.
7 Pasolini began to translate the *Oresteia* in 1960 at the request of Vittorio Gassman. He did the work with passion and, given the tight production schedule, had to work quickly, relying, as he himself says, on instinct. He used three sources: *Eschyle*, vol. 2, texte établi et traduit par Paul Mazon (Paris: Les Belles Lettres, 1948); *The Oresteia of Aeschylus*, ed. George Thompson (Cambridge: University Press, 1938); Eschilo, *Le tragedie*, ed. Mario Untersteiner (Milan: Istituto Editoriale Italiano, 1947). He ignored other fine translations, such as that at the time by Manara Valgimigli. The text was published as *Orestiade* by the Istituto Nazionale del Dramma Antico for classical performances in the Greek theatre of Syracuse, Urbino, 1960, and with variations in Eschilo, *Orestiade*, in *Quaderni del Teatro Popolare Italiano*, no. 2 (Turin: Einaudi, 1960) and 1985 (in the series: *Scrittori tradotti da scrittori*). The publication by the Teatro Popolare Italiano includes, in addition to the text, other materials related to the staging and some critical essays. The editions by Einaudi and Urbino are almost contemporaneous, but the latter is based on a more advanced state of Pasolini's work and is therefore reproduced in the *Teatro* collection of the Meridiani Mondadori, which I use here.

The relationship with the inspiration of *Pilade*, a few years later, is clear if we observe the following: Pasolini sought in his work on language to modify 'sublime tones into civic' and reasoning tones (Pasolini, *Teatro*, 1008) and together with Vittorio Gassman he sought to distance himself from the archaeological tendency. The materials for the performance, staged and directed by Vittorio Gassman and Luciano Lucignani during the 16th cycle of classical productions at the Greek theatre of Syracuse from 19 May to 5 June 1960, are found not only in the Einaudi text cited but also in the *Notiziario quindicinale* of the Teatro Popolare Italiano, ed. Vittorio Gassman, in the journal of the Istituto Nazionale del Dramma Antico, *Dioniso* 24 (1960): 189–95. The cast included: Vittorio Gassman (Agamemnon and Orestes), Olga Villi (Clytemnestra), Valentina Fortunato (Cassandra, Electra, Athena), Arnaldo Ninchi (Pylades). Some scholarly critics (for example Enzo Degan in the *Rivista di filologia e istruzione classica*) picked up errors, but others grasped the novelty of the work and its anthropological and social significance. An example was Massimo Fusillo, *La Grecia secondo Pasolini* (Rome: Carocci, 2007), in the chapter: 'L'Orestea: utopia di una sintesi'. This perceptive essay emphasizes the innovative and even provocative energy of Pasolini's translation in the sixties, noting its political and anthropological scope at a time when the prevailing view was still idealistic and classical. Fusillo grasped the weight of a political vision, a metaphor for a reflection on contemporary society that in those years believed it was possible to achieve 'a synthesis between primitive culture and modern rationality' (142), with confidence 'in the recovery of ancient cultures and the rejection of uniformity' (145). The translation, not philologically accurate, is 'aimed at a theatrical performance: the primary goal is to establish a new relationship with the public', and is proof against omissions, simplifications, oversights and contrivance. It was a creative translation supported by the underlying political-anthropological interpretation which paved the way for Pasolini's following works. Fusillo writes: 'In reality, the stylistic level of this translation is far from prosaic or humdrum: eliminating classical coldness does not mean eliminating the sublime, and indeed it seems that Pasolini has a highly fascinating affinity for the archaic power of Aeschylus' language. Despite the ideological contrivances introduced here and there, Aeschylus' images have not lost their expressiveness' (149). Some examples of semantic slanting are restored to consistency with Pasolini's ideological system and the cultural horizon of modern audiences. It was an important training for later works inspired by ancient tragedy.

8 *Edipo Re*, written and directed by Pier Paolo Pasolini. Produced by Alfredo Bini. It is based on Sophocles' *Oedipus the King*. The performers were: Franco Citti (Oedipus), Silvana Mangano (Jocasta), Alida Valli (Merope), Carmelo Bene (Creontes), Julian Beck (Tiresias), Luciano Bartoli (Laius), Francesco Leonetti (servant of Laius), Ahmed Bellachmi (Polybus), Giandomenico Davoli (shepherd of Polybus), Ninetto Davoli (Anghelos-Angelo), Pier Paolo Pasolini (the guide of the supplicant people). See: 'La sceneggiatura di Pier Paolo Pasolini', in *Edipo re: Un film di Pier Paolo Pasolini* (Milan: Garzanti, 1967).

9 *Appunti per un'Orestiade africana* (1968–69) was directed, filmed and commented on by Pasolini and produced by Gian Vittorio Baldi and IDI Cinematografica (Rome), I Film dell'Orso. The screenplay can be read in Pier Paolo Pasolini, *Tutte le opere: Per il cinema*, ed. Walter Siti and Franco Zabagli (Milan: Mondadori, I Meridiani, 2001), vol. 1, 1175–1204, with a *Nota per l'ambientazione dell'Orestiade in Africa* (1968–69) and a note on *L'Atene bianca* (1968).

10 'Voyages, coffrets magiques aux promesses rêveuses, vous ne livrerez plus vos trésors intacts. Une civilisation proliférante et surexcitée trouble à jamais le silence des mers. Les parfums des tropiques et la fraîcheur des êtres sont viciés par une fermentation aux relents suspects, qui mortifie nos désirs et nous voue à cueillir des souvenirs à demi corrompus. [...] L'humanité s'installe dans la monoculture; elle s'apprête à produire la civilisation en masse, comme la betterave. Son ordinaire ne comportera plus que ce plat'. Claude Lévi-Strauss, *Tristes tropiques*, in Œuvres, Edition établie par Vincent Debaene, Frédéric Keck, Marie Mauzé et Martin Rueff (Paris : Gallimard, 2008), 25–6.

11 See note 5 in the introduction.

12 'PYLADES. And here I am, alone. / Alone with a boy who ran down from the mountain in a hurry, / as if he was going to his first holiday feast / – strong, friendly and joyful even when he brings the news / of our tragedy – and with an old man, / who walked step by step from the city, / mulling over the tragedy in his heart, / full of modesty.' (Episode 9; Pasolini, *Teatro*, 452)

13 Pasolini, *Affabulazione, Pilade*, 234.

14 Ibid., 122.

15 'A God enlightened me [...] She is called Athena [...] She is the last of the Gods. She was not known / in ancient times. Her port / is not lost in the darkness of centuries. / She has come to light today amid us. / As if we had conceived her ourselves. / Her hour is not the dawn or the twilight; / but it is the heart of the day, and her worship / does not call for shrines set apart in the fields; / her places are rather markets, squares, / banks, schools, stadiums, ports, / factories. The young know her better than we. / It is in the crowd, in the light / that she appears [...] She has not known the waiting within the womb [...] She does not know anything about this ordeal / of flesh that grows and of a nothing that gains the form / of what it should look like: she did not have / or mother who was crazy or too humble / a mother the slave of her father, a tiger / bloody, or cow obedient. / She had only her father [...] She does not remember. / She knows only reality. / What she knows, the world is.' (Episode 1; Pasolini, *Teatro*, 363–4)

16 Ibid., 367.

17 The Church was aware of this and approached it with Vatican Council II and the kindly, paternal image of Pope John XXIII, whom Pasolini loved, but the process followed its rapid course.

18 For further analysis of this situation see: Achille Abridge, ed., *Classi sociali e strati nel mutamento culturale* (La Scuola: Brescia, 1976); Giorgio Galli, *I partiti politici italiani, 1943–2000* (Milan: Rizzoli, 2001); Paul Ginsborg, *Storia d'Italia dal dopoguerra a oggi* (Turin: Einaudi, 1989; 2006); Paul Ginsborg, *Storia d'Italia 1946–1966: Famiglia, società e stato* (Turin: Einaudi 1998); Giovanni Sabbatucci and Vittorio Vidotto, eds, *Storia d'Italia* (Bari: Laterza, 1997–99), vols 5 and 6; Paolo Sylos Labini, *Saggio sulle classi sociali* (Rome-Bari: Laterza, 1974).

19 'It was an army that had no weapons, but olive branches [...]. Grace and authority acted together / It was Athena, who came first, and behind, / with flowers brought from the fields,

the Eumenides. / At that triumphant invasion, / the people, as always, were uncertain / drunk with life. / But first, the scientists, the inventors, / the manufacturers of the instruments of labour, / those that transform everyday lives, / day after day enlarging the man in his nature; / then the men who express the lives of others, / in verse, in images, in music; / finally, headed by Orestes, came those who, elected by the people, / govern the city / and joined the procession. [...] A new life began [...], The city grew / more than it had grown through all the centuries / of its life. Work yielded unforeseen fruits. / Buildings, factories, bridges, gleamed whitely, / made of clear materials never seen before. [...] It seemed that more than a new idea of mankind, / a new idea of life / had entered people's minds. [...] Athena had created a new city.' (Episode 8; Pasolini, *Teatro*, 447–8).

20 George Didi-Huberman notes this implicit quotation by Pasolini of Dante's *Inferno*, canto 26, lines 25–33 ('Quante 'l villan ch'al poggio si riposa, [...] / vede lucciole giù per la vallea, / forse colà dov'e' vendemmia e ara: / di tante fiamme tutta risplendea / l'ottava bolgia, sì com'io m'accorsi / tosto che fui là 've 'l fondo parea') in an interesting essay: *Survivance des lucioles* (Paris: Les Éditions de Minuit, 2009), 10.

21 1 February 1975, 'L'articolo delle lucciole' (in the *Corriere della Sera*: 'Il vuoto del potere in Italia') in Pier Paolo Pasolini, *Tutte le opere: Saggi sulla politica e sulla società*, ed. Walter Siti and Silvia De Laude (Milan: Mondadori, I Meridiani, 1999, 405).

22 Ibid., 408.

23 Pasolini, *Affabulazione, Pilade*, 195.

24 'In the water churned up amid the clouds of smoke, / I see the shape of a body: it is not an animal, / a sheep, or a pig: no, it's a boy, / it's a child, naked; its limbs / have been amputated and float, / tossed all together and confused in the water. / Now rises a foot, the foot that jumped joyfully / on the fields outside the small town / on hill or plain, together with his classmates. / Now surfaces a tuft of hair, either brown or blond. / I do not know, the color is lost in nothingness. And now rises to view / the member, still unripe, already strong, / to say that this was his miserable mystery. The confidence / of his timid and mature manhood, / so far from the tomb!' (Episode 5; Pasolini, *Teatro*, 423).

25 'There is tragedy in it, in spite of everything, because the most profound reason of both aestheticism and humour is the terror of death. [...] What happens to him is not an intimate drama, but a tragedy. The event therefore lies outside the scope of all: on the stage of a world that is mysterious but real. He lives through this tragedy *en plein air* with a real lack of awareness, as its innocent and aggressive victim.' Pier Paolo Pasolini, 'La sceneggiatura di Pier Paolo Pasolini', in *Edipo re: Un film di Pier Paolo Pasolini* (Milan: Garzanti, 1967), 14–15.

26 For example: 'His father looks at him, standing out clearly in his uniform as a petit-bourgeois soldier, against the sky traversed by swallows. He listens to his inner voice, high and solemn as in a tragedy' (ibid., 50).

27 In sequence 34, which corresponds to the first episode in Sophocles, and repeats in part its dialogue, it is significant that the film omits the strong reference to *dike* which Oedipus makes in his solemn speech to the people afflicted by the plague (verse 274).

28 Pasolini, 'La sceneggiatura', 143.

29 Ibid.

30 The theme of time emerges, on occasion obsessively, early in Pasolini's work, from the first poems in Friulian dialect (*La meglio gioventù* [Florence: Sansoni, Biblioteca di Paragone, 1954]). It comprised 1) *Poesie a Casarsa*, 2) *Dov'è la mia patria*, 3) *Tal còur di un frut*. The collection was published 20 years later with variations as part of a larger book: *La nuova gioventù* (Turin: Einaudi, 1975). His mother tongue brings him viscerally into contact with the world in which he grew up and which satisfied his anthropological interest. In peasant life and the rhythms of the countryside he perceived the eternal return of time on itself, mingling with the rhythm of the seasons, the coexistence of the old with the new, the old man in the child, death in life, the eternal return of the same which conveys an impression of the immobility and insignificance

of human life. This impression, precocious in Pasolini's mind, left its mark, as I have tried to bring out in this analysis. Likewise, in the same work there emerges the theme of pity for his youth wounded and trampled on and the theme of death. See, for example, the poems 'Il nini muàrt' (10; The dead boy); 'Tornant al paìs' (18; Returning to the village): 'Ti viens cà di nualtris, / ma nualtris si vif, / a si vif quiès e muàrs / coma n'aga ch'a passa / scunussuda entra i bars' ('You come here among us, but we others live, live and die quietly, like water passing unknown amid the bushes'); 'La domènia uliva' (35; Palm Sunday); 'La not di maj' (A May night): 'Tal to vuli frugàt / drenti di un rèit / di rujas insanganadis / i no jot un Passàt [...] vita sensa distìn, / puartade via cu'cuarp: / di fi' doventàt pari / dal spolèr al sgivìn' ('In your eye consumed in a network of bloody wrinkles, / I do not see a Past [...] life without destiny, / carried away with the body: / from son become a father, / from the fire to the clod of earth'); 'I dis robàs' (113; The stolen days): 'No finirà il dizùn dal timp?' (Will time's hunger never end?). He explored this theme and over the years it returned with a deeper awareness, as in the collection *Le ceneri di Gramsci*, issued in 1957. Hence in 'Canto popolare': 'And if we turn to that past / which is our privilege, another procession / of the people comes singing: recovered / is our movement right from the Christian / origins, but that song / remains behind, unmoving. / It is repeated unchanged. / In the nights not torches, but globes / of light, and the outer city seems / the same, no different, no different the new boys' (784). See Pier Paolo Pasolini, *Tutte le opere: Tutte le poesie*, ed. Walter Siti (Milan: Mondadori, Meridiani, 2003). On this theme see also Pasolini's beautiful and moving youthful play (1944) in Friulian dialect: *I Turcs tal Friul* (The Turks in Friuli). It was issued in the volume *Teatro* in *Tutte le opere*.
31 Pasolini, 'La sceneggiatura', 129.
32 Ibid., 133.
33 Sophocles is very explicit in this respect, both in the fourth stasimon of *Oedipus the King* and the fourth stasimon of *Antigone*.
34 Enrico Medda, 'Rappresentare l'arcaico: Pasolini ed Eschilo negli Appunti per un'Orestiade africana', in *Il mito greco nell'opera di Pasolini*, Atti del Convegno Internazionale, Udine/Casarsa della delizia, 24–26 October 2002, ed. Elena Fabbro (Udine: Forum, 2004), 109–26. The essay points out that Pasolini's approach to the Greek text is not be rigorously philological or historiographical, but poetic. Naturally it cannot be maintained that the *Oresteia* represents the transition from tyranny to the phase of democracy. Likewise, I would add, Pasolini's approach to Africa is poetic and a projection of a hope, rather than a political-anthropological analysis of the first decade of independence. The bibliography for the history of Africa and its postcolonial problems is extensive. See, for example, Robert O. Collins, James McDonald and Erik Kristofer Ching, *Problems in African History* (Princeton, NJ: M. Wiener, 2001); Frederick Cooper, *Africa Since 1940: The Past of the Present* (Cambridge: Cambridge University Press, 2002); Paul Nugent, *Africa Since Independence: A Comparative History* (Basingstoke: Palgrave Macmillan, 2004).
35 Pier Paolo Pasolini, *Appendice a Orestiade*, in *Teatro*, 1009.
36 'In his 1962 pamphlet, *Ujamah: The Basis of African Socialism*, Nyerere expressed his aversion to the untrammelled individualism of Western capitalist society, and argued for the extension of a communication ethic, which he believed still existed in rural society, to the nation as a whole. The challenge was to encourage individuals to perceive their interests as lying within the pursuit of the collective good rather than in opposition in the rest of society' (Nugent, *Africa Since Independence*, 141).
37 Pasolini translates Aeschylus: 'I understand your anger: you are older than me. / But if your experience is greater, / God gave me the gift of reason. / Go, go to another country! / You will regret this. I know that the future / days will bring greatness to my people: / and if you're here in the glorious centre / of this city, you will see processions / of men and women bearing you gifts / as among no other people in the world' (Pasolini, *Per il cinema*, 1195).
38 It is hardly necessary to point out that Pasolini, as an artist, was not interested in problematizing the situation in Africa or exercising a lucidly prophetic faculty which elsewhere (for example

in dealing with the Italian situation) he certainly did not lack. His eye and his sensibility found a source of energy, vitality and patience in Africa, during a phase when it still succeeded in resisting the anthropological disaster completed elsewhere and achieved a harmonious integration between consciousness of the tragic and the love of life that Pasolini learned from Greek tragedy. His awareness overlooked the dangers that loomed over Africa and would soon be manifested: the elites in power, trained in Western culture, but rooted in African culture, guided by high ideals, overthrown by elites of a very different kind, often tribal; the balkanization, secessionism, tribalism; the second colonization and the brutal exploitation of riches, especially petroleum; the ungovernable growth of cities; the public–private confusion; the repercussions of the imbalances and European tensions; hunger, poverty, disease; the slow progress toward education; the inequalities that contravened the declarations of principles so radical and advanced for the times by the heroic leaders of the early struggles.

Chapter 8   The Apocalypse of a Civilization: From *Akropolis* to *Apocalypsis cum figuris* by Jerzy Grotowski

1 'What is possible? First confrontation with myth rather than identification. In other words, while retaining our private experiences, we can attempt to incarnate myth, putting on its ill-fitting skin to perceive the relativity of our problems, their connection to the 'roots', and the relativity of the 'roots' in the light of today's experience.' Jerzy Grotowski, *Towards a Poor Theatre* (Holstebro: Odin Teatrets Forlag, 1968), 23.
2 Ludwik Flaszen, *Wyspiański's Akropolis*, in *The Grotowski Sourcebook*, ed. Richard Schechner and Lisa Wolford, (London/New York: Routledge, 1977), 62–70.
3 The cast was Zygmunt Molik (Singer, Jacob, Priam), Rena Mirecka (Rebecca, Cassandra), Antoni Jahołkowski (Isaac, guard), Ryszard Cieślak (Esau, Hector), Zbigniew Cinkutis (Laban, angel, Paris), Stanisław Ścierski (Lia, Elena) and Andrzej Paluchiewicz (a woman, Rachel, a member of the tribe, Hecuba).
4 The sources for the reconstruction of the production are: the viewing of a replica in Paris in the sixties; the film *Akropolis*, directed by James MacTaggart, produced by Lewis Freedman (New York: Arthur Singer Films, 1968), shot near London, with an introduction by Peter Brook; the script kindly provided by the head of The Grotowski Institute Archives, Bruno Chojak, who also edited the references in the text and to whom I wish to express my gratitude. Without the script this critical discourse would not be possible. Another source is the press review kept in the same archive.

A unique and valuable source was an interview granted me by Ludwik Flaszen, in Paris in August 2012 over a number of sessions. I am deeply moved when I remember those hours and I am infinitely grateful to Flaszen (encountered more than thirty years after our first meeting during a Grotowskian laboratory at the Venice Biennale in 1975) for the generosity, acuteness, clarity, passion and depth of his accounts. I thank him for all this and for introducing me to the director of the archive.

To this should be added the important collection: Ludwik Flaszen, *Grotowski and Company*, trans. Andrzej Wojtasik with Paul Allain, edited and with an introduction by Paul Allain with the editorial assistance of Monika Blige and with a tribute by Eugenio Barba (Wrocław: Icarus, 2010).

I wish to thank Annamaria Guglielmi for the script translated from Polish into Italian, making possible the quotations that appear here translated into English.

Special thanks are due to my student Stefania Balzano, who presented a thesis in modern philology at the Catholic University of Milan (academic year 2008–09) on '*Akropolis* e il Teatro Laboratorio di Grotowski' under my supervision and who intelligently read and examined the above documents at their locations. I am indebted to her for the clarification of certain elements of this reconstruction. An appendix to her thesis contains a full translation into Italian of the script.

I wish to remember the late Sisto Dalla Palma, president of the Centro di Ricerca per il Teatro (CRT) in Milan, who brought Grotowski to Milan and introduced, in his course at the university, the appreciation of his theatre and the laboratory theatre method, enabling their implications and fruitfulness to be fully understood.

Other studies useful for a reconstruction of the production are: Robert Findlay, 'Grotowski's Akropolis: A Retrospective', *Modern Drama* 27, no. 1 (March 1984); Jennifer Kumiega, *The Theatre of Grotowski* (London: Methuen, 1987); James Slowiak and Jairo Cuesta, *Jerzy Grotowski* (London: Routledge, 2007), in the series Routledge Performance Practitioners.

5   The literature in this field is obviously extensive. Readers should consult at least: Daniel R. Schwarz, *Imagining the Holocaust* (New York: St Martin's Press, 1999); Christopher William Edgar Bigsby, *Remembering and Imagining the Holocaust: The Chain of Memory* (Cambridge: Cambridge University Press, 2006).

6   In the great narrative of his experience of a concentration camp, Primo Levi speaks of 'our nights' and the prisoners' dreams. 'Our restless sleep was often interrupted by noisy and futile disputes, by curses, by kicks and blows delivered blindly to ward off some harassing and inevitable contact.' *If This Is a Man* (London: Abacus, 2008), 24.

In their broken sleep, they were tormented by hunger and the exhaustion of 'tired beasts'. They experienced nightmares, and yet it was better than the moment of waking:

> Some nights drag on. The dream of Tantalus and the dream of the story are woven into a texture of more indistinct images: the suffering of the day, made up of hunger, blows, cold, exhaustion, fear and promiscuity, turns at night time into shapeless nightmares of unheard-of violence, which in free life would only occur during a fever. One wakes up at every moment, frozen with terror, shaking in every limb, under the impression of an order shouted out in a voice full of anger in a language not understood. The procession to the bucket and the thud of bare heels on the wooden floor turn into another symbolic procession: it us again, gray and identical [...]. We try in vain, when the nightmare itself or the discomfort wakes us, to extricate the various elements and drive them back, separately, out of the field of our present attention [...]. But as soon as we close our eyes, once again we feel our brain start up, beyond our control; it knocks and hums incapable of rest, it fabricates phantasms and terrible symbols, and without rest projects and shapes their images as a gray fog onto the screen of our dreams. (68)

Of the memoir writers, Grotowski definitely knew Tadeusz Borowski, a writer who survived the concentration camp (*This Way for the Gas, Ladies and Gentlemen*, trans. Barbara Vedder [New York: Penguin Classics, 1992]), from whose work he took a fragment which furnished the epigraph to the original programme notes of *Akropolis*. But it is Primo Levi who is particularly capable of helping us appreciate how appropriate Grotowski's approach is in this matter. Levi's work has a tension that is intellectual, not sentimental and not impressionistic, an essential rigour that comes very close to Grotowski's need to understand aspects of the human spirit when faced with the extreme, the limits of the human, not to join the line of those who exploit indignation and pity.

Note the epigraph to his book: 'Consider if this is a man / Who works in the mud / Who does not know peace / Who fights for half a loaf / Who dies for a yes or a no. / Consider if this is a woman, / Without hair and a name / Without the strength to remember / Eyes empty and womb cold / Like a frog in winter.'

7   See the section devoted to 'The Dream Work', in *The Interpretation of Dreams*, in *The Standard Edition of the Complete Psychological Works of Sigmund Freud*, ed. and trans. James Strachey, with Anna Freud (London: The Hogarth Press and The Institute of Psycho-analysis, 1953).

8   Where it is prohibited to write and communicate, to preserve the fragments of memory, to evade controls and prohibitions, a story is torn up to be saved. Levi still remembers: 'From the outside door, secretly and looking around surreptitiously, the storyteller comes in. He is seated on Wachsmann's bunk and at once gathers around him a small, attentive silent crowd. He

chants an interminable Yiddish rhapsody [...]. From the few words that I understand it must be a song that he composed himself, in which he has enclosed all the whole life of the Lager [...]' (*If This Is a Man*, 64).
9. I take this phrase from the important book by Tzvetan Todorov, *Facing the Extreme* (London: Phoenix. 2000).
10. Flaszen, *Wyspiański's Akropolis*, 68.
11. A precise and fully documented analysis of Wyspiański's play and its relation to Grotowski's work can be found in Magda Romanska, *The Post-traumatic Theatre of Grotowski and Kantor: History and Holocaust in 'Akropolis' and 'Dead Class'* (London: Anthem Press, 2012).
12. Flaszen told me that the aims of Grotowski and the group included shaking off the indifference and numbness favoured by incipient consumerism, even under communism.
13. 'Exercises,' in *Action culturelle du sud-est* 6, supplement, 1–13. 'A certains moments dans *Akropolis* nous avons cherché comment retrouver une expression humaine qui ne soit pas sentimentale dans une situation tragique: des prisonniers dans un camp d'extermination. Jouer cela sur certaines notes émotives cela manque de pudeur et de proportion. Comment retrouver alors une expression corporelle qui soit assez froide comme base ? Nous avons pris certains éléments de pantomime, nous les avons changés, cette pantomime n'est pas restée une pantomime classique. Nous avons laissé les éléments froids de la pantomime. Ils ont toujours été transformés de l'intérieur et transgressés par les impulsions vivantes de l'acteur [...] après l'application de différents types d'exercices plastiques de systèmes bien connus: de Delsarte, de Dalcroze e d'autres, pas à pas nous avons commencé à envisager les exercices dits plastiques comme une 'conjunctio oppositorum' entre la structure et la spontanéité.'
14. Slowiak and Cuesta, *Jerzy Grotowski*, 104–5.
15. In the chapter titled 'A Place for Moral Life?' in Todorov's fine book cited above we read, 'Haven't we learnt all too well this sad and simple truth, namely that in extreme situations all traces of moral life evaporate as men become beasts locked in a mortal struggle for survival?' (31).
16. 'Here the struggle to survive is without respite, because everyone is desperately and ferociously alone' (Levi, *If This is a Man*, 94).
17. 'A body that has been exploited to the utmost with a number tattooed on it to save on dog tags, with just enough sleep at night to work during the day, and just enough time to eat. And just enough food so it will not die wastefully. As for actual living, there is only one place for it – a piece of the bunk. The rest belongs to the camp, the Fatherland. But not even this small space, nor the shirt you wear, nor the spade you work with are your own. If you get sick, everything is taken away from you: your clothes, your cap, your "organized" scarf, your handkerchief. If you die – your gold teeth, already recorded in the camp inventory, are extracted. Your body is burned and your ashes are used to fertilize the fields or fill in the ponds. Although in fact so much fat and bone is wasted in the burning, so much flesh, so much heat! But elsewhere they make soap out of people, and lampshades out of human skin, and jewellery out of bones' (*This Way for the Gas, Ladies and Gentlemen*, 131).
18. Flaszen, *Wyspiański's Akropolis*, 66.
19. 1 Cor 13.
20. In general on Grotowski and his method see, apart from the texts cited here in the other notes: Raymonde Temkine, *Grotowski*, trans. Alex Szogyi (New York: Avon Books, 1972); Eugenio Barba, *La terre de 'Cendres et diamants': Mon apprentissage en Pologne*, trans. Éliane Deschamps-Pria (Saussan: L'Entretemps, 2000); Peter Brook, *Avec Grotowski* (Arles: Actes Sud, 2008); Franco Ruffini, *Craig, Grotowski, Artaud* (Rome/Bari: Laterza, 2009); Marco De Marinis, *Il teatro dell'altro* (Florence: La casa Usher, 2011).
21. Grotowski, *Towards a Poor Theatre*, ed. Eugenio Barba (New York: Routledge, 2002), 21.
22. Grotowski, *Towards a Poor Theatre*.
23. Ibid., 21.
24. Ibid., 16.

25 Ibid., 25.
26 This means, as Grotowski explained many times, transcending the everyday and rediscovering unity of thought and feeling, the psychophysical unity of conscious and unconscious, of impulse and expression, of the present and the depths deposited in our being over time.
27 Grotowski, *Towards a Poor Theatre*, 52.
28 See: *LEI: Lessico Etimologico Italiano*, ed. Max Pfister (Mainz: Akademic der Wissenschaften und der Literatur, 1991).
29 The following analysis is based on attendance at productions, the first time in Venice, on an island in the lagoon (San Giacomo in Palude, a former convent, only accessible for the occasion, during the Biennale Teatro 1975), and the second time at the auditorium of the Palazzo Reale in Milan in March 1979 for the CRT in Milan. To this should be added: the reconstruction of the production by Jennifer Kumiega in *Theatre of Grotowski*, ch. 5; the video recording made by Ermanno Olmi, which can be viewed at the video library of the CRT; and the program notes, the press review, and the photographs kept at the CRT. The archive of the CRT retains, in the documentation for the production it hosted, an illuminating transcription of a round table with the participation of Jerzy Grotowski, Ermanno Olmi, Sisto Dalla Palma and Franco Laera. The theme was the nature of the audio-visual document that the Italian director had created at the invitation of the president of the CRT after lengthy negotiations with the Polish director, who was very much against the idea. Olmi clearly knows that 'there are memories that rest outside the instruments which we normally trust to preserve these memories'. *Apocalypsis* travels in the memory of everyone, even those who have not seen it, yet he chose a television recording. Why television and not film? Why did both Olmi and Grotowski choose the former, the direct medium, without any prior knowledge on the part of the production cameramen and mix engineer and without the actors being able to see themselves from the outside and intervene on the takes and editing? The choice fell on the medium of television in order to meet the stringent conditions of the theatre laboratory, for the sake of greater immediacy, and to ensure that the entry of the camera does not alter the field and the balance or undermine the already difficult relations between actors and audience. The actors entered the television studio and there, excluding everything that might bother them and without changing their positions, they created their 'theatrical' space. When the time came to choose, Grotowski and Olmi opted for the first editing – crude, uncertain, unbalanced – in which the blurred and perhaps even shaky shots of the television medium produced a record that was more respectful of the theatrical event, while the second editing began to present the performance as a function of the televisual work and not as an act of witness.
30 Kumiega, *Theatre of Grotowski*, 89.
31 According to the account by Flaszen 'in all the performances before *Apocalypsis*, roles were divided more or less as it happens in other theatres' (*Wyspiański's Akropolis*, 90).
32 On training and Grotowski's method see – in addition to the fundamental contribution by the same director (*Towards a Poor Theatre*; It. trans. *Per un teatro povero* [Rome: Bulzoni, 1970]) and the volume by Kumiega cited above (also found in an Italian edition: *Jerzy Grotowski: La ricerca nel teatro e oltre il teatro 1959–1984* [Florence: La Casa Usher, 1989]) – Lisa Wolford and Richard Schechner, eds, *The Grotowski Sourcebook* (London/New York: Routledge, 1997); Thomas Richards, *Al lavoro con Grotowski sulle azioni fisiche* (Milan: Ubulibri, 1993); and Jerzy Grotowski and Ludwik Flaszen, *Il Teatr Laboratorium di Jerzy Grotowski 1959–1969*, with an essay by Eugenio Barba, ed. Ludwik Flaszen and Carla Pollastrelli, with Renata Molinari (Pontedera: Fondazione Pontedera Teatro, 2001).
33 Kumiega, *Theatre of Grotowski*, 90.
34 The quotation from the conversation with Eric Forsythe is given in Flaszen, *Wyspiański's Akropolis*, 91.
35 In the Slavic tradition, the figure of the Simpleton comes from afar. It is related to the figure of the 'fool of God', the 'fool in Christ', which in the Orthodox church combined acceptance

of the most degrading abjection of Eastern monasticism with the imitation of Christ, despised and suffering. Russian hagiographic literature is full of holy fools, despised, insane, poor in spirit, or simulators of folly and transgressors of common sense in order to bear witness to the divergence or the foolishness of earthly values that imprison, exalt and deceive mankind. He tells the truth paradoxically, not in a discursive, logical language, but with his whole body. To this line belongs Grotowski's character the Simpleton. For a discussion of the issues consult: Louis Bouyer, *La spiritualità bizantina e ortodossa* (Bologna: Dehoniane, 1968); Giuseppe Manzoni, *La spiritualità della chiesa ortodossa russa* (Bologna: EDB, 1993); Georgij Fedotov, *I santi dell'antica Russia*, ed. and trans. by Maria Pia Pagani, preface by Gabriele De Rosa, afterword by Sisto Dalla Palma (Milan: Aquilegia Edizioni, 2000). A concise and useful summary of the problem can be read in Maria Pia Pagani, 'I venerabili folli di Russia', *Ricerche di storia sociale e religiosa* 28, no. 56 (1999), 83–91.
36 Ludwik Flaszen, 'Il Teatr Laboratorium e la ricerca teatrale', *Sipario* 404 (1980): 10–13.
37 Flaszen, *Grotowski and Company*, 116–17.
38 Ibid., 12.
39 The stage writing is a continuous flow through a montage of associations which, for ease of description, can be schematized as follows: 1) entrance of the actors and identification of members of the troupe – Peter designates the Saviour, who is the Simpleton – the relation of the Simpleton to the different characters and the various 'evangelical' situations, evoked by gestures and parables with irony and blasphemy: Lazarus, Mary Magdalene, Judas, John; 2) the 'procession' – the death and resurrection of Lazarus; 3) the betrayal of Peter and the great prostitute; 4) farewell and the Passion; 5) the last interview: Peter and the Simpleton; 6) the expulsion.
40 The text was transcribed and translated directly from the video recording by Margherita Bagicalupo. It was checked against the appendix '*Apocalypsis cum figuris*: Translation and Personal Account' in the volume by Kumiega, *Theatre of Grotowski*, 239ff. The latter was based on a Polish script and checks on most of the sources. The Gospel passages quoted in the Italian translation follow the edition: *The Holy Bible, Containing the Old and New Testaments* (New York: Collins, 1954). The same edition was used for the passages from the Old Testament.
41 Jn 10:1.
42 Jn 11:43.
43 Jn 21:16–17.
44 Jn 13: 6–7; 10; 19; 21; 33; 36.
45 There have been numerous adaptations of Dostoevsky's novels for the stage since 1870: the Moscow Arts Theatre staged many of his works including *The Brothers Karamazov* (1910) and *The Demons* (1913). After the Stalinist period in Russia the plays returned to the stage on numerous occasions, notably: *The Gambler* by Anatolij Vasil'ev in 1997. Outside Russia, in Poland, the many adaptations by Andrew Waida are essential (*The Devils*, 1971). In France there were the famous productions of *The Brothers Karamazov* by Jacques Copeau (1911) and *Crime and Punishment* by Gaston Baty in the thirties, the recent dramatic reading of *Notes from the Underground* by Patrice Chéreau (2003) and a new version of *The Demons* by Albert Camus (1959). Also notable was *Passions* by Thierry Salmon (1990). Other notable adaptations were *The Demons* by Lev Dodin (1991) and Peter Stein (2010) and *The Grand Inquisitor* by Peter Brook (2004). In Italy Giorgio Strehler directed adaptations in which he was preceded by the authors Corrado Alvaro with *The Brothers Karamazov* (1948) and Diego Fabbri with *The Demons* (1961). In close relation to *Apocalypsis cum figuris* was *Min fars us* (1972) at the Odin Teatret. The cinema, as is well known, has also drawn on Dostoevsky. *Le notti bianche* (1957) by Luchino Visconti and *The Idiot* (1951) by Akira Kurosawa are unforgettable.
46 Mikhail Bakhtin, *Problemy poetiki Dostoevskogo*, English translation *Problems of Dostoevsky's Poetics* (Minnesota: University of Minnesota Press, 1984).
47 The text used here is Thomas Stearn Eliot, *Collected Poems 1909–1962* (London: Faber & Faber, 1963), 93–104.

48 Magda Romanska, *Post-traumatic Theatre*.
49 Ibid., 96.
50 In this and subsequent quotations from the works of Eliot, square brackets indicate the parts of the text omitted or added in the Teatr Laboratorium text.
51 It is highly interesting to observe in the area of dramatic representation of the Slavic tradition, in both theatre and film, related to literature, the recurrent theme of the Second Coming, the return of Christ to a world that no longer waits for him, does not recognize him, rejects and kills him again. With regard to the analysis presented here, there may be a certain pregnancy in the reference that leads from Dostoevsky and Grotowski to the recent films of Andrei Zvyagintsev: *Vozvrashcheniye* (*The Return*), which was awarded the Leone d'Oro at the Venice Film Festival in 2003. The director, a former actor in the theatre and then at the start of his career, recognizes Tarkovsky as his master. In his symbolic film he presents, behind the seemingly familiar story of a father's return, after many years, to his sons and the dynamics that develop, an intense and profound reflection on the one who returns (associated with Christ partly through the evocation of the image by Mantegna). He is not recognized, his severe lessons of independence, courage and freedom seem to be rejected, radically so by at least one of his two sons, and he is pushed or driven to a second death. The secret remains hidden; the 'treasure', symbolically foreshadowed in the box dug up on the island and then abandoned and denied, remains undiscovered. The men, precisely the children to whom they had spoken, again remain deaf.
52 For a summary of these elements I recommend the introduction to Simone Weil, *Oeuvres complètes*, ed. André A. Devaux and Florence de Lussy (Paris: Gallimard, 1988).
53 'Treny Jeremiasza, fragmenty II Lamentagi, I Noktruru', in *Breviarium Romanum* (Rrym, 1960), str. 436.
54 Lam 2:8; 10–11.
55 This is a brief summary of the episode. The two brothers Karamazov, the logical and disenchanted intellectual Ivan and the 'saintly' Alyosha, have a long conversation. After meeting and suddenly understanding each other instinctively, learning to love each other and to love life, a close bond develops between them. What concerns them above all else is 'to solve the eternal problems'. As with all Russians, in their interpretation, the most urgent problems are the existence of God, immortality, the sense of sorrow, the mystery of innocent suffering, the foundations of morality, the basis of the condemnation of crime, the improbability of justice and the impossibility of redemption, the commandment to love (figured in Christ's love for mankind), seen as 'a kind of miracle impossible on earth', the love of cruelty, the temptation to rebel, and forgiveness. Ivan reveals himself to Alyosha, first as a listener, through an account of a poem which he has composed and has imprinted in his mind. It is a sacred poem set in the sixteenth century, in the genre of Italian, French and Russian performances (in the age before Peter the Great). Christ appears onstage, although he does not say a word. For 15 centuries troubled humanity awaits him and prays for him to manifest himself as promised. He then appears to the people, who are oppressed and sinful but also feel a childlike love for him. The action is set in Seville at the time of the fires of the Inquisition. He heals the suffering and the crowd is moved to a frenzy of tears and joy. But the Grand Inquisitor passes by in his coarse black monk's habit and with the gaunt, aged, livid appearance of a figure by El Greco, burning with anger, and has him put in prison. At night he goes to speak to him in his cell. Of course, what takes place is perhaps a dream, a fantasy, the materialization of soul-searching, probably in the spirit of a 'theatrical meditation', the spiritual exercises of Ignatius of Loyola or the 'hallucination of a ninety-year-old […] exalted by the *auto da fé* of the previous day, with its hundred heretics burned alive' (398), who finally says what he has kept pent up within him for 90 years. Christ wanted to make people free through truth. But freedom is too heavy a burden. Men have laid it down at the foot of the institution of power in which the mission entrusted to Peter has been dissolved. (In part 4, ch. 7 of *The Idiot* Dostoevsky puts into the mouth of Prince Myshkin a vibrant tirade against the betrayal of Christianity and the opening of the road to atheism paradoxically inherent in the Catholic institution, developed as organizational-legal-hierarchical machinery inherited from the Roman Empire.) It gave

them bread and security through authority, the illusion of miracle and mystery, in exchange for renouncing a freedom that cannot endure, 'because they are weak, filled with vices, inconsistent and seditious' (402) and freedom is beyond their strength. ('There is nothing more seductive for man than freedom of conscience, but there is also nothing most excruciating' [404].) They have yielded to the temptations of Satan that Christ rejected. 'Already for a long time we are not with you, but with *him*', says the Grand Inquisitor to the unspeaking Christ on his reappearance. He gave the flock the happiness of being weak. It is satisfied. The Grand Inquisitor will again burn, the powerful man will again kill Christ, driving him from his world to which he returned only to cause trouble. He does not fear him and love him. His eyes are open and he does not 'wish to serve madness' (412).

56 It will be recalled that Dostoevsky's work itself evoked painting, with the twofold reference to Holbein's *Dead Christ* (with deep, realistic scars on the body of human suffering, the image of prolonged agony and the scandal of endless suffering inflicted on an innocent), and in *The Idiot*, both in the words of Hippolytus (part 3, ch. 6) and in the words of the Prince when visiting Rogozin (part 2, ch. 4).

57 He is a wholly good man who has already achieved complete unity, harmony and transparency, albeit in a state of estrangement from the world, of which his illness and the 'mythical' Switzerland from which he comes are emblems. The duplicity of the 'man from underground' (a halved nature, a rope stretched between high and low, a compound of bad faith, a creature unresolved) is in him completely resolved into unity, without duplicity or zones of darkness, without pretensions, without unconscious pressures and suspicions. He is candid and penetrating, direct and honest, gentle but not weak. He is courageous, generous, acute and lucid, without malice. He loves outcasts and children, exposes duplicity, understands unhappiness, perceives dignity and pride despite appearances, is indifferent to slander, cannot be turned from his efforts to redeem the evil, is moved by pity and seeks beauty.

58 'The production was based on the text *El príncipe constant* by the great seventeenth-century Spanish playwright, Pedro Calderòn de la Barca, in a famous Polish version by Słovacki. However the director's task is not to perform *The Constant Prince* the way it was written. Grotowski presents his own vision of the drama which would be considered a variation of the original play's subject. The performance is a specific study on the phenomenon of *constancy*' (Flaszen, *Grotowski and Company*, 110). The première of the famous production was in Wrocław on 14 November 1965.

59 The allusion is to a dangerous journey in which man gradually achieves an integrated unity, through the progressive enlargement of the self which assimilates the repressed contents of the individual, which, unless dominated, lead to an archaic indistinctness. The process of individuation curbs both the danger of drowning in archaic structures and the danger of crystallization in the stereotype, the mask. The keystone of this process is the symbolic activity: raising, accepting, living, subjecting to critical scrutiny, assimilating the symbol into consciousness, synthesis and operative reality, open to the future, which becomes the backbone of this inquiry of the ego in quest of its *potential*.

60 In *Apocalypsis* the radicalization of the conflict between Simon Peter, head of the temporal church, and the Simpleton needs to be problematized in terms of the historical context. Of course the nineteenth-century point of view bound up with the controversy between Catholicism and the Orthodox church, Slavophilia and the West, supported by Dostoevsky, bears heavily on the situation represented by Grotowski. It seems not to accept the great process of democratization, of reconciliation to an original spirituality and defence of the weak, the repositioning of Christ at the centre of the Conciliar and post-Conciliar church and its message. It will be recalled that Vatican Council II, convened in 1962, came to an end in 1965.

61 Kumiega, *Theatre of Grotowski*, 57.

A Provisional Epilogue   Between the Experience and the Representation of the Tragic: Towards a Performative Theatre

1 On the problem of evil and genocide see: Christopher Bigsby, *Remembering and Imagining the Holocaust: The Chain of Memory* (Cambridge: Cambridge University Press, 2006); Bernard Bruneteau, *Il secolo dei genocidi* (Bologna: Il Mulino, 2005; French translation: *Le siècle des génocides* (Paris: Armand Colin, 2004); Leonidas Donskis, *Amore per l'odio: La produzione del male nelle società moderne*, preface by Zygmunt Bauman (Trento: Erikson, 2008); English translation: *Forms of Hatred: The Troubled Imagination in Modern Philosophy and Literature* (Amsterdam/New York: Rodopi, 2003); Alexander Leben Hinton, ed., *Annihilating Difference: The Anthropology of Genocide* (Berkeley: University of California Press, 2002); *I concetti del male*, ed. Pier Paolo Portinaro (Turin: Einaudi, 2002); James Waller, *Becoming Evil: How Ordinary People Commit Genocide and Mass Killing* (Oxford: Oxford University Press, 2002).
2 I have dealt with this question in: Annamaria Cascetta, ed., 'Verso un teatro performativo', special issue, *Comunicazioni sociali*, no. 1 (2014).
3 'Le plus urgent ne me paraît pas tant de défendre une culture dont l'existence n'a jamais sauvé un homme du souci de mieux vivre et d'avoir faim, que d'extraire de ce que l'on appelle la culture, des idées dont la force vivante est identique à celle de la faim.' ('The most urgent seemed not so much to defend a culture that has never saved a man from worrying how to live better and not go hungry, but rather to extract what we call culture from ideas whose living force is identical to that of hunger.') Antonin Artaud, 'Le théâtre et son double', in *Œuvres complètes*, vol. 4 (Paris: Gallimard 1978), 9.
4 Ibid., 25.
5 'La terrorisante apparition du Mal qui dans les Mystères d'Éleusis était donnée dans sa forme pure, et était vraiment révélée, repond au temps noir de certaines tragédies antiques que tout vrai théâtre doit retrouver. Si le théâtre essentiel est comme la peste, ce n'est pas parce qu' il est contagieux, mais parce que comme la peste il est la révélation, la mise en avant, la poussée vers l'extérieur d'un fond de cruauté latente par lequel se localisent sur un individu ou sur un peuple toutes les possibilités perverses de l'esprit.' (The terrifying apparition of Evil, which in the Mysteries of Eleusis was presented in its pure form, and was really revealed, responds to the dark time of certain ancient tragedies that all true theatre has to rediscover. If the essence of theatre is like the plague, it is not because it is contagious, but because like the plague it is the revelation, the bringing out, the outward projection of the latent cruelty, locating in an individual or a people all the perverse possibilities of the mind) (Ibid., 29).
6 Ibid., 37.
7 Ibid., 77.
8 The text of the production, *Rwanda 94: Une tentative de réparation symbolique envers les morts*, à *l'usage des vivants*, has been published by Éditions Théâtrales (Paris, 2002); the Italian tour of the work was accompanied by a very full programme: *Italy for Rwanda 1994–2004*, ed. Antonio Calbi (Milan: Teatri 90 Edizioni, 2004). Other contributions can be read in the monographic number of *Alternatives théâtrales* 67–8 (April 2001); *Europe* 84, nos 926–7 (June–July 2006): 115–39 contains a contribution by Jacques Delcuvellerie ('Écrire l'extrême: La littérature et l'art face aux crimes de masse').
9 See Gérard Prunier, *The Rwanda Crisis: History of a Genocide* (London: Hurst, 1995).
10 The issue was recently dealt with by a performance presented at the Festival d'Avignon in 2013 by the Swiss director Milo Rau: *Hate Radio*. Rau 'pratique depuis quelques années avec sa société de production, l'International Institute of Political Murder, un théâtre du réel esthétiquement assez élaboré et qui cherche l'intervention dans la vraie vie' (Fabienne Darge, *Le Monde*, 24 July 2013, 10; [Rau] has been practising for some years now with his production company, the International Institute of Political Murder, an aesthetically highly elaborate reality theatre, which seeks to intervene in real life). The work reconstructs a programme broadcast by RTLM (Radio-Télévision des Milles Collines) which helped guide the genocide in Rwanda. It is built

upon real testimonies, including those of a survivor on the stage, thus reducing to a minimum the boundary between presence and performance.

11 Yolande Mukagasana has presented her testimony in a series of works: Yolande Mukagasana and Patrick May, *La mort ne veut pas de moi: Document* (Paris: Éditions Fixot, 1997); Yolande Mukagasana and Patrick May, *N'aie pas peur de savoir* (Paris: Éditions Laffont, 1999); Yolande Mukagasana, *Les blessures du silence: Témoignages du génocide au Rwanda*, photography by Alain Kazinierakis (Arles: Actes Sud, 2001).

12 'J'en voulais au soleil qui brillait sur ce pays. J'en voulais a tout.' She relates how she escaped, her urge to bear witness and her pity. 'Je ne veux ni terrifier ni apitoyer, je veux témoigner. Uniquement témoigner. Ces hommes qui m'ont fait subir les pires souffrances je ne les hais ni les méprise, j'ai même pitié d'eux' (Groupov, *Rwanda 94*, 25).

13 Ibid., 33; 'Je suis mort, ils m'ont tué. / Je ne dors pas, je ne suis pas en paix.'

14 'Les morts, entre autres choses, ne supportent plus ce langage indéfini, sans victimes et sans bourreaux. Une 'tragédie', vous voyez? Qui dit tragédie dit fatalité, destin inéluctable. L'apparition vient d'insister fortement sur la définition du crime: un génocide' (ibid., 45).

15 Ibid., 51–55. 'Regardez-les, mais méfiez-vous / Ces appareils qui propagent / l'information / Ce sont eux qui infectent les / coeurs / Et souillent les esprits. / Une hyène rusée se met à / beugler / à la manière d'une vache. / Nous sommes dans leur / tanière / S'il vous plaît, soyez vigilants.'

16 Ibid., 66.

17 Ibid., 80.

18 Ibid., 86.

19 'En vérité tous les Tutsis périront; / ils disparaîtront de ce pays. [...] Parce qu'on les tue comme les rats' (ibid., 127).

20 'À travers nous l'humanité / vous regarde tristement. [...] Nous sommes, à jamais, ce nuage accusateur. / Morts, c'est pour l'éternité que nous réclamons notre dû. [...] Je ne suis pas en paix' (ibid., 146).

21 'Sur la colline de Muyira / Couverte de forêts et de buissons / Vivaient avant le génocide / De nombreux hommes forts. [...]'

22 Virgilio Melchiorre, *Ideologia, utopia, religione* (Milan: Rusconi, 1980), 306.

23 Paul Ricoeur, *Finitude et culpabilité* (Paris: Montaigne, 1960), 10, cited by Melchiorre, *Ideologia, utopia, religione*, 307.

24 An extraordinarily powerful book that helps us understand what happened and how far it is thematized in the work of Delcuvellerie is Jean Hatzfeld, *Une saison de machete* (Paris: Éditions du Seuil, 2003). During a long stay in the penitentiary of Nyamata in Rwanda, the author, a journalist and writer, collected the testimony of ten people who played an important part in these planned murders and he organized them into a long and disquieting account which is moving by its naked truth, without rhetorical or literary encrustations, like certain expressions in the writings of Primo Levi and Peter Weiss. The sons of peasants and farmers themselves or in some rare cases former teachers, minor public officials or soldiers, members of a brigade band, seemingly innocuous, they became the most zealous executors of that *boulot*, meaning the 'work' of genocide which for some months replaced the normal work of the fields.

25 Elie, one of the interviewees in Hatzfeld, says, 'On devait faire vite, on n'avait pas droit aux congés, surtout pas les dimanches, on devait terminer. On avait supprimé toutes les cérémonies. On était tous embauchés à égalité pour un seul boulot, abattre tous les cancrelats' (ibid., 19; We had to work fast. All leave was cancelled, especially on Sundays. We had to make an end of it. We cancelled all the services. We were all set to work on a single job, killing all the cockroaches).

26 Ibid., 161. 'Moi je sais que Dieu seul peut comprendre ce que nous avons fait.'

27 Ibid., 162. 'Dieu gardait le silence et les églises puaient des cadavres qu'on avait délaissés dedans.'

28 For the study of this question, important for the contemporary theatre, I would refer the reader to the volume: Annamaria Cascetta and Laura Peja, eds, *La prova del Nove: Scritture per la scena e temi epocali nel secondo Novecento* (Milan: Vita e Pensiero, 2005). Among the sources are: the film by Luc de Hensch, *Une république devenue folle: Rwanda 1894–1994*; the film by Anne Van Der Wée, *Les morts ne sont pas morts*; the book by Colette Braeckman, *Histoire d'un génocide*; oral accounts of witnesses collected on site; archive material broadcast on French Rwandese radio and television and the BBC.

29 Jacques Decuvellerie, 'Dramaturgie', *Alternatives théâtrales* 67–8 (April 2001), 53 (50–56). '[…] une étroite symbiose entre texte, jeu et musique. Pas du tout dans le sens de l'opéra, plutôt des tragédies antiques.'

30 See Georges Banu, 'Rwanda 94, un événement', *Alternatives théâtrales* 67–8 (April 2001), 21 (21–23).

31 Decuvellerie, 'Dramaturgie', 56. 'Elle joue sur une limite. […] Cela n'a rien du charme ou des aberrations de la spontanéité, et cela se sent: qu'elle n'est pas une comédienne, mais que ceci est bien une forme élaborée. Elle est ce qu'elle dit mais elle "joue" un rôle d'elle-même, elle est en représentation dans cette représentation-ci.'

32 Dante, *Inferno*, 126.

33 One key source of the work is Peter Weiss's *Die Ermittlung* (1965).

34 'Mais une heure après l'assaut, je mangeais.' The quotations are taken from the script of the French version (*Ruhe monologen*), supplied to me by Muziektheater Transparant.

35 'Je trouve la vie militaire fantastique. Tout l'appareil militaire est grandiose en soi. Ce qu'une armée peut faire. La masse! Chez les SS, on était toujours supérieur à l'ennemi, vous voyez? On était toujours supérieur.'

36 'On ne tire pas un trait sur un quart de sa vie.'

37 They are (with titles in French of the translation by Jean-Claude Poyet appended to the programme) 'Vorüber die stöhnende Klage' ('Finie, la plainte gémissante!' D. 53), 'Ein jugendlicher Maienschwung' ('Un souffle de verdure adolescent', D. 61), 'Der Entfernten' ('À celle qui est au loin', D. 331), 'Widerhall' ('Écho', D. 428), 'Räuberlied' ('Chant de brigands', D. 435), 'Der Geistertanz' ('La danse des esprits', D. 494), 'Ruhe, schönstes Glück der Erde' ('Paix, bonheur suprême de la terre', D. 657), 'Wein und Liebe' ('Le vin et l'amour', D. 901), 'Die Nacht' ('La nuit', D. 983 c).

38 'Paix, bonheur suprême de la terre, / Paix, descends en nous bénissant, / Afin qu'en nous soit silence, / Comme sous les fleurs repose un / tombeau. […] Accorde ta paix à la terre, / verse sur elle ton baume apaisant, / Afin que l'âme guérisse / Et s'élève au-dessus du tombeau' (the translation cited is by Poyet).

39 Peter Brook clarifies the idea of 'necessary theatre':

> In the theatre we always return to the same point: it is not enough for writers and actors to experience this compulsive necessity, audiences must share it too. So in this sense it is not just a question of wooing an audience. It is an even harder matter of creating works that evoke in audiences an undeniable hunger and thirst.
>
> A true image of necessary theatre-going I know is a psychodrama session in an asylum. […] Two hours after any session begins all the relations between the people present are slightly modified, because of the experience in which they have been plunged together. As a result something is more animated, something flows more freely, some embryonic contacts are being made between previously sealed-off souls. When they leave the room, they are not quite the same as when they entered. […] Today, it is hard to see how a vital theatre and a necessary one can be other than out of tune with society – not seeking to celebrate the accepted values, but to challenge them. The artist is not there to indict, nor to lecture, nor to harangue, and least of all to teach. He is part of them. *The Empty Space* (London: Penguin 1968), 148–50.

INDEX

Aeschylus 6, 8, 9, 41, 48, 51, 54, 103, 114, 157, 219n7
Africa, freedom of 115
Agamennon (Aeschylus) 6, 12, 51
Akropolis (Grotowski) 118–27
Alighieri, Dante 110, 138, 158
Allain, Paul 223n4
Alonge, Roberto 18
Alvaro, Corrado 227n45
American Civil War 56
ancient Greek tragedy 6–12
anthropological transformation 101–3
Antigone (Sophocles) 6
Antoine, André 42
Apocalypsis cum figuris (Grotowski) 127–45
Appia, Adolphe 43
Aquinas, Thomas 41
Arendt, Hannah 75
Aristotle 1, 9, 11, 85, 106
Arnold, Albert James 75
ars una 117
Artaud, Antonin 148
Ash Wednesday (Eliot) 130, 136, 138–9

Bacigalupo, Margherita 227n40
Bagimont, Colette 150, 153
Baker, George Pearce 48
Bakhtin, Mikhail 135
Balzano, Stefania 223n4
Banu, Georges 157
Barba, Eugenio 118, 223n4
Barbieri, Gato 114
Baty, Gaston 227n45
Baudelaire, Charles 93
Beauvoir, Simone de 80
Beckett, Samuel 5, 72, 91, 93–9, 130, 145, 148
Being and Nothingness (Sartre) 85
Bergman, Ingmar 27, 94
Berlau, Ruth 73
Beyond the Pleasure Principle (Freud) 57
Birth of Tragedy, The (Nietzsche) 17

Blige, Monica 223n4
Bloch, Ivan 62
Borowski, Tadeusz 126, 224n6, 225n17
Bouyer, Louis 227n35
Boyer, Régis 27, 201n7, 202n12, 204n39
Brandes, Georg Morris 17
Brecht, Bertolt 5, 59–63, 68–70, 72–4, 158, 210n3, 211n10, 211nn12–13, 212nn17–19, 212n26, 212nn30–31, 213n32, 213n39
Brook, Peter 43, 161, 223n4, 227n45, 232n39
Brothers Karamazov, The (Dostoevsky) 130, 134, 140, 143
Bruegel, Pieter 32, 43
Buddenbrooks (Mann) 19
Burri, Alberto 157

Cahiers (Camus) 75
Calderòn de la Barca, Pedro 229n58
Caligula 216nn41–2
Caligula (Camus) 75–90
Camus, Albert 5, 75–81, 84–6, 88–90, 140, 214n11, 214n16, 214n18, 215n19, 215n40, 216n47, 216n51, 216n53, 217n54, 227n45
Carnets (Camus) 75
Chaplin, Charlie 98
Chéreau, Patrice 227n45
Choephori, The (Aeschylus) 6, 51
Chojak, Bruno 223n4
Christianity 31
Christ's Passion 110
Christus patiens 142
Cieślak, Ryszard 118–19, 121, 143
Cinkutis, Zbignieu 120
Citti, Sergio 218n3
Claudel, Camille 35
Claudel, Paul 5, 31–2, 35–6, 39–42, 44–5, 158, 206n12, 206n14, 206n23, 206n26, 207nn27–8, 207n30, 207n40, 208n41–2
Clausewitz, Carl von 62, 211n9
Cold War 95
Communist Manifesto (Marx, Engels) 62

Confessions (St Augustin) 96
Constant Prince, The (Grotowski) 143–4
Copeau, Jacques 34, 42, 77–8, 227n45
Courage Model 1949 (Brecht) 73
Croce, Benedetto 102
Cuesta, Jairo 125, 223n4

Dalcroze, Jacques 41, 125
Dalla Palma, Sisto 223n4, 226n29, 227n35
Darge, Fabienne 230n10
Darwin, Charles 15
De Laude, Silvia 218n1
De Martino, Ernesto 103
De Pauw, Josse 158–60
De Rosa, Gabriele 227n35
Death of Tragedy, The (Steiner) 2
Degan, Enzo 219n7
Delcuvellerie, Jacques 149, 157–8
Delsarte, François 125
Descartes, René 89, 95
Dessau, Paul 60
Di Benedetto, Vincenzo 11–12,
Dodin, Lev 227n45
Dostoevsky, Fyodor Mikhailovich 129–30, 132, 135–7, 140–43, 227n45, 228n51, 228n55, 229n56, 229n60
Dramaticules (Beckett) 98
Dullin, Charles 34–5, 42

Ecclesiastes (Bible) 40, 63
El Greco (Dominikos Theokopoulos) 228n55
Electra complex 57
Eliot, Thomas Stearns 31, 130, 136–43, 228n50
Endgame (Beckett) 91–9
Engels, Friedrich 62
Epic-political theatre 158
Étranger, L' (Camus) 75, 77–8
Eumenides, The (Aeschylus) 6, 51
Euripides 5
Ezekiel (Bible) 69

Fabbri, Diego 227n45
Fabien, Michèle 218n1
Farewell to Arms, A (Hemingway) 56
Faulkner, William 54
Fedotov, Georgij 227n35
Ferrone, Siro 60
figura Christi 31, 39, 144
Findlay, Robert 223n4
Fitzgerald, Francis Scott Key 54

Flaszen, Ludwik 117–18, 123–4, 126, 129–30, 140, 223n4, 225n12, 226n31, 229n58
Fortunato, Valentina 219n7
Freedman, Lewis 223n4
Freud, Sigmund 11, 15, 48, 57, 122, 208n22, 209n24
Fusillo, Massimo 219n7
Future of War, The (Bloch) 62

Galindo, Christiane 75
Gassman, Vittorio 219n7
Genocide 147
Gernet, Louis 9, 201n25
Gerontion (Eliot) 141
Ghosts (Ibsen) 15–30
Gide, André 77
Gontarski, Stanley E. 217n4
Grapes of Wrath (Steinbeck) 54
Great Gatsby, The (Fitzgerald) 54
Grenier, Jean 85
Grimmelshausen, Hans Jakob Christoffel von 69
grotesque tragedy 88
Grotowski, Jerzy 117–18, 124–31, 133, 137, 140, 143–4, 147–8, 157, 223n1, 223n4, 224n6, 225n12, 226n26, 226n29, 227n35, 227n39, 228n51, 229nn57–60
Guglielmi, Annamaria 223n4
guilt 15, 25
Gurawski, Jerzy 118
Gustavus Adolphus 66–8

Habyarimana, Juvénal 149, 156
Haerdter, Michael 217n4
Happy Days (Beckett) 98
Hatzfeld, Jean 156, 231nn24–5
Hébertot, Jacques 36, 76
Hegel, Georg Wilhelm Friedrich 94
Heidegger, Martin 4
Hemingway, Ernest 56
Hill, Heinar 73
Himmler, Heinrich 159
Hitler, Adolf 159
Holbein, Hans the Younger 229n56
Homme révolté, L' (Camus) 89
Humour 97–8
Hurwicz, Angelica 74

Ibsen, Henrik 5, 15–17, 25, 27–9, 48, 201n1, 202n8, 203n23, 203n28, 205n40

INDEX

Iceman Cometh, The (O'Neill) 57
Idiot, The (Dostoevsky) 143
Ignatius of Loyola 228n55
Iliad (Homer) 120
Imperative of Responsibility (Jonas) 97
Isaiah 34, 40, 43

Jahołkowski, Antoni 118, 120,
Jansen, Tom 159
Jeremiah 69, 141–2
Jesus Christ 31, 37, 40, 44, 63, 70, 110,
    114, 117, 119, 130–31, 133, 140, 161,
    227n35, 228n51, 228n51, 228n55,
    229n60
Jeune fille Violaine, La (Claudel) 31
Jonas, Hans 97
Jouvet, Louis 34
Jung, Carl Gustav 48, 57

Kamali 150
Kapital, Das (Marx) 62
Kazinierakis, Alain 231n11
Keaton, Buster 98
Khrushchev, Nikita Sergeevič 144
Kierkegaard, Søren 1–2, 5, 15–18, 98,
    200nn9–10, 201n5
Kumiega, Jennifer 129, 144, 223n4, 226n29,
    227n40
Kurosawa, Akira 227n45

Laera, Franco 226n29
Lanza, Diego 11
Leibniz, Gottfried Wilhelm 95
Leo XIII 41
Lettres à un ami allemand (Camus) 80
Levi, Primo 122, 126, 224n6, 224n8, 231n24
Lévi-Strauss, Claude 103
Levy Bruhl, Lucien 103
limits 1, 4, 13, 93, 96, 100, 147
List, Garrett 157
Long Day's Journey into Night (O'Neill) 57–8
Longhi, Roberto 218n3
Lucignani, Luciano 219n7
Lugné-Poe, Aurélien 42
Luxemburg, Rosa 62

MacPherson, Coleen 218n1
MacTaggart, James 125, 223n4
Malentendu, Le (Camus) 76, 80
Mallarmé, Stéphane 44
Malraux, André 77

Mann, Thomas 19
Mantegna, Andrea 110, 228n51
Manzoni, Giuseppe 227n35
Maritain, Jacques 31, 41
Marx, Karl 59, 62
Marxism 59
Maselli, Titina 218n1
May, Patrick 231n11
Mazon, Paul 219n7
Medda, Enrico 115, 222n34
Meglio gioventù, La (Pasolini) 111
Mein Kampf (Hitler) 62
Melchiorre, Virgilio 155
Mémoires improvisées (Camus) 34
Métamorphose de la tragédie, La (Omesco) 2
Milhaud, Darius 41
Mirecka, Rena 119, 121
Mitterrand, François-Marie 150, 154
modernity, transition to 15
modern tragedy 5
Modern Tragedy (Williams) 199n6
Molik Zygmunt 118–21
Moses 96
mother (archetype) 158
Mother Courage and Her Children (Brecht) 59–74
Mourning Becomes Electra (O'Neill) 47–58
Mukagasana, Yolande 149–50, 155,
    158, 231n11
Murray, Yvonne 114
Mutter, Die (Brecht) 69, 71
Muyango 150, 157
mysterium iniquitatis 39
Myth de Sisyphe, Le (Camus) 75, 78

Nausée, La (Sartre) 78
Nazi era 143
Nazi Germany 60, 122
nihilism 86, 89
nihilistic assumption 97
Nietzsche, Friedrich 1, 16–18, 48, 85
Ninchi, Arnaldo 219n7
Notes for an African Oresteia (Pasolini) 103, 112,
    114, 116
Nugent, Paul 222n36
Nyerere, Julius 115, 222n36

Oedipus complex 57
Oedipus rex (Pasolini) 103, 112
Oedipus the King (Sophocles) 6, 8, 9, 12
Œtly, Paul 76
Olmi, Ermanno 226n29

O'Neill, Carlotta 47, 57
O'Neill, Eugene 5, 47–8, 51, 54–8, 209n23, 210n26
On War (Clausewitz) 62
Oresteia, The (Aeschylus) 6, 102–103, 106, 114–15
Oxenstierna, Axel Gustavsson 64

Pagani, Maria Pia 227n35
Paluchiewicz, Andrzej 119, 121
Paolozza, Adam 218n1
Paradise (Dante) 138
Pasolini, Pier Paolo 5, 101–3, 105–7, 109–16, 218n1, 218n3, 219n7, 220n12, 220n15, 220n17, 221n19, 221nn24–7, 221n30, 222n34, 222n37–8
performative theatre 147
Persians, The (Aeschylus) 157
Peste, La (Camus) 80, 89, 90
Peter the Great 228n55
Petersburski, Jerzy 118
Philipe, Gérard 76
philosophical-anthropological pessimism 56–7, 96
Pia, Pascal 77
Poetics (Aristotle) 11
Polish October 144
'poor theatre' 122, 126
Pope John XXIII 220n17
Pope St Gregory 34
Pope St Leo 34, 43
postdramatic theatre 147
psychoanalysis 57
Pylades (Pasolini) 101–16

Rau, Milo 230n10
Ricoeur, Paul 155
Rimbaud, Jean-Arthur 44
ritual 158
Romilly, Jacqueline de 10
Roofthooft, Dirk 159
Ruhe (Muziektheater Transparant) 158–61
Rwanda 94 (Groupov) 147–58

sacrifice 38
Salmon, Thierry 227n45
Sartre, Jean-Paul 80, 85, 94, 217n11
Savage, Archie 114
Schiller, Friedrich 69, 212n29
Schopenhauer, Arthur 48, 57–8, 99, 210n25
Schubert, Franz 158, 160

Ścierski, Stanisław 119, 120
Shakespeare, William 88, 95
Sherman, William Tecumseh 55
Siti, Walter 218n1
Sleutelaar, Armando 159
Sleutelaar, Hans 159
Słovacki, Juliusz 229n58
Slowiak, James 125, 223n4
social drama 147
Socrates 98
Sophocles 6, 8–9, 112–13, 200n17, 221n27, 222n33
Sound and the Fury, The (Faulkner) 54
St Augustin 96, 98, 148
St John 40, 128, 130, 133, 140, 153
St Luke 40, 43, 130, 136
St Matthew 40, 130, 136
St Paul 32, 39, 126, 138
St Peter 32
Stalin, Visarionovic Dzugasvili 77
Stanislawski, Konstantin Sergeevič 127
Steinbeck, John Ernst 54
Steiner, George 106, 199n5
Strehler, Giorgio 227n45
Strindberg, Johan August 48
Suetonius 85
Supernatural Knowledge (Weil) 140
Szajna, Jósef 118
Szondi, Peter 1

Tarkovsky, Andrei 228n51
Tayor, Charles 102
Testori, Giovanni 31
theatre laboratory 122
theatre of cruelty 148
theatrical machine 29
Thirty Years War 64–5, 68
Thompson, George 219n7
Tidings Brought to Mary, The (Claudel) 31–45
Tilly, Jean t'Serclaes 67, 70
Todorov, Tzvetan 225n15
Totem and Taboo (Freud) 57
Towards a Poor Theatre (Grotowski) 127
Tristes Tropiques (Lévi-Strauss) 103, 116
Trojan War 115
Trojan Women (Euripides) 5

Unersteiner, Mario 219n7

Valgimigli, Manara 219n7
Vasil'ev, Anatolij 227n45

Vedder, Barbara 224n6
Vernant, Jean Pierre 9
Vidal-Naquet, Pierre 9
Villi, Olga 219n7
Visconti, Luchino 227n45

Waida, Andrew 227n45
Waiting for Godot (Beckett) 93–4, 96
Wallenstein (Schiller) 69
Wallenstein, Albrecht Wenzel Eusebius von 68
Waste Land, The (Eliot) 130
Weigel, Helene 70, 73–4
Weil, Simone 130, 140–42
Weiss, Peter 231n24

Wijs, Carly 159
Wilhelmi, Ruth 73
Williams, Raymond 2, 199n6
Własta, Andrzej 118
Wojtasik, Andrzej 223n4
Wojtyla, Karol 143
World as Will and Representation (Schopenhauer) 58
World War I 12–13, 61
World War II 13, 62, 159
Wyspiański, Stanislaw 117–19, 123–4, 126
Wyszynski, Stefan 143

Zvyagintsev, Andrei 228n51

www.ingramcontent.com/pod-product-compliance
Lightning Source LLC
Chambersburg PA
CBHW021823300426
44114CB00009BA/292